Caldera OpenLinux and Netfinity® Server Integration Guide

Jakob Carstensen, Ivo Gomilsek, Lenz Grimmer,
Jay Haskins, and Joe Kaplenk

International Technical Support Organization

www.redbooks.ibm.com

Caldera OpenLinux and Netfinity® Server Integration Guide

ISBN 0-13-089771-X

The ITSO Networking Series

Red Hat Linux and Netfinity® Server Integration Guide
   by Carstensen, Haskins, Gomilsck, Grimmer, and Kaplenk

Caldera OpenLinux and Netfinity® Server Integration Guide
   by Carstensen, Gomilsek, Grimmer, Haskins, and Kaplenk

SuSE Linux and Netfinity® Server Integration Guide
   by Carstensen, Grimmer, Gomilsek, Haskins, and Kaplenk

JAVA™ 2 Network Security, Second Edition
   by Pistoia, Reller, Gupta, Nagnur, and Ramani

A Guide to Virtual Private Networks
   by Murhammer, Bourne, Gaidosch, Kunzinger, Rademacher, and Weinfurter

TCP/IP Tutorial and Technical Overview, Sixth Edition
   by Murhammer, Atakan, Bretz, Pugh, Suzuki, and Wood

Understanding Optical Communications
   by Dutton

Asynchronous Transfer Mode (ATM)
   by Dutton and Lenhard

High-Speed Networking Technology
   by Dutton and Lenhard

www.security: How to Build a Secure World Wide Web Connection
   by Macgregor, Aresi, and Siegert

Internetworking over ATM: An Introduction
   by Dorling, Freedman, Metz, and Burger

Inside APPN and HPR
   by Dorling, Lenhard, Lennon, and Uskokovic

Caldera OpenLinux and Netfinity® Server Integration Guide

Jakob Carstensen ■ Ivo Gomilsek ■
Lenz Grimmer ■ Jay Haskins ■
Joe Kaplenk

IBM

Prentice Hall PTR, Upper Saddle River, New Jersey 07458
www.phptr.com

© Copyright International Business Machines Corporation 1997, 1999, 2000. All rights reserved.

Note to U.S. Government Users—Documentation related to restricted rights—Use, duplication or disclosure is subject to restrictions set forth in GSA ADP Schedule Contract with IBM Corp.

First Edition (December 1999)

This edition applies to preparing for or installing Caldera OpenLinux 2.3 or Caldera OpenLinux eServer.

Comments may be addressed to:
IBM Corporation, International Technical Support Organization
Dept. HZ8 Building 678
P.O. Box 12195
Research Triangle Park, NC 27709-2195

When you send information to IBM, you grant IBM a non-exclusive right to use or distribute the information in any way it believes appropriate without incurring any obligation to you.

Published by Prentice Hall PTR
Prentice-Hall, Inc.
Upper Saddle River, NJ 07458

Prentice Hall books are widely used by corporations and government agencies for training, marketing, and resale.
The publisher offers discounts on this book when ordered in bulk quantities. For more information, contact Corporate Sales Department, Phone 800-382-3419; FAX: 201-236-7141, E-mail: corpsales@prenhall.com; or Write:

Prentice Hall PTR
Corporate Sales Department
One Lake Street
Upper Saddle River, NJ 07458

Take Note! Before using this information and the product it supports, be sure to read the general information in Appendix F, "Special Notices" on page 313.

Printed in the United States of America

10 9 8 7 6 5 4 3 2 1

ISBN   0-13-089771-X

Prentice-Hall International (UK) Limited, *London*
Prentice-Hall of Australia Pty. Limited, *Sydney*
Prentice-Hall Canada Inc., *Toronto*
Prentice-Hall Hispanoamericana, S.A., *Mexico*
Prentice-Hall of India Private Limited, *New Delhi*
Prentice-Hall of Japan, Inc., *Tokyo*
Pearson Education Asia Pte. Ltd.
Editora Prentice-Hall do Brasil, Ltda., *Rio de Janeiro*

Contents

Preface......xiii
The team that wrote this redbook......xiii
Comments welcome......xv

Chapter 1. Linux installation......1
1.1 Knowing your hardware......1
1.2 Hardware considerations......1
    1.2.1 Adaptec SCSI controller......2
    1.2.2 IBM ServeRAID controller......2
    1.2.3 IBM token-ring network adapters......2
1.3 Updating the BIOS and ServeRAID controller firmware......2
1.4 Making the CD-ROM bootable......2
1.5 Basic Linux installation......3
1.6 Installation with ServeRAID......33
    1.6.1 Installing ipsutils.rpm......34
    1.6.2 The ipssend commands......36
    1.6.3 Replacing a defunct drive......48
    1.6.4 Replacing a defunct drive with disabled Hot Spare Rebuild......49
    1.6.5 Replacing a defunct drive with a hot spare drive installed......49
    1.6.6 Using the Ipsmon utility......55
    1.6.7 Using the Ipsadm utility......55
1.7 Installing and configuring token-ring network cards......61

Chapter 2. Basic system administration......65
2.1 Log in to the system......65
2.2 Using the Window Manager......68
2.3 Getting the X-Windows terminal window......69
2.4 Accessing COAS - Caldera Open Administration System......70
2.5 Adding and removing software packages using kpackage......72
    2.5.1 Uninstalling a package......74
    2.5.2 Installing a package......75
2.6 Package management using RPM......77
2.7 System menu......78
2.8 Accounts......79
    2.8.1 Managing accounts......81
    2.8.2 Managing groups......85
2.9 Daemons (services)......88
2.10 Filesystem......89
    2.10.1 Mounting an NFS volume......90
2.11 Hostname......90
2.12 Resources......91

2.13 Time. 92
2.14 Peripherals menu 93
2.15 Mouse 94
2.16 Printer 95
    2.16.1 Adding a new printer. 96
    2.16.2 Removing a printer 98
    2.16.3 Edit a printer. 98
2.17 Network menu 99
2.18 Ethernet interfaces 100
    2.18.1 Adding a new network interface 101
    2.18.2 Removing a network interface. 103
2.19 Name resolution settings 103
    2.19.1 Name resolution order and sources 104
    2.19.2 Defining a DNS server 104
2.20 Manipulating kernel modules 106
    2.20.1 Loading a new module 107
    2.20.2 Unloading a new module 108
2.21 Configuring X-Windows 108

Chapter 3. General performance tools in Linux 109
3.1 General configuration hints. 109
3.2 System monitoring / performance test tools 111

Chapter 4. Samba. 123
4.1 What can you do with Samba? 123
4.2 Setting up the Samba server 123
    4.2.1 Configuring the Samba server 125
    4.2.2 Starting and stopping the Samba server. 133
    4.2.3 Starting Samba as startup service 134
    4.2.4 Using SWAT. 135
4.3 Sources and additional information. 153

Chapter 5. DNS - Domain Name Service 155
5.1 Installation of software 157
5.2 DNS sample configuration 157
5.3 Configuration tips 162

Chapter 6. DHCP - Dynamic Host Configuration Protocol 163
6.1 What is DHCP? 163
6.2 Why should I use DHCP? 163
6.3 Implementation on Linux 163

Chapter 7. Apache and IBM HTTP Server 167
7.1 The IBM HTTP server. 168

7.2 Apache HTTP Server installation 169
7.3 IBM HTTP Server installation 170
      7.3.1 Activating IBM HTTPD on system bootup 173
      7.3.2 Setting up the Administration Server. 173
7.4 General performance tips 178

Chapter 8. Sendmail. 181
8.1 What is Sendmail? 181
8.2 What you can do with Sendmail 181
8.3 Before you begin 181
8.4 Network configuration. 183
8.5 Setting up the DNS configuration 184
      8.5.1 Setting up the root DNS 184
      8.5.2 Setting up the DNS for the first subdomain 187
      8.5.3 Setting up the DNS for the second subdomain 190
      8.5.4 Setting up Sendmail 193
      8.5.5 Setting up the mail client 196
8.6 Sources of additional information 198

Chapter 9. LDAP - Lightweight Directory Access Protocol 199
9.1 What is LDAP? 199
      9.1.1 Directory Services 199
      9.1.2 X.500 200
9.2 How can I use LDAP? 200
9.3 LDAP basics. 200
      9.3.1 LDIF files 201
9.4 Implementation on Linux 201
      9.4.1 Downloading and installing OpenLDAP. 203
      9.4.2 Roaming Profiles for Netscape 204
      9.4.3 Starting OpenLDAP server 206
      9.4.4 Configuring Netscape 206
9.5 Sources of additional information 209

Chapter 10. NIS - Network Information System 211
10.1 What is NIS? 211
10.2 How can I use NIS? 211
10.3 Implementation on Linux 211
      10.3.1 NIS Server 212
      10.3.2 NIS Client 215
10.4 Sources of additional information 219

Chapter 11. NFS - Network File System 221
11.1 The NFS process 221
11.2 Allowing NFS access to data 224

11.3 Accessing data remotely with NFS 226
11.4 Allowing NFS access to data with GUI 227

Chapter 12. Packet filtering with IP Chains. 229
12.1 What is packet filtering? 229
12.2 What can you do with Linux packet filtering? 229
12.3 What do you need to run packet filtering?. 230
12.4 Network configuration for a packet filtering implementation 230
12.5 How to permanently enable IP Forwarding 232
12.6 Your first IP Chains success. 233
12.7 How packets travel through a gateway 234
12.8 Using IP Chains 235
    12.8.1 How to create a rule 236
    12.8.2 Making the rules permanent 238
12.9 Sources of additional information 238

Chapter 13. Backup and Recovery 239
13.1 Microlite BackupEDGE. 239
    13.1.1 Installing Microlite BackupEDGE 240
    13.1.2 Configuring the tape devices 241
    13.1.3 Defining the devices for making backups 247
    13.1.4 Initializing the tape 250
    13.1.5 Your first backup 252
    13.1.6 Restoring single files or directories. 255
    13.1.7 Master and incremental backups 258
    13.1.8 Restoring master and incremental backups 260
    13.1.9 Performing scheduled backups. 262
13.2 Microlite RecoverEDGE 265
    13.2.1 Creating the RecoverEDGE boot disks 266
    13.2.2 Recovering from total crash 273
13.3 More information on Microlite 274
13.4 BRU. 274
    13.4.1 Installing BRU. 274
    13.4.2 Basic commands 275
    13.4.3 X interface 276
    13.4.4 The big buttons. 277
    13.4.5 Summary 281

Appendix A. RAID levels. 283
A.1 What is RAID? 283
    A.1.1 RAID-0 284
    A.1.2 RAID-1 and RAID-1E 285
    A.1.3 RAID-10 286
    A.1.4 RAID-5 287

A.1.5 RAID-5 enhanced 291
A.1.6 Orthogonal RAID-5 293
A.1.7 Performance 294
A.1.8 Recommendations 296
A.1.9 Summary 297

Appendix B. Working video modes for IBM Netfinity servers 299

Appendix C. Recommendations for disk partitions 301

Appendix D. Hardware issues for IBM Netfinity servers 303

Appendix E. Sample smb.conf SAMBA configuration file 305

Appendix F. Special notices 313

Appendix G. Related publications 317
G.1 International Technical Support Organization publications 317
G.2 Redbooks on CD-ROMs. 317
G.3 Other publications. 317
G.4 Referenced Web sites 318

How to get IBM Redbooks 321
IBM Redbooks fax order form 322

List of abbreviations 323

Index 325

IBM Redbooks evaluation 329

Preface

Caldera OpenLinux 2.3 and OpenLinux eServer are the latest editions of the popular Caldera Linux distribution. OpenLinux 2.3 and eServer are the fully tested, proven, stable and supported Linux distributions for corporate and home use. OpenLinux delivers reliability, ease of installation and administration, high performance, security, and robust applications. This version of OpenLinux includes the latest version of LIZARD (Linux Wizard), the powerful but simple-to-use graphical installation program. LIZARD automatically detects all supported hardware and helps you to get OpenLinux up and running quickly.

Assumptions about you

This redbook will help you install and configure OpenLinux on your IBM Netfinity servers; furthermore it will help you understand, install and configure a wide range of different services, such as Samba, Apache and LDAP among others.

Do I need to be a Linux expert to use this guide? The answer to that question is "No". This redbook is aimed at beginners and intermediate Linux users and for all Windows NT users who are used to the safe and convenient graphical user interface.

The team that wrote this redbook

This redbook was produced by a team of specialists from around the world working at the International Technical Support Organization, Raleigh Center.

Jakob Carstensen is an Advisory Specialist for Netfinity Servers at the International Technical Support Organization, Raleigh Center. He manages residencies and produces redbooks. His most recent publication was *Linux for WebSphere and DB2 Servers*. Before joining the ITSO, he worked in Denmark both for the IBM PC Institute teaching TechConnect and Service Training courses, and for IBM PSS performing level-2 support of Netfinity products. He has a Bachelor of Electronic Engineering degree and has worked for IBM for the past nine years.

Ivo Gomilsek is a Product Specialist for PC Hardware in IBM Slovenia. He is IBM Certified Professional Server Specialist, Red Hat Certified Engineer, OS/2 Warp Certified Engineer and Certified Vinca Co-StandbyServer for Windows NT Engineer. Ivo was a member of the team that wrote the redbook *Implementing Vinca Solutions on IBM Netfinity Servers*. His areas of expertise

xiii

include IBM Netfinity servers, network operating systems (OS/2, Linux, Windows NT) and Lotus Domino Servers. During his career he has worked as a Systems Engineer in PSG and is now working in Product Support Services (PSS) as level-2 support for IBM Netfinity servers, and high availability solutions for IBM Netfinity servers and Linux. Ivo has been employed at IBM for three years.

Lenz Grimmer is a Software Engineer at SuSE GmbH in Nuremberg, Germany. He belongs to the distribution development team and is responsible for a number of packages on the distribution. He has five years of experience with Linux (since Kernel 0.99.xx) and holds a degree in Computer Science from the Berufsakademie in Mannheim, Germany. Before he started working for SuSE in April 1998, he worked as a system administrator for a local Internet service provider that used Linux exclusively for its servers. His areas of expertise include setting up different Linux services such as Apache, Samba and Squid. In addition to trying to be helpful on several SuSE mailing lists, he has written the SuSE FAQ, which is available online at
http://www.suse.com/Support/Doku/FAQ/

Jay Haskins is a Systems Architect for IBM Global Services Enterprise Architecture and Design in Seattle, Washington. He has been a Linux and Open Source advocate for more than five years and currently spends most of his time developing dynamic monitoring tools using Perl and the Apache Web server. Before joining IBM, Jay worked in several different areas of the information technology field including UNIX system administration, database design and development, Windows application development, and network administration.

Joe Kaplenk is a Senior Systems Management Integration Professional for IBM Global Services/DAAS in Lisle, Illinois. He has 20 years of experience in the computer field. He holds a degree in Physics from the University of Utah. His areas of expertise include UNIX system administration and computer science education. He has written several books on UNIX and Linux system administration, including the *UNIX System Adminstrator's Interactive Workbook* and the *Linux Network Administrator's Interactive Workbook,* both published by Prentice-Hall, as well as contributing articles to Linux journals. He has worked with IBM for three years. He has also been teaching Computer Science part-time at the College of DuPage in Glen Ellyn, Illinois for 16 years and UNIX administration for seven years.

Thanks to the following people for their invaluable contributions to this project:

Erik Ratcliffe, Caldera Systems

Thanks to the following people from the International Technical Support Organization, Raleigh Center:

Gail Christensen
Shawn Walsh
Linda Robinson
David Watts
Rufus Credle
Margaret Ticknor
Mike Haley

Thanks to the following IBM employees:

Egan Ford, Advanced Technical Support
Karl Schultz, Netfinity ServerProven
Julie Briddon, Marketing Communications
Bo Brun, PC Institute

Comments welcome

Your comments are important to us!

We want our redbooks to be as helpful as possible. Please send us your comments about this or other redbooks in one of the following ways:

- Fax the evaluation form found in "IBM Redbooks evaluation" on page 329 to the fax number shown on the form.
- Use the online evaluation form found at http://www.redbooks.ibm.com/
- Send your comments in an Internet note to redbook@us.ibm.com

Chapter 1. Linux installation

This chapter describes in detail the basic installation necessary to install and run Caldera OpenLinux 2.3 and Caldera OpenLinux eServer beta release on IBM Netfinity servers. We also show what steps you need to carry out before the installation, to avoid problems during the installation.

1.1 Knowing your hardware

Before you install Caldera OpenLinux, you should be familiar with the hardware in the computer. You at least need information about the following components in your computer:

- Hard drives - interface type (SCSI or IDE) and size
- CD-ROM - interface type (SCSI or IDE) and the manufacturer
- SCSI adapter - manufacturer and model number
- Display Adapter - manufacturer and model number
- Mouse - mouse type and connector type
- Network card - manufacturer and model number
- RAM - the amount of RAM in your system
- Monitor - manufacturer and model number

For the monitor in particular, it is good to know all technical specifications.

For IBM Netfinity servers and other IBM products, including monitors and SCSI adapters, the ultimate source for all information is:

```
ftp://ftp.pc.ibm.com/pcicrse/psref
```

Here you will find the PSREF (Personal Systems Reference) sheets for all IBM PC products, both current and withdrawn. You can also find a lot of useful information at the following internet resources:

```
http://www.pc.ibm.com/support
http://www.pc.ibm.com/us/netfinity/tech_library.html
```

1.2 Hardware considerations

In this section we describe how to handle hardware found in IBM Netfinity servers, when installing Caldera OpenLinux.

1.2.1 Adaptec SCSI controller

All versions of the Adaptec SCSI controllers used in IBM Netfinity servers are supported in kernels 2.2.10 and above, which are used in Caldera OpenLinux 2.3 and Caldera OpenLinux eServer.

1.2.2 IBM ServeRAID controller

All versions of the IBM ServeRAID controller used in IBM Netfinity servers are supported in Caldera OpenLinux 2.3 and Caldera OpenLinux eServer.

1.2.3 IBM token-ring network adapters

IBM ISA, PCMCIA and PCI token-ring network adapters are supported in kernels 2.2.10 and above, which are used in Caldera OpenLinux 2.3 and Caldera OpenLinux eServer.

1.3 Updating the BIOS and ServeRAID controller firmware

Before starting the installation it is important to have the latest level of microcode for all your hardware components. You can download the latest BIOS, diagnostic updates and ServeRAID controller firmware for your IBM Netfinity server from:

http://www.pc.ibm.com/support

For the networking products, you will find all the latest available code at:

http://www.networking.ibm.com

> **Note**
>
> Always update the BIOS of the IBM Netfinity server to the latest level, and update all adapters with the latest firmware before installing.

1.4 Making the CD-ROM bootable

If you want to use the CD-ROM for booting the system to start the installation make sure the CD-ROM is in the boot sequence before any hard drive devices. You can modify this in the IBM Netfinity server BIOS. To do this follow these steps:

1. Power on the server.
2. When you see the IBM logo press F1 to enter the setup utility.
3. From the setup utility select **Start Options > Startup Sequence**.

4. Make sure that your CD-ROM is in the boot sequence before the first hard disk device.
5. Press Esc until you come to the setup utility main window and select **Save Settings.**
6. Press **Enter** to confirm saving the current settings.
7. Exit the setup utility.

> **Note**
>
> Making the CD-ROM bootable can also be done by loading the default settings from the setup utility, but be aware that all other settings will be set to default as well.

1.5 Basic Linux installation

In this section we will describe how to install the Caldera OpenLinux 2.3 and Caldera OpenLinux eServer on IBM Netfinity servers. To successfully complete the installation follow these steps:

1. Insert Caldera OpenLinux 2.3 or Caldera OpenLinux eServer into the CD-ROM drive of your IBM Netfinity server. When the CD is started, you will see a window similar to Figure 1.

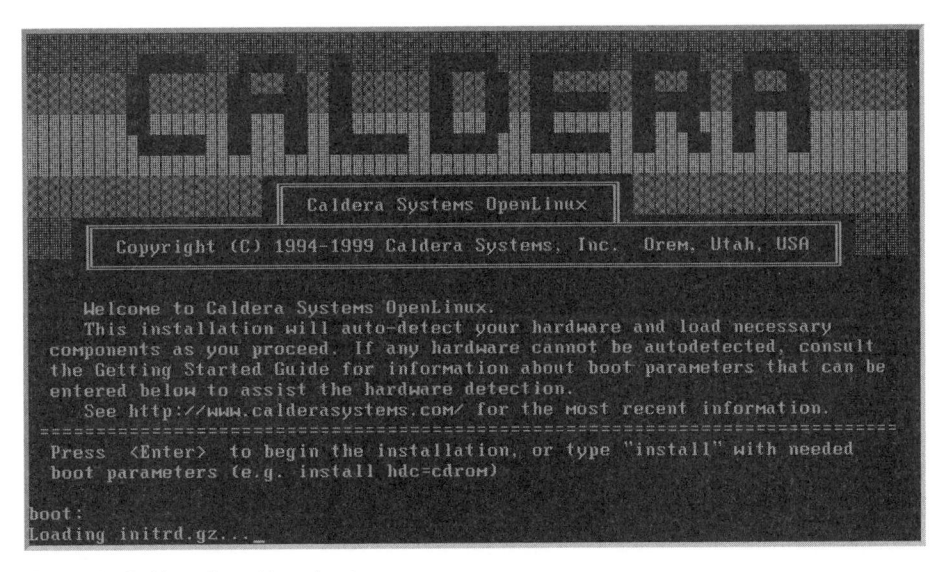

Figure 1. Caldera OpenLinux bootup

After the initial ramdisk and kernel are loaded you will see a window similar to Figure 2.

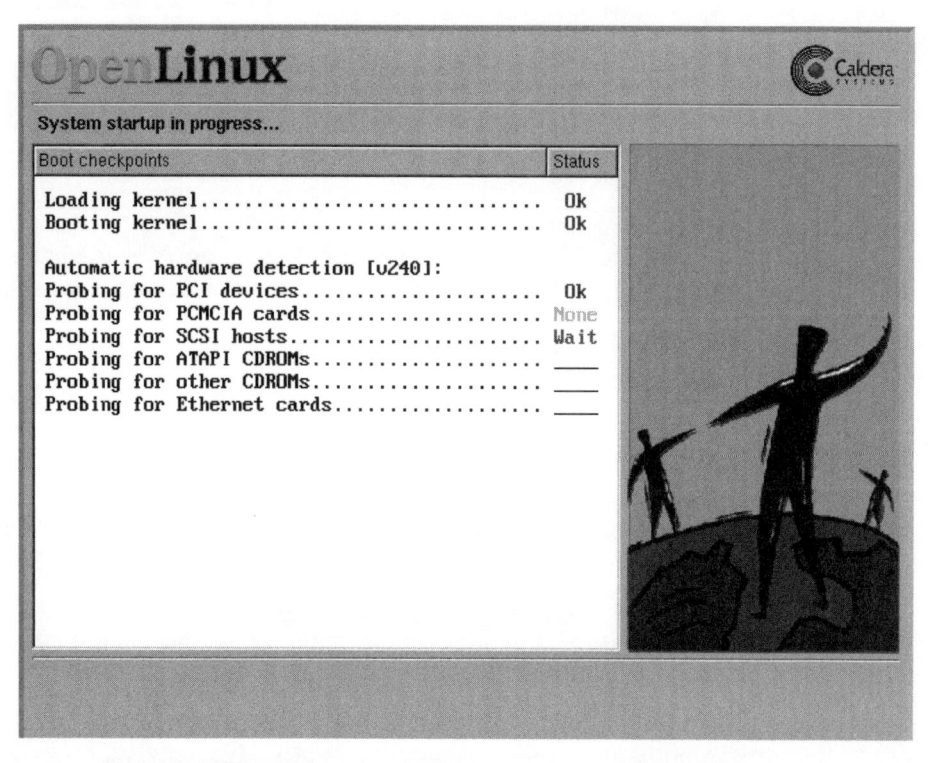

```
OpenLinux                                            Caldera
System startup in progress...
 Boot checkpoints                                  Status
Loading kernel...............................  Ok
Booting kernel...............................  Ok

Automatic hardware detection [v240]:
Probing for PCI devices....................  Ok
Probing for PCMCIA cards...................  None
Probing for SCSI hosts.....................  Wait
Probing for ATAPI CDROMs...................  ____
Probing for other CDROMs...................  ____
Probing for Ethernet cards.................  ____
```

Figure 2. Hardware detection

When all the hardware is detected you will see a window similar to Figure 3.

4 Caldera OpenLinux and Netfinity Server Integration Guide

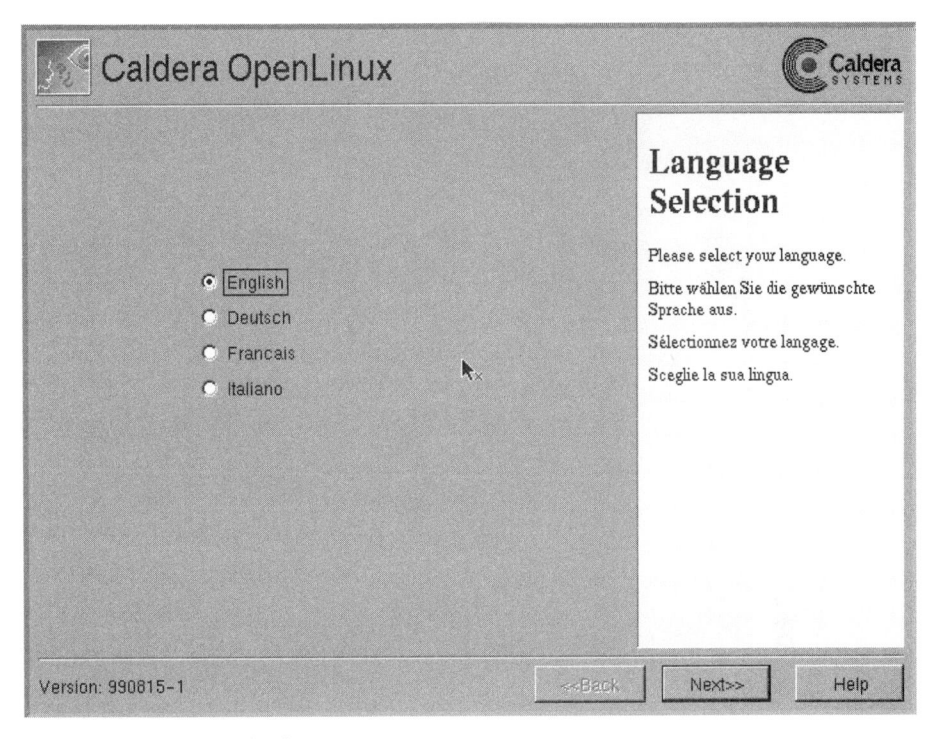

Figure 3. Language selection

Select a language and click **Next** to continue. You will see a window similar to Figure 4.

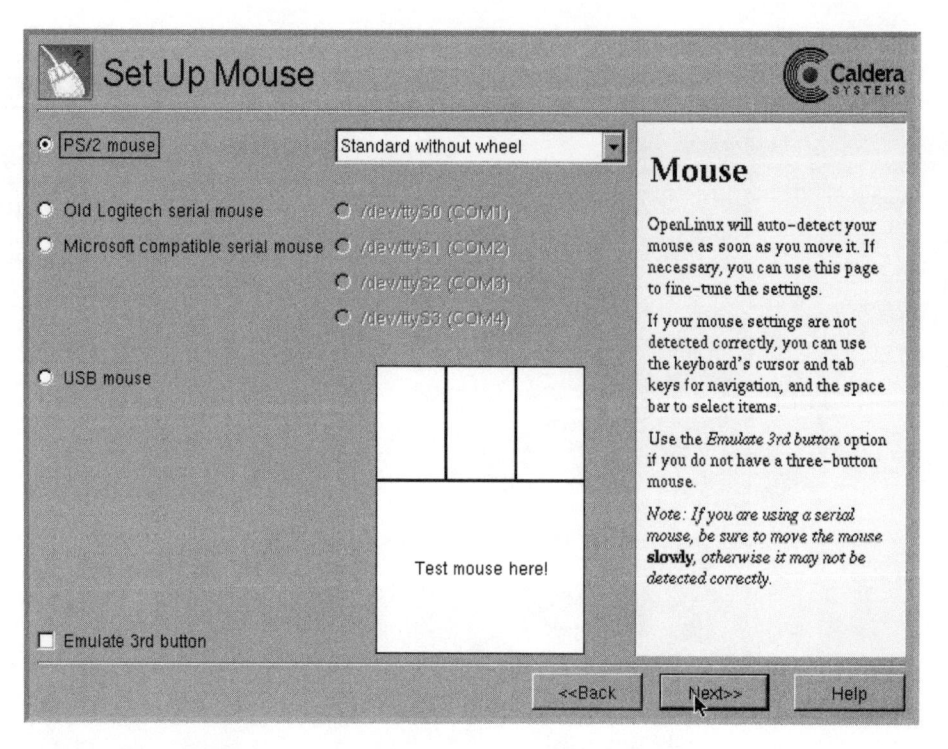

Figure 4. Mouse setup

2. Here you select your mouse type and settings. When you are finished, click **Next** to continue. You will see a window similar to Figure 5.

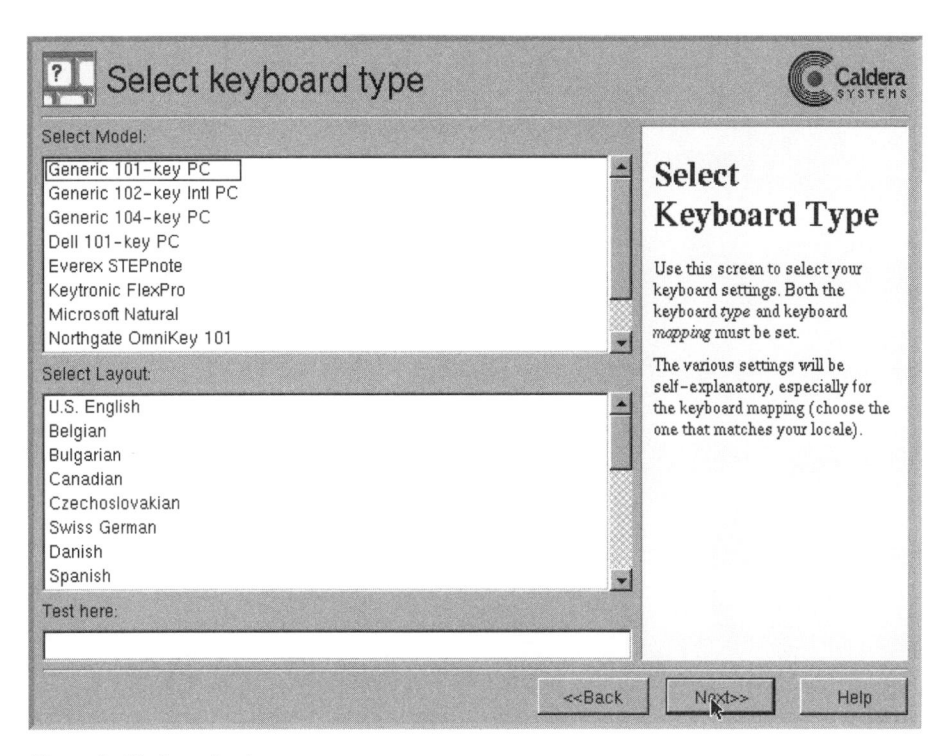

Figure 5. Keyboard setup

3. In this window you select the keyboard type and layout. Click **Next** to continue. You will see a window similar to Figure 6.

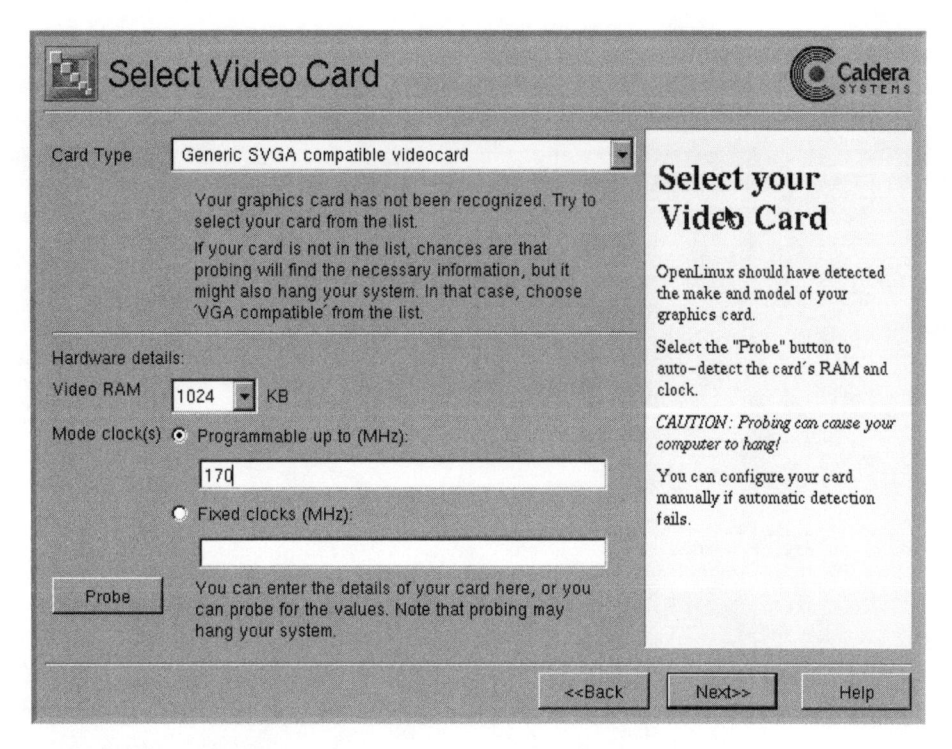

Figure 6. Video card setup

4. Here you select the XFree server you will use for your video card. Before selecting your XFree video server check Appendix B, "Working video modes for IBM Netfinity servers" on page 299. When defining the card type, the install program automatically picks up the XFree server that supports that card. The best way is to select, from the Card Type scroll box, the XFree server that supports the card you are using. After you have selected the XFree server you want, you need to specify the amount of Video RAM and also the Mode clock. If you do not know the exact values, you can click **Probe** to search for the details of the graphic card.

Note

Before successfully probing for the card, you need to specify the correct XFree server for your card.

If you click **Probe**, you will see a window similar to Figure 7. If you select the VGA XFree server, the installation procedures will continue with step 11.

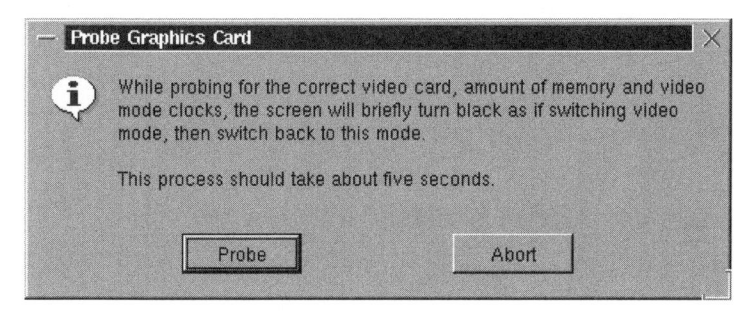

[Dialog: Probe Graphics Card — While probing for the correct video card, amount of memory and video mode clocks, the screen will briefly turn black as if switching video mode, then switch back to this mode. This process should take about five seconds. Buttons: Probe | Abort]

Figure 7. Before probing for the video card

5. Click **Probe** to start probing for the card. The window will briefly turn black. When probing is finished, you will see a window similar to Figure 8.

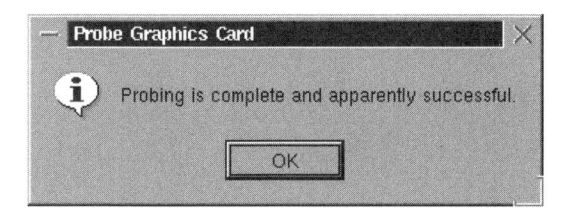

[Dialog: Probe Graphics Card — Probing is complete and apparently successful. Button: OK]

Figure 8. After successfully probing for the card

6. If for some reason the video card cannot be recognized correctly, you need to type in the settings manually. If you do not know the correct settings, select the VGA XFree server and you can fine-tune XFree after the installation is completed. Click **OK** to return to the video card setup window. Click **Next** to continue. You will see a window similar to Figure 9.

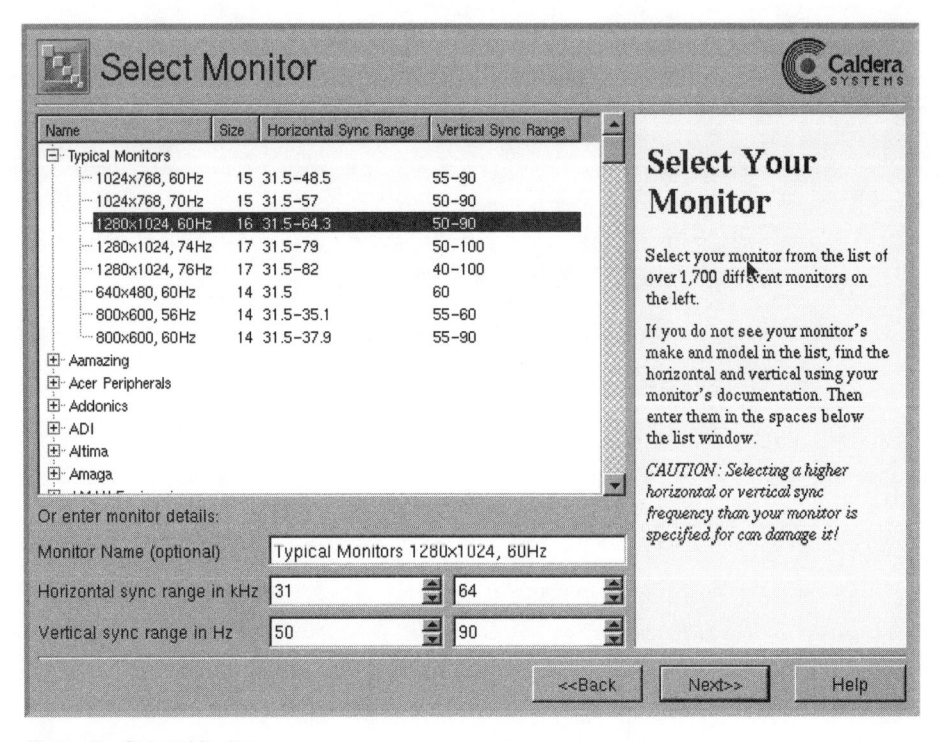

Figure 9. Select Monitor

7. Select the monitor type you are using. If there is no exact match for your monitor model, select one of the Typical Monitors. Use the one nearest to the one you are using. Click **Next** to continue, and you will see a window similar to Figure 10.

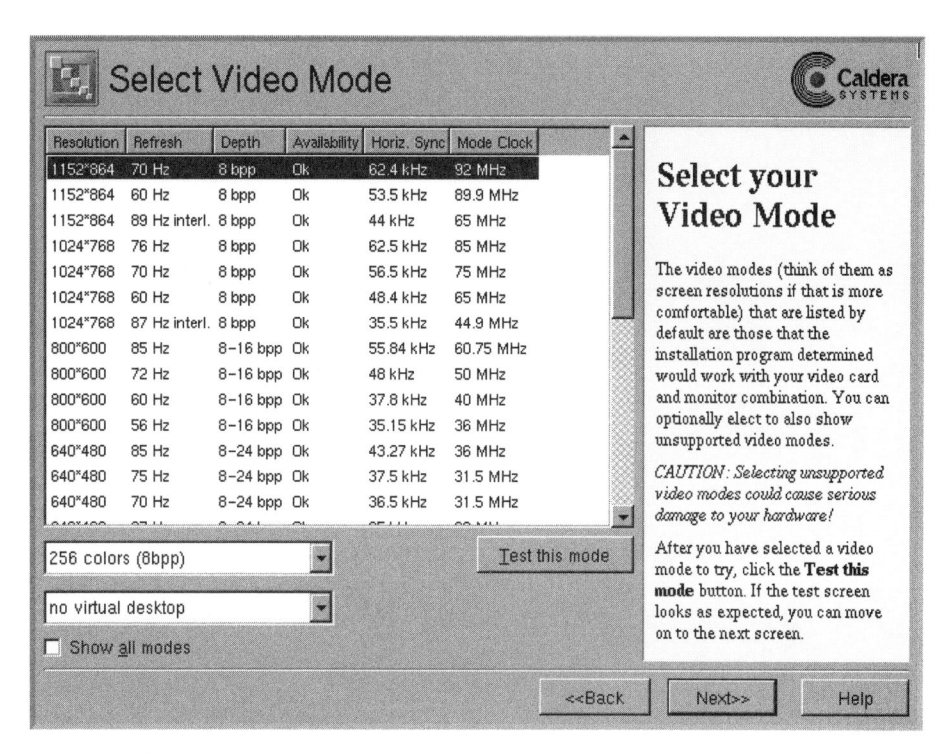

Figure 10. Selecting Video Mode

8. In this window you select the video mode, color depth and the virtual desktop size you prefer. You can find working modes for IBM Netfinity servers in Appendix B, "Working video modes for IBM Netfinity servers" on page 299. Depending on the amount of memory on the video card, color depth and resolution, you can have a virtual desktop. This is a feature of the XFree servers. By default only the modes that are compatible with the selected video card and monitor are displayed. If you are an experienced user you can check the **Show all modes** option to see all available video modes. You can test the selected video mode by clicking **Test this mode.** You will see a window similar to Figure 11.

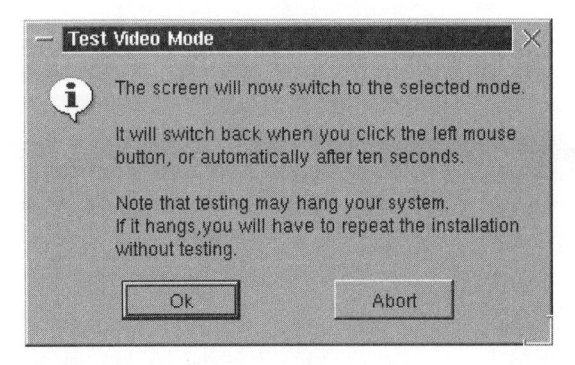

Figure 11. Test the video mode

9. Click **OK** to start the test. If you have selected a working mode for your hardware, you will get a clear demo image and a message how to get back to the installation process. This image will disappear after 10 seconds if you do nothing. After you have successfully tested your video mode you will be back to the window similar to Figure 10. Click **Next** to continue the installation. You will see a window similar to Figure 12.

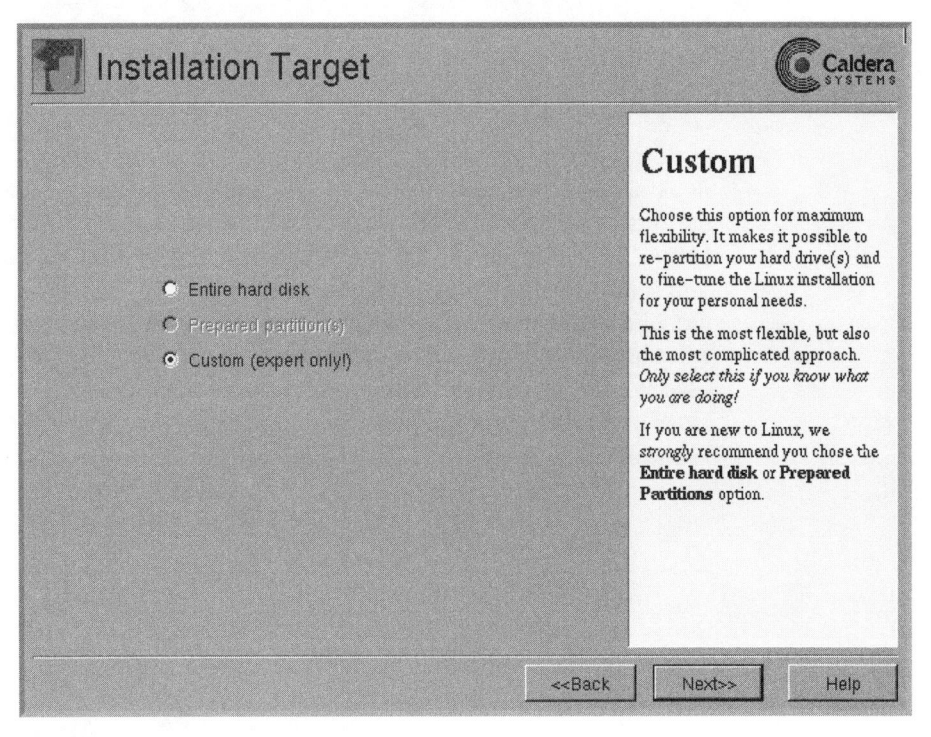

Figure 12. Choosing installation target

12 Caldera OpenLinux and Netfinity Server Integration Guide

10. At this point you can select the type of partitioning you want to use. You have three options:

- **Entire hard disk**: this option is initially selected if no previous Linux installation is found on the system. It means that the whole disk will be used for the Caldera OpenLinux installation.

- **Prepared partition(s)**: this option is enabled only when a previous Linux installation is found on the hard disk. If you choose this option, the installation process will use the existing partitioning.

- **Custom (expert only!)**: use this option if you want to create your own partition scheme.

In our case we selected **Custom**. Click **Next** to continue the installation. You will see a window similar to Figure 13.

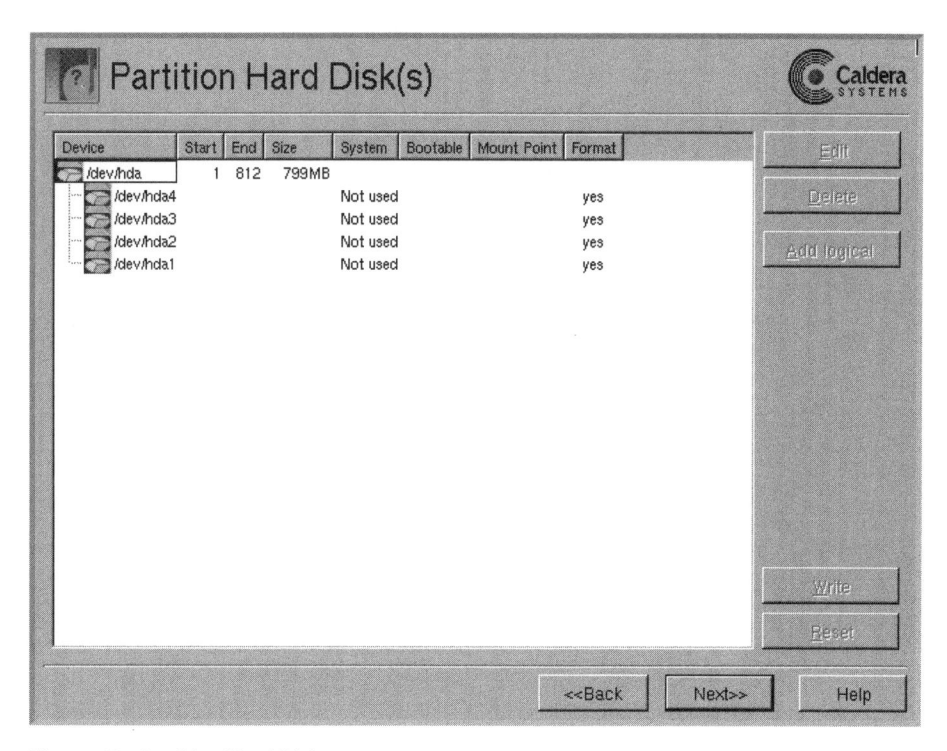

Figure 13. Partition Hard Disk

11. Here you can create, delete, or modify partitions. To create a new partition select an entry that indicates it is "Not used" and click **Edit**, and you will see a window similar to Figure 14.

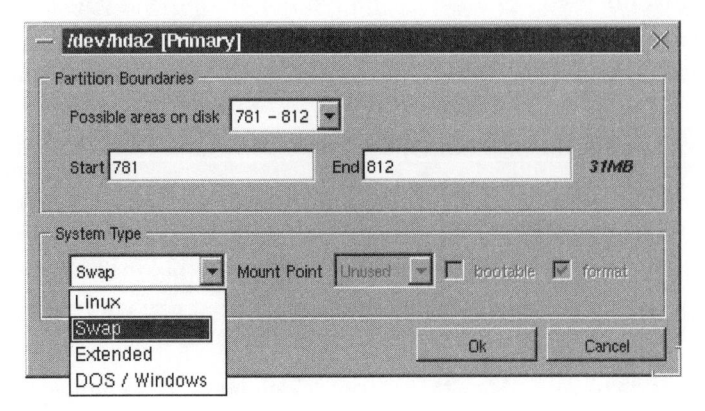

Figure 14. Creating new partition

As you can see in Figure 14, you can create four types of partitions:

- Linux
- Swap
- Extended
- DOS/Windows

For successfully installing Caldera OpenLinux you need to create at least one Linux and one swap partition. But we recommend that you create more Linux partitions for the installation files:

- One small partition for "/boot" mounting point, around 20 MB for kernel images
- Partition for "/" mounting point (ROOT), at least 1GB
- Partition for "/home" mounting point; the size depends on your needs
- Partition for "/usr", mounting point; the size depends on your needs
- Partition for "/var", mounting point; the size depends on your needs
- Partition for "/opt", mounting point; the size depends on your needs

For the Linux type of partitions, you can select the mounting point by clicking the arrow to the right of the Mount Point field, and you will see a window similar to Figure 15.

> **Note**
>
> Refer to Appendix C, "Recommendations for disk partitions" on page 301 for our recommendations regarding disk partitions.

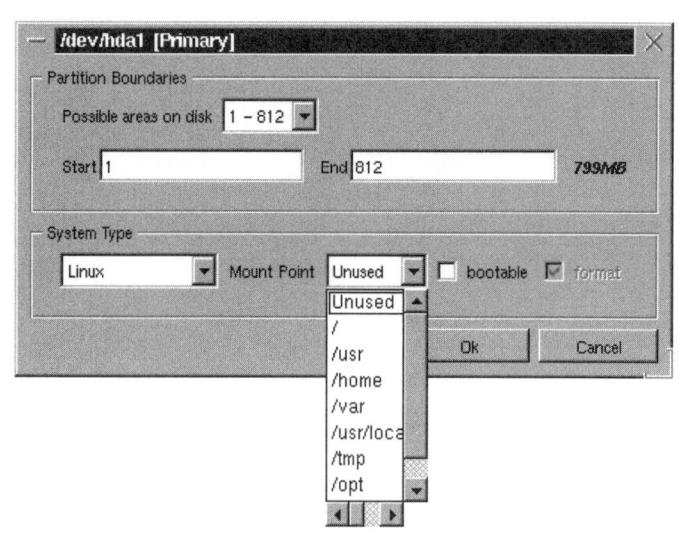

Figure 15. Select mounting point

If the mount point you need is not available, you can easily type in whatever you need. That is the case for the "/boot" mount point. If you want the partition you are creating to be bootable, select the **bootable** checkbox.

12. When you have selected the mount point and defined the size of the partition click **OK** to save the selections you made. You will see a window similar to Figure 16.

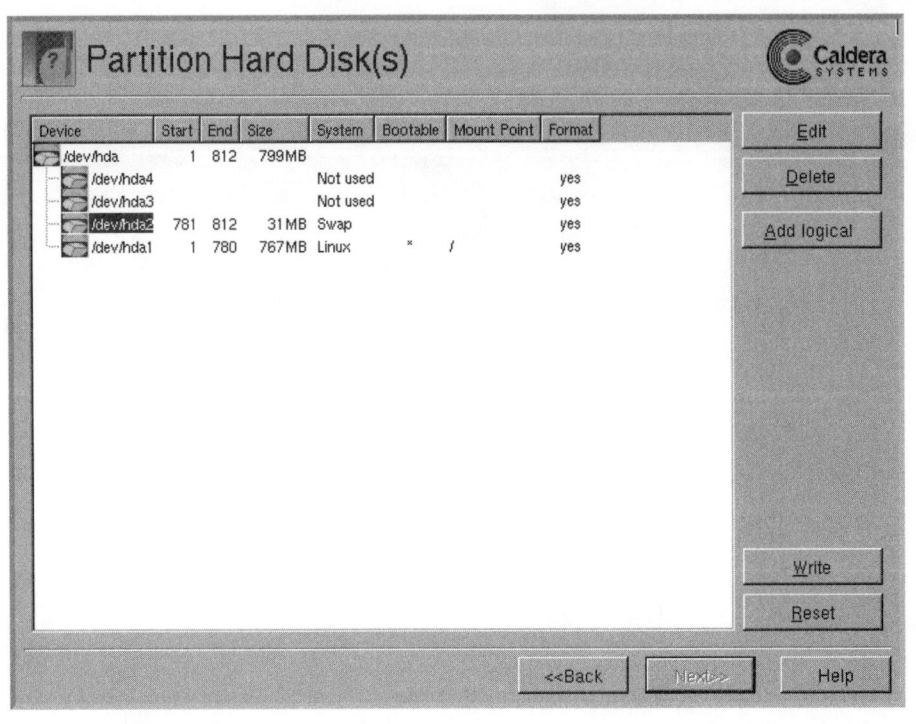

Figure 16. After defining partitions

If you need to create more that four partitions on one physical disk, this can be done by creating an extended partition with more logical drives in it. To create an extended partition you need to use the Extended type as the partition type.

13. To create an extended partition select an unused partition entry and click **Edit**, and you will see a window similar to Figure 14 on page 14.
14. Select **Extended** as the partition type and define the partition size. Click **OK** to continue, and you will see a window similar to Figure 17.

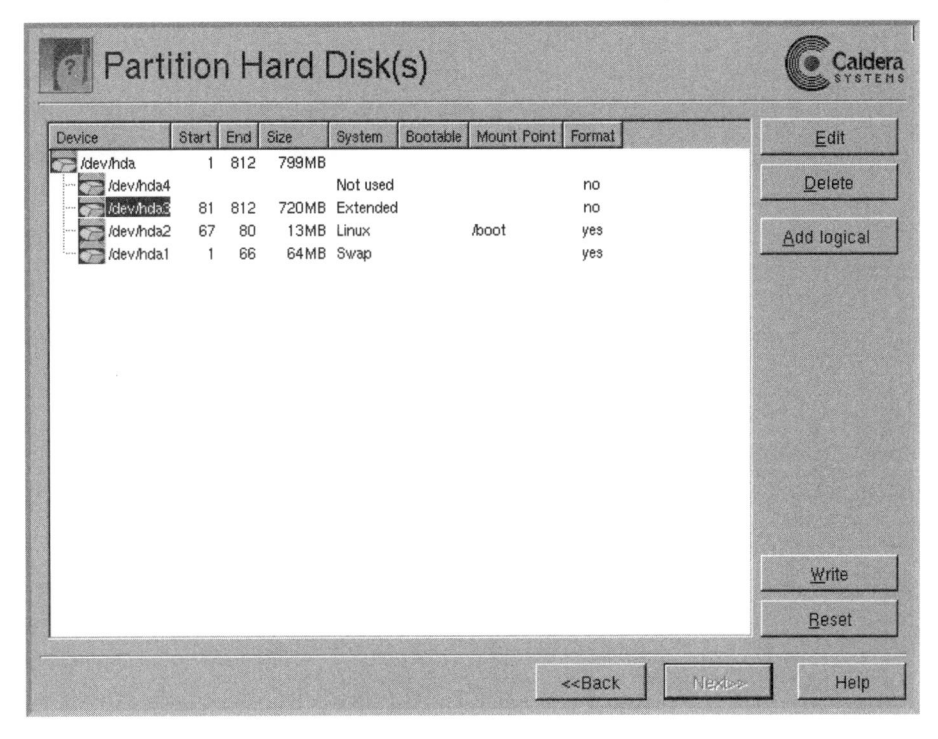

Figure 17. After creating an extended partition

As you can see in our example, there is an extended partition under device "/dev/hda3".

15. To create logical drives inside an extended partition, select the extended partition and click **Add logical.** You will see a window similar to Figure 18.

Figure 18. Add a logical partition

Chapter 1. Linux installation   **17**

16. Here you specify the size and mount point of the logical partition. Then you click **OK** to continue. You will see a window similar to Figure 19.

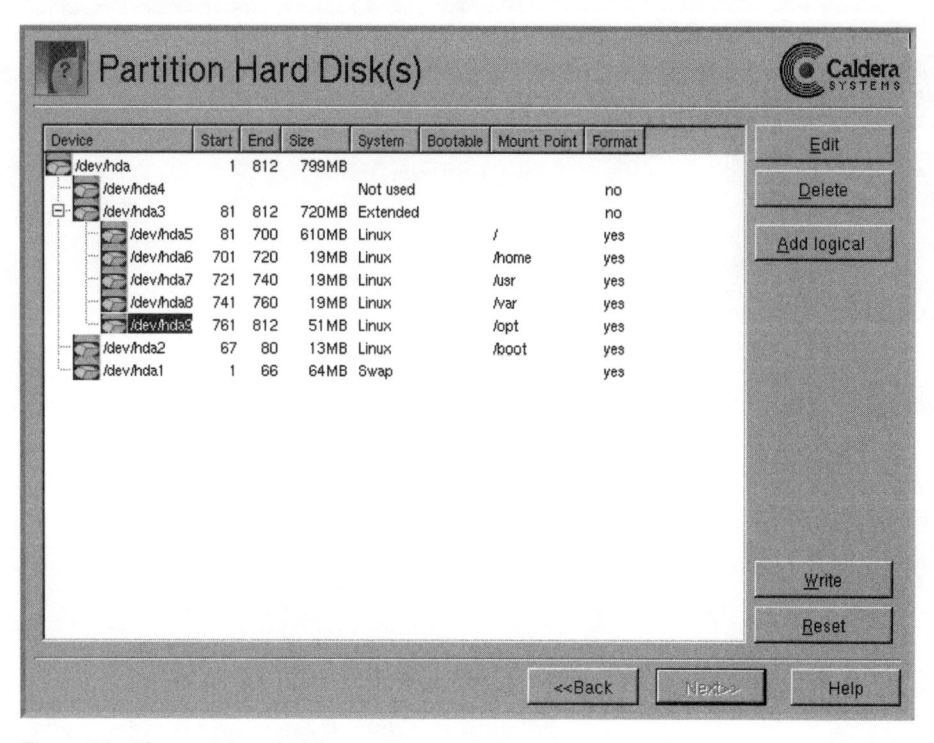

Figure 19. After creating partitions

17. The partitions you have just created are not yet written to the disk, so you can still make changes. You can click the **Reset** button to restore the original configuration. When you are finished with the changes click **Write** to commit the changes to the disk drive. Click **Next** to continue. If you forget to assign "/" (the root partition), you will see a window similar to Figure 20, and you proceed on step 19. Otherwise, you will see a window similar to Figure 21 on page 20 and you continue at step 20.

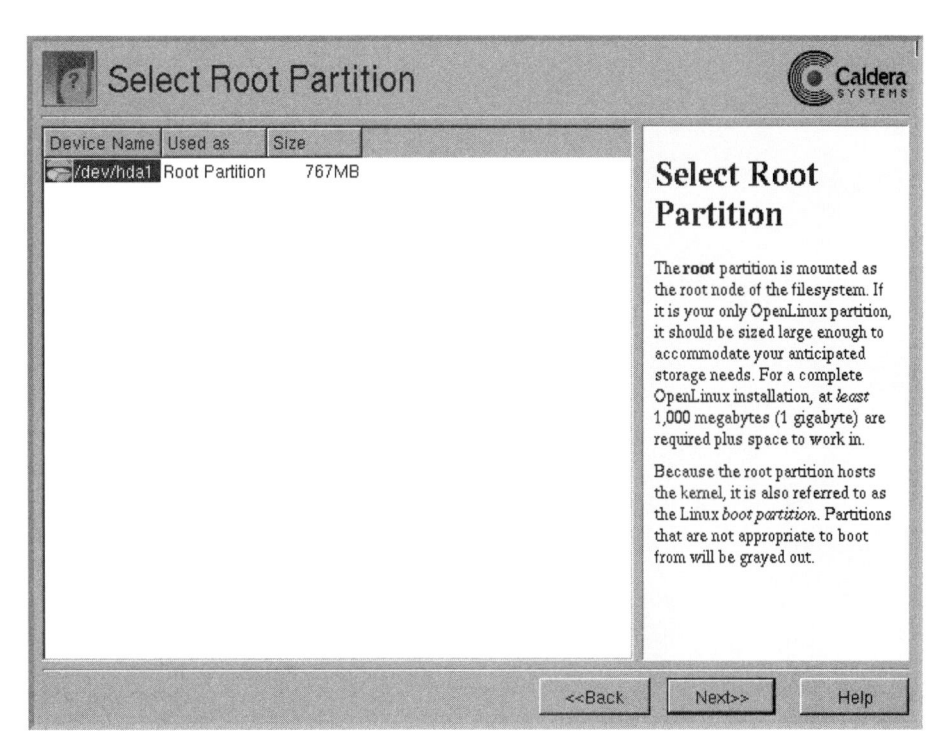

Figure 20. Selecting root partition

18. Select the partition that will be used for the root mounting point "/". Click **Next** to continue. You will see a window similar to Figure 21.

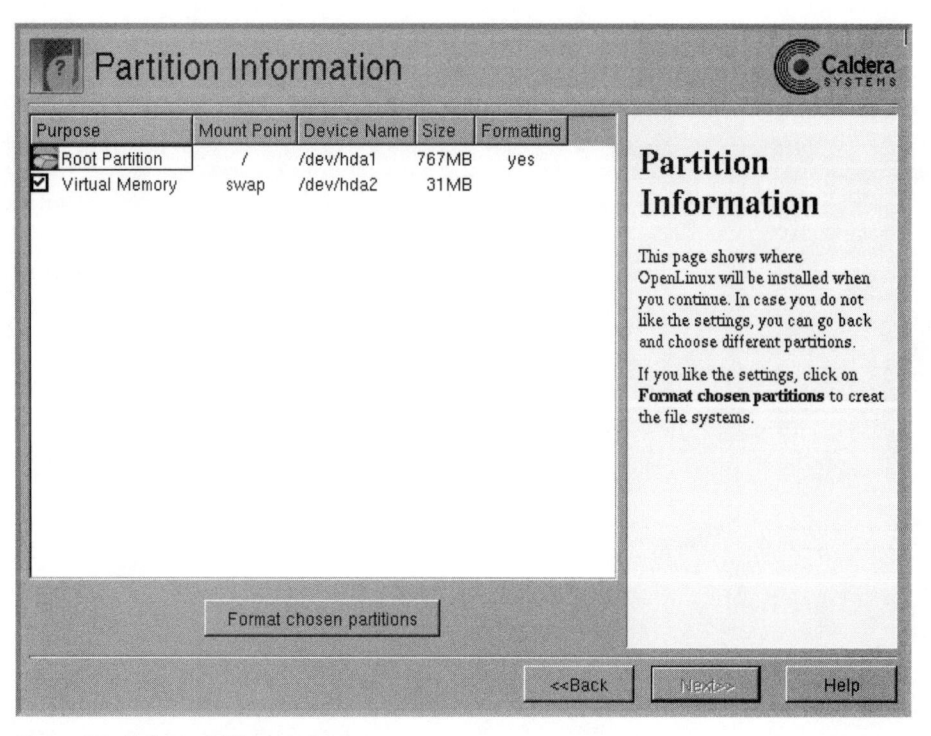

Figure 21. Select partitions to format

19. Before you can start installing the file system it has to be created on the target partitions. Do this by formatting the partitions. In this window you can select which partitions you want to format. Some partitions (for example "/" - the root partition) will be formatted by default and you cannot choose not to format them. To start formatting, click **Format chosen partitions.** You will see a window similar to Figure 22.

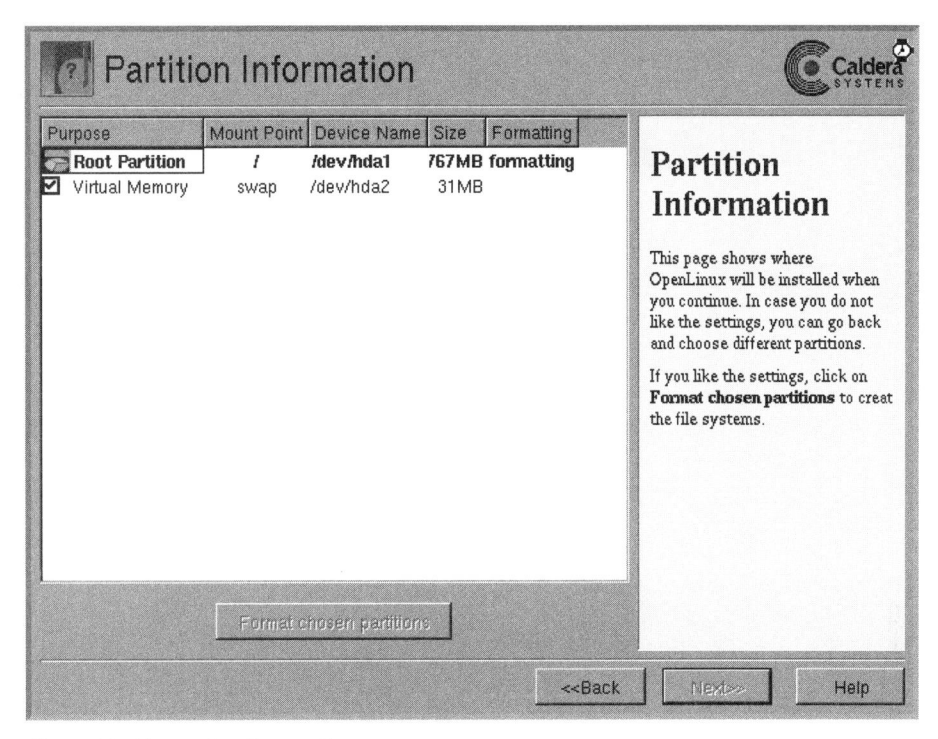

Figure 22. Formatting the partitions

After the partitions are formatted, you will see a window similar to Figure 23.

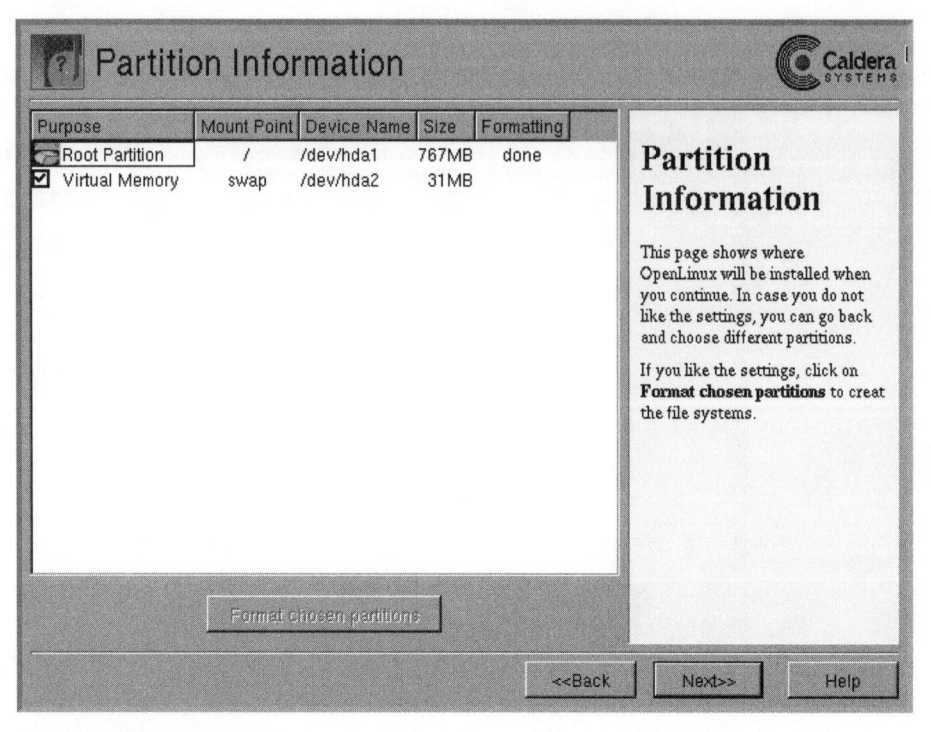

Figure 23. After formatting

20. Click **Next** to proceed with the installation. You will see a window similar to Figure 24.

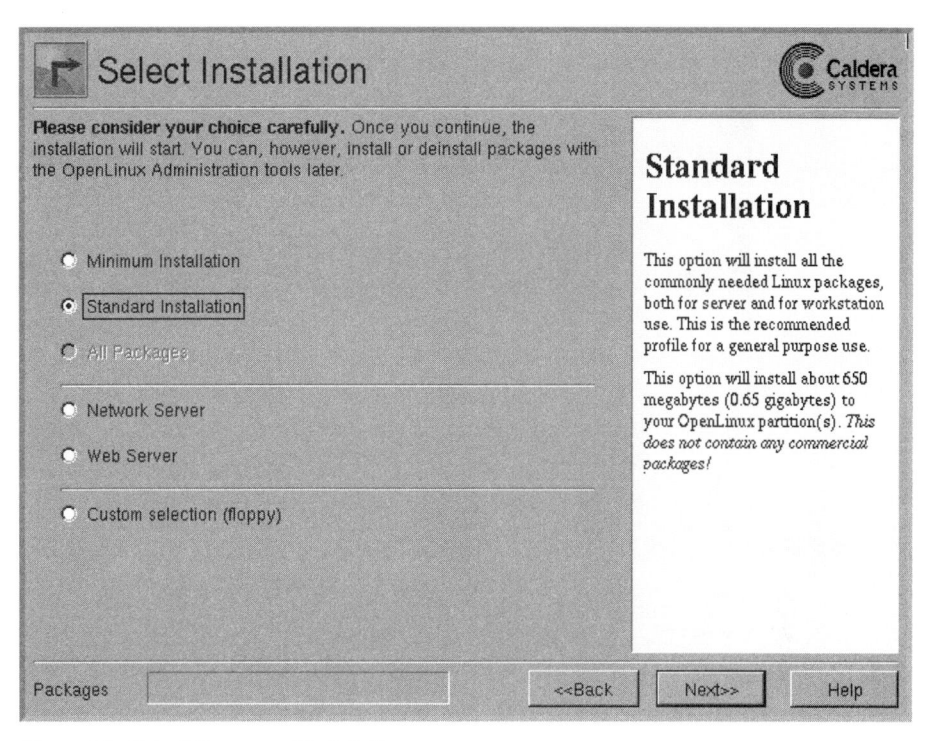

Figure 24. Select the type of installation

21. Here you select the installation type, and define which packages will be installed. If some options are grayed out, it means you do not have enough free space available for the installation. You can click the **Back** button to go back and change the partitions to meet your needs. After selecting the type of installation, click **Next** to continue. The packages will start installing in the background; Linux is a real multitasking operating system. You can see the progress in the Packages field. You will see a window similar to Figure 25.

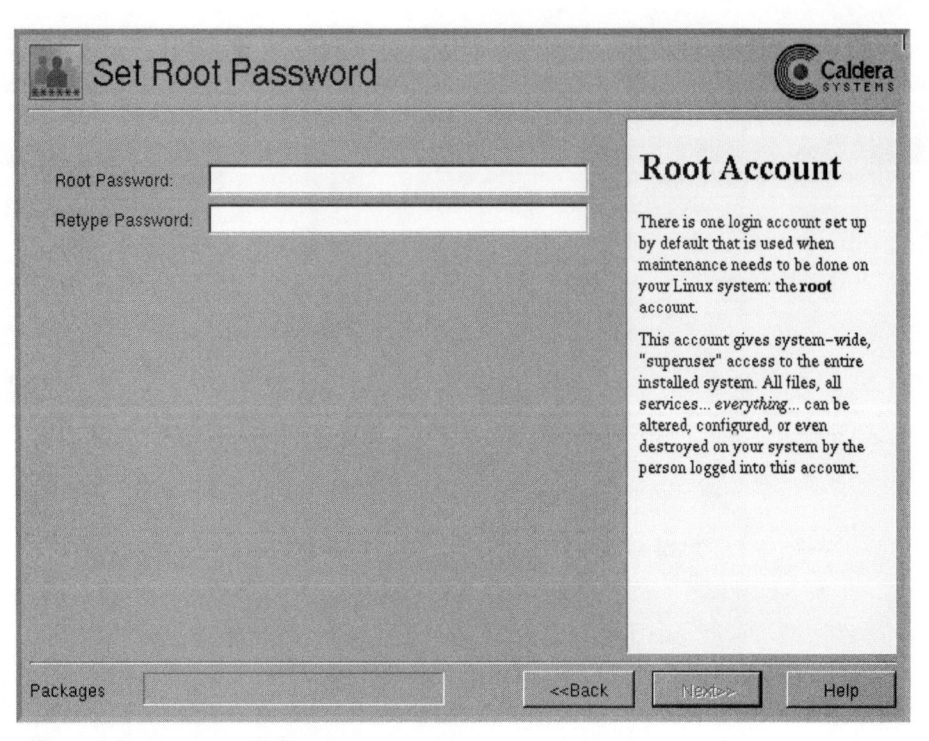

Figure 25. Defining root password

22. In this window you define your root account password. The root user will manage your system. After you entered the password, click **Next** to continue. You will see a window similar to Figure 26.

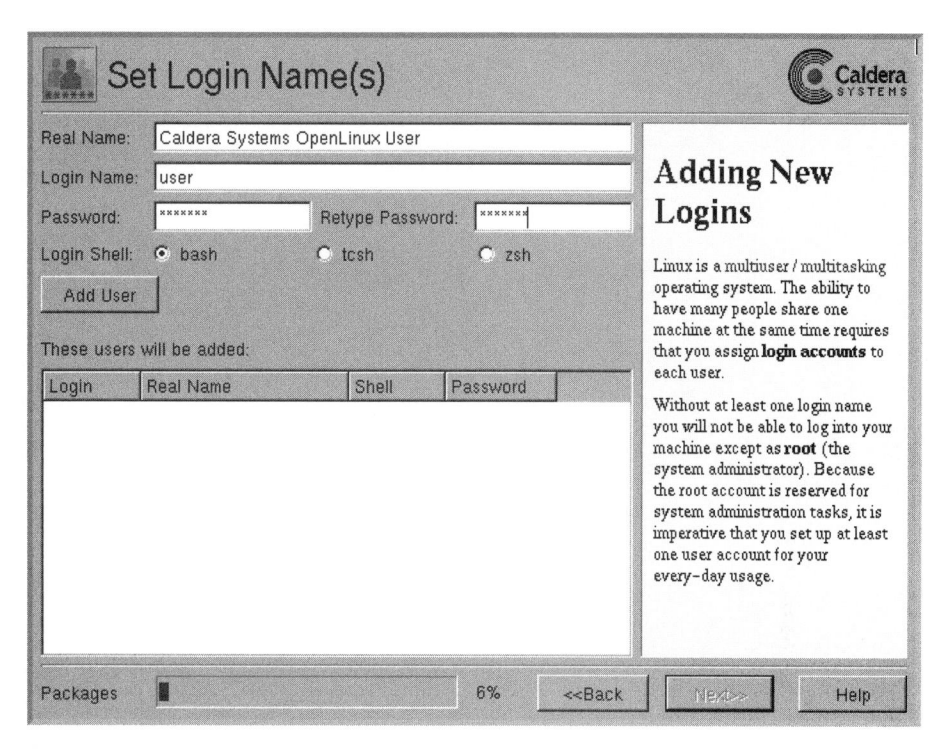

Figure 26. Defining users

23. You need to create at least one user to continue with the installation. To add a new user, fill in all fields and click **Add User.** You will see a window similar to Figure 27.

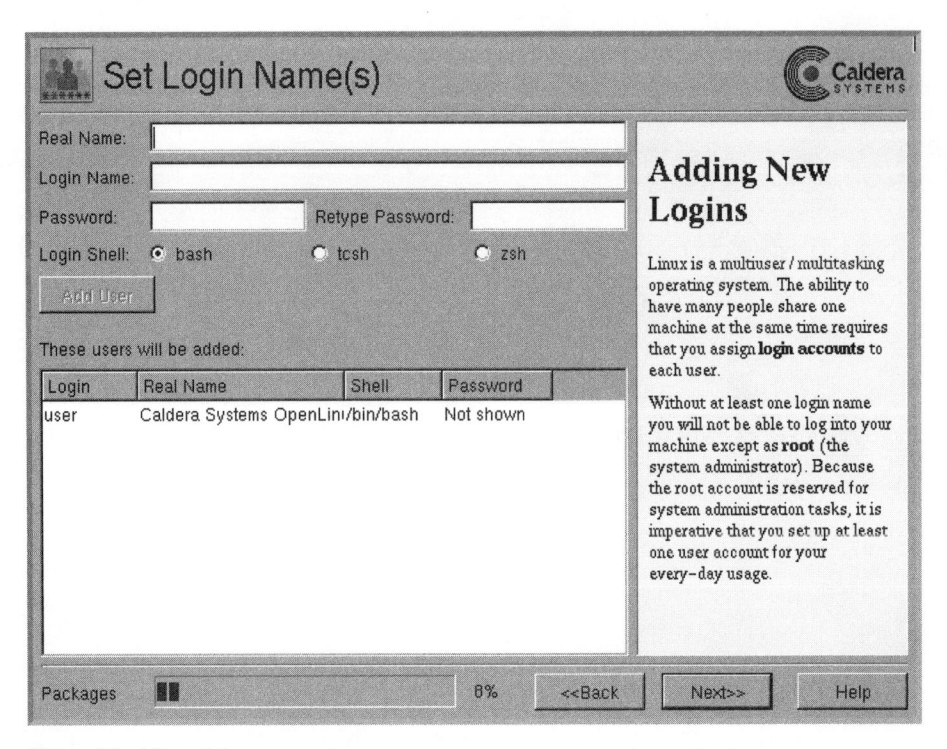

Figure 27. After adding new user

24. You can see which users have been created already. To continue with the installation, click **Next,** and you will see a window similar to Figure 28.

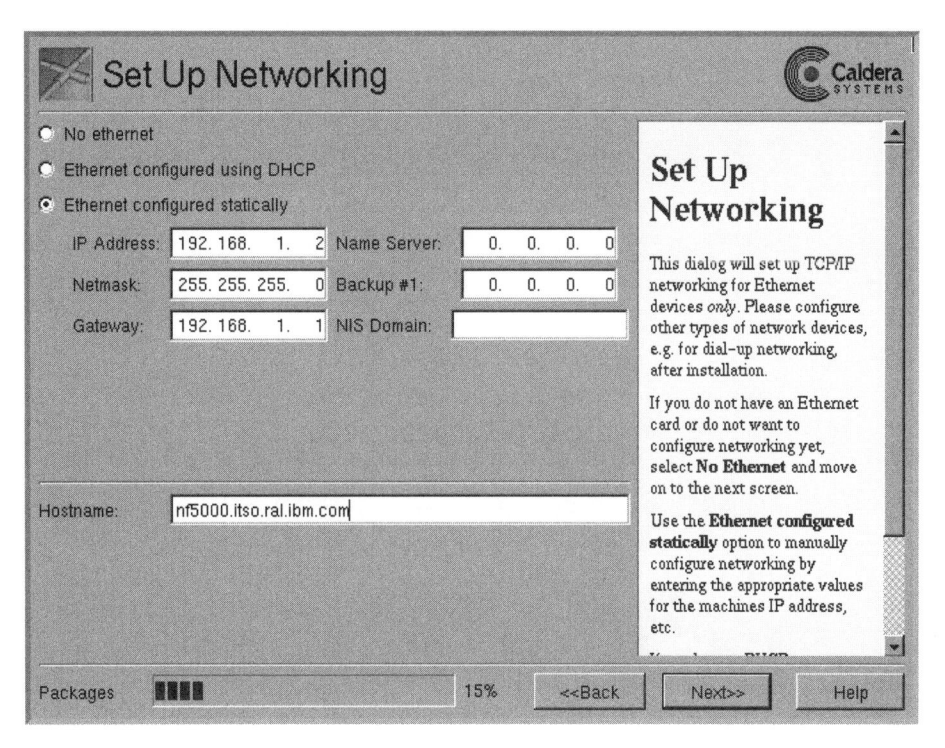

Figure 28. Set up networking

25. If your network card was recognized by the kernel, you can set it up here. The setup can be done only for Ethernet cards. You have three options:

    a. **No Ethernet**: use this option if you do not have a network card or the card is not supported, as for example token-ring. You can still configure token-ring cards later.

    b. **Ethernet configured using DHCP**: use this option when you use a DHCP server to define the IP addresses of the clients.

    c. **Ethernet configured statically**: use this option when you have a static IP address.

    On this page you also define the hostname of the computer you are installing on. All the settings can later be modified using Caldera Open Administration System (COAS). When you have typed in all needed data, click **Next** to continue. You will see a window similar to Figure 29.

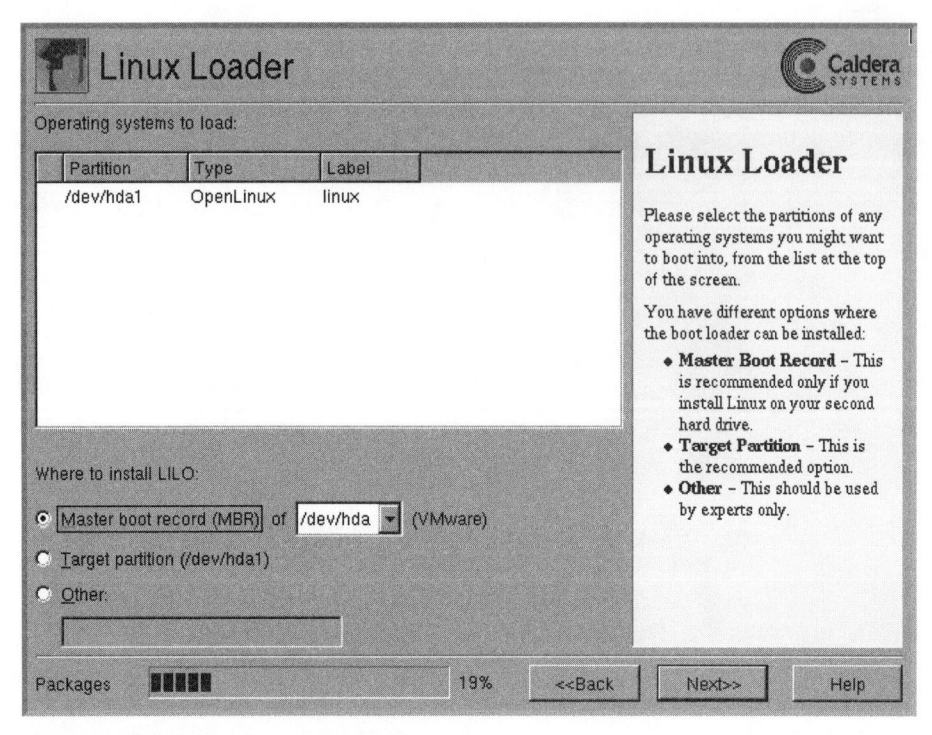

Figure 29. Configuring the Linux Loader

26. The Linux operating system is loaded by the Linux Loader (LILO). In this window you specify where the LILO will be installed. You have three options:

    a. **Master boot record (MBR)**: the LILO will reside on the first bootable physical hard drive. You use this option when Linux is the only operating system on the system or if you want to use the LILO for booting other operating systems as well.

    b. **Target partition:** in this case the LILO is set up in the boot record of the installation partition, the one that was defined as bootable. You choose this option when you are using another operating system loader (Boot Manager, System Commander, etc.), and you will be booting Linux with it.

    c. **Other:** this is the option for experienced users only.

    After you have selected your option, click **Next** to continue. You will see a window similar to Figure 30.

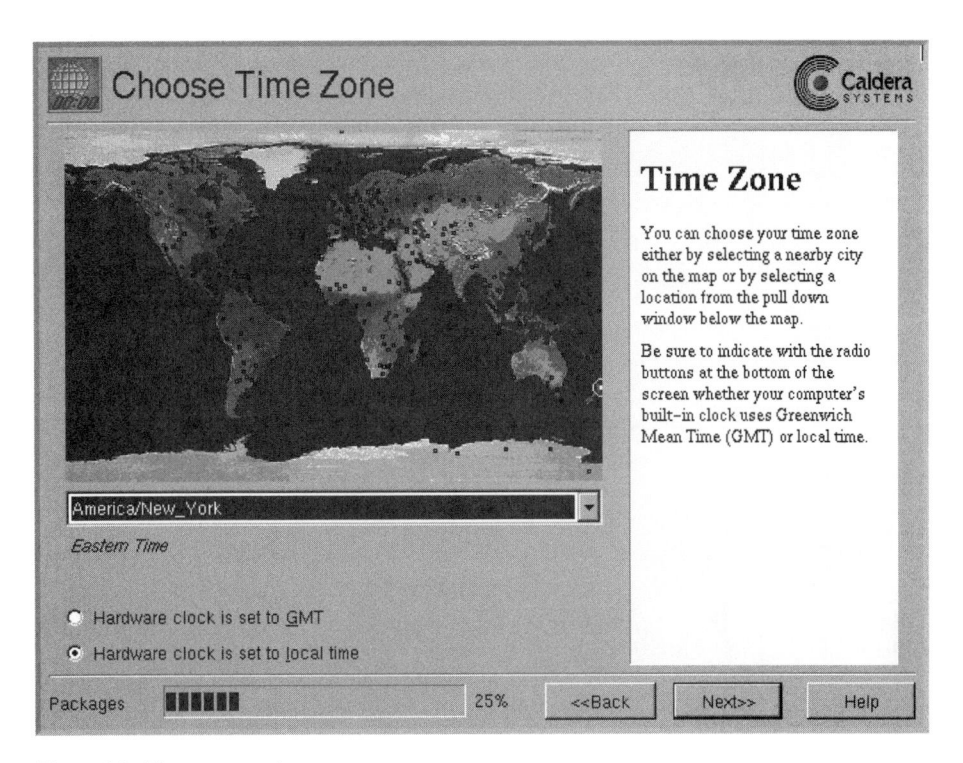

Figure 30. Time zone setup

27. Select your time zone and define how the hardware clock should be set. Click **Next** to continue, and you will see a window similar to Figure 31.

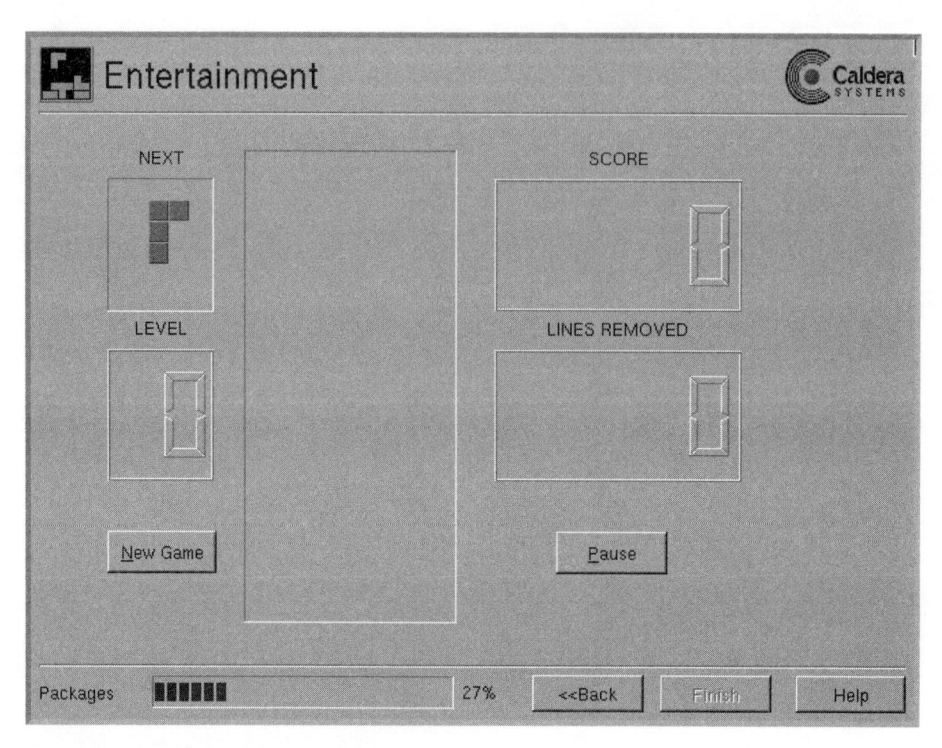

Figure 31. Entertainment during installation

28. While waiting for all the packages to be installed, you can entertain yourself by playing Tetris - the ultimate game. The installation is completed when the Finish button becomes selectable. Click **Finish** to continue, and you will see a window similar to Figure 32.

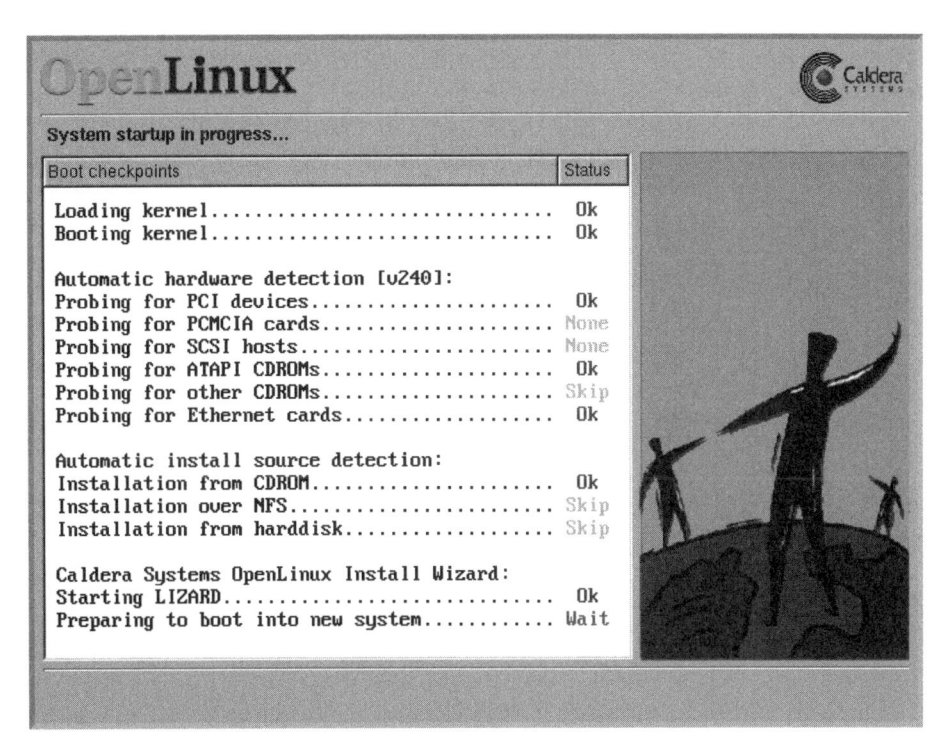

Figure 32. Booting after installation

When the system boots up you will see a window similar to Figure 33.

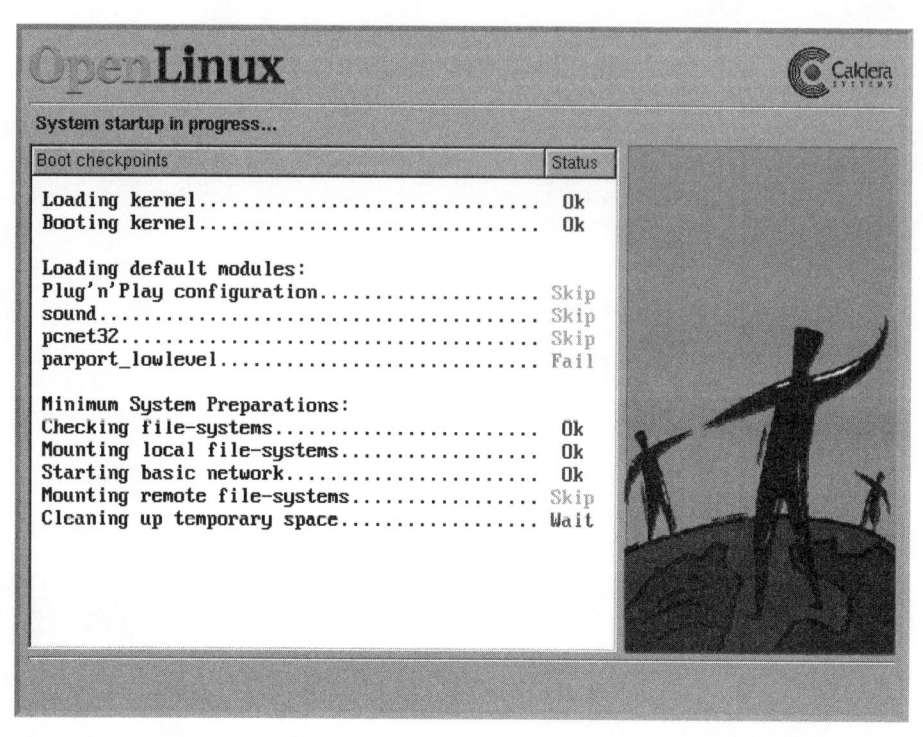

Figure 33. Starting up the operating system

When all the services are started, you will see a logon window similar to Figure 34.

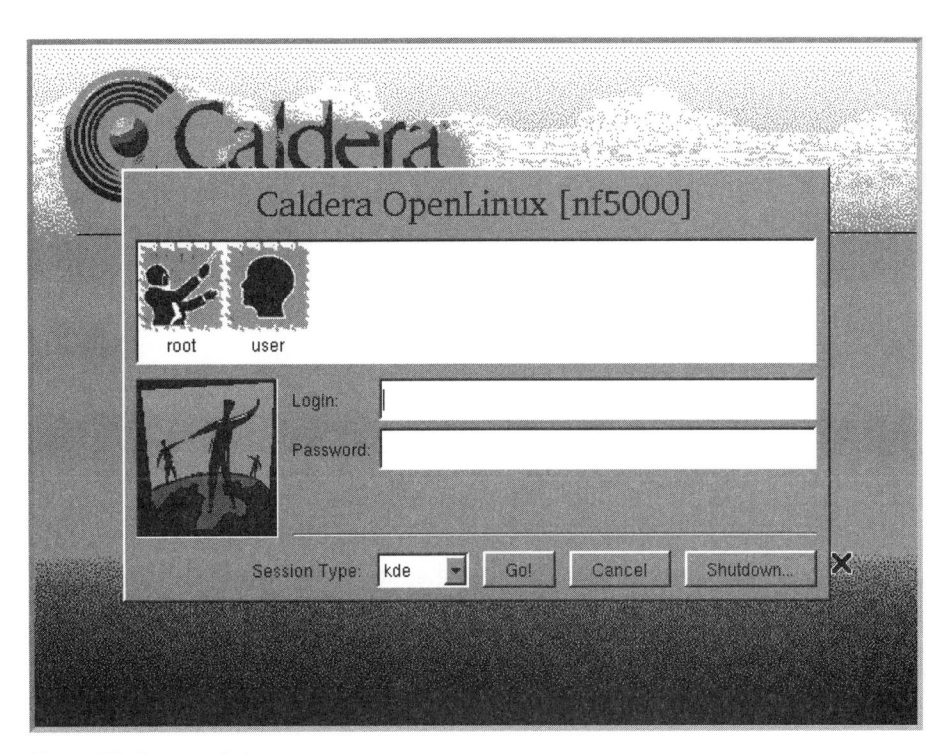

Figure 34. Logon window

Congratulations, your Caldera OpenLinux system is now ready to use!

1.6 Installation with ServeRAID

In this section we will describe how to install Caldera OpenLinux products on the IBM Netfinity servers with the IBM ServeRAID controller and how to use the features of the IBM ServeRAID controller. The IBM ServeRAID controller is a high-performance RAID controller. In the current version of the Linux driver all ServeRAID adapter versions are supported. Before you start the installation, you need to define the RAID arrays and the logical drives. The logical drives are represented to the operating system as if they were physical disk drives. For more information on RAID levels and performance issues, see Appendix A, "RAID levels" on page 283.

> **Stop**
>
> Before installing Caldera OpenLinux on the IBM Netfinity server with an IBM ServeRAID controller, you need to define RAID arrays and logical drives. You can do this with ServerGuide, which comes with all IBM Netfinity servers, or with the ServeRAID DOS Configuration diskette, which is available at `http://www.pc.ibm.com/support`.
>
> We strongly recommend that you use hot spare hard disks in your system to secure your data the best possible way.

All Caldera OpenLinux distributions from Version 2.3 support the ServeRAID SCSI controller. To install the operating system, follow the procedure in 1.5, "Basic Linux installation" on page 3. Your Logical disk drives defined in the RAID array will appear as SCSI drives in the installation program.

After you have installed the system get the utilities for RAID administration from:

```
http://www.developer.ibm.com/welcome/netfinity/serveraid.html
```

From that site you can download the following files:

- `ips-100.tgz`: this file contains the kernel patch for the 2.2.x kernel, which enables the support for IBM ServeRAID adapter in those kernels,
- `ipsutils.rpm`: this file contains the Linux utilities for IBM ServeRAID SCSI adapter,
- `009n012.exe`; this file contains the WIN32 Administration Client, which can be used to remotely configure and monitor the ServeRAID controller used in Linux installation,

1.6.1 Installing ipsutils.rpm

To successfully install the ipsutils package you have to be logged in as "root". After you have downloaded the ipsutil.rpm package you need to install it. The ipsutil package is a standard Red Hat Package Manager (RPM) package. Caldera OpenLinux uses RPM for installing packages, so the RPM utility is already installed on your system. To check if your RPM utility is working, open a terminal window in the KDE graphic environment and execute this command:

```
rpm --version
```

Your RPM is working if your output looks something like this:

```
RPM version 2.5.5.OL
```

More GUI-oriented users will probably want to use the kpackage tool, which is part of KDE graphic environment and is used for installing packages. But if you try to install the ipsutils.rpm with this tool you will see a window similar to Figure 35.

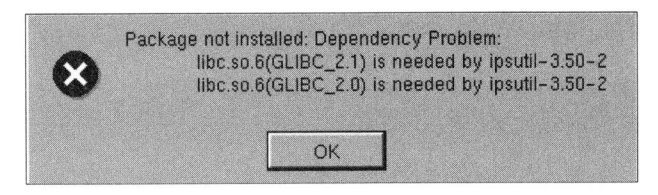

Figure 35. Error installing ipsutils.rpm with kpackage

Experienced users will recognize that this is a dependencies problem, but even if you try to install without enabling the **Check Dependencies** option, as you can see in Figure 36, you will still get the same error.

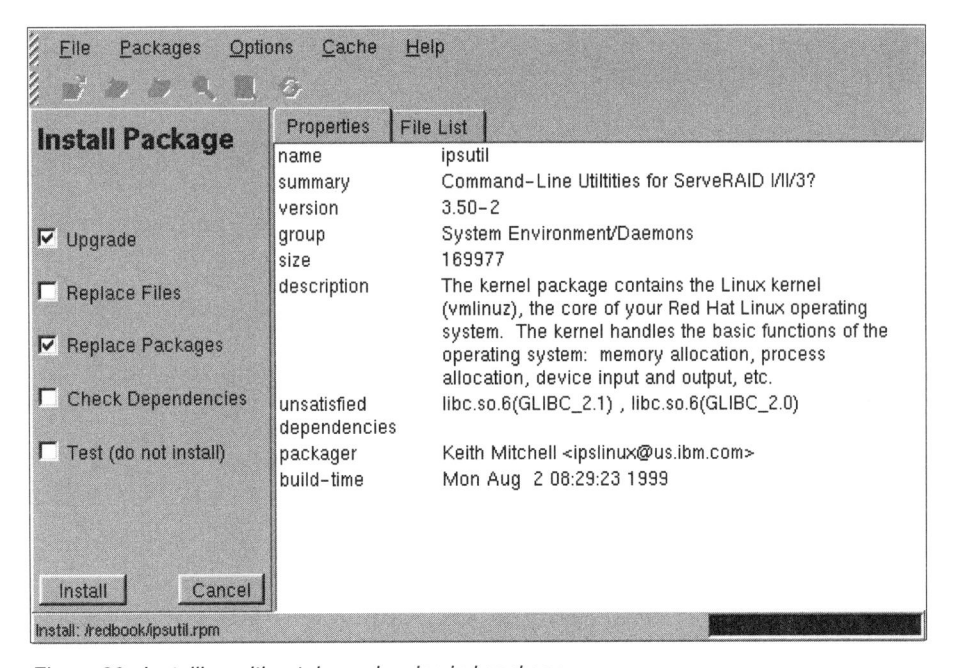

Figure 36. Installing without dependencies in kpackage

This is because ipsutils.rpm displays the copyright message before installing. So the only way to install the package is to execute the following command from a terminal:

```
rpm -Uhv --nodeps ipsutil.rpm
```

This assumes that your current directory is where the ipsutil.prm file resides. The necessary files will be installed in the /usr/bin directory. To see if the utilities are working, type the following command:

```
ipssend
```

You will see output similar to Figure 37.

```
Licensed Material - Property of IBM Corporation
IBM ServeRAID Command Line Interface v3.50.17
Copyright (C) IBM Corporation 1996 - 1999
All Rights Reserved
US Government Restricted Rights - Use, Duplication, or Disclosure
Restricted by GSA ADP Schedule Contract with IBM Corporation


Usage: IPSSEND <Command> <Param 1> ... <Param N>
Help : IPSSEND <Command> for specific help on any command.
       Command    | Param 1   | Param 2       | Param 3  | Param 4      | Param 5
       ---------- | --------- | ------------- | -------- | ------------ | ----------
       AUTOSYNC   | Controller| Logical Drive | NOPROMPT |              |
       BACKUP     | Controller| Filename      | NOPROMPT |              |
       DEVINFO    | Controller| Channel       | SCSI ID  |              |
       DRIVEVER   | Controller| Channel       | SCSI ID  |              |
       ERASEEVENT | Controller| Options       |          |              |
       GETCONFIG  | Controller| Options       |          |              |
       GETEVENT   | Controller| Options       |          |              |
       GETSTATUS  | Controller|               |          |              |
       HSREBUILD  | Controller| Options       |          |              |
       INIT       | Controller| Logical Drive | NOPROMPT |              |
       INITSYNC   | Controller| Logical Drive | NOPROMPT |              |
       REBUILD    | Controller| Channel       | SCSI ID  | New Channel  | New SCSI ID
       RESTORE    | Controller| Filename      | NOPROMPT |              |
       SETSTATE   | Controller| Channel       | SCSI ID  | New State    |
       SYNCH      | Controller| Scope         | Scope ID |              |
       UNATTENDED | Controller| Options       |          |              |
       UNBLOCK    | Controller| Logical Drive |          |              |
```

Figure 37. Ipssend command output

As you can see, `ipssend` supports quite a lot of commands for dealing with the IBM ServeRAID controller. In this section we will cover the ones that are necessary in order to use the ServeRAID controller efficiently.

1.6.2 The ipssend commands

In this section we cover the different options of the `ipssend` command.

1.6.2.1 The getconfig command
This command is used to get the configuration information of the IBM ServeRAID controller, the logical drives and the physical drives. The `getconfig` command has the following syntax:

```
ipssend getconfig <Controller> <Options>
```

The parameters are explained in Table 1.

Table 1. getconfig command parameters

Parameter	Description
Controller	Number of controller (1 to 12)
Options	AD for Controller Information
	LD for Logical Drive Information
	PD for Physical Device Information
	AL (default) for All Information

To get all information about the first ServeRAID controller, execute the following command:

    ispsend getconfig 1

You will see a window similar to Figure 38.

```
Found 1 IBM ServeRAID Controller(s).
Read Configuration has been initiated for Controller 1...
--------------------------------------------------------------------------
Controller Information
--------------------------------------------------------------------------
   Firmware Version                     : 2.88.10
   Boot Block Version                   : 97139
   Date of Configuration Written        : 6/25/1999
   Controller Configuration ID          : Null Config
   SCSI Channel Description             : 3 parallel SCSI wide
   Host Interface Description           : 1 32 bit PCI
   Initiator IDs (Channel/SCSI ID)      : 1/7  2/7  3/7
   Maximum Physical Devices             : 30
   Defunct Disk Drive Count             : 0
   Logical Drives/Offline/Critical      : 2/0/0
   Rebuild Rate (Low/Medium/High)       : High
   Read Ahead                           : Adaptive
   Unattended Mode (Yes/No)             : No
   Concurrent Commands Supported        : 128
   Configuration Update Count           : 14
--------------------------------------------------------------------------
Logical Drive Information
--------------------------------------------------------------------------
 Logical Drive Number 1
   Status of Logical Drive              : Okay (OKY)
   Raid Level                           : 5
   Size (in MB)                         : 100
   Write Cache Status                   : Write Through (WT)
   Number of Chunks                     : 3
   Stripe Unit Size                     : 16K
   Access Blocked                       : No
   Part of Array                        : A
 Logical Drive Number 2
   Status of Logical Drive              : Okay (OKY)
   Raid Level                           : 5
   Size (in MB)                         : 17256
   Write Cache Status                   : Write Through (WT)
   Number of Chunks                     : 3
   Stripe Unit Size                     : 16K
   Access Blocked                       : No
   Part of Array                        : A

   Array A Stripe Order (Channel/SCSI ID)  : 1,0 1,4 1,3
--------------------------------------------------------------------------
Physical Device Information
--------------------------------------------------------------------------
   Channel #1:
      Initiator at SCSI ID 7
      Target on SCSI ID 0
         Device is a 16 bit, Fast SCSI, tag queuing Hard Disk
         SCSI ID                        : 0
         PFA (Yes/No)                   : No
         State                          : Online (ONL)
```

Figure 38. Executing ipssend getconfig 1

In this output you can see all information about the ServeRAID configuration. If you want information only about the controller itself, execute this command:

    ispsend getconfig 1 ad

You will see output similar to Figure 39.

```
[root@nf5500 /root]# ipssend getconfig 1 ad

Found 1 IBM ServeRAID Controller(s).
Read Configuration has been initiated for Controller 1...
--------------------------------------------------------------------------------
Controller Information
--------------------------------------------------------------------------------
   Firmware Version                        : 2.88.10
   Boot Block Version                      : 97139
   Date of Configuration Written           : 6/25/1999
   Controller Configuration ID             : Null Config
   SCSI Channel Description                : 3 parallel SCSI wide
   Host Interface Description              : 1 32 bit PCI
   Initiator IDs (Channel/SCSI ID)         : 1/7  2/7  3/7
   Maximum Physical Devices                : 30
   Defunct Disk Drive Count                : 0
   Logical Drives/Offline/Critical         : 2/0/0
   Rebuild Rate (Low/Medium/High)          : High
   Read Ahead                              : Adaptive
   Unattended Mode (Yes/No)                : No
   Concurrent Commands Supported           : 128
   Configuration Update Count              : 14
Command Completed Successfully.
```

Figure 39. Executing ipssend getconfig 1 ad

To get information about logical drives execute this command:

   ipssend getconfig 1 ld

You will get output similar to Figure 40.

```
[root@nf5500 /root]# ipssend getconfig 1 ld

Found 1 IBM ServeRAID Controller(s).
Read Configuration has been initiated for Controller 1...
--------------------------------------------------------------------------------
Logical Drive Information
--------------------------------------------------------------------------------
 Logical Drive Number 1
   Status of Logical Drive          : Okay (OKY)
   Raid Level                       : 5
   Size (in MB)                     : 100
   Write Cache Status               : Write Through (WT)
   Number of Chunks                 : 3
   Stripe Unit Size                 : 16K
   Access Blocked                   : No
   Part of Array                    : A
 Logical Drive Number 2
   Status of Logical Drive          : Okay (OKY)
   Raid Level                       : 5
   Size (in MB)                     : 17256
   Write Cache Status               : Write Through (WT)
   Number of Chunks                 : 3
   Stripe Unit Size                 : 16K
   Access Blocked                   : No
   Part of Array                    : A

   Array A Stripe Order (Channel/SCSI ID)  : 1,0  1,4  1,3
Command Completed Successfully.
```

Figure 40. Executing ipssend getconfig 1 ld

From this output you can get all information about the logical drives:

- Drive status
- RAID Level
- Size
- Write Cache Status
- Number of Chunks
- Stripe Unit Size
- Access
- Array

To get detailed information about a physical drive, execute this command:

    ipssend getconfig 1 pd

You will see output similar to Figure 41.

```
[root@nf5500 /root]# ipssend getconfig 1 pd

Found 1 IBM ServeRAID Controller(s).
Read Configuration has been initiated for Controller 1...
----------------------------------------------------------------------
Physical Device Information
----------------------------------------------------------------------
   Channel #1:
      Initiator at SCSI ID 7
      Target on SCSI ID 0
         Device is a 16 bit, Fast SCSI, tag queuing Hard Disk
         SCSI ID                       : 0
         PFA (Yes/No)                  : No
         State                         : Online (ONL)
         Size (in MB)/(in Sectors):      8678/17773888
         Device ID                     : IBM-PCCODGHS09Y 035168164E69
      Target on SCSI ID 3
         Device is a 16 bit, Fast SCSI, tag queuing Hard Disk
         SCSI ID                       : 3
         PFA (Yes/No)                  : No
         State                         : Online (ONL)
         Size (in MB)/(in Sectors):      17357/35548048
         Device ID                     : IBM-PCCODGHS18Y 0351680EE209
      Target on SCSI ID 4
         Device is a 16 bit, Fast SCSI, tag queuing Hard Disk
         SCSI ID                       : 4
         PFA (Yes/No)                  : No
         State                         : Online (ONL)
         Size (in MB)/(in Sectors):      8678/17773888
         Device ID                     : IBM-PCCODGHS09Y 04206816F8A1
      Target on SCSI ID 15
         Device is a 16 bit, Fast SCSI, tag queuing Unknown Device
         SCSI ID                       : 15
         PFA (Yes/No)                  : No
         State                         : Stand By (SBY)
         Size (in MB)/(in Sectors):         0/         0
         Device ID                     : SDR     GEM200  2    1
   Channel #2:
      Initiator at SCSI ID 7
Command Completed Successfully.
```

Figure 41. Executing ipssend getconfig 1 pd

1.6.2.2 The getstatus command

This command is used to retrieve the current status of the IBM ServeRAID controller. The `getstatus` command has the following syntax:

```
ipssend getstatus <Controller>
```

The parameters are explained in Table 2.

Table 2. getstatus command parameters

Parameter	Description
Controller	Number of controller (1 to 12)

To get the status of first ServeRAID controller in your IBM Netfinity server, execute this command:

```
ipssend getstatus 1
```

You will see output similar to Figure 42.

```
[root@nf5500 /root]# ipssend getstatus 1

Found 1 IBM ServeRAID Controller(s).
Background Command Progress Status for controller 1...
    Current/Most Recent Operation  : Rebuild
    Source logical drive           : 1
    Target logical drive           : 1
    Rebuild Rate                   : High
    Status                         : Successfully Completed
    Logical Drive Size (in Stripes): 552192
    Number of Remaining Stripes    : 0
    Percentage Complete            : 100.00%
Command Completed Successfully.
```

Figure 42. Executing ipssend getstatus 1

If the ServeRAID controller is in the middle of rebuilding a drive, you will see output similar to Figure 43.

```
[root@nf5500 /root]# ipssend getstatus 1

Found 1 IBM ServeRAID Controller(s).
Background Command Progress Status for controller 1...
    Current/Most Recent Operation  : Rebuild
    Source logical drive           : 1
    Target logical drive           : 1
    Rebuild Rate                   : High
    Status                         : In Progress
    Logical Drive Size (in Stripes): 3200
    Number of Remaining Stripes    : 2070
    Percentage Complete            : 35.31%
Command Completed Successfully.
```

Figure 43. Executing ipssend getstatus 1 during rebuilding of a drive

1.6.2.3 The devinfo command

This command is used to retrieve the current status of the devices connected to the IBM ServeRAID controller. The `devinfo` command has the following syntax:

    ipssend devinfo<Controller> <Channel> <SCSI ID>

The parameters are explained in Table 3.

Table 3. devinfo command parameters

Parameter	Description
Controller	Number of controller (1 to 12)
Channel	Channel of Device (1 to 3)
SCSI ID	SCSI ID of Device (0 to 15)

To get the status of a device with SCSI ID 0 on channel 1 on the first ServeRAID controller in your IBM Netfinity server, execute the command:

    ipssend devinfo 1 1 0

You will see output similar to Figure 44.

```
[root@nf5500 linux]# ipssend devinfo 1 1 0

Found 1 IBM ServeRAID Controller(s).
Device Information has been initiated for controller 1...
        Device is a 16 bit, Fast SCSI, tag queuing Hard Disk
        Channel                 : 1
        SCSI ID                 : 0
        PFA (Yes/No)            : No
        State                   : Hot Spare (HSP)
        Size (in MB)/(in Sectors):      8678/17773888
        Device ID               : IBM-PCCODGHS09Y 035168164E69
Command Completed Successfully.
```

Figure 44. Executing ipssend devinfo 1 1 0

If the ServeRAID controller is in the middle of rebuilding a drive, you will see output similar to Figure 45.

```
[root@nf5500 /root]# ipssend devinfo 1 1 0

Found 1 IBM ServeRAID Controller(s).
Device Information has been initiated for controller 1...
        Device is a 16 bit, Fast SCSI, tag queuing Hard Disk
        Channel                 : 1
        SCSI ID                 : 0
        PFA (Yes/No)            : No
        State                   : Rebuild (RBL)
        Size (in MB)/(in Sectors):      8678/17773888
        Device ID               : IBM-PCCODGHS09Y 035168164E69
Command Completed Successfully.
```

Figure 45. Executing ipssend devinfo 1 1 0 during rebuilding of a drive

1.6.2.4 The hsrebuild command

This command is used for setting the state of the Hot Swap Rebuild option. The `hsrebuild` command has the following syntax:

    ipssend hsrebuild <Controller> <Options>

The parameters are explained in Table 4.

Table 4. hsrebuild command parameters

Parameter	Description
Controller	Number of controller (1 to 12)
Options	ON: enable Hot Swap Rebuild
	?: Display status of Hot Swap Rebuild feature

With this command you can retrieve or set the Hot Swap Rebuild feature. If the Hot Swap Rebuild feature is ON, it means that if one drive in the RAID array fails, rebuilding of this drive will start automatically when you replace the failed drive with new one. This can improve the safety of your data.

> **Note**
>
> The Hot Swap Rebuild feature should not be confused with a hot spare drive. A hot spare drive means that a drive is in a waiting state as long as the RAID array is in an Okay state. Once the RAID array becomes in a Critical state, the hot spare drive is enabled and the data from the defunct drive automatically get rebuilt onto the hot spare drive, disregarding the Hot Swap Rebuild setting.

To retrieve the information about the Hot Swap Rebuild status on the first ServeRAID controller, execute this command:

```
ipssend hsrebuild 1 ?
```

You will see output similar to Figure 46.

```
[root@nf5500 linux]# ipssend hsrebuild 1 ?

Found 1 IBM ServeRAID Controller(s).
Set Hot Swap Rebuild has been initiated for controller 1...
Hot Swap Rebuild is ON for controller 1.
```

Figure 46. Executing ipssend hsrebuild 1 ?

To enable the Hot Swap Rebuild option, execute this command:

```
ipssend hsrebuild 1 on
```

You will see output similar to Figure 47.

```
[root@nf5500 linux]# ipssend hsrebuild 1 on

Found 1 IBM ServeRAID Controller(s).
Set Hot Swap Rebuild has been initiated for controller 1...
Hot Swap Rebuild is already ON for controller 1.
```

Figure 47. Executing ipssend hsrebuild 1 on

1.6.2.5 The setstate command

With the setstate command you redefine the state of a physical device from the current state to the designated state. The setstate command has the following syntax:

```
ipssend setstate <Controller> <Channel> <SCSI ID> <New State>
```

The parameters are explained in Table 5.

Table 5. setstate command parameters

Parameter	Description
Controller	Number of controller (1 to 12)
Channel	Channel of device (1 to 3)
SCSI ID	SCSI ID of device (0 to 15)
New State	EMP (Empty) RDY (Ready) HSP (Hot Spare) SHS (Standby Hot Spare) DDD (Defunct Disk Drive) DHS (Defunct Hot Spare) RBL (Rebuild) SBY (Standby) ONL (Online)

Stop

Extreme caution must be taken when executing this command! For example, redefining a defunct (DDD) device to online (ONL) without going through a rebuild is extremely dangerous.

Before changing the state of a physical device, you can check the current status with this command:

```
ipssend getconfig 1 pd
```

With this command you will see all physical devices, except empty ones, on the first IBM ServeRAID controller. For example if you want to set the state of device on the first ServeRAID controller, channel 1 and SCSI ID 1 to RDY - Ready, execute this command:

```
ipssend setstate 1 1 1 rdy
```

You will see output similar to Figure 48.

```
[root@nf5500 /root]# ipssend setstate 1 1 1 rdy

Found 1 IBM ServeRAID Controller(s).
Set Device State has been initiated for Controller 1...
Command Completed Successfully.
```

Figure 48. Executing ipssend setstate 1 1 1 rdy

You can verify the change of the device state by executing this command:

```
ipssend getconfig 1 pd
```

1.6.2.6 The synch command

This command is used to synchronize the parity information on redundant logical drives. If the parity information is inconsistent, it will automatically be repaired. The synch command has the following syntax:

```
ipssend synch <Controller> <Scope> <Scope ID>
```

The parameters are explained in Table 6.

Table 6. synch command parameters

Parameter	Description
Controller	Number of controller (1 to 12)
Scope	Drive for a single logical drive
Scope ID	Number of logical drive (1 to 8)

> **Note**
> We recommend that you use this command on a weekly basis.

1.6.2.7 The unattended command

This command is used to alter the unattended mode of the ServeRAID controller. The unattended command has the following syntax:

```
ipssend unattended <Controller> <Options>
```

The parameters are explained in Table 7.

Table 7. unattended command parameters

Parameter	Description
Controller	Number of controller (1 to 12)
Options	ON: enable unattended mode
	OFF: disable unattended mode
	?: display status of unattended mode feature

If you want to see the current status of the first ServeRAID controller, execute this command:

```
ipssend unattended 1 ?
```

You will see output similar to Figure 49.

```
[root@nf5500 /]# ipssend unattended 1 ?
Found 1 IBM ServeRAID Controller(s).
Set Unattended Mode has been initiated for controller 1...
Unattended Mode is set off.
```

Figure 49. Executing ipssend unattended 1 ?

If you want to set the unattended mode to ON, execute this command:

    ipssend unattended 1 on

1.6.2.8 The rebuild command

This command starts a rebuild to the designated drive. The `rebuild` command has the following syntax:

    ipssend rebuild <Controller> <Channel> <SCSI ID> <New Channel> <New SCSI ID>

The parameters are explained in Table 8.

Table 8. Rebuild command parameters

Parameter	Description
Controller	Number of controller (1 to 12)
Channel	Channel of defunct drive (1 to 3)
SCSI ID	SCSI ID of defunct drive (0 to 15)
New Channel	Channel of new drive (1 to 3)
New SCSI ID	SCSI ID of new drive (0 to 15)

This operation is valid for disk arrays containing one or more logical drives in a Critical (CRT) state. For example, if you want to rebuild a defunct drive on SCSI ID 1 on channel 1 on the first ServeRAID controller to a new drive on SCSI ID 0 on the same channel, you will execute this command:

    ipssend rebuild 1 1 1 1 0

You will see output similar to Figure 50.

```
[root@nf5500 linux]# ipssend rebuild 1 1 1 1 0

Found 1 IBM ServeRAID Controller(s).
Rebuild Drive has been initiated for controller 1...
Rebuilding Logical Drive #1:
.........10% Done
.........20% Done
.........30% Done
.........40% Done
.........50% Done
.........60% Done
.........70% Done
.........80% Done
.........90% Done
.........Done Logical Drive #1
Rebuilding Logical Drive #2:
```

Figure 50. Executing ipssend rebuild 1 1 1 1 0

1.6.3 Replacing a defunct drive

When a physical drive in a RAID array becomes defunct you will see a light signal on the drive. You can simulate a defunct drive by executing the following command:

```
ipssend setstate 1 1 4 ddd
```

In this case we are simulating that the drive with SCSI ID 4 on channel 1 on the first ServeRAID controller is defunct. The following steps should be taken to replace the defunct drive:

1. Physically replace the defunct drive with a good drive.

2. The IBM ServeRAID controller will start rebuilding the drive automatically.

> **Note**
>
> Automatically rebuilding will work only on ServeRAID II and III. And Enable Hot Spare Rebuild must be set to Enabled!

You can check the progress of rebuilding the logical drives on the first IBM ServeRAID controller with this command:

```
ipssend getstatus 1
```

You will see output similar to Figure 43 on page 41.

If the rebuild is not completed successfully, you will see output similar to Figure 51.

```
[root@nf5500 /root]# ipssend getstatus 1

Found 1 IBM ServeRAID Controller(s).
Background Command Progress Status for controller 1...
   Current/Most Recent Operation   : Rebuild
   Source logical drive            : 1
   Target logical drive            : 1
   Rebuild Rate                    : High
   Status                          : Drive Failed
      Channel Number is            : 1
      SCSI ID Number is            : 0
   Logical Drive Size (in Stripes) : 552192
   Number of Remaining Stripes     : 302692
   Percentage Complete             : 45.18%
Command Completed Successfully.
```

Figure 51. Failed rebuild

1.6.4 Replacing a defunct drive with disabled Hot Spare Rebuild

When you have disabled the Hot Spare Rebuild function in the IBM ServeRAID controller configuration, the following steps should be taken to replace the defunct drive. In our example, the drive with SCSI ID 1 on channel 1 on the first ServeRAID controller is defunct.

1. Physically replace the defunct drive with a working one.

2. Execute the following command to start rebuilding the drive:

   ipssend setstate 1 1 1 rbl

   You will see output similar to this:

```
[root@nf5500 /root]# ipssend setstate 1 1 1 rbl

Found 1 IBM ServeRAID Controller(s).
Set Device State has been initiated for Controller 1...
Command Completed Successfully.
```

Figure 52. Forced rebuild of the defunct drive

You can check the progress of rebuilding the logical drives on first IBM ServeRAID controller with this command:

   ipssend getstatus 1

You will see output similar to Figure 43 on page 41.

1.6.5 Replacing a defunct drive with a hot spare drive installed

When you have configured the hot spare drive in your IBM ServeRAID configuration, the defunct physical drive is automatically rebuilt to the hot spare drive. Follow these steps to replace the defunct physical drive and set it as a hot spare drive:

1. You find out that there is a defunct physical drive in you RAID array on the first ServeRAID controller. In our example the physical drive on SCSI ID 1 on channel 1 was defined as a hot spare drive. You can check this by executing the command:

   `ipssend getconfig 1 pd`

   You will see output similar to Figure 53.

```
[root@nf5500 /]# ipssend getconfig 1 pd

Found 1 IBM ServeRAID Controller(s).
Read Configuration has been initiated for Controller 1...
--------------------------------------------------------------------------------
Physical Device Information
--------------------------------------------------------------------------------
   Channel #1:
      Initiator at SCSI ID 7
      Target on SCSI ID 0
         Device is a 16 bit, Fast SCSI, tag queuing Hard Disk
         SCSI ID                        : 0
         PFA (Yes/No)                   : No
         State                          : Online (ONL)
         Size (in MB)/(in Sectors):      8678/17773888
         Device ID                      : IBM-PCCODGHS09Y 035168164E69
      Target on SCSI ID 1
         Device is a 16 bit, Fast SCSI, tag queuing Hard Disk
         SCSI ID                        : 1
         PFA (Yes/No)                   : No
         State                          : Rebuild (RBL)
         Size (in MB)/(in Sectors):      8678/17773888
         Device ID                      : IBM-PCCODGHS09Y 04206816F8A1
      Target on SCSI ID 3
         Device is a 16 bit, Fast SCSI, tag queuing Hard Disk
         SCSI ID                        : 3
         PFA (Yes/No)                   : No
         State                          : Online (ONL)
         Size (in MB)/(in Sectors):      17357/35548048
         Device ID                      : IBM-PCCODGHS18Y 0351680EE209
      Target on SCSI ID 4
         Device is a 16 bit, Fast SCSI, tag queuing Hard Disk
         SCSI ID                        : 4
         PFA (Yes/No)                   : No
         State                          : Defunct Hot Spare (DHS)
         Size (in MB)/(in Sectors):      8678/17773888
         Device ID                      : IBM-PCCODGHS09Y 0420681924B4
      Target on SCSI ID 15
         Device is a 16 bit, Fast SCSI, tag queuing Unknown Device
         SCSI ID                        : 15
         PFA (Yes/No)                   : No
         State                          : Stand By (SBY)
         Size (in MB)/(in Sectors):      0/       0
         Device ID                      : SDR     GEM200  2   1
   Channel #2:
      Initiator at SCSI ID 7
Command Completed Successfully.
```

Figure 53. After failing the drive in RAID array

As you can see, the hot spare drive is already rebuilding and the defunct drive is in Defunct Hot Spare (DHS) state.

2. Remove the defunct drive from the server. In our example this is the drive with SCSI ID 4 on channel 1.

3. Set the state of the drive to Empty (EMP) with the command:

   ```
   ipssend setstate 1 1 4 emp
   ```

   You will see output similar to Figure 54.

```
[root@nf5500 /]# ipssend setstate 1 1 4 emp

Found 1 IBM ServeRAID Controller(s).
Set Device State has been initiated for Controller 1...
Command Completed Successfully.
```

Figure 54. Setting the DHS to EMP

You can check the result of this operation by executing this command:

```
ipssend getconfig 1 pd
```

You will see output similar to Figure 55.

```
[root@nf5500 /]# ipssend getconfig 1 pd

Found 1 IBM ServeRAID Controller(s).
Read Configuration has been initiated for Controller 1...
----------------------------------------------------------------
Physical Device Information
----------------------------------------------------------------
   Channel #1:
      Initiator at SCSI ID 7
      Target on SCSI ID 0
         Device is a 16 bit, Fast SCSI, tag queuing Hard Disk
         SCSI ID                  : 0
         PFA (Yes/No)             : No
         State                    : Online (ONL)
         Size (in MB)/(in Sectors):   8678/17773888
         Device ID                : IBM-PCCODGHS09Y 035168164E69
      Target on SCSI ID 1
         Device is a 16 bit, Fast SCSI, tag queuing Hard Disk
         SCSI ID                  : 1
         PFA (Yes/No)             : No
         State                    : Rebuild (RBL)
         Size (in MB)/(in Sectors):   8678/17773888
         Device ID                : IBM-PCCODGHS09Y 04206816F8A1
      Target on SCSI ID 3
         Device is a 16 bit, Fast SCSI, tag queuing Hard Disk
         SCSI ID                  : 3
         PFA (Yes/No)             : No
         State                    : Online (ONL)
         Size (in MB)/(in Sectors):   17357/35548048
         Device ID                : IBM-PCCODGHS18Y 0351680EE209
      Target on SCSI ID 15
         Device is a 16 bit, Fast SCSI, tag queuing Unknown Device
         SCSI ID                  : 15
         PFA (Yes/No)             : No
         State                    : Stand By (SBY)
         Size (in MB)/(in Sectors):      0/      0
         Device ID                : SDR    GEM200  2   1
   Channel #2:
      Initiator at SCSI ID 7
Command Completed Successfully.
```

Figure 55. After removing defunct drive

As you can see, there is no entry for the defunct drive anymore.

4. Insert a new drive into the server. In our example this will be the same location as the defunct drive.
5. Set the state of that drive to Ready (RDY) with this command:

    ipssend setstate 1 1 4 rdy

You will see output similar to Figure 56.

```
[root@nf5500 /]# ipssend setstate 1 1 4 rdy

Found 1 IBM ServeRAID Controller(s).
Set Device State has been initiated for Controller 1...
Command Completed Successfully.
```

Figure 56. Setting the new drive state to RDY

With setting the state to Ready (RDY) the drive is started.

> **Note**
>
> All new drives must first be set to ready (RDY).

You can check the result of this operation by executing this command:

    ipssend getconfig 1 pd

You will see output similar to Figure 57.

```
[root@nf5500 /]# ipssend getconfig 1 pd

Found 1 IBM ServeRAID Controller(s).
Read Configuration has been initiated for Controller 1...
--------------------------------------------------------------------------------
Physical Device Information
--------------------------------------------------------------------------------
   Channel #1:
      Initiator at SCSI ID 7
      Target on SCSI ID 0
         Device is a 16 bit, Fast SCSI, tag queuing Hard Disk
         SCSI ID                   : 0
         PFA (Yes/No)              : No
         State                     : Online (ONL)
         Size (in MB)/(in Sectors) :    8678/17773888
         Device ID                 : IBM-PCCODGHS09Y 035168164E69
      Target on SCSI ID 1
         Device is a 16 bit, Fast SCSI, tag queuing Hard Disk
         SCSI ID                   : 1
         PFA (Yes/No)              : No
         State                     : Rebuild (RBL)
         Size (in MB)/(in Sectors) :    8678/17773888
         Device ID                 : IBM-PCCODGHS09Y 04206816F8A1
      Target on SCSI ID 3
         Device is a 16 bit, Fast SCSI, tag queuing Hard Disk
         SCSI ID                   : 3
         PFA (Yes/No)              : No
         State                     : Online (ONL)
         Size (in MB)/(in Sectors) :   17357/35548048
         Device ID                 : IBM-PCCODGHS18Y 0351680EE209
      Target on SCSI ID 4
         Device is a 16 bit, Fast SCSI, tag queuing Hard Disk
         SCSI ID                   : 4
         PFA (Yes/No)              : No
         State                     : Ready (RDY)
         Size (in MB)/(in Sectors) :    8678/17773888
         Device ID                 : IBM-PCCODGHS09Y 0420681924B4
      Target on SCSI ID 15
         Device is a 16 bit, Fast SCSI, tag queuing Unknown Device
         SCSI ID                   : 15
         PFA (Yes/No)              : No
         State                     : Stand By (SBY)
         Size (in MB)/(in Sectors) :       0/       0
         Device ID                 : SDR     GEM200   2   1
   Channel #2:
      Initiator at SCSI ID 7
Command Completed Successfully.
```

Figure 57. After setting the state to RDY

As you can see, the new drive appears as a Ready (RDY) device, in our example under SCSI ID 4 on channel 1.

6. Change the state of the new drive to Hot Spare (HSP) with this command:

   ipssend setstate 1 1 4 hsp

   You will see output similar to Figure 58.

```
[root@nf5500 /]# ipssend setstate 1 1 4 hsp

Found 1 IBM ServeRAID Controller(s).
Set Device State has been initiated for Controller 1...
Command Completed Successfully.
```

Figure 58. Changing the state to HSP

You can check the result of this operation by executing this command:

```
ipssend getconfig 1 pd
```

You will see output similar to Figure 59.

```
[root@nf5500 /]# ipssend getconfig 1 pd

Found 1 IBM ServeRAID Controller(s).
Read Configuration has been initiated for Controller 1...
----------------------------------------------------------------
Physical Device Information
----------------------------------------------------------------
   Channel #1:
      Initiator at SCSI ID 7
      Target on SCSI ID 0
         Device is a 16 bit, Fast SCSI, tag queuing Hard Disk
         SCSI ID                   : 0
         PFA (Yes/No)              : No
         State                     : Online (ONL)
         Size (in MB)/(in Sectors) :   8678/17773888
         Device ID                 : IBM-PCCODGHS09Y 035168164E69
      Target on SCSI ID 1
         Device is a 16 bit, Fast SCSI, tag queuing Hard Disk
         SCSI ID                   : 1
         PFA (Yes/No)              : No
         State                     : Rebuild (RBL)
         Size (in MB)/(in Sectors) :   8678/17773888
         Device ID                 : IBM-PCCODGHS09Y 04206816F8A1
      Target on SCSI ID 3
         Device is a 16 bit, Fast SCSI, tag queuing Hard Disk
         SCSI ID                   : 3
         PFA (Yes/No)              : No
         State                     : Online (ONL)
         Size (in MB)/(in Sectors) :  17357/35548048
         Device ID                 : IBM-PCCODGHS18Y 0351680EE209
      Target on SCSI ID 4
         Device is a 16 bit, Fast SCSI, tag queuing Hard Disk
         SCSI ID                   : 4
         PFA (Yes/No)              : No
         State                     : Hot Spare (HSP)
         Size (in MB)/(in Sectors) :   8678/17773888
         Device ID                 : IBM-PCCODGHS09Y 0420681924B4
      Target on SCSI ID 15
         Device is a 16 bit, Fast SCSI, tag queuing Unknown Device
         SCSI ID                   : 15
         PFA (Yes/No)              : No
         State                     : Stand By (SBY)
         Size (in MB)/(in Sectors) :      0/        0
         Device ID                 : SDR     GEM200  2   1
   Channel #2:
      Initiator at SCSI ID 7
Command Completed Successfully.
```

Figure 59. After setting the state to HSP

Congratulations! You have just installed a brand new the new hot spare drive and it is ready to use.

1.6.6 Using the Ipsmon utility

The ipsmon utility is part of the ipsutils.rpm package. It can be used to monitor the current status of the IBM ServeRAID controller. The `ipsmon` command has the following syntax:

```
ipsmon <-f:filename> <-s>
```

The parameters are explained in Table 9.

Table 9. Ipsmon parameters

Parameter	Description
-f:filename	Specifies a filename to report messages; default filename is ipsmon.log
-s	Specifies if messages should only be logged to the standard output device

If you want to monitor the IBM ServeRAID controller activity on the standard console, execute this command:

```
ipsmon -s
```

You will see output similar to Figure 60.

```
[root@nf5500 /root]# ipsmon -s

Licensed Material - Property of IBM Corporation
IBM ServeRAID Controller Monitor v3.50.17
Copyright (C) IBM Corporation 1996 - 1999
All Rights Reserved
US Government Restricted Rights - Use, Duplication, or Disclosure
Restricted by GSA ADP Schedule Contract with IBM Corporation

Found 1 IBM ServeRAID Controller(s)
Oct 12 1999 12:14:04 EDT INF000:A1C-SID-- No controller errors detected

Oct 12 1999 12:14:09 EDT INF001:A1C-SID-- rebuild started
```

Figure 60. ipsmon utility

1.6.7 Using the Ipsadm utility

With the ipsadm utility, you can remotely administer your IBM ServeRAID controller from any WIN32-based workstation. As we explained in the beginning of 1.6, "Installation with ServeRAID" on page 33, you can download the WIN32 based administration client. The WIN32 client is in the file

009n012.exe. By executing this file on any WIN32-based workstation, you will create the installation diskette for the IBM ServeRAID Administration and Monitoring Program. After you have created the diskette, run setup.exe from the diskette. This will install the IBM ServeRAID Administration and Monitoring Program on your WIN32-based workstation. You start the program by running IBM ServeRAID administration. You will see a window similar to Figure 61.

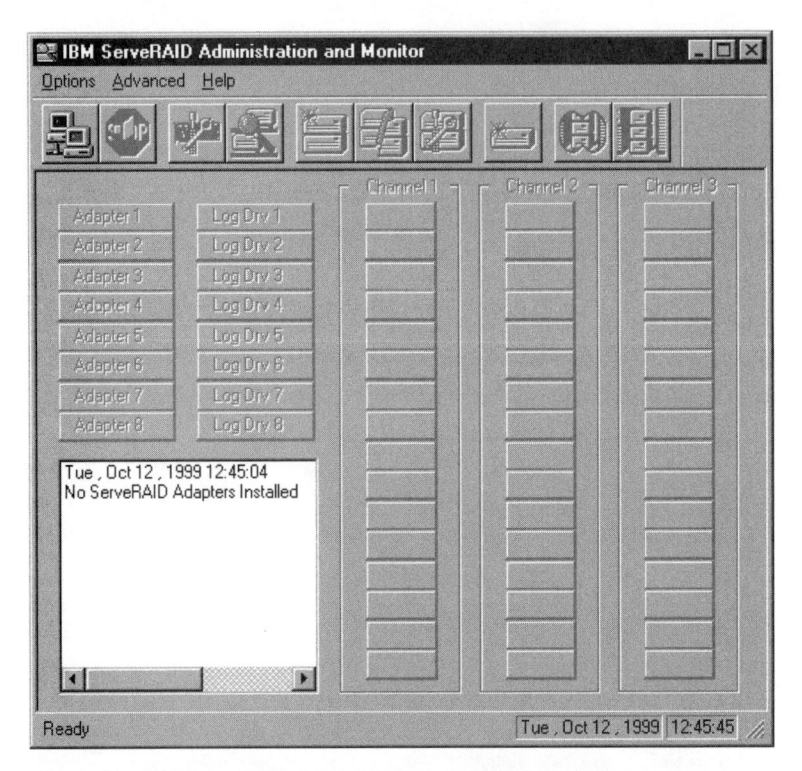

Figure 61. IBM ServeRAID Administration and Monitor window

To be able to remotely access the IBM ServeRAID controller in the IBM Netfinity server running Linux, you need to run the ipsadm utility on that server. The ipsadm utility is basically a background server listening for TCP/IP connections on port 1087 on one side and interacting with the IBM ServeRAID controller on the other side. So it basically accepts the commands from the IBM ServeRAID Administration and Monitoring Program and passes them on to the IBM ServeRAID controller. The ipsadm command has the following syntax:

```
ipsadm [-p:port#] [-f:filename] [-s:security file] [-d] [-er]
```

The parameters are described in Table 10.

Table 10. ipsadm parameters

Parameter	Description
-p:port#	Defines a port number for server communication
-f:filename	Specifies a filename to report messages
-s:security file	Specifies a filename to check for valid username:password
-d	Disables logging information to the display
-er	Displays all errors and warnings

In our example, we created a /etc/ips.pwd password file with the following entries:

```
nf5500:password
```

Where `nf5500` is the user ID for accessing the IBM ServeRAID controller and the password is `password`. To start the ipsadm utility execute this command:

```
ipsadm -s:/etc/ips/pwd
```

In our example we used the created password file. You will see output similar to Figure 62.

```
[root@nf5500 /root]# ipsadm -s:/etc/ips.pwd

Licensed Material - Property of IBM Corporation
IBM ServeRAID Administration & Monitoring Server Utility v3.50.17
Copyright (C) IBM Corporation 1996 - 1998
All Rights Reserved
US Government Restricted Rights - Use, Duplication, or Disclosure
Restricted by GSA ADP Schedule Contract with IBM Corporation

TCP/IP networking protocol initiated on port number 1087.
Using /etc/ips.pwd for username/password file.
Security enabled.
Not logging to a file.
Tue Oct 12 12:18:39 EDT 1999 --> IBM ServeRAID Administration Server started
Tue Oct 12 12:18:39 EDT 1999 --> Successfully created parent socket.
Tue Oct 12 12:18:39 EDT 1999 --> Bind to socket successful.
Tue Oct 12 12:18:39 EDT 1999 --> Listening for connection...
```

Figure 62. Starting ipsadm utility

To remotely connect to the IBM ServeRAID controller follow these steps:

1. In the IBM ServeRAID Administration and Monitoring Program select **Options.** You will see a window similar to Figure 63.

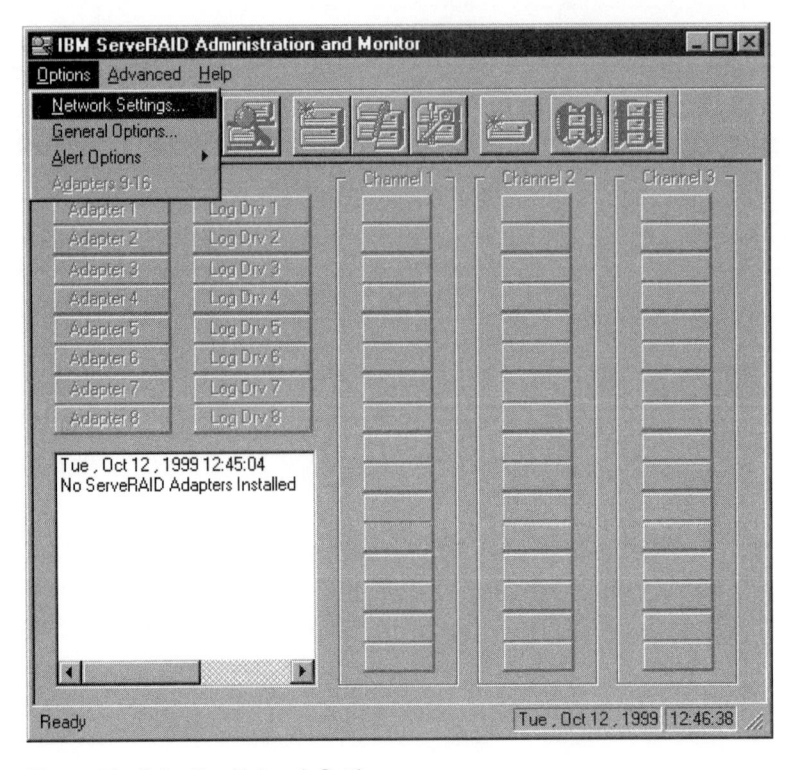

Figure 63. Selecting Network Settings

2. Select **Network Settings...**, and you will see a window similar to Figure 64.

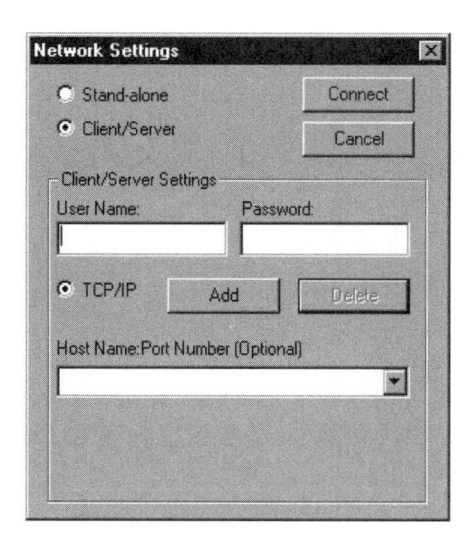

Figure 64. Network Settings

3. Select the **Client/Server** option, as you can see in Figure 64.

4. In the Host Name:Port Number(Optional) field, type in the host name or the IP address of the IBM Netfinity server running the ipsadm utility. The port number is optional and needs to be supplied if you change the default port on the server side. Click **Add** to add the host. You will see a window similar to Figure 65.

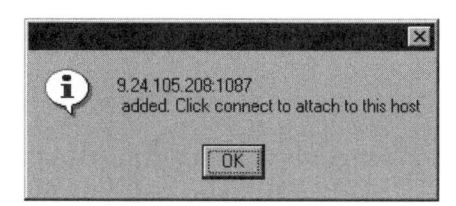

Figure 65. Host added

5. Click **OK** to return to the Network Settings window. You will see a window similar to Figure 66.

Chapter 1. Linux installation   59

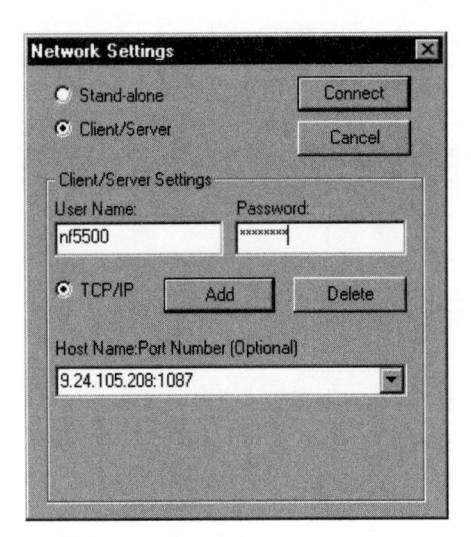

Figure 66. After the host is added

6. In the User Name field, type in the user ID you defined in your password file and in the Password field, type in the password. Click **Connect** to connect to the server with the IBM ServeRAID controller. You will see a window similar to Figure 67.

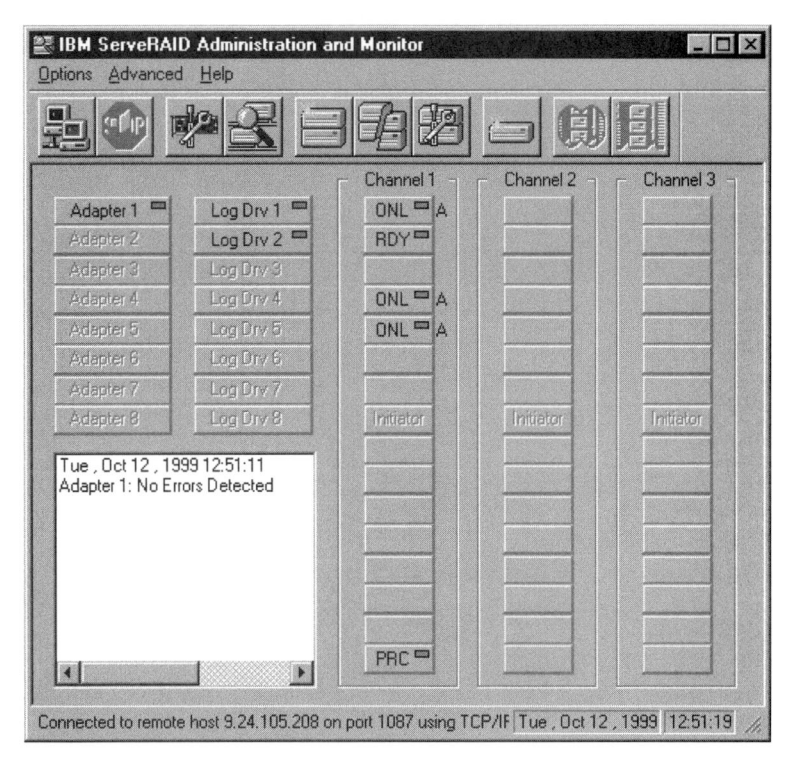

Figure 67. Connected to the server

Congratulations! You can now manage your IBM ServeRAID controller remotely.

1.7 Installing and configuring token-ring network cards

In Caldera OpenLinux there is no way to graphically add and configure token-ring cards. To successfully install and configure token-ring cards, follow these steps:

1. Install a token-ring card (PCI or ISA) in a free slot in your IBM Netfinity server.

2. Start the system and from COAS start **Kernel** tools as described in 2.20, "Manipulating kernel modules" on page 106. To skip the probing of new hardware, click **Done**. When the tool is started, you will see a window similar to Figure 68.

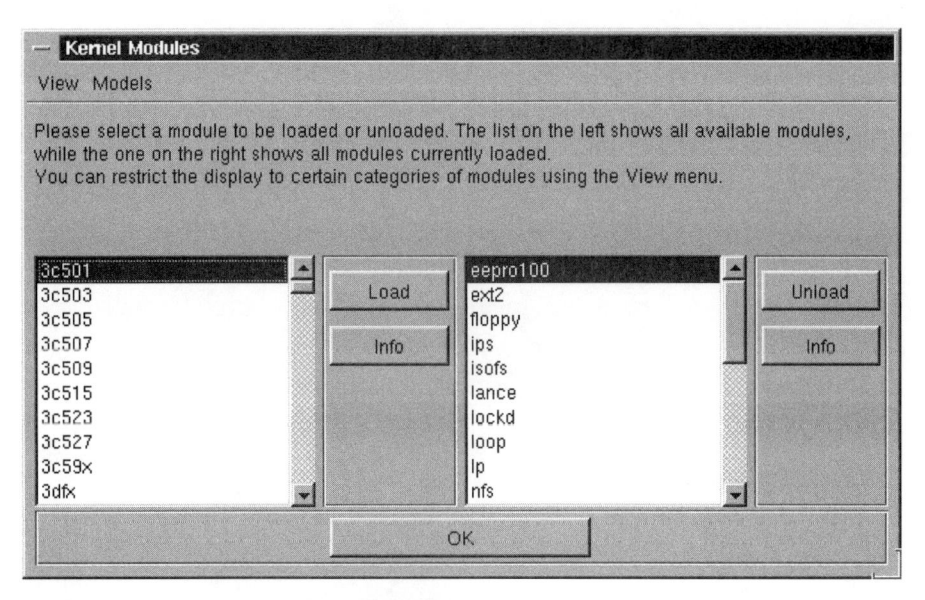

Figure 68. Loading the module for token-ring card

3. Load the appropriate module for your card:

- **olympic** - this is the module for a PCI token-ring network card.
- **ibmtr** - this is the module for an ISA token-ring network card.

In our example we used the **olympic** module for the PCI token-ring network card. Select the module and click **Load,** and you will see a window similar to Figure 69.

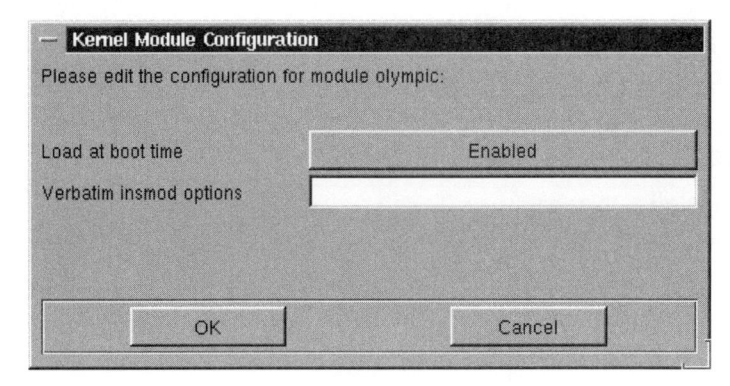

Figure 69. Loading the module for PCI token-ring network card

> **Note**
>
> When using the IBM Turbo 16/4 ISA adapter you must set it to auto 16/4 compatibility mode. This is done by using the LANAID diskette and running this command:
>
> `LANAIDC /fast=auto16`
>
> If you are not sure, run `LANAIDC /view`.

4. Click **OK** to load the module. If the module is loaded successfully the window will close and you will see a green light on the back of the network card.

5. You need to create a network script for the token-ring network card. In our example we are assuming that this is the first token-ring network card in your server. With your favorite editor create the file:

   `/etc/sysconfig/network-scripts/ifcfg-tr0`

   The file should look like this:

   ```
   DEVICE=tr0
   IPADDR=9.24.104.202
   REMIP=0.0.0.0
   NETMASK=255.255.255.0
   BROADCAST=9.24.104.255
   MTU=1500
   GATEWAY=9.24.104.1
   ONBOOT=yes
   ```

   You need to adapt all addresses to your configuration.

> **Note**
>
> Caldera OpenLinux does not support DHCP for the token-ring cards. If you want to have DHCP running on your token-ring card you need to download the DHCP client that supports the token-ring cards from `http://www.isc.org/` and configure the /etc/sysconfig/network-scripts/ifup-dhcp script to use the new client.

If you want to use DHCP with your network card then you have to add an additional line to the `/etc/sysconfig/network-scripts/ifcfg-tr0` file:

`DYNAMIC=dhcp`

Chapter 1. Linux installation   **63**

In case you have more than one token-ring card in your server, you need to create the configuration file for each of them. The file names will look like this:

ifcfg-tr0, ifcfg-tr1, ifcfg-tr2 and so on.

6. Restart the network with the following commands:

```
/etc/rc.d/init.d/network stop
/etc/rc.d/init.d/network start
```

Congratulations! Your token-ring network card is now working and is ready for some heavy traffic.

Chapter 2. Basic system administration

This chapter will give you an overview of how to perform the most common administrative tasks on a Caldera OpenLinux System. Most of these tasks can be done with the Caldera Open Administration System (COAS), Caldera's OpenLinux graphical-oriented configuration and administration tool. However, you may still perform these tasks using the command-line tools.

> **Stop**
>
> Be careful when you are editing configuration files on your own. If you edit configuration files with an editor, make sure to maintain the format of the file. If you change the format of a configuration file, COAS may not be able to understand the configuration information and you cannot use COAS for future configuration.

2.1 Log in to the system

Before you can use any Linux system you need to log in to the system. Whenever you start Caldera OpenLinux, you will see a login window similar to Figure 70.

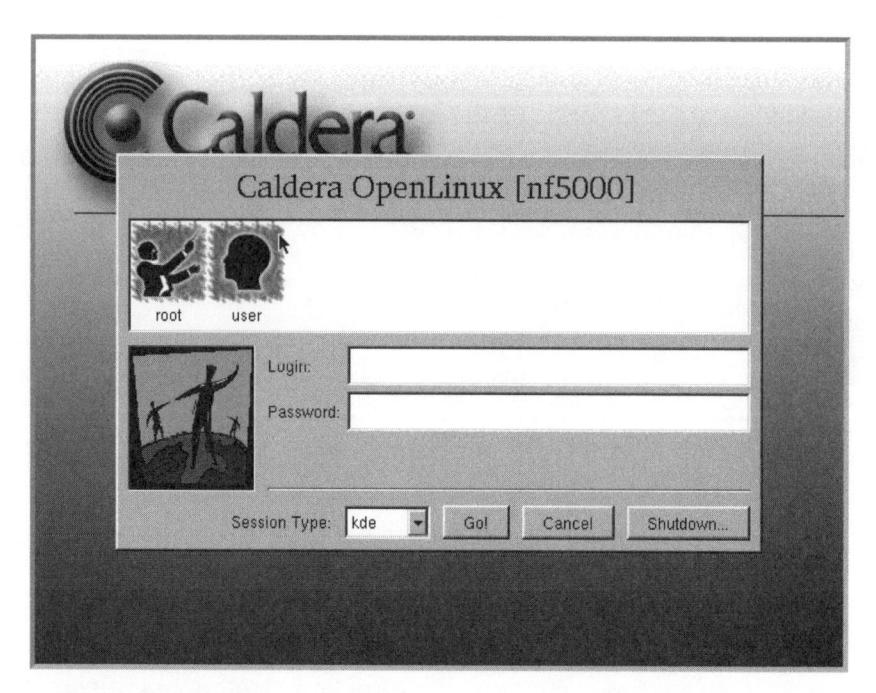

Figure 70. Login window

If you wish to use a text-based user interface, you can press Ctrl-Alt-Fx, where x is the number from 1 to 6, , to switch to a text console. For example to switch to console 1, you need to press Ctrl-Alt-F1, and you will see a window similar to Figure 71.

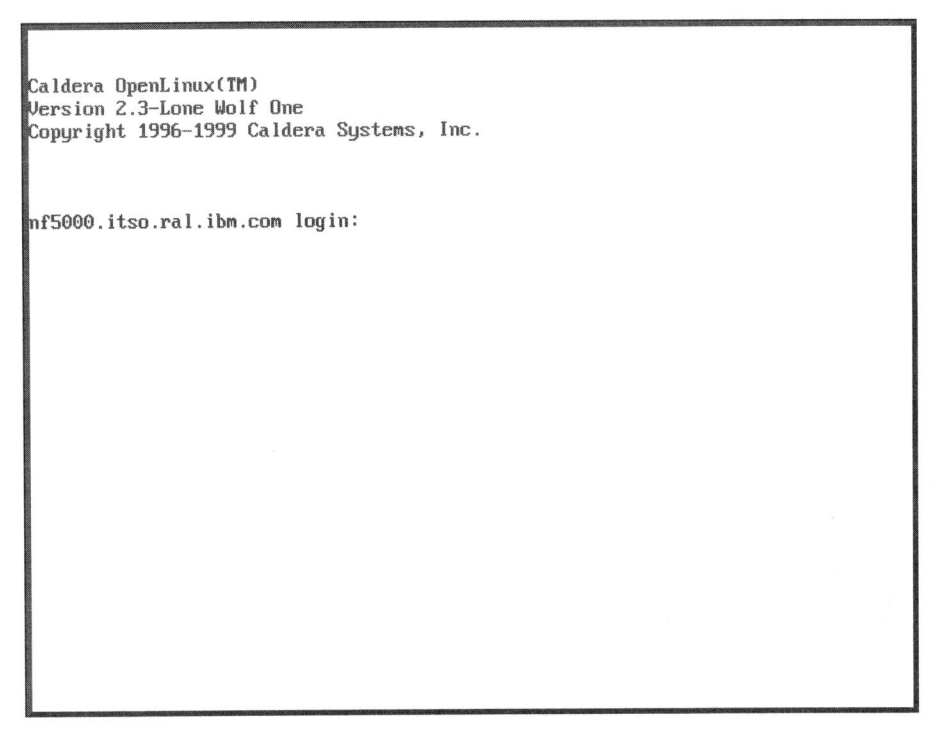

```
Caldera OpenLinux(TM)
Version 2.3-Lone Wolf One
Copyright 1996-1999 Caldera Systems, Inc.


nf5000.itso.ral.ibm.com login:
```

Figure 71. Text-based user interface

If you want to switch back to the graphical interface press Alt-F8. This means that you are switching to the console number 8. Caldera OpenLinux uses this console for the graphical user interface. To start working with Caldera OpenLinux, you need to log on with either a graphical or a text-based user interface. To start the graphical user interface type in the username and password in the window similar to the one in Figure 70, and click **Go!**. You will see a window similar to Figure 72.

Figure 72. KDE Window Manager

2.2 Using the Window Manager

Once you are logged into the system through the graphical user interface you will see a window similar to Figure 72, which is controlled by the Window Manager. Caldera OpenLinux uses the KDE Windows Manager. You can get more information about KDE on:

    http://www.kde.org

At the bottom of the window you can see the toolbar that is used for accessing all available functions. It has pull-down menus, icons and buttons. You can use them for accessing the features of the operating system and applications.

> **Note**
>
> We recommend that you use more than 8bpp color definitions for your XFree86 server setup; otherwise, you will have problems with missing colors when you open more programs.

In the following sections we will describe how to use some basic tools in the graphical environment and especially how to customize your Caldera OpenLinux system by using COAS.

2.3 Getting the X-Windows terminal window

In order to run commands from the command line when you have the GUI Windows-based window in front of you, you need to create a terminal window. You can do this by clicking the icon representing the terminal window, circled in Figure 73.

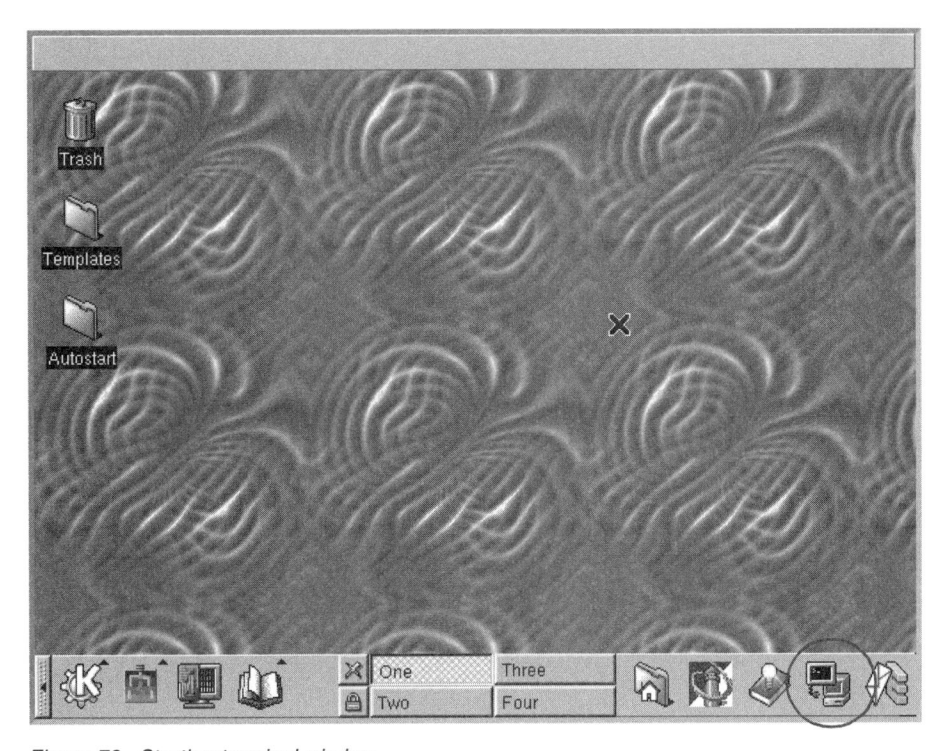

Figure 73. Starting terminal window

Chapter 2. Basic system administration **69**

After the terminal window is started, you will see a window similar to Figure 74.

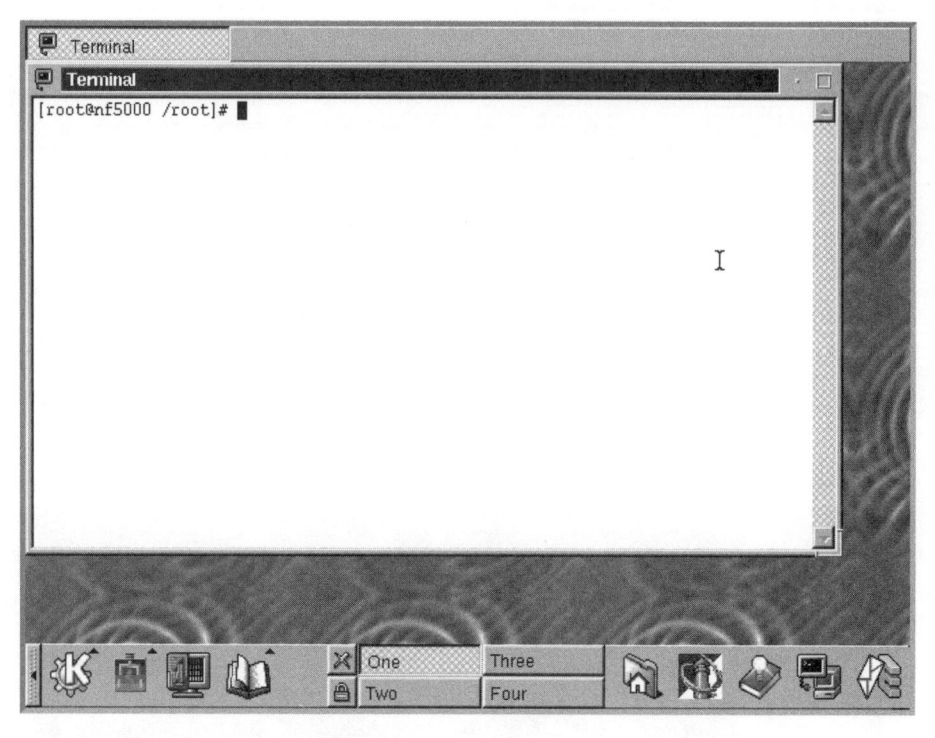

Figure 74. Terminal window in KDE

In this terminal window you can access the system from a command-line prompt as in a text-based interface. The command line prompt gives you more flexibility than menus, but you can do most of the basic things from the menu system. It is a matter of personal choice.

2.4 Accessing COAS - Caldera Open Administration System

All the administration tasks in Caldera OpenLinux are performed through the use of COAS. You can access the COAS tools by clicking the **COAS** icon on the KDE toolbar, circled in Figure 75.

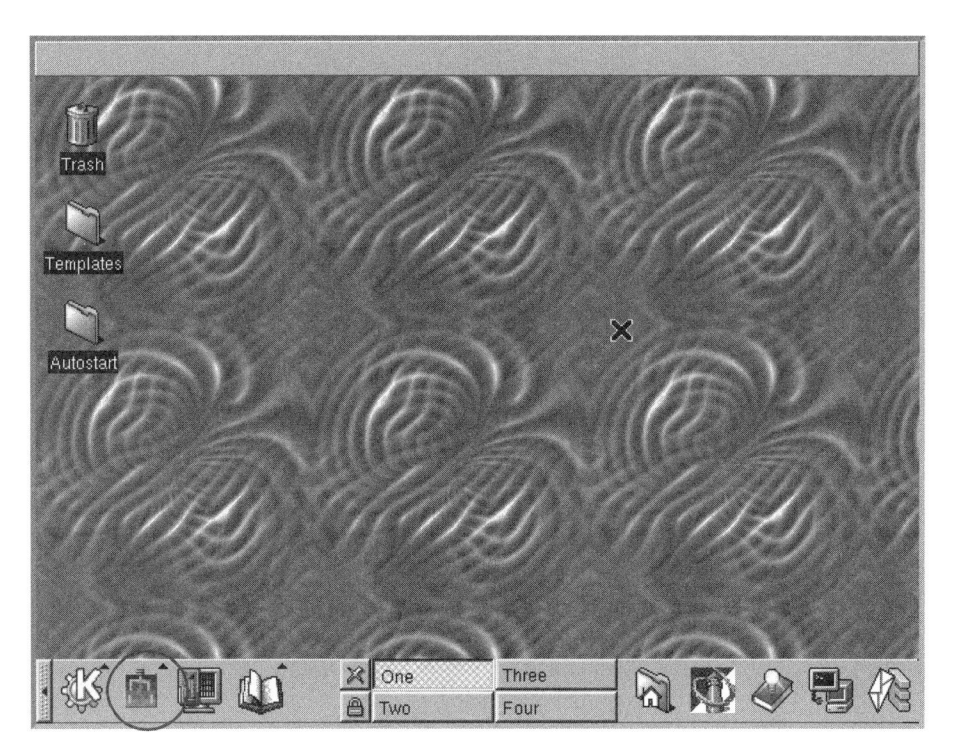

Figure 75. Accessing the COAS tools

After you click the **COAS** icon, you will see a window similar to Figure 76.

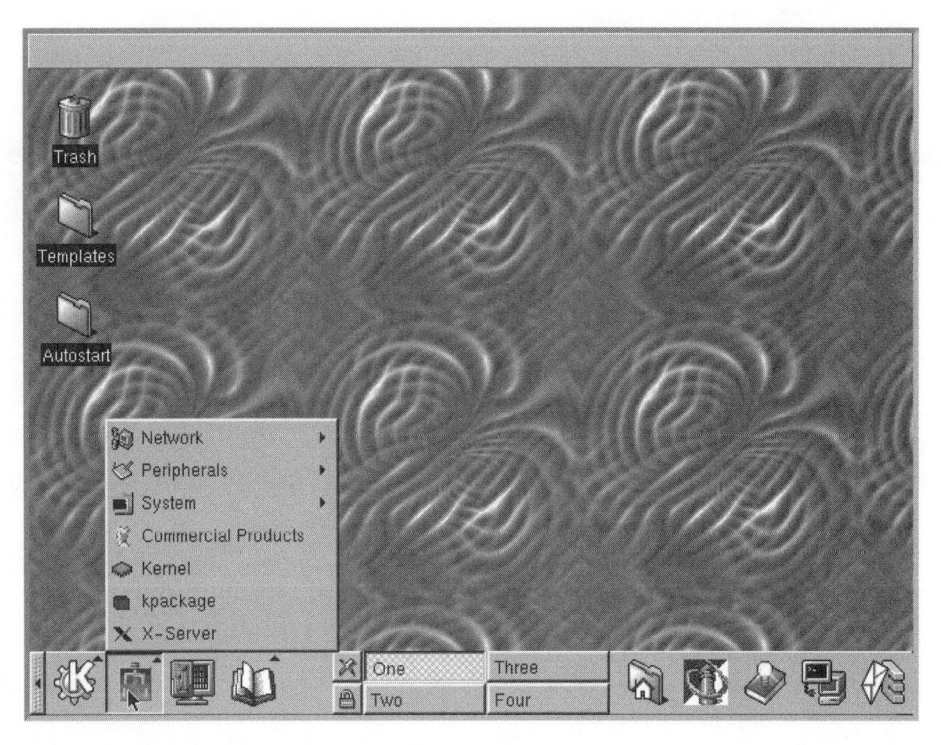

Figure 76. COAS tools

You can see you have several tools available. We will discuss them in the following sections.

2.5 Adding and removing software packages using kpackage

If you want to add or remove software once Caldera OpenLinux is installed or just check if the software is installed, you can do this by using the kpackage tool in COAS. You can start kpackage by selecting **kpackage** from the COAS tools menu, as you can see in Figure 77.

Figure 77. Starting kpackage

When kpackage is started, you will see a window similar to Figure 78.

Chapter 2. Basic system administration

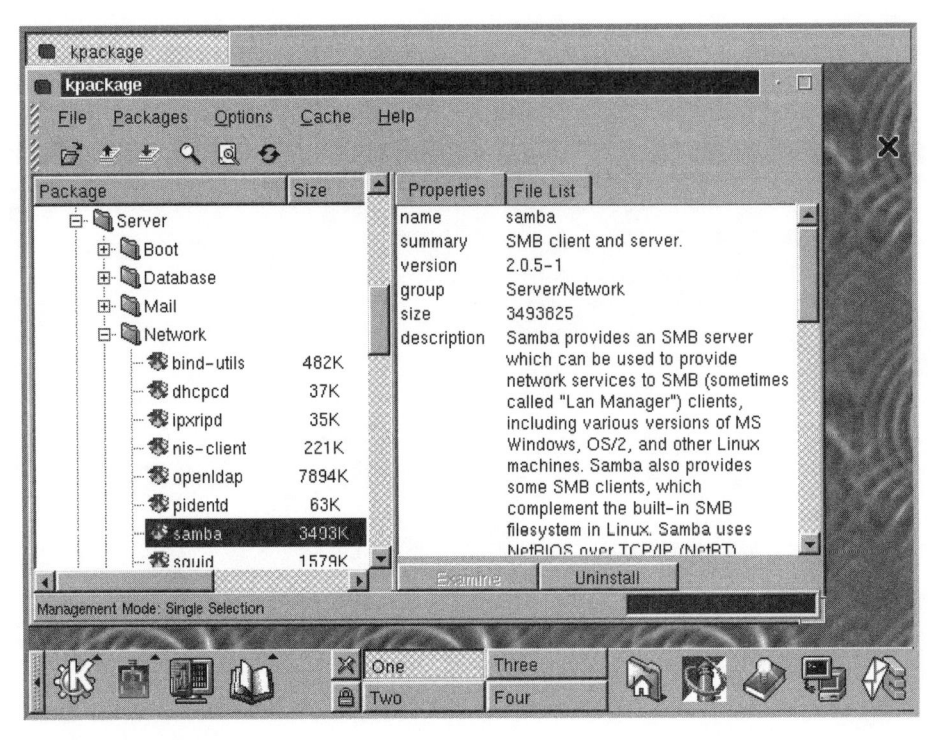

Figure 78. kpackage

2.5.1 Uninstalling a package

If you want to uninstall a package, select the desired package and click **Uninstall.** You will see a window similar to Figure 79.

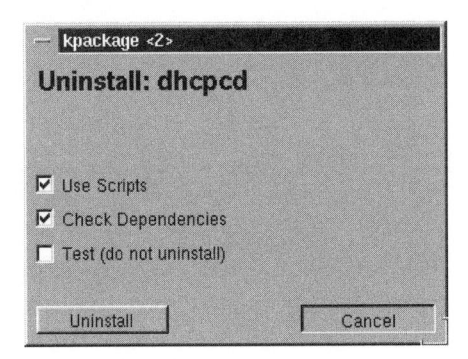

Figure 79. Uninstalling a package

Before you uninstall a package, you can change the options, but we suggest that you leave the default settings unchanged. After you have adjusted the settings, click **Uninstall** to continue. After the dependencies are checked, the package will be uninstalled.

2.5.2 Installing a package

To install a package, click **File > Open**, and you will see a window similar to Figure 80.

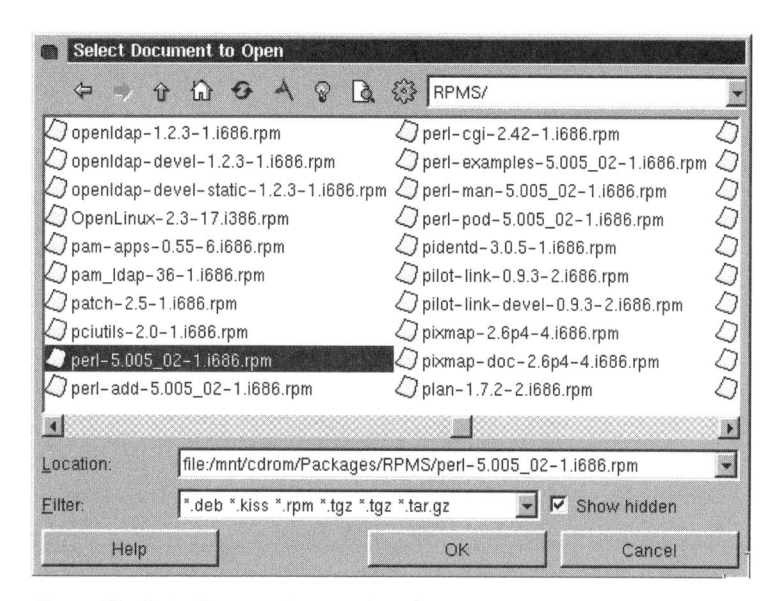

Figure 80. Selecting a package to install

Here you can select the packages you wish to install from any available system directory.

Note

If you want to install packages from a CD-ROM, you must mount the CD-ROM drive before you can access the files on it. This can be done with the command `mount /mnt/cdrom` from a command prompt.

After you have selected the package, click **OK** to continue. You will see a window similar to Figure 81.

Chapter 2. Basic system administration   75

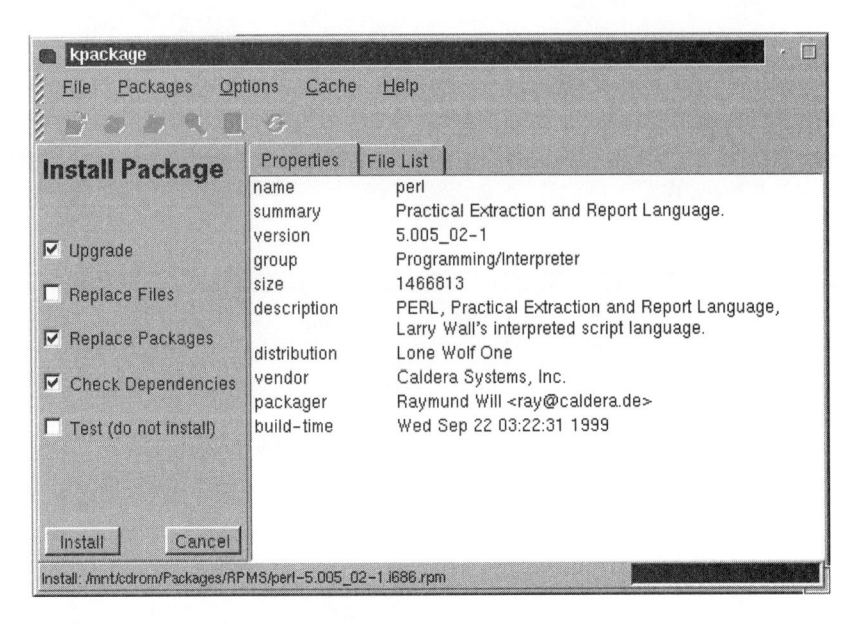

Figure 81. Description on a new package

In this window you see the description of the package. Select the **File List** option to see which files are included with the package. Before you actually install packages, you can adjust the installation options. The options are:

- **Upgrade** - this is used if you are installing a package that is already installed
- **Replace File** - if there are files in the same location already, they will be replaced automatically
- **Replace Packages** - packages are updated in the packages database
- **Check Dependencies** - check if all dependencies are satisfied
- **Test (do not install)** - perform a test installation

After you have selected your options, click **Install** to install the package. After the package is installed it will appear in the package list, as you can see in Figure 82.

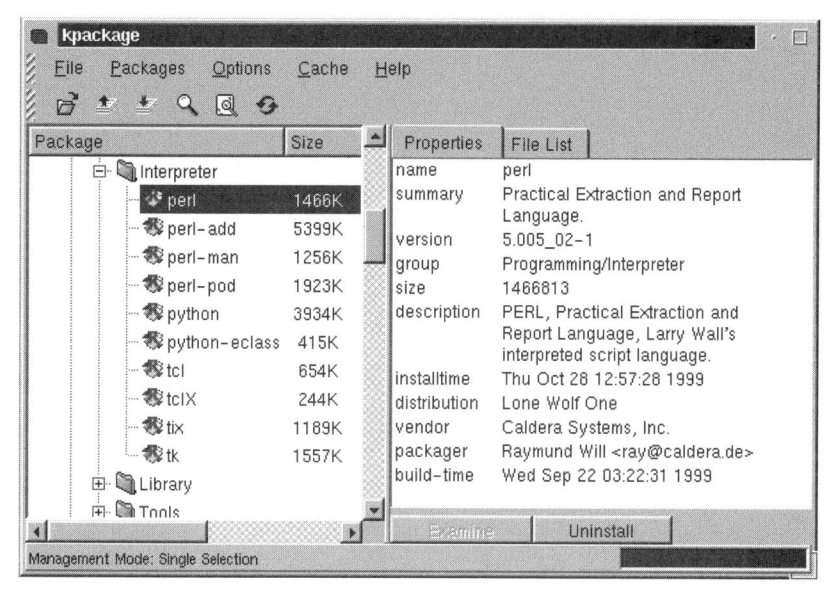

Figure 82. After the installation

2.6 Package management using RPM

Package management can also be done directly with the RPM package manager on the command line. The command line in the graphical interface can be accessed through the terminal window as we described in 2.3, "Getting the X-Windows terminal window" on page 69. Table 11 shows some of the most frequently used versions of the rpm commands.

Table 11. Basic RPM commands

Command	Description
`rpm -q <package>`	If a package is installed, check version and build number of the installed package.
`rpm -qi <package>`	Obtain more information about an installed package.
`rpm -qa`	List all installed packages.
`rpm -qf <filename>`	Determine the (installed) package that `<file>` belongs to.
`rpm -Uhv <package.rpm>`	Update/Install the file `package.rpm` showing a progress bar.

Command	Description
`rpm -F -v ./*.rpm`	Update (freshen) all currently installed packages using the RPM files in the current directory.
`rpm --help`	Get help about the different options and parameters.

> **Note**
>
> After you install packages using RPM, you may need to run some additional configuration programs. Programs such as Apache need to be customized to your particular environment and require some post-installation maintenance. Some of these packages can be configured from the graphical interface by selecting other icons. Other packages have their own configuration tools.

More information and options about RPM can be found in the manual page (`man rpm`), the RPM how-to file (less /usr/doc/howto/en/RPM-HOWTO.txt.gz) and at the RPM Web site at http://www.rpm.org. You can also display a short overview by running `rpm --help`..

2.7 System menu

In the System menu of the COAS tools, you can access the following tools:

- **Accounts** - for managing the accounts
- **Daemons** - for managing the startup programs
- **Filesystem** - for mounting devices and NFS volumes
- **Hostname** - for setting hostnames
- **Resources** - for checking the hardware resources
- **Time** - for setting the time and time zone

The System menu is shown in Figure 83.

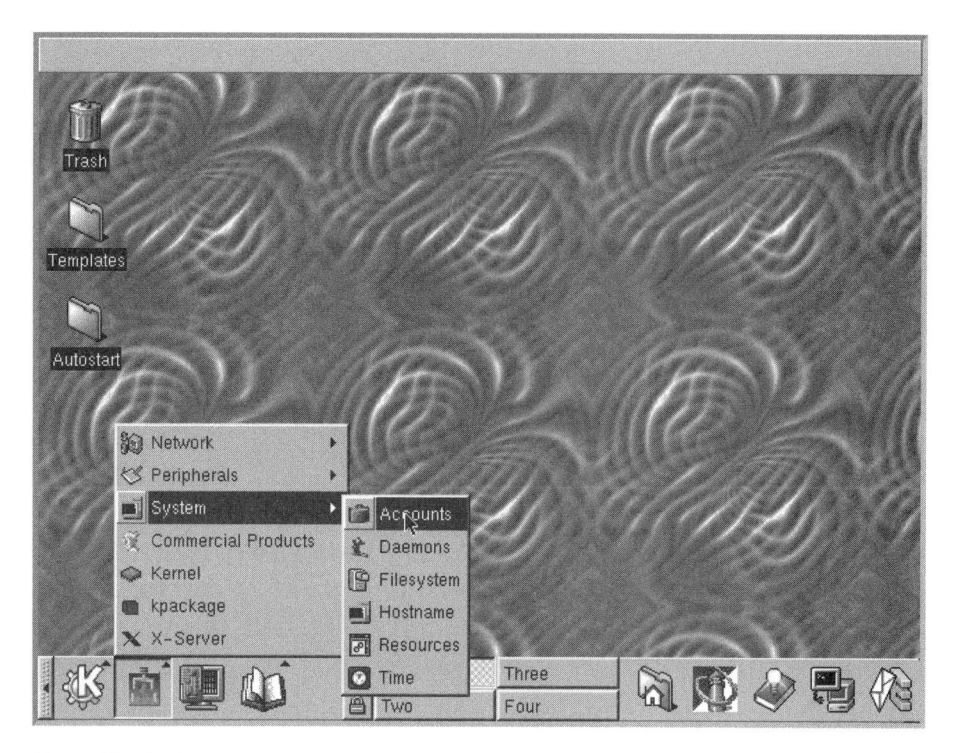

Figure 83. System menu

To start the tools from the System menu, select the tool you want. At the initial window, click **OK** to continue.

2.8 Accounts

This tool is used to manipulate the user accounts. After the tool is started, you will see a window similar to Figure 84.

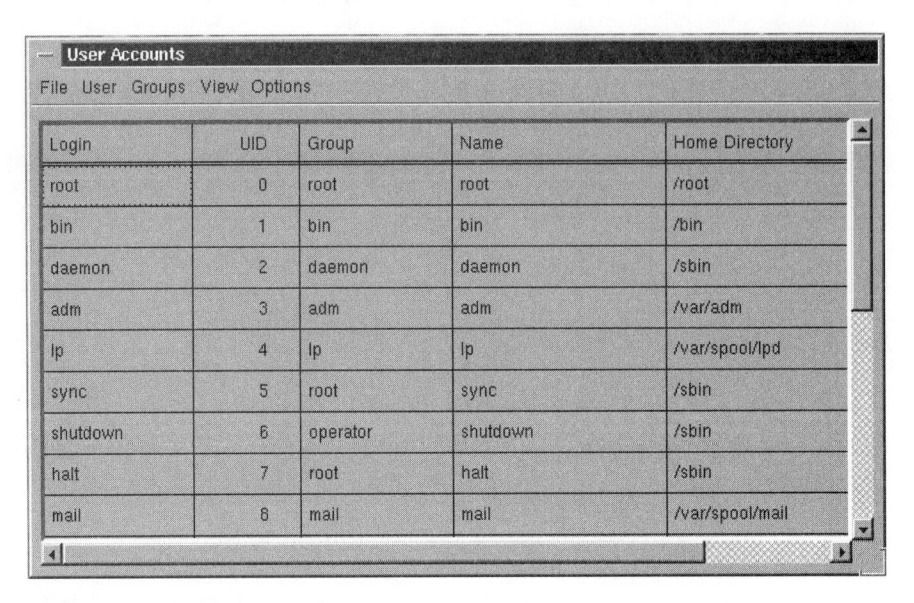

Login	UID	Group	Name	Home Directory
root	0	root	root	/root
bin	1	bin	bin	/bin
daemon	2	daemon	daemon	/sbin
adm	3	adm	adm	/var/adm
lp	4	lp	lp	/var/spool/lpd
sync	5	root	sync	/sbin
shutdown	6	operator	shutdown	/sbin
halt	7	root	halt	/sbin
mail	8	mail	mail	/var/spool/mail

Figure 84. Account management

Here you can manage users and groups. In the following sections we will describe how to perform these tasks.

In the View menu, you have two options for displaying users:

- **All users** - all users will be displayed
- **Regular users** - only regular users will be displayed

In the Options menu, you have three options to choose from:

- **Preferences** - here you define the global preferences for creating users and groups. If you select this option you will see a window similar to Figure 85.

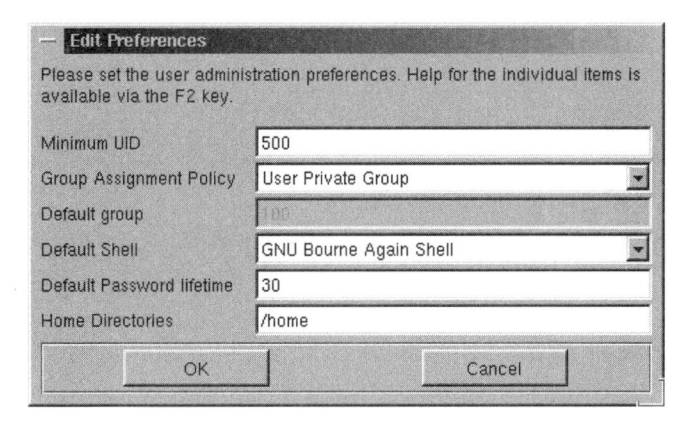

Figure 85. Setting the preferences for creation

Define your preferences and click **OK** to store them.

- **Enable/Disable shadow passwords** - here you can enable or disable shadow passwords.

- **Enable/Disable NIS lookups** - here you can enable or disable NIS lookups.

2.8.1 Managing accounts

In this section we explain how to manage accounts. We cover adding a new user, deleting a user and editing an existing user.

To create a new user follow these steps:

1. To add a new user, select **User > Create User**. You will see a window similar to Figure 86.

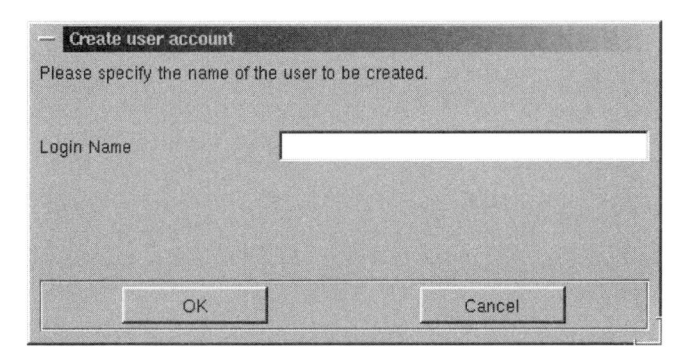

Figure 86. Login name for the new user

Chapter 2. Basic system administration 81

2. Type in the unique login name of the new user and click **OK** to continue, and you will see a window similar to Figure 87.

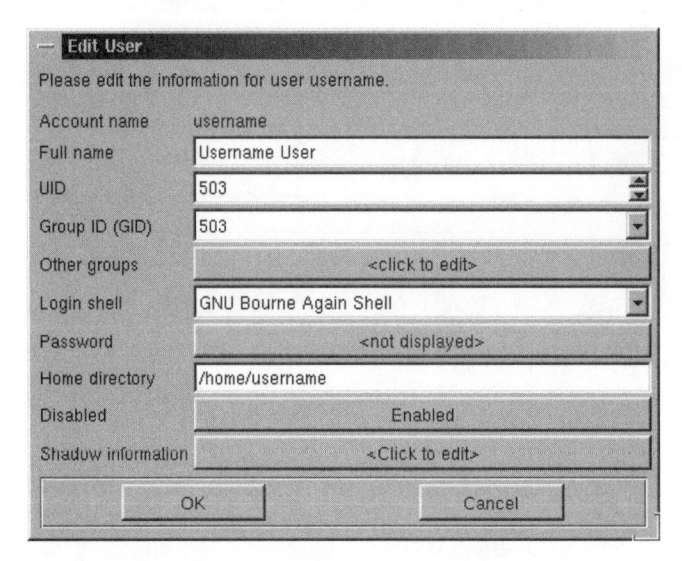

```
─ Edit User
Please edit the information for user username.
Account name    username
Full name       Username User
UID             503
Group ID (GID)  503
Other groups              <click to edit>
Login shell     GNU Bourne Again Shell
Password                  <not displayed>
Home directory  /home/username
Disabled                  Enabled
Shadow information        <Click to edit>
        OK                        Cancel
```

Figure 87. Specifying parameters for the new user

Here you need to specify the following:

- **Full name** - this is the description of the user

- **UID** - this is the number by which the system knows you. It only attaches this number to file and directory ownership and uses /etc/passwd to convert this to a username when listing the attributes. Generally UID numbers are unique and the system programs will usually prevent you from creating more than one username with the same UID. This can usually be overridden by specifying options to the commands to create IDs.

- **GID** - this is a unique number assigned to a group. In Caldera OpenLinux each user has its own default group. The default GID is the next available and the GID numbers are starting at 500.

- **Other groups** - each user can be a member of one or more groups. You can specify these groups here. If you click the button you will see a window similar to Figure 88.

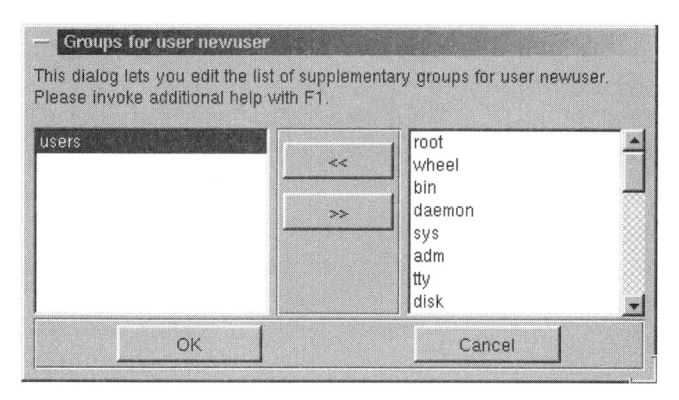

Figure 88. Specifying other groups for the user

When you have added all the groups you want, click **OK** to continue.

- **Login shell** - the shell that is started when the user logs in.
- **Password** - the password used to log in with. To define a password, click the button labeled **<not displayed>** and you will see a window similar to Figure 89.

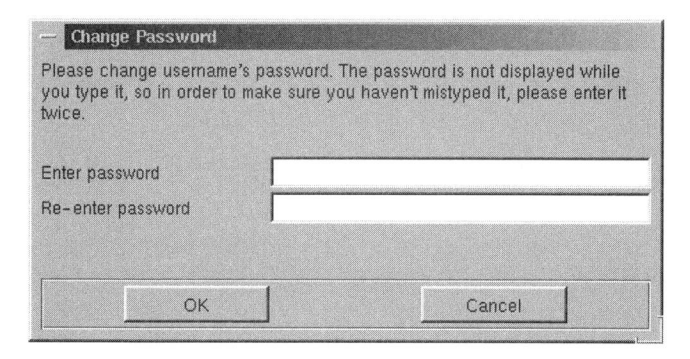

Figure 89. Specifying the password for the new user

Type in the password for the user and click **OK** to continue.

Note

Caldera OpenLinux uses shadow passwords by default.

- **Home directory** - this is the user's home directory. It is the first place a user goes to when logging in. It contains files and programs that are owned and used by that user.

Chapter 2. Basic system administration **83**

- **Disabled/Enabled** - with this you define if an account is enabled or disabled. You can toggle this value by clicking the button.
- **Shadow information** - here you define the password properties: expiration, change timeframe, etc. If you want to change the default values, click the button and you will see a window similar to Figure 90.

Figure 90. Password properties for the new user

When you have edited the properties, click **OK** to save them.

3. After you have typed in all necessary information for the new user, click **OK** to actually create the new user.

2.8.1.1 Deleting a user

When you want to delete a user, select the user from the list and click **User > Delete User**. You will see a window similar to Figure 91.

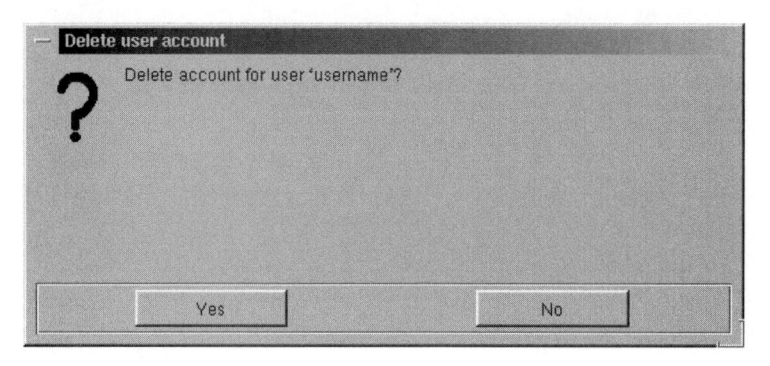

Figure 91. Deleting a user

Click **Yes** to delete the user.

2.8.1.2 Editing a user

When you want to edit a user, select the user from the list and choose **User > Edit User**. You will see a window similar to Figure 92.

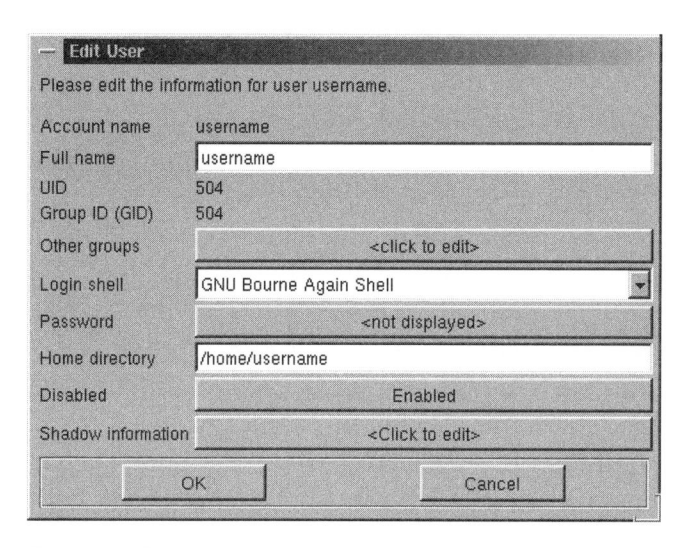

Figure 92. Edit a user

Here you can modify the following attributes of a user:

- Other groups
- Login shell
- Password
- Home directory
- Disabled/Enabled
- Shadow information

We described these attributes in 2.8.1, "Managing accounts" on page 81. When you are done, click **OK**.

2.8.2 Managing groups

You can access the tool for managing groups by selecting **Accounts > Groups > Manage groups**. You will see a window similar to Figure 93.

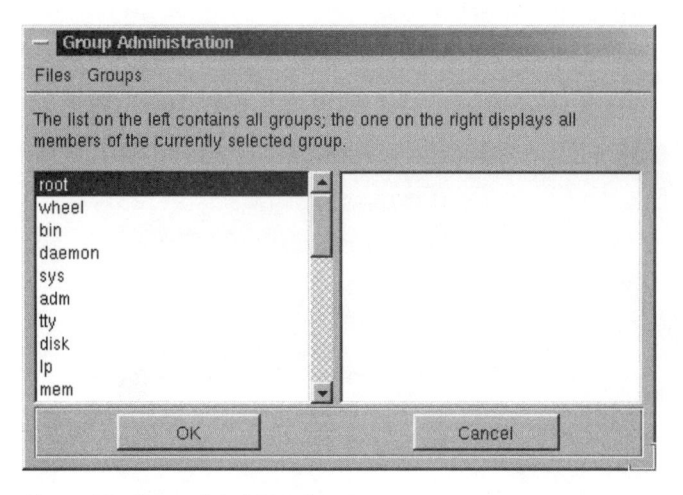

Figure 93. Group Administration

Here you can perform operations related to the groups.

2.8.2.1 Creating a new group
You can create a new group by selecting **Groups > Create Group**. You will see a window similar to Figure 94.

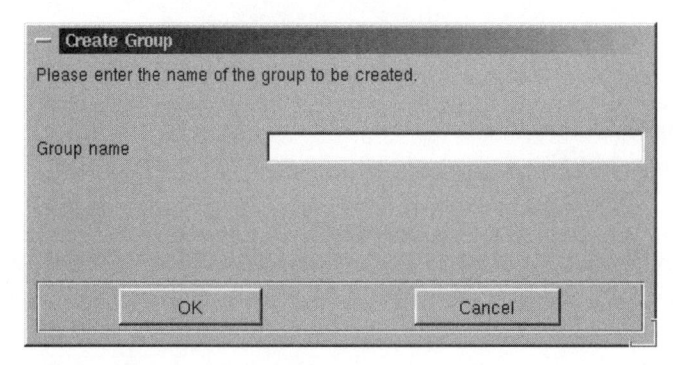

Figure 94. Creating a new group

Type in the name of the new group and click **OK** to create it.

2.8.2.2 Deleting a group
Select the group you want to delete from the list of all the groups and choose **Groups > Delete Group**. You will see a window similar to Figure 95.

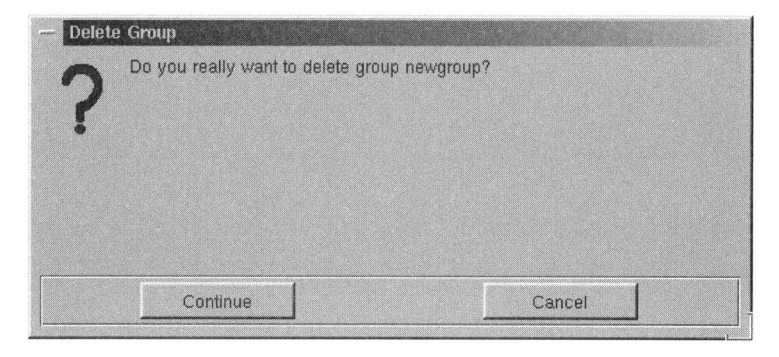

Figure 95. Deleting a group

Click **Continue** to actually delete a group.

2.8.2.3 Rename a group
Select the group you want to rename from the list of all the groups and choose **Groups > Rename Group.** You will see a window similar to Figure 96.

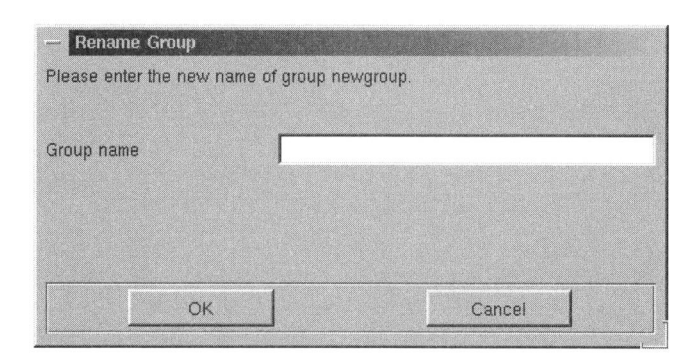

Figure 96. Renaming a group

Type in the new name for the group and click **OK** to rename it.

2.8.2.4 Merge a group
You have the option to merge users from one group to another. Select the group to which you want to merge another and choose **Groups > Merge Group**. You will see a window similar to Figure 97.

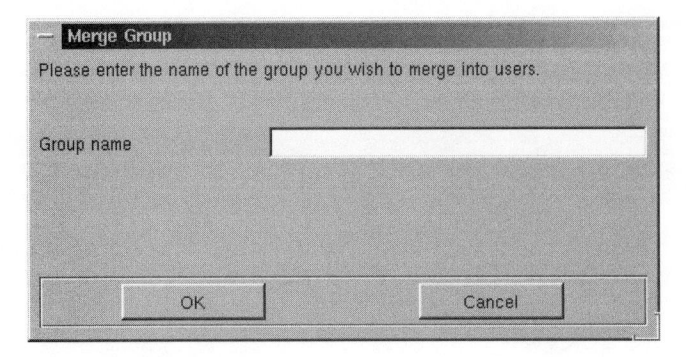

Figure 97. Merge a group

Type in the name of the group you want to merge in. Click **OK** to continue.

2.8.2.5 Group membership

You can change the members of a group. To change the members of a desired group select the group from the list of all the groups and choose **Groups > Group Membership**. You will see a window similar to Figure 98.

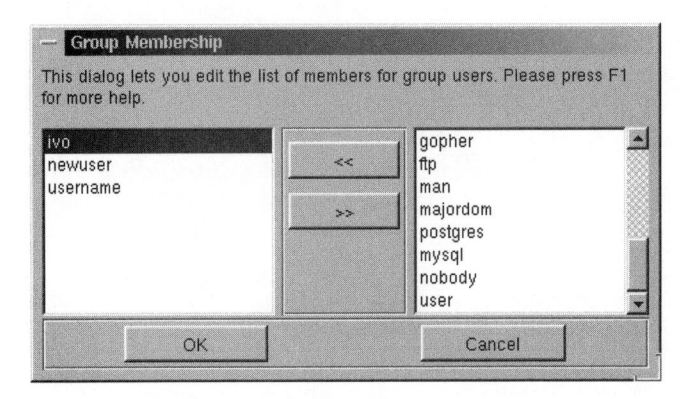

Figure 98. Group membership

You can add or remove users from a group. Click **OK** to save your changes.

2.9 Daemons (services)

This tool is used to manipulate the daemons that will start at the server startup. After the tool is started you will see a window similar to Figure 99.

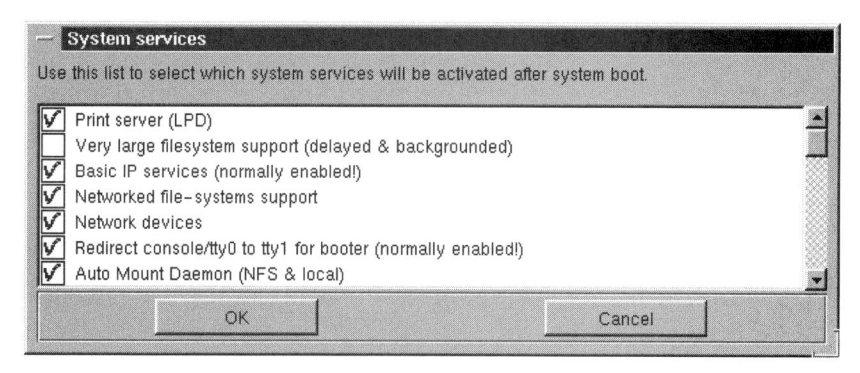

Figure 99. System services

Here you define which services (daemons) will be started at the server startup. When you are finished, click **OK** to save your changes.

2.10 Filesystem

Here you can mount or unmount the devices and connect to the NFS servers. After the tool is started, you will see a window similar to Figure 100.

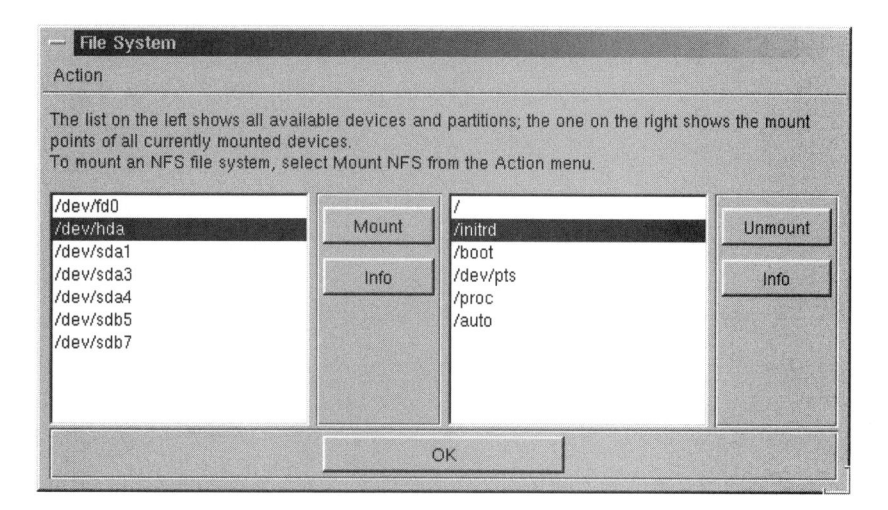

Figure 100. Filesystems

On the left side you see unmounted devices. If you want to mount the device, select it from the list and click **Mount.**

Chapter 2. Basic system administration **89**

On the right side you see mounted devices. If you want to unmount an already mounted device, select it from the list and click **Unmount.**

By selecting the mounted or unmounted device and clicking **Info,** you will see the information about the particular device.

2.10.1 Mounting an NFS volume

You can mount an NFS file system by choosing **Action > Mount NFS**. You will see a window similar to Figure 101.

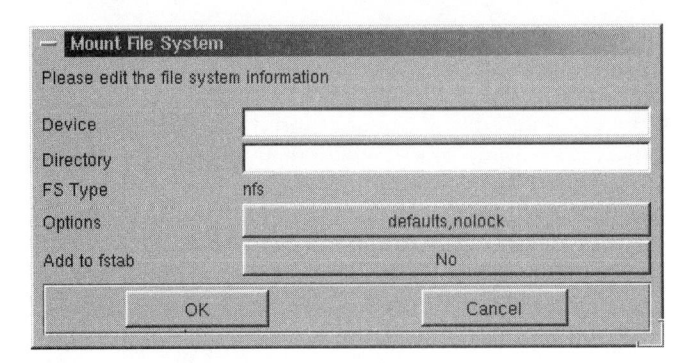

Figure 101. Mounting an NFS volume

Type in the required values and click **OK** to mount the NFS volume.

2.11 Hostname

Here you can change the hostname of your Linux server. After the tool is started you will see a window similar to Figure 102.

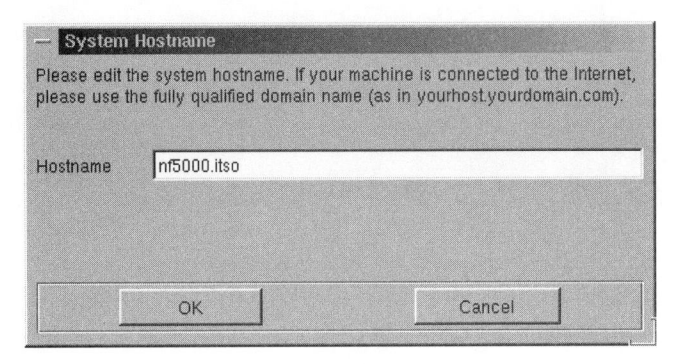

Figure 102. Changing the hostname

Type in the new hostname and click **OK** to save it.

2.12 Resources

With this tool you can examine hardware resources. After the tool is started you will see a window similar to Figure 103.

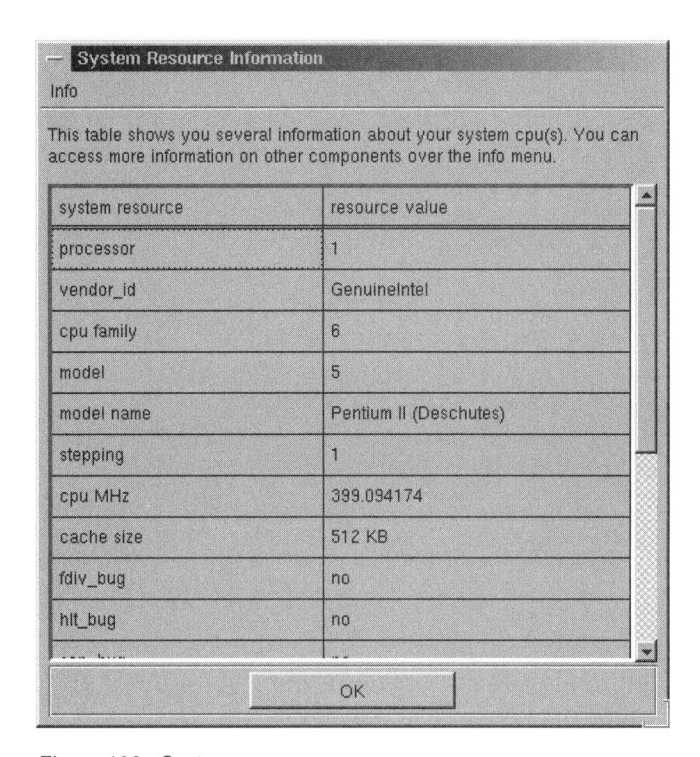

Figure 103. System resources

Here you can get information about the following resources:

- Block devices
- Character devices
- Interrupts
- System load average
- IOports
- DMA

To access this information, select the appropriate option from the Info menu. For example if you select **Interrupts**, you will see a window similar to Figure 104.

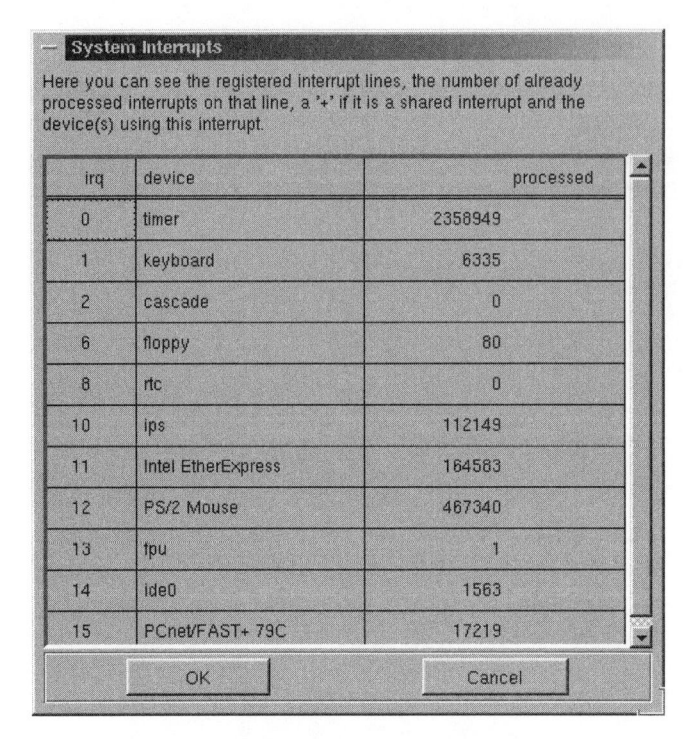

Figure 104. System interrupts

2.13 Time

Here you can set the time and time zone. After the tool is started, you will see a window similar to Figure 105.

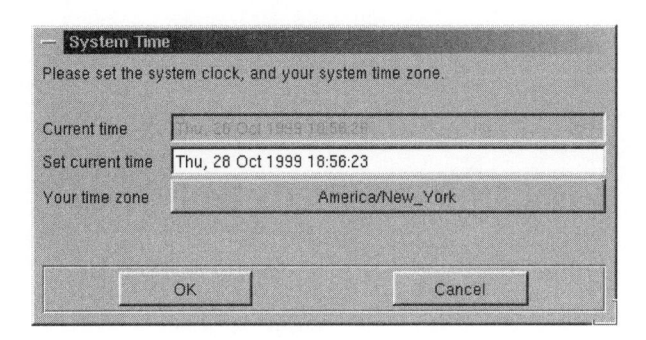

Figure 105. Setting the time

Type in the current time. If you also want to change the time zone, click the button for it. You will see a window similar to Figure 106.

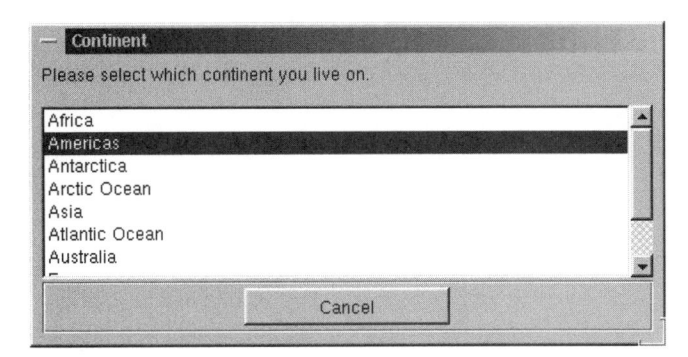

Figure 106. Setting the time zone

Select your region and you will be presented with the time zones for that region. Select the one that matches your city. After that you will be back in the System Time panel. Click **OK** to save the changes.

2.14 Peripherals menu

In the Peripherals menu of the COAS tools you can access the following tools:

- **Mouse** - for managing the mouse
- **Printers** - for managing the printers

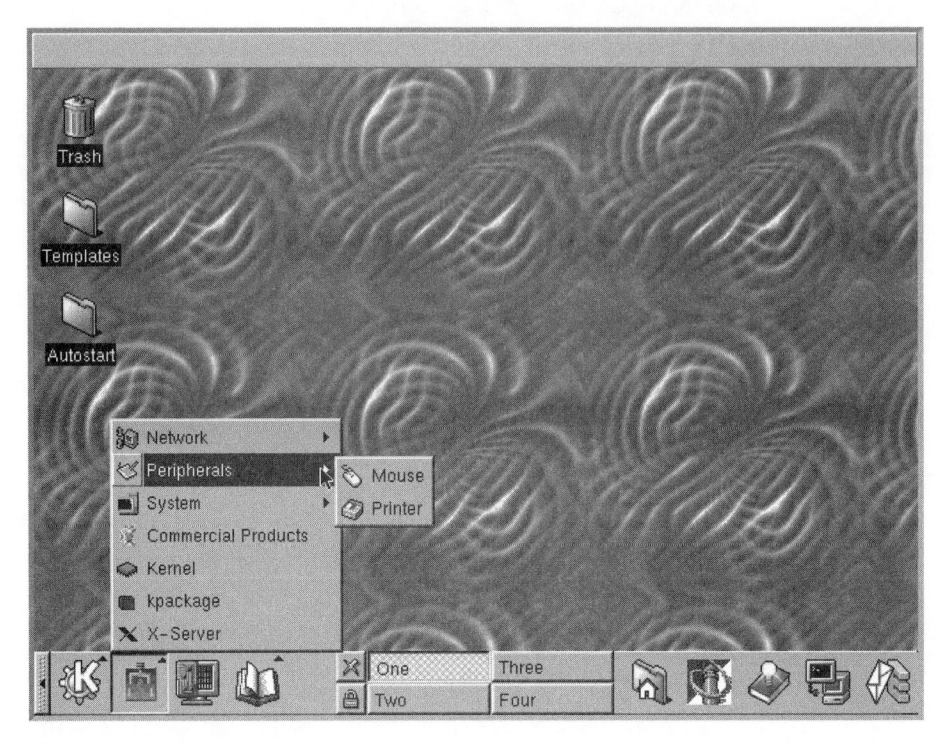

Figure 107. Peripherals menu

To start the tool from Peripherals menu, select the tool you want. At the initial dialog, click **OK** to continue.

2.15 Mouse

This tool is used to configure the behavior of the mouse in the tex- based user interface. After the tool is started you will see a window similar to Figure 108.

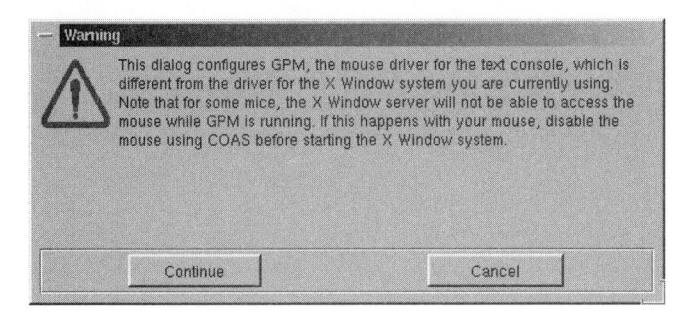

Figure 108. Warning before configuring the mouse

As you can see from the warning, this tool is used for configuring the GPM to enable additional features for mouse usage in the text-based interface. Click **Continue** to continue with the configuration. You will see a window similar to Figure 109.

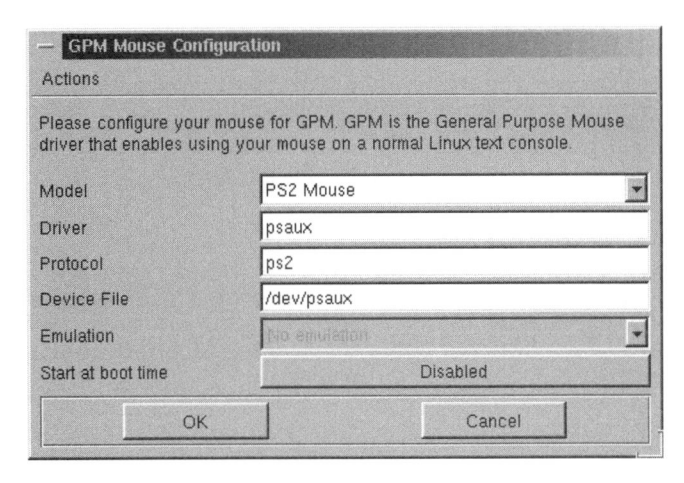

Figure 109. GPM Mouse Configuration

Select the configuration parameters that meet your needs and click **OK** to continue. On the next window, click **Save** to save your settings.

> **Note**
>
> If you did not install the GPM package, you will receive the error message that the daemon cannot be started.

2.16 Printer

This tool is used to configure the printers you want to use in your Caldera OpenLinux system. After the tool is started, you will see a window similar to Figure 110.

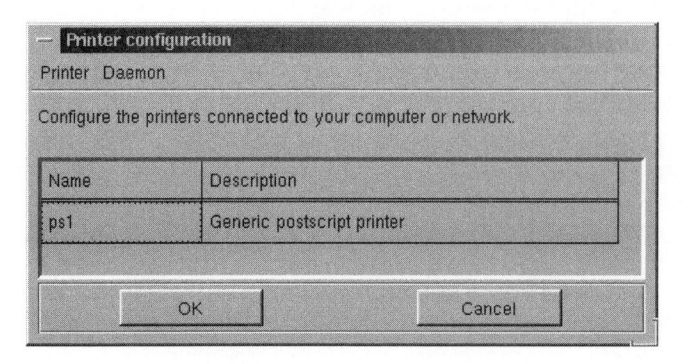

Figure 110. Printer configuration

Here you can manage printers. In the following sections we will describe how to perform these tasks.

From the Daemon menu you can **Start** or **Stop** the printer daemon.

> **Note**
>
> You can only print documents if the daemon is running.

2.16.1 Adding a new printer

You can add a new printer to your system by selecting **Printer > Add**. You will see a window similar to Figure 111.

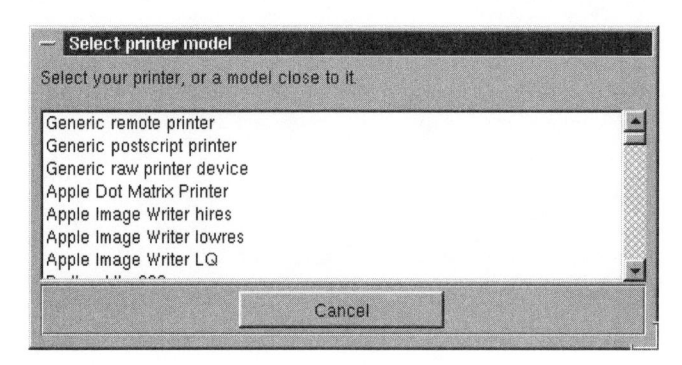

Figure 111. Selecting a printer model

Select your model from the list. After that you will see a window similar to Figure 112.

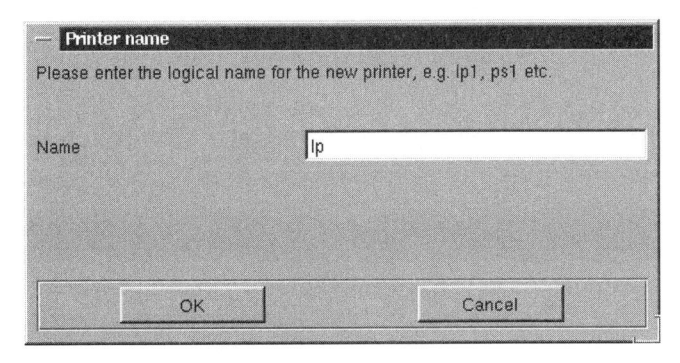

Figure 112. Defining printer logical name

Here you define the logical name of the printer. This name is then used in all printer definitions. Click **OK** to continue, and you will see a window similar to Figure 113.

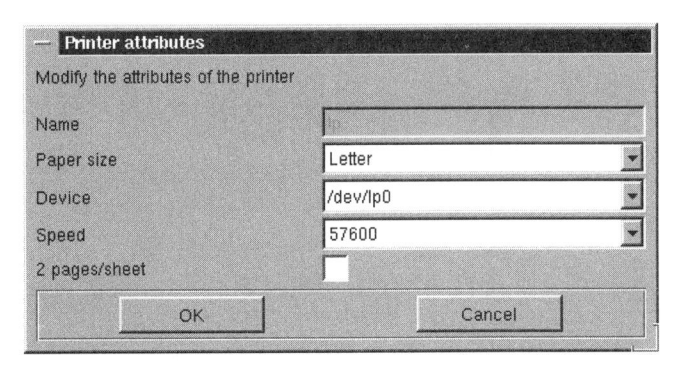

Figure 113. Printer attributes

Here you define printer attributes:

- **Paper size**
- **Device** - this is the physical device to which the printer is connected. This is usually the parallel port, and /dev/lp0 is the first parallel port in your server.
- **Speed** - this is the speed for the data traveling over the device to which the printer is connected.

These attributes are related to the printer driver you choose, so all drivers will not have the same options.

After you have defined all attributes for your printer driver click **OK** to continue. On the next window select **Save** to save your configuration. The installation program will then ask you if it should create the printer queue for your new printer. Click **OK** to create the queue. The printer daemon will be stopped so that the queue can be created and then it will be restarted again.

2.16.2 Removing a printer

You can remove a printer from your system by selecting the printer, which is to be removed, from the list of installed printers and select **Printer > Remove**. You will be asked if you really want to remove the printer twice. Answer **OK** both times if you really want to remove the printer.

2.16.3 Edit a printer

If you want to edit the properties of the installed printer, select the printer from the list and choose **Printer > Edit**. You will see a window similar to Figure 114

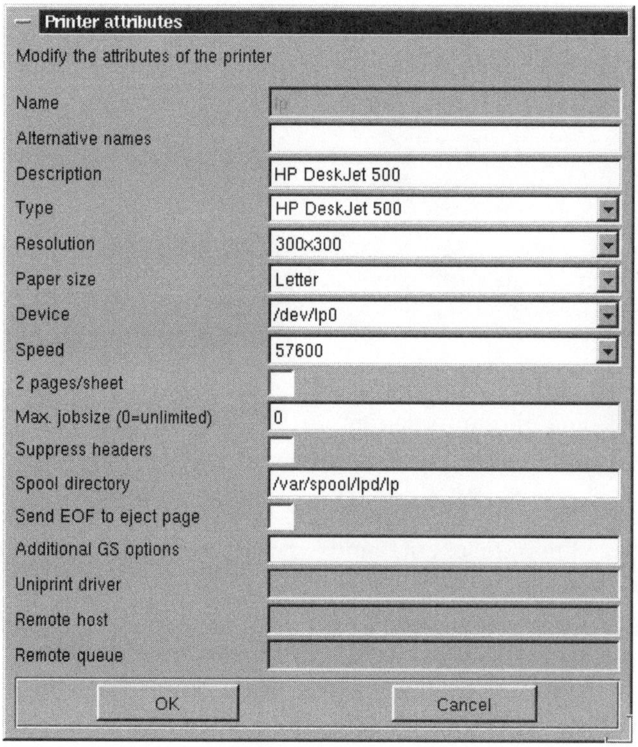

Figure 114. Printer attributes

Edit the preferences you want and click **OK** to continue. On the next window click **Save** to save the changes.

2.17 Network menu

From the Network menu of the COAS tools, you can access the following tools:

- **TCP/IP** - for managing TCP/IP settings.
- **Ethernet interfaces** - for Ethernet Network Interface Cards (NICs).
- **Mail Transfer** - for managing the Mail Transfer Agent (MTA). You can find more information on how to set up MTA on your server in Chapter 8, "Sendmail" on page 181.

The COAS tools menu is shown in Figure 107 on page 94.

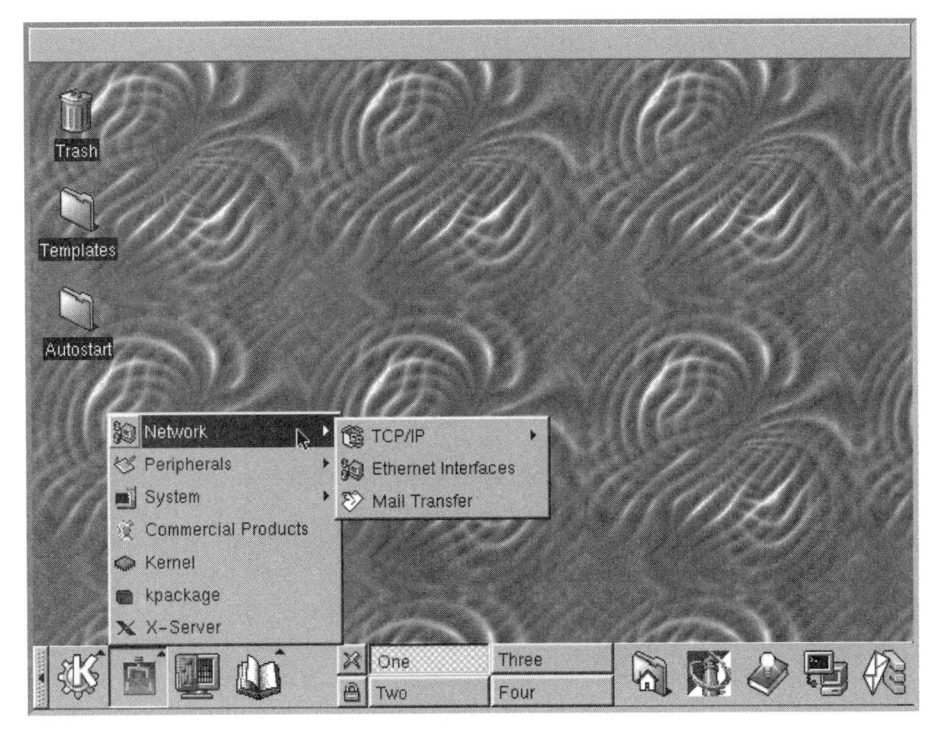

Figure 115. Network menu

To start the tools from the Network menu select the tool you want. At the initial window, click **OK** to continue. If you select **TCP/IP,** you will be presented with two options, as you can see in Figure 116.

Chapter 2. Basic system administration **99**

Figure 116. TCP/IP menu

- **NIS** - for setting the NIS client options. You can get more information on how to set up an NIS client or server in Chapter 10, "NIS - Network Information System" on page 211.

- **Resolver** - to set up the TCP/IP resolving settings.

2.18 Ethernet interfaces

With this tool you can configure your Ethernet NICs. After you start the tool you will see a window similar to Figure 117.

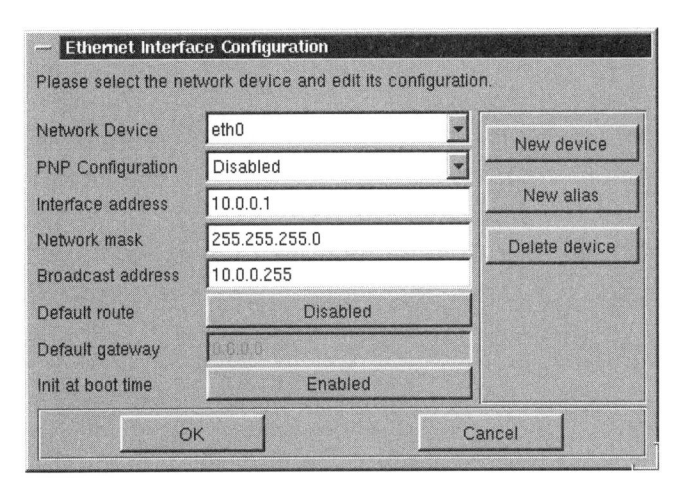

Figure 117. Ethernet Interface Configuration window

If you configured your Ethernet NIC during installation you will see the current configuration. There are several configuration options available:

- **Network device** - this is the name of the network device as it is recognized by the kernel.

- **PNP Configuration** - here you can select if the adapter is configured automatically from a DHCP server by selecting the **DHCP** option, or manually by selecting the **Disabled** option.

- **Interface address** - here you define the IP address of the interface.

- **Network mask** - here you define the subnet mask for the interface.

- **Broadcast address** - here you define the broadcast IP address. This is by default calculated from subnet mask.

- **Default route** - here you enable or disable the default route.

- **Default gateway** - if you enabled default routing, you need to specify the IP address of the router here.

- **Init at boot time** - here you specify if the interface should be initialized during system startup.

2.18.1 Adding a new network interface

If you have installed a new Ethernet interface you can add it to the system configuration by clicking **New device.** You will see a window similar to Figure 118.

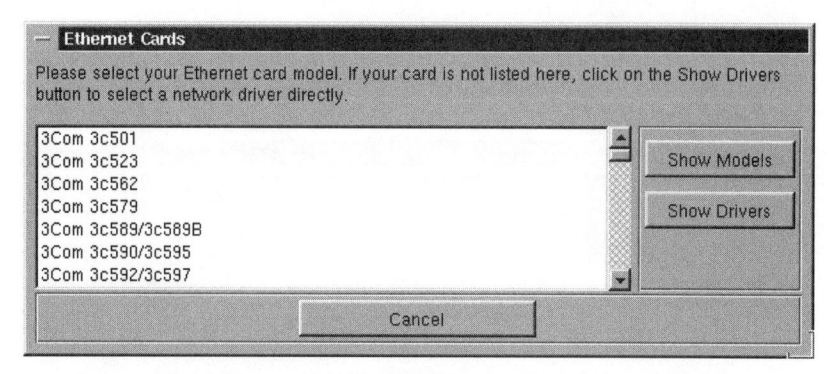

Figure 118. Selecting the type of the Ethernet card

If you do not find the driver for your Ethernet card among the listed models, you may try to check all available drivers. To see all drivers click **Show Drivers.** Select your model/driver by clicking the appropriate one, and you will see a window similar to Figure 119.

Figure 119. Defining hardware parameters

Here you define the hardware parameters for the driver for your Ethernet NIC. When you are done, click **OK** to continue. The setup utility will try to load the module you selected. If the loading of the module is successful, your new interface definition will now be available for additional setup. You will see a window similar to Figure 117 on page 101. Define parameters to meet your needs and click **OK** to continue. On the next window click **Save** to save the configuration.

2.18.2 Removing a network interface

If you want to delete the definition for a Ethernet NIC, click **Delete device** from the dialog shown in Figure 117 on page 101. Then click **OK** to close the configuration window. On the next window, click **Save** to save the changes you just made.

If you have more than one Ethernet NIC adapter and you want to remove the adapter eth1 for example, follow these steps:

1. Stop the interface by executing the command:

    /sbin/ifdown eth1

2. Delete the file /etc/sysconfig/network-scripts/ifcfg-eth1 by executing the command:

    rm /etc/sysconfig/network-scripts/ipcfg-eth1

This procedure can be used for all adapters when you have multiple adapters defined.

2.19 Name resolution settings

You can access the tool for name resolution settings by clicking **Network > TCP/IP > Resolver**. When you start the tool you will see a window similar to Figure 120.

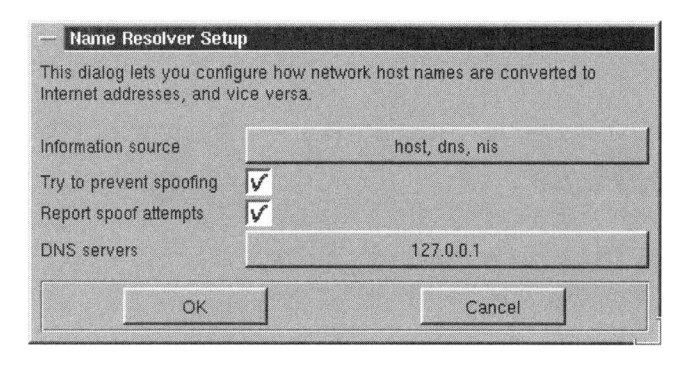

Figure 120. Name resolution setup

Here you can define how the name resolution is performed on your system. You have four options here:

- **Information source** - here you define the order and sources for the name resolution.
- **Try to prevent spoofing**

Chapter 2. Basic system administration **103**

- **Report spoof attempts**
- **DNS servers** - the defined IP addresses of the DNS servers

2.19.1 Name resolution order and sources

You can change the name resolution order and sources by clicking the button to the right of **Information sources.** You will see a window similar to Figure 121.

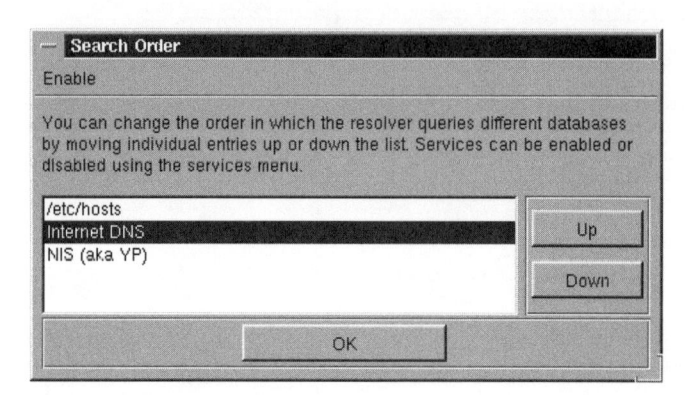

Figure 121. Search order

The search order can be changed by moving the name resolution resources up and down. If you want to enable or disable a particular name resolution source you can do this by selecting **Enable** and selecting the source you want to enable or disable. If a source is currently enabled, you can disable it and vice versa. When you are done, click **OK** to continue and on the next window select **Save** to save the changes.

2.19.2 Defining a DNS server

You can define a DNS server by clicking the button to the right of the **DNS servers** button. You will see a window similar to Figure 122.

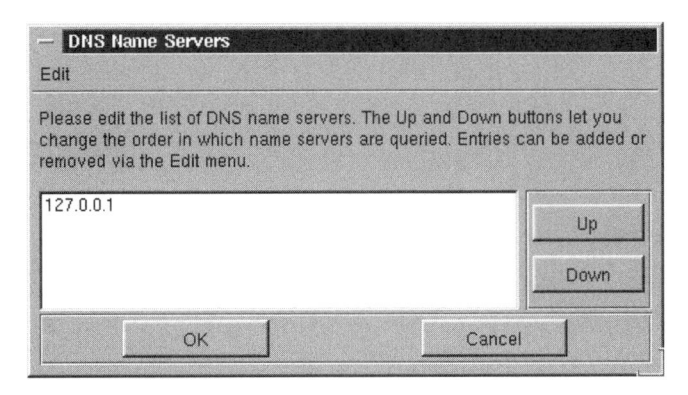

Figure 122. DNS servers

If you have more than one DNS server defined you can reorder them by moving them up and down. The top-most server will be accessed first and so on.

2.19.2.1 Add a new DNS server
If you want to add a new DNS server select **Edit > Add server**. You will see a window similar to Figure 123.

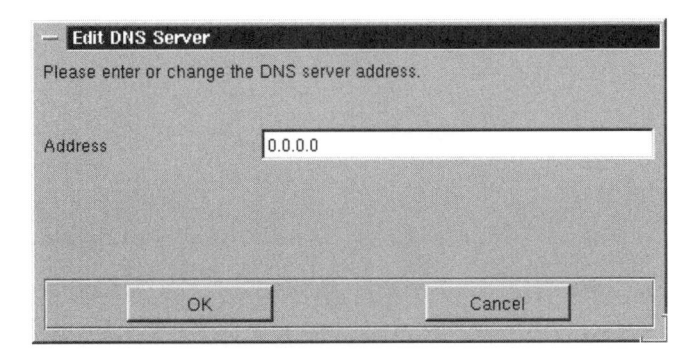

Figure 123. Specifying a DNS server

Type in the IP address of the DNS server and click **OK** to go back to the previous window.

2.19.2.2 Remove a DNS server
If you want to remove a DNS server select it from the list and choose **Edit > Remove server**.

2.19.2.3 Change a DNS server

If you want to change a DNS server's IP address select it from the list and choose **Edit > Edit server**. You will see a window similar to Figure 123. Type in the new IP address of the server and click **OK** to go back to the previous window.

2.20 Manipulating kernel modules

You can manage kernel modules in Caldera OpenLinux by using the kernel configuration tool from the COAS tools. You can start it by selecting the **Kernel** from the COAS tools menu. When the Kernel tool is started, you will see a window similar to Figure 124.

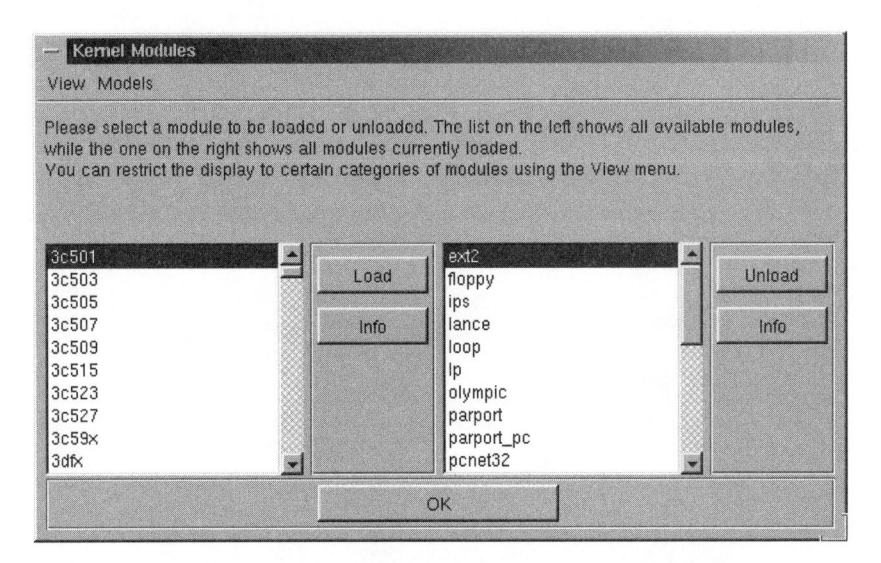

Figure 124. Kernel modules

On the left side you can see all available modules and on the right side you can see loaded modules. By default all modules are displayed, but if you want to display just one kind of module, you can do this by selecting the following options from the View menu:

- All drivers
- Arcnet drivers
- CD-ROM drivers
- Ethernet drivers
- Misc drivers
- Network drivers
- SCSI drivers

- SCSI host adapter drivers
- Sound drivers
- Token-ring drivers
- ISDN drivers
- Multimedia drivers

If you want to get information about a particular module select the module from either side and click **Info.**

2.20.1 Loading a new module

When you install a new piece of hardware you need to load the appropriate module if you want the hardware to be useful. In Linux, drivers can be loaded or unloaded without restarting the system. It may take some time to get used to this if you are used to another popular operating system. To load a new module select the module from the left side and click **Load.** You will see a window similar to Figure 125.

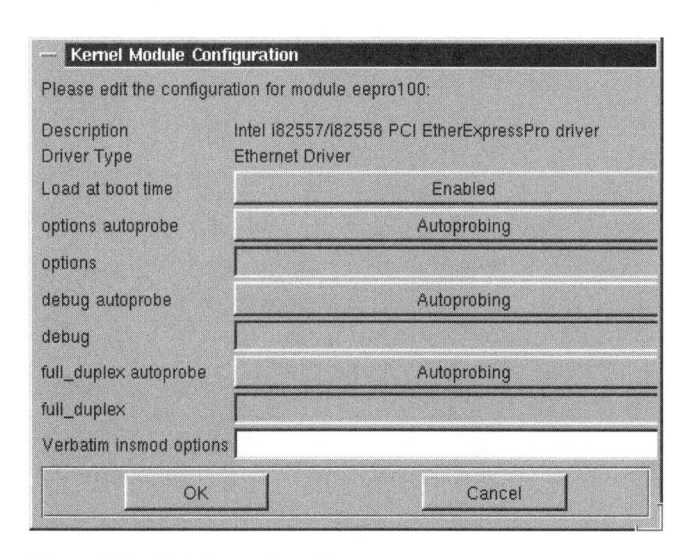

Figure 125. Module configuration

Each module has several hardware-related options and an option to load at boot time. If you want to load a module at boot time, click the button to the right of the Load at boot time field to specify your preferred setting. Click **OK** to actually load the module. If the module is loaded successfully, it will appear on the left side where the loaded modules are displayed.

2.20.2 Unloading a new module

If you want to unload an already loaded module, select it from the left side and click **Unload.** You will be asked if you really want to unload the module. Click **OK** to unload the module. If the module has been enabled to load at system startup, you will see a window similar to Figure 126.

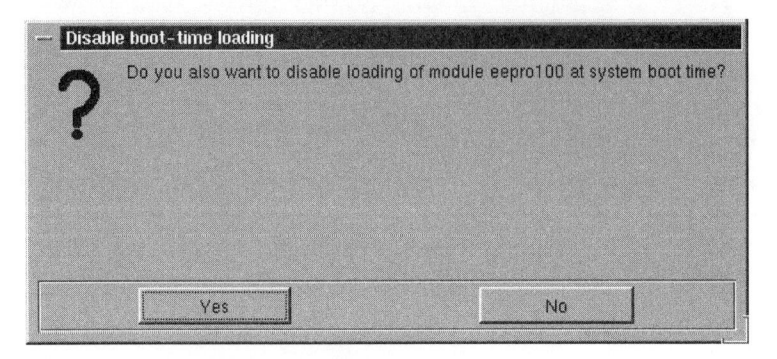

Figure 126. Disabling loading at startup

Here you can decide if you will also disable the startup loading of the module. Select **Yes** or **No** to continue. After that the module will be unloaded.

2.21 Configuring X-Windows

If for whatever reason you need to change the X-Windows setup after installation, you can do this by clicking **X-server** from the COAS tools menu. The configuration procedure is the same as in the installation process. Refer to 1.5, "Basic Linux installation" on page 3 for more information.

Chapter 3. General performance tools in Linux

Linux offers a great variety of ways to optimize your system for maximum performance. Apart from the general fact that it is always good to have as much RAM and the fastest CPU as possible, there are some additional parameters to tune a Linux system. This section is intended as a collection of useful hints and tools, but without getting into too much detail about them. Please refer to the respective documentation and references. You should also note that using some of these hints may render your system unstable; use them at your own risk and only if you know what you are doing.

3.1 General configuration hints

These are some general tips for tweaking your system to maximize performance.

Recompile your programs and the Linux kernel with all available compiler optimization flags (for example, -funroll-loops, -fomit-frame-pointer, -O6) and all architecture-specific compiler options for your hardware architecture. This may increase the size of binaries or make them unable to run on some processors, but you can gain a lot of speed in comparison with the binaries shipped in the distribution. Alternatively you could use special compilers for your architecture (for example, pgcc), which offer even more sophisticated optimization options.

Create swap partitions of equal priority but different hard disk drives to allow load balancing. Please note that it need to be different devices! Using two different partitions on one hard disk will have the reverse effect. Even better, try to avoid swapping at all by adding more memory. A busy server should never need to swap, as this would severely degrade the overall performance.

If you are running a heavily loaded server with a lot of parallel processes, you might run into the Linux kernel's limit of running processes (512 by default). This maximum number of tasks is configurable in the kernel sources, so you have to recompile the kernel after changing this value. This value is defined in the file /usr/src/linux/include/linux/tasks.h:

```
#define NR_TASKS        512
```

You can increase this value up to 4090 processes, if necessary.

Linux offers a filesystem mount option that is called noatime. The atime is a timestamp of the last access time (reading and writing) for a certain file. This option can be added to the mount options in /etc/fstab. When a filesystem is mounted with this option, read accesses to files will no longer result in an update of the inode access time information. This information is usually not very interesting on a file or Web server, so the lack of updates to this field is not relevant. The performance advantage of the noatime flag is that it suppresses write operations to the filesystem for files that are simply being read. Since these write accesses add additional overhead, this can result in measurable performance gains. Instead of specifying this as a mount option that would apply to the whole filesystem, you can use the command `chattr` to set this flag on single files or directories. For example:

```
chattr -R +A /var/spool/news
```

This command would set the noatime flag recursively on all files below the news spool directory (a very common practice on busy news servers). See the manual page chattr(1) for more information.

You can use the hdparm tool to tune some hard disk drive parameters. Unfortunately most of them only work on IDE systems (which should be avoided in server systems, anyway), but the option `-a` works for SCSI, too. The manual page describes it as follows: "This option is used to get/set the sector count for filesystem read-ahead. This is used to improve performance in sequential reads of large files, by prefetching additional blocks in anticipation of them being needed by the running task. The default setting is 8 sectors (4KB). This value seems good for most purposes, but in a system where most file accesses are random seeks, a smaller setting might provide better performance. Also, many drives have a separate built-in read-ahead function, which alleviates the need for a filesystem read-ahead in many situations." For example, to set the sector count read-ahead of your first SCSI disk to 4 sectors (2 KB), you would use the following command:

```
hdparm -a 4 /dev/sda
```

See the hdparm manual page for a complete list of available options.

The freely available tool Powertweak is a nice utility for tuning PCI chipset optimizations. It is expected to be extended to be a general performance tweaking tool similar to Powertweak on MS Windows. See `http://linux.powertweak.com` for more info about it.

You should also disable all unused services and daemons, especially network-related services. This has several advantages: fewer open services need fewer system resources (file descriptors, memory) and the system is less vulnerable to external attacks against known security holes. A good starting point is the /etc/inetd.conf file. Comment out all services you don't need, or disable inetd completely.

The Linux /proc filesystem offers a lot of entry points for run-time optimization without recompiling the kernel. This directory does not physically exist on your hard drive; it is mapped as a virtual directory. Most of the files contained herein are readable and contain various system information. Other files can be edited with a regular text editor to set a certain kernel parameter. See /usr/src/linux/Documentation/sysctl/README in the Linux kernel sources for a detailed description of the tunable parameters (including filesystem, virtual memory, etc.).

There are some special TCP options that can be disabled in a local network with high signal quality and bandwidth, since they are mostly intended for lossy connections (see /usr/src/linux/net/TUNABLE in the Linux kernel sources for a detailed list):

To disable TCP timestamps, enter:

```
echo 0 > /proc/sys/net/ipv4/tcp_timestamps
```

To disable window scaling, enter:

```
echo 0 > /proc/sys/net/ipv4/tcp_window_scaling
```

To disable selective acknowledgments, enter:

```
echo 0 > /proc/sys/net/ipv4/tcp_sack
```

To tune the default and maximum window size (only if you know what you are doing), enter:

/proc/sys/net/core/rmem_default - default receive window

/proc/sys/net/core/rmem_max - maximum receive window

/proc/sys/net/core/wmem_default - default send window

/proc/sys/net/core/wmem_max - maximum send window

The following Web sites offer a lot of additional helpful hints about tuning and performance issues on Linux:

http://tune.linux.com

http://www.tunelinux.com

3.2 System monitoring / performance test tools

This section introduces a small collection of useful tools, among the many available, to monitor your Linux system or to gather system information.

To get an overview of all running processes and the system load, run the command `top` in a terminal session.

```
11:53am  up  3:57,  1 user,  load average: 0.00, 0.00, 0.00
34 processes: 33 sleeping, 1 running, 0 zombie, 0 stopped
CPU states:  0.0% user,  1.6% system,  0.0% nice, 98.4% idle
Mem:    62968K av,   59196K used,    3772K free,   17408K shrd,   15164K buff
Swap: 125996K av,       0K used,  125996K free                  33768K cached

  PID USER     PRI  NI  SIZE  RSS SHARE STAT LIB %CPU %MEM  TIME COMMAND
  515 root     20   0   792  792   628 R      0  1.6  1.2  0:01 top
    1 root      0   0   196  196   168 S      0  0.0  0.3  0:04 init
    2 root      0   0     0    0     0 SW     0  0.0  0.0  0:00 kflushd
    3 root      0   0     0    0     0 SW     0  0.0  0.0  0:00 kupdate
    4 root      0   0     0    0     0 SW     0  0.0  0.0  0:00 kpiod
    5 root      0   0     0    0     0 SW     0  0.0  0.0  0:00 kswapd
    6 root      0   0     0    0     0 SW     0  0.0  0.0  0:00 md_thread
   76 root      0   0   648  648   536 S      0  0.0  1.0  0:00 syslogd
   79 root      0   0   016  016   392 S      0  0.0  1.2  0:00 klogd
  116 at        0   0   552  552   456 S      0  0.0  0.8  0:00 atd
  121 root      0   0   452  452   376 S      0  0.0  0.7  0:00 gpm
  132 root      0   0  1592 1592  1488 S      0  0.0  2.5  0:00 httpd
  135 root      0   0   624  624   528 S      0  0.0  0.9  0:00 lpd
  137 wwwrun    0   0  1592 1592  1500 S      0  0.0  2.5  0:00 httpd
  138 wwwrun    0   0  1592 1592  1500 S      0  0.0  2.5  0:00 httpd
  139 wwwrun    0   0  1592 1592  1500 S      0  0.0  2.5  0:00 httpd
  140 wwwrun    0   0  1592 1592  1500 S      0  0.0  2.5  0:00 httpd
  141 wwwrun    0   0  1592 1592  1500 S      0  0.0  2.5  0:00 httpd
```

Figure 127. Example output of top

The `top` command updates the process list in regular intervals. To change this interval, press S and enter the desired number of seconds between each update. If you want to sort the processes by memory consumption, press M. To exit from top, press Q. This will bring you back to the command line.

Similar to the `top` command, the `pstree` command displays a hierarchical structure of all currently running processes:

```
[root@nf5000 /] # pstree
init-+-atd
     |-cron
     |-dhclient
     |-gpm
     |-httpd---22*[httpd]
     |-httpd---httpd
     |-inetd-+-in.telnetd---login---bash---make---make---make---make---gcc-+-as
     |       |                                                             |-cc1
     |       |                                                             `-cpp
     |       `-in.telnetd---login---bash---pstree
     |-kflushd
     |-klogd
     |-kpiod
     |-kswapd
     |-kupdate
     |-login---bash
     |-lpd
     |-md_thread
     |-5*[mingetty]
     |-nmbd
     |-nscd---nscd---5*[nscd]
     |-sendmail
     |-smbd---smbd
     `-syslogd
```

If you are running a graphical desktop like KDE, which is used in Caldera OpenLinux, you can also use windows-based tools such as KTop, the KDE Task Manager:

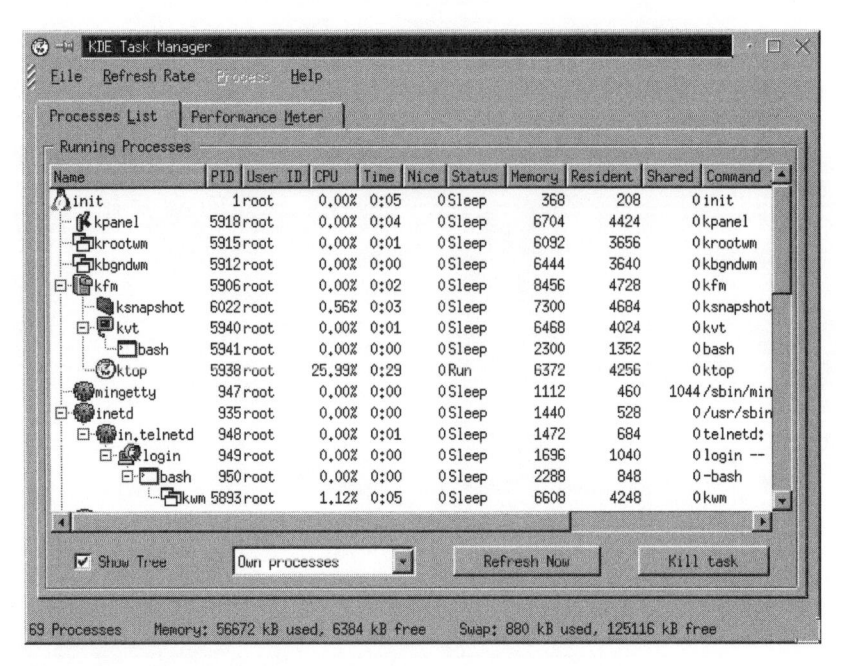

Figure 128. KDE Task Manager: Process List

The `KTop` command offers two different views. It can either display a process list (similar to the `top` and `pstree` commands), or you can switch to the performance meter, which displays the system load and memory usage over a longer time period.

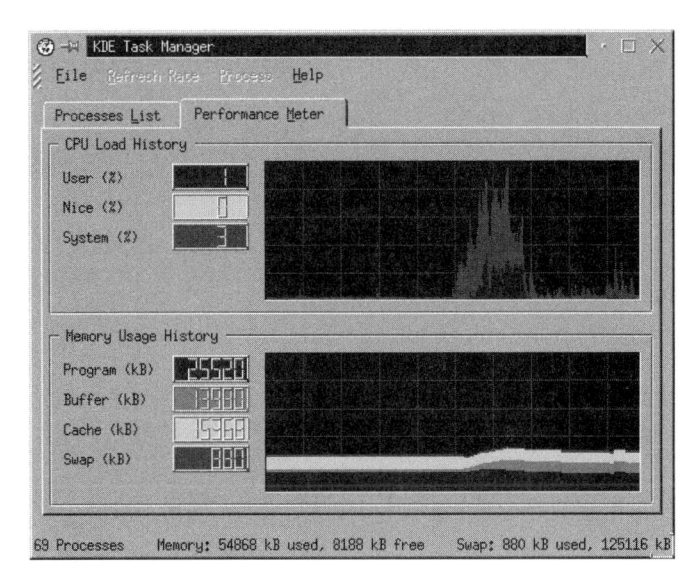

Figure 129. KDE task manager: performance meter

The Lothar project currently works on a very sophisticated hardware detection and configuration tool. The Web site can be found at:

```
http://www.linux-mandrake.com/lothar/
```

Figure 130 on page 116 shows Lothar's graphical front end on the Lothar Web site.

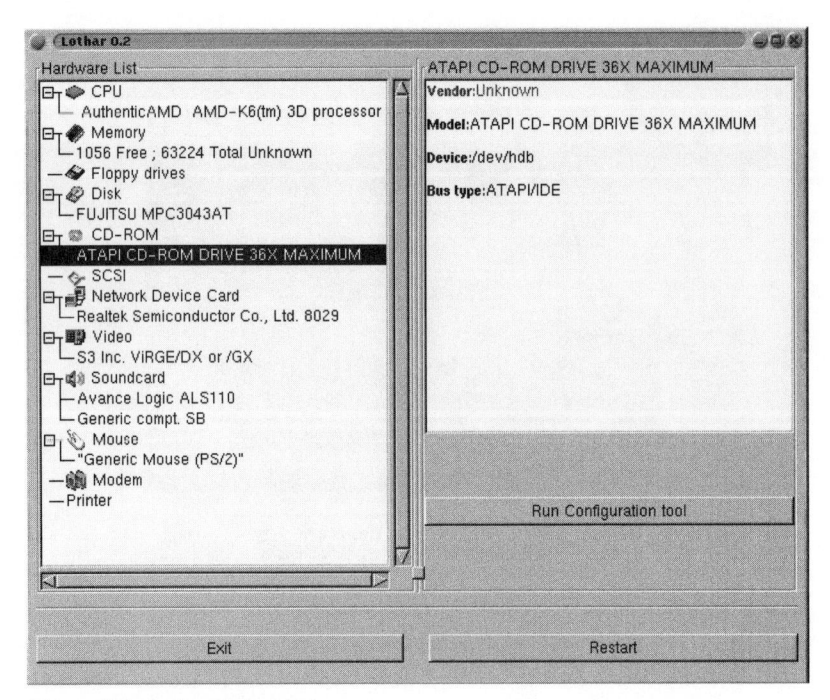

Figure 130. Lothar main window

The KDE control center also gives you a lot of information about your system by reading a number of informative files in the /proc filesystem. They can also be displayed in a regular text viewer (for example, `more`, `less` or `cat`):

The /proc/cpuinfo file contains information about your CPU (for example, vendor, Mhz, and flags such as mmx). For example:

```
[root@nf5000 /] # cat /proc/cpuinfo
processor         : 0
vendor_id         : GenuineIntel
cpu family        : 6
model             : 5
model name        : Pentium II (Deschutes)
stepping          : 2
cpu MHz           : 513.953346
cache size        : 512 KB
fdiv_bug          : no
hlt_bug           : no
sep_bug           : no
f00f_bug          : no
coma_bug          : no
fpu               : yes
fpu_exception     : yes
cpuid level       : 2
wp                : yes
flags             : fpu vme de pse tsc msr pae mce cx8 sep mtrr pge mca cmov pat p
se36 mmx osfxsr
bogomips          : 313.75
```

The /proc/interrupts file lists all interrupts used by Linux. Note that this shows interrupts only from devices that have been detected by the kernel! If a device will not be detected because of a resource conflict, you have to resolve this conflict manually (for example, by changing the BIOS setup). For example:

```
[root@nf5000 /] # cat /proc/interrupts
           CPU0
  0:      548029         XT-PIC   timer
  1:         557         XT-PIC   keyboard
  2:           0         XT-PIC   cascade
  8:           2         XT-PIC   rtc
  9:         371         XT-PIC   PCnet/PCI II 79C970A
 12:          68         XT-PIC   PS/2 Mouse
 13:           0         XT-PIC   fpu
 14:      198235         XT-PIC   ide0
 15:           3         XT-PIC   ide1
NMI:           0
```

The /proc/ioports file contains all allocated device I/O ports. Here the same rule applies. Only devices that are actually detected by the kernel are listed here. For example:

```
[root@nf5000 /] # cat /proc/ioports
0000-001f : dma1
0020-003f : pic1
0040-005f : timer
0060-006f : keyboard
0070-007f : rtc
0080-008f : dma page reg
00a0-00bf : pic2
00c0-00df : dma2
00f0-00ff : fpu
0170-0177 : ide1
01f0-01f7 : ide0
02e8-02ef : serial(auto)
02f8-02ff : serial(auto)
0376-0376 : ide1
03c0-03df : vga+
03e8-03ef : serial(auto)
03f6-03f6 : ide0
03f8-03ff : serial(auto)
1000-101f : PCnet/PCI II 79C970A
1020-1027 : ide0
1028-102f : ide1
```

The /proc/meminfo file displays information about memory (for example, memory used, free memory, and swap size). You can also use the `free` command to display this information. For example:

```
[root@nf5000 /] # cat /proc/meminfo
        total:    used:    free:  shared: buffers:  cached:
Mem:  64569344 62578688  1990656 54308864 18792448 27807744
Swap: 129019904   102400 128917504
MemTotal:     63056 kB
MemFree:       1944 kB
MemShared:    53036 kB
Buffers:      18352 kB
Cached:       27156 kB
SwapTotal:   125996 kB
SwapFree:    125896 kB
[root@nf5000 /] # free
             total       used       free     shared    buffers     cached
Mem:         63056      61124       1932      53068      18352      27164
-/+ buffers/cache:      15608      47448
Swap:       125996        100     125896
```

The /proc/mounts file shows all currently mounted partitions. The `mount` command without parameters will display similar information. For example:

```
[root@nf5000 /] # cat /proc/mounts
/dev/root / ext2 rw 0 0
proc /proc proc rw 0 0
/dev/hda1 /boot ext2 rw 0 0
devpts /dev/pts devpts rw 0 0
[root@nf5000 /] # mount
/dev/hda3 on / type ext2 (rw)
proc on /proc type proc (rw)
/dev/hda1 on /boot type ext2 (rw)
devpts on /dev/pts type devpts (rw,gid=5,mode=0620)
```

The /proc/partitions file displays all existing partitions on all devices. You can also use `fdisk -1` to display this information. For example:

```
[root@nf5000 /] # cat /proc/partitions
major minor  #blocks  name

   3     0   1023907  hda
   3     1      6016  hda1
   3     2    126000  hda2
   3     3    891072  hda3
   3    64   1023907  hdb
   3    65   1023088  hdb1
  22     0 1073741823 hdc
[root@nf5000 /] # fdisk -1

Disk /dev/hda: 32 heads, 63 sectors, 1015 cylinders
Units = cylinders of 2016 * 512 bytes

   Device Boot    Start       End    Blocks   Id  System
/dev/hda1   *         1         6      6016+  83  Linux
/dev/hda2             7       131    126000   82  Linux swap
/dev/hda3           132      1015    891072   83  Linux

Disk /dev/hdb: 32 heads, 63 sectors, 1015 cylinders
Units = cylinders of 2016 * 512 bytes

   Device Boot    Start       End    Blocks   Id  System
/dev/hdb1             1      1015   1023088+  83  Linux
```

The /proc/pci file gives information about all your PCI devices. You can also use the command `lspci`. Please note that the /proc/pci file is obsolete and will be replaced by /proc/bus/pci/* in the future. For example:

```
[root@nf5000 /] # cat /proc/pci
PCI devices found:
  Bus  0, device   0, function  0:
    Host bridge: Intel 82439TX (rev 1).
      Medium devsel.  Master Capable.  No bursts.
  Bus  0, device   7, function  0:
    ISA bridge: Intel 82371AB PIIX4 ISA (rev 8).
      Medium devsel.  Master Capable.  No bursts.
  Bus  0, device   7, function  1:
    IDE interface: Intel 82371AB PIIX4 IDE (rev 1).
      Medium devsel.  Fast back-to-back capable.  Master Capable.  Latency=64.
      I/O at 0x1020 [0x1021].
  Bus  0, device  15, function  0:
    Display controller: Unknown vendor Unknown device (rev 0).
      Vendor id=15ad. Device id=710.
      Medium devsel.  Fast back-to-back capable.  Master Capable.  Latency=64.
      I/O at 0x1030 [0x1031].
      Non-prefetchable 32 bit memory at 0xfc000000 [0xfc000000].
      Non-prefetchable 32 bit memory at 0xfb000000 [0xfb000000].
  Bus  0, device  16, function  0:
    Ethernet controller: AMD 79C970 (rev 16).
      Medium devsel.  Fast back-to-back capable.  IRQ 9.  Master Capable.  Laten
cy=64.  Min Gnt=6.Max Lat=255.
      I/O at 0x1000 [0x1001].
      Non-prefetchable 32 bit memory at 0xfd000000 [0xfd000000].
[root@nf5000 /] # lspci
00:00.0 Host bridge: Intel Corporation 430TX - 82439TX MTXC (rev 01)
00:07.0 ISA bridge: Intel Corporation 82371AB PIIX4 ISA (rev 08)
00:07.1 IDE interface: Intel Corporation 82371AB PIIX4 IDE (rev 01)
00:0f.0 Display controller: Unknown device 15ad:0710
00:10.0 Ethernet controller: Advanced Micro Devices 79c970 [PCnet LANCE] (rev 10
)
```

The /proc/swaps file displays information about all active swap partitions. For example:

```
[root@nf5000 /] # cat /proc/swaps
Filename                        Type            Size    Used    Priority
/dev/hda2                       partition       125996  56      -1
```

The /proc/version file displays some version information about the Linux kernel. The command `uname -a` will display similar information. For example:

```
[root@nf5000 /] # cat /proc/version
Linux version 2.2.12 (root@m20.calderasystems.com) (gcc version
egcs-2.91.66 19990314 (egcs-1.1.2 release)) #1 SMP Thu Sep 23
22:09:31 MDT 1999
[root@nf5000 /] # uname -a
Linux nf5000.itso 2.2.12 #1 SMP Thu Sep 23 22:09:31 MDT 1999 i686
unknown
```

If you want to obtain some information about your SCSI devices, take a look at the files below /proc/scsi.

Apart from configuring numerous parameters of your hard drive, the command hdparm can also be used to perform hard disk performance tests with the command hdparm -tT <device>. For example:

```
[root@nf5000 /] # hdparm -tT /dev/hda

/dev/hda:
 Timing buffer-cache reads:   64 MB in  0.68 seconds =94.12 MB/sec
 Timing buffered disk reads:  32 MB in 29.51 seconds = 1.08 MB/
[root@nf5000 /] # hdparm -c1 /dev/hda

/dev/hda:
 setting 32-bit I/O support flag to 1
 I/O support  =  1 (32-bit)
[root@nf5000 /] # hdparm -tT /dev/hda

/dev/hda:
 Timing buffer-cache reads:   64 MB in  0.67 seconds =95.52 MB/sec
 Timing buffered disk reads:  32 MB in 12.92 seconds = 2.48 MB/sec
```

Another popular hard disk performance test is bonnie, found at (http://www.textuality.com/bonnie/). Note, however, that these tests are mostly useful for testing different parameter settings on one machine as a relative measure, not as a comparison between different systems.

To test the throughput of your network, you can either use netperf, found at http://www.netperf.org/netperf/NetperfPage.html, or bing.

Chapter 4. Samba

If you look at any English dictionary, Samba is defined as a Brazilian dance, but Samba in Linux is something completely different. Samba is an implementation of a Server Message Block (SMB) protocol server that can be run on almost every variant of UNIX in existence. Samba is an open source project, just like Linux. The entire code is written in C so it is easily ported to all flavors of UNIX. Samba is a tool for the peaceful coexistence of UNIX and Windows on the same network on the level of file and print sharing over the NetBIOS protocol. It allows UNIX systems to move into a Windows "Network Neighborhood" without causing a mess. With Samba, UNIX servers are acting like any other Windows server, offering their resources to the SMB clients. Recently SMB was renamed by Microsoft to Common Internet File System (CIFS).

4.1 What can you do with Samba?

- With Samba, a Linux server can act as a file/print server for Windows networks. It can replace expensive Windows NT file/print server in this role, creating a less expensive solution.
- Samba can act as a NetBIOS name server (NBNS) in a Windows world, where it is referred to as WINS - Windows Internet Name Service.
- Samba can participate in NetBIOS browsing and master browser elections.
- Samba can provide a gateway for synchronizing UNIX and Windows NT passwords.
- With Samba client software, you can access any shared directory or printer on Windows NT servers or Samba servers and allow UNIX machines to access Windows NT files.
- With Samba File System (SMBFS) you can mount any share from a Windows NT server or Samba server in your directory structure (this is available only on Linux).

4.2 Setting up the Samba server

You can check if the Samba package is installed by running kpackage. To start kpackage click the **K** sign on the panel, select **COAS** and then **kpackage**.

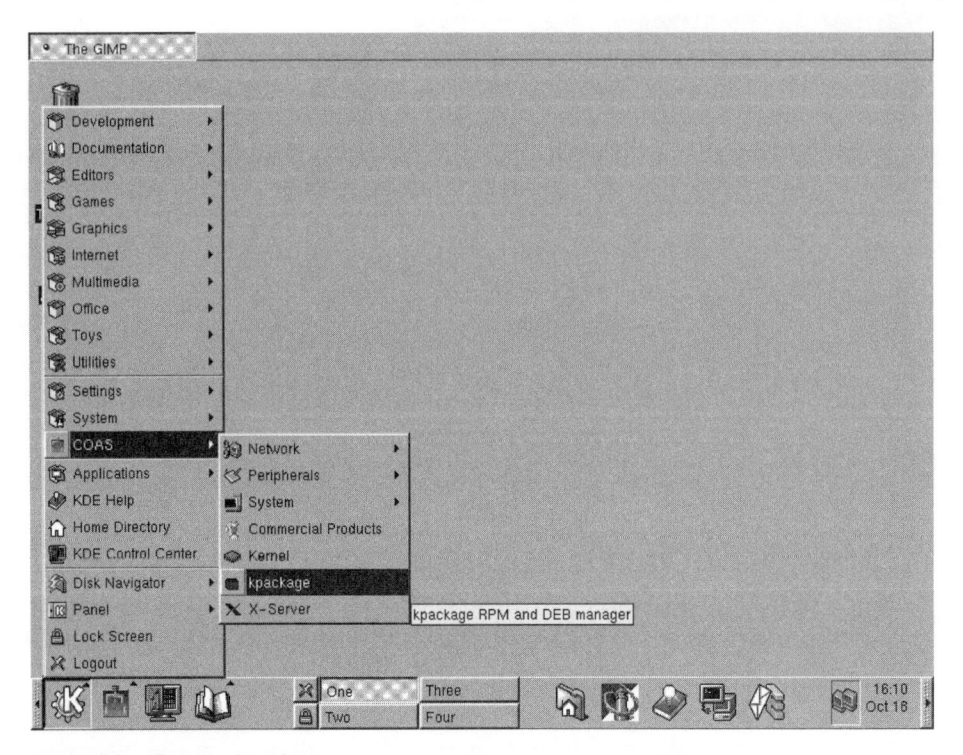

Figure 131. Starting kpackage

When kpackage is started, search for the **Server** section and then under this find the **Network** section and expand it. If the Samba package is installed you will see a window similar to Figure 132.

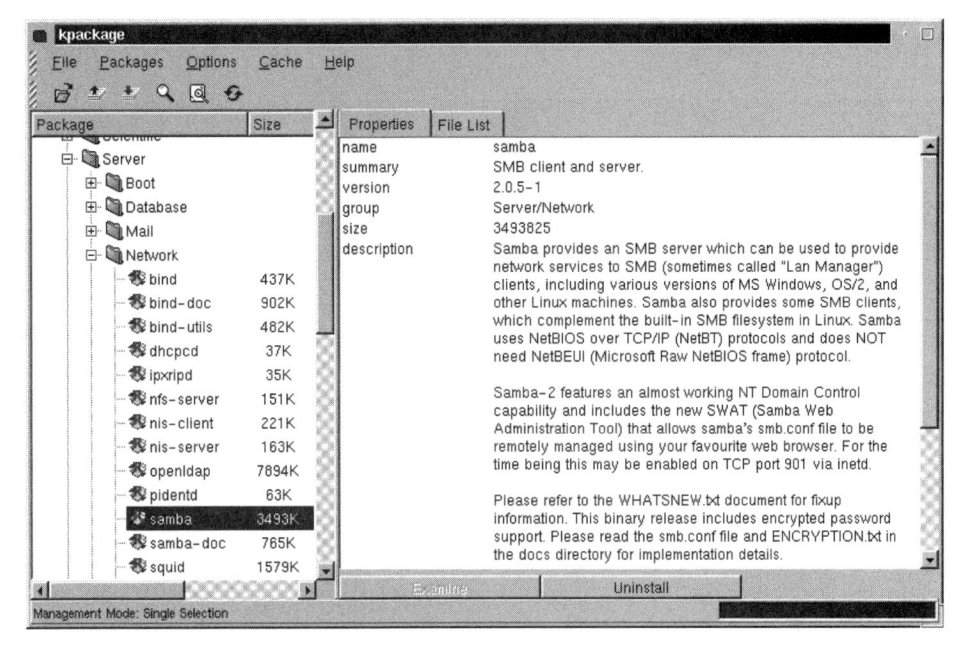

Figure 132. Checking for the Samba package

As you can see in Figure 132, the Samba package is installed.

4.2.1 Configuring the Samba server

In this section we will explain how to configure Samba so it can participate as a file/print server in an existing Window network or be just a stand-alone file/print server for Windows and Linux clients.

Before you can start using Samba you need to configure the smb.conf file. This file is the heart of the Samba server. When the Samba package is installed in Caldera OpenLinux the sample configuration file is installed as the /etc/samba.d/smb.conf.sample file.

In Caldera OpenLinux, Samba by default uses the smb.conf file in the directory /etc/samba.d. To begin with, it is enough just to make a copy of the sample file by executing the command:

```
cp /etc/samba.d/smb.conf.sample /etc/samba.d/smb.conf
```

The SAMBA configuration file smb.conf is divided into two main sections:

1. Global Settings - here you set up parameters that affect the connection parameters.

2. Share Definitions - here you define shares. A share is a directory on the server that is accessible over the network and shared among users. This section has three subsections:

   a. Homes - in this subsection you define the user's home directories.

   b. Printers - in this subsection you define the available printers.

   c. Shares - this subsection can have more entries, one for each share you want to define.

In the following sections we will describe how to modify the smb.conf file to efficiently and simply use Samba as a file/print server. We explain only the most necessary parameters. If you need more information, see the manual entry for the smb.conf file or the Samba project Web site at:

    http://www.samba.org

You can find our smb.conf configuration file in Appendix E, "Sample smb.conf SAMBA configuration file" on page 305.

4.2.1.1 Setting the NetBIOS parameters

The NetBIOS parameters are part of the Global Section. When you open your smb.conf file you will see something similar to this:

```
#==================== Global Settings ========================

[global]
        netbios name = NF5000

        workgroup = LINUX

        server string = Samba Server on Caldera OpenLinux
```

The parameters are described in Table 12.

Table 12. NetBIOS parameters

Parameter	Description
netbios name	The Samba server is known by this name on the network. This parameter has the same meaning as the Windows NT computer name. If you do not specify anything it defaults to the server's host name.
workgroup	This parameter specifies in which Window NT domain or workgroup the Samba server will participate. It is equivalent to Windows NT domain or workgroup name.
server string	This is the description string of the Samba server. It has the same role as the Windows NT description field.

4.2.1.2 Global printing settings

In the smb.conf file you will see something similar to this:

```
load printers = yes

printcap name = /etc/printcap

printing = lprng
```

The parameters are described in Table 13.

Table 13. Printing parameters

Parameter	Description
load printers	This parameter controls if Samba loads all printers in the printcap file for browsing.
printcap name	With this parameter you tell Samba the location of the printcap file. The default value is /etc/printcap.
printing	This parameter tells Samba what printing style to use on your server. Caldera OpenLinux by default uses the LPRNG printing style.

4.2.1.3 Global security settings

In your smb.conf file you will see something similar to this:

```
security = user
;   password server = <NT-Server-Name>
encrypt passwords = yes
smb passwd file = /etc/samba.d/smbpasswd
```

The parameters are described in Table 14.

Table 14. Security parameters

Parameter	Description
security	This parameter has four possible values: share, user, server, domain
password server	In the case of server or domain security level this server is used for authorization. For the parameter value you use the server NetBIOS name.
encrypt passwords	By setting this parameter to yes, you enable Samba to use the Encrypted Password Protocol, which is used in Windows NT Service Pack 3 and in Windows 98. This is needed to communicate with those clients.

Parameter	Description
`smb passwd file`	This parameter tells Samba where encrypted passwords are saved.

The security modes are as follows:

- Share - for this security mode, clients only need to supply the password for the resource. This mode of security is the default for Windows 95 file/print server. It is not recommended for use in UNIX environments, because it violates the UNIX security scheme.

- User - the user/password validation is done on the server that is offering the resource. This mode is most widely used.

- Server - the user/password validation is done on the specified authentication server. This server can be a Windows NT server or another Samba server.

- Domain - this security level is basically the same as the server security level, with the exception that the Samba server becomes a member of a Windows NT domain. In this case the Samba server can also participate in such things as trust relationships.

Because Windows NT 4.0 Service Pack 3 or later, Windows 95 with the latest patches, and Windows 98 use the encrypted passwords for accessing NetBIOS resources, you need to enable your Samba server to use the encrypted passwords. Before you start the Samba server for the first time, you need to create a Samba encrypted passwords file. This can be done with the mksmbpasswd utility. The recommended way is to first create the user accounts in Linux and then create the Samba password file with the command:

```
cat /etc/passwd | /usr/sbin/mksmbpasswd > /etc/samba.d/smbpasswd
```

This creates the Samba password file from the Linux password file.

> **Note**
>
> Use the same filename you specified for creating the Samba password file in the smb.conf configuration to tell the Samba server where the password file is.
>
> By default the passwords for the Samba users are undefined. Before any connection is made to the Samba server, users need to create their passwords.

Now you need to specify the password for all users. If you are changing or specifying a password for a user, you can do this by executing the command:

    /usr/bin/smbpasswd -U username

You will see a window similar to Figure 133.

```
[root@nf5000 /]# /usr/bin/smbpasswd -U user
New SMB password:
Retype new SMB password:
Password changed for user user.
[root@nf5000 /]#
```

Figure 133. Specifying the password for Samba user

> **Note**
>
> Anyone with access to /usr/bin/smbpasswd can change passwords for the Samba users.

Another way is to have each Samba user change the password for himself, by remotely connecting to the Samba server and executing the command:

    /usr/bin/smbpasswd

The output will be similar to Figure 133. If a Samba user already has defined a password he will need to type the old password before he can change to a new password.

If you want to add a Samba server user later, this can be done with the following command:

    /usr/sbin/smbpasswd -a username password

This will add a new user to the Samba password file.

> **Note**
>
> You have to be logged on as root if you want to manage other users. If you are logged on as a user, you can only change your own password. The smbpasswd utility uses the location of the password file from the smb.conf configuration file.

4.2.1.4 Global name resolution settings

In your smb.conf file you will see something similar to this:

Chapter 4. Samba **129**

```
name resolve order = wins lmhosts bcast
wins support = yes
;   wins server = w.x.y.z
```

The parameters are described in Table 15.

Table 15. Name resolution parameters

Parameter	Description
`name resolve order`	With this parameter you specify how the Samba server resolves NetBIOS names into IP addresses. The preferred value is `wins lmhosts bcast`. Refer to the manual page of the smb.conf file for more information.
`wins support`	If this option is enabled the Samba server will also acts as a WINS server.
`wins server`	With this parameter you tell Samba which WINS server to use.

Note

Samba can act as a WINS server or a WINS client, but not both. So only one of the parameters (`wins support` or `wins server`) can be set at the same time. If you specify the IP address of WINS server, then `wins support` must be set to no.

4.2.1.5 Creating shares

In the previous section we explained how to prepare general configuration parameters. But a Samba server can be useful when you offer resources to the users. In this section we will explain how to create a share. The simple share section in the smb.conf file looks similar to this:

```
[redbook]
    comment = Redbook files
    path = /redbook
    browseable = yes
    printable = no
    writable = yes
    write list = @users
```

Table 16 describes the most important parameters for creating a share.

Table 16. Share parameters

Parameter	Description
comment	This describes the function of the share.
admin users	This parameter is used to specify the users who have administrative privileges for the share. When they access the share they perform all operations as root.
path	Defines the full path to the directory you are sharing.
browseable	If this parameter is set to yes, you can see the share when you are browsing the resources on the Samba server. The value can be yes or no.
printable	This parameter specifies if the share is a print share. The value can be yes or no.
write list	Users specified in this list have write access to the share. If the name begins with @ it means a group name.
writable	This parameter specifies if the share is writable. The value can be yes or no.
read list	Users specified in this list have read access to the share. If the name begins with @ it means a group name.
read only	If this is set to yes, share is read only. The value can be yes or no.
valid users	This parameter specifies which users can access the share.

By using these parameters you can easily set up a new share. Each share definition starts with the share name in brackets "[]". Below this name you can specify the values for the share parameters.

4.2.1.6 Share permissions

Although you can control the share permissions with share parameters, UNIX permissions are applied before the user can access files on the share. So you need to take care of UNIX permissions, so the user also has access to the shared directory under UNIX.

When a user creates a new file on the shared directory, the default create mask used is 0744. For directory creation, the default create mask is 0755. If you want, you can force a different creation mask. The parameters for doing this are explained in Table 17.

Table 17. Create mask parameters

Parameter	Description
create mask	This is used for file creation to mask against UNIX mask calculated from the DOS mode requested.
directory mask	This is used for directory creation to mask against UNIX mask calculated from the DOS mode requested.

4.2.1.7 Creating shares for home directories

For handling home directories Samba has a special share section called [homes]. This share definition is used for all home directories, so you do not need to create separate shares for each user.

When a client requests a connection to a file share, existing file shares are scanned. If a match is found, that share is used. If no match is found, the requested share is treated as a username and validated by security. If the name exists and the password is correct, a share with that name is created by cloning the [homes] section. The home share definition uses the same parameters as a normal share definition. The following is an example of a home share definition in the smb.conf configuration file:

```
[homes]
comment = Home Directories
path = %H
valid users = %S
browseable = no
writable = yes
create mode = 0700
directory mode = 0700
```

As you can see, we used some variables in this definition, which are explained in Table 18.

Table 18. Variable description

Parameter	Description
%H	This variable represents the home directory of the user.
%S	The name of the current service, which is, in the case of home share, equal to username.

As you can see in the example, we used creation masks for the files and the directories in such a way that we forced all new files or directories to be accessible only by the owner of the home directory.

4.2.1.8 Creating a printer share

A Samba server uses the same procedure for printer shares as for the home shares. If all share definitions and usernames are tested against the requested share name and the matched definition is still not found, Samba searches for a printer with that name (if the [printers] section exists). If the match is found in the printer definitions that [printers] share section is cloned with the name of the requested service, which is really a printer name. The following is an example of the printers definition in the smb.conf configuration file:

```
[printers]
comment = All Printers
path = /var/spool/samba
browseable = no
# Set public = yes to allow user 'guest account' to print
guest ok = no
writable = no
printable = yes
create mask = 0700
```

As you can see the [printers] section is just another share definition, because when a user prints they basically copy the data into a spool directory, after that the data is handled by the local printing system. The only big difference between a printer share and other share definitions is that the printable parameter is set to "yes". This means that a user can write a spool file to the directory specified under the share definition. If the share is printable, then it is also writable by default.

4.2.2 Starting and stopping the Samba server

You can start the Samba server by executing the command:

/etc/rc.d/init.d/samba start

You will see output similar to the following:

```
[root@nf5000 /root]# /etc/rc.d/init.d/samba start
Starting samba:   smbd nmbd.
```

As you can see, two daemons are started: smbd and nmbd. Smbd is the actual Samba server and nmbd is the WINS server.

The Samba server can be stopped by executing the command:

`/etc/rc.d/init.d/samba stop`

Whenever you make modifications to the smb.conf configuration file, you must restart the Samba server.

4.2.3 Starting Samba as startup service

You can configure your boot process so Samba is started at the boot. You can do this by using the System Daemon configuration tool. To start the System Daemon configuration tool click the **K** sign on the panel, select **COAS**, then **System** and at the end **Daemons**. You will see a window similar to Figure 134.

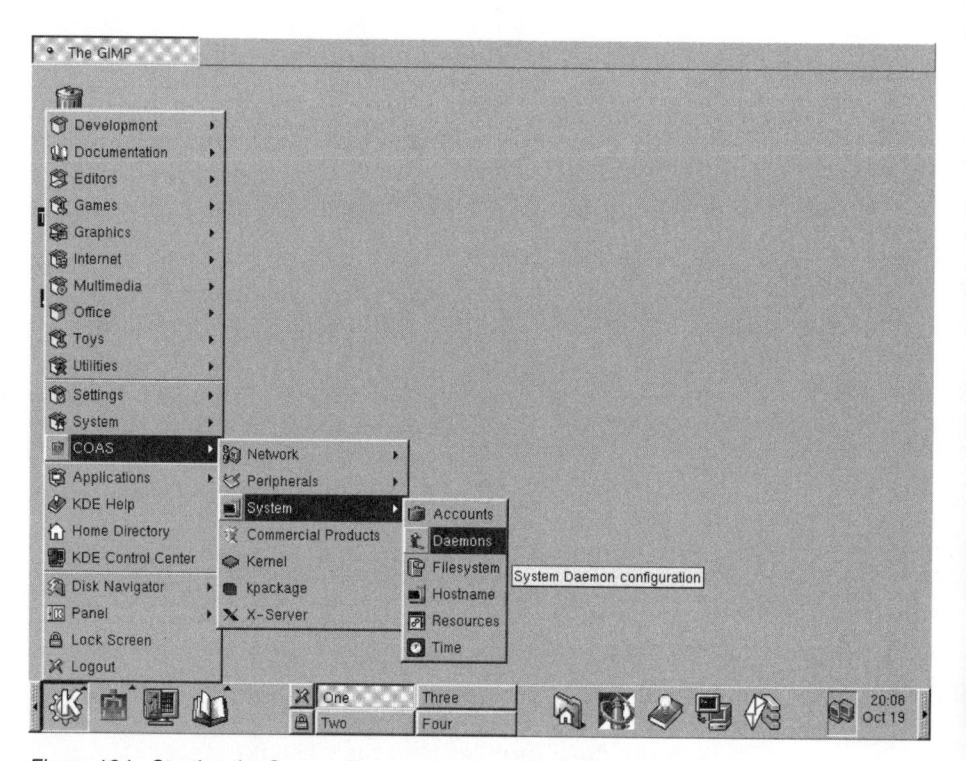

Figure 134. Starting the System Daemon configuration tool

After the System Daemon configuration tool is started you will see a welcome window to COAS administration tools. Click **OK** to continue. You will see a window similar to Figure 135.

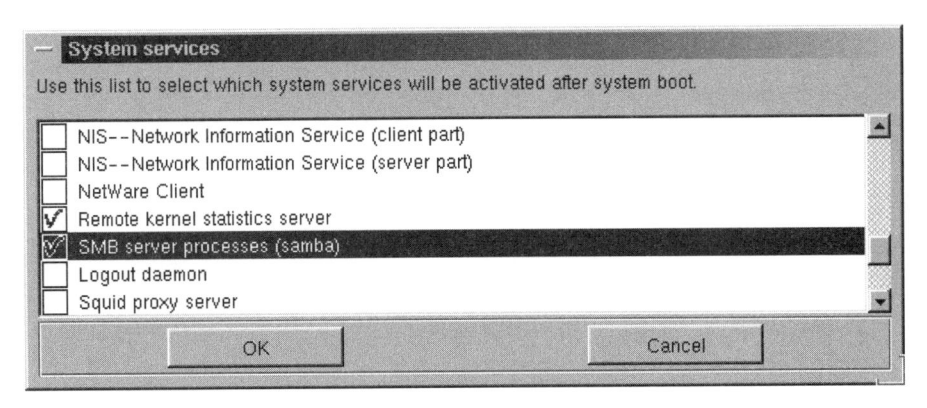

Figure 135. Selecting Samba to start as a boot process

Select **SMB server process (Samba)** on the list. Click **OK** to save your new settings.

When the Linux server is restarted, the Samba server will be started automatically.

4.2.4 Using SWAT

The Samba Web Administration Tool (SWAT) allows the remote configuration of the smb.conf configuration file through a Web browser. That means you can configure Samba in a GUI-like environment. SWAT itself is a small Web server and CGI scripting application, designed to run from inetd, provides access to the smb.conf configuration file.

An authorized user with the root password can configure the smb.conf configuration file via Web pages. SWAT also places help links to all configurable options on every page, which lets an administrator easily understand the effect of the changes.

Before using SWAT you must check the following.

1. In the /etc/services file you must have the following line:

    ```
    swat 901/tcp
    ```

2. In the /etc/inetd.conf file you must have the following line:

    ```
    swat stream tcp nowait.400 root /usr/sbin/tcpd swat
    ```

    As you can see, SWAT is started with a TCP wrapper, so you can control who can access the SWAT service with the /etc/hosts.deny file. For example, if you want to access SWAT locally only, your /etc/hosts.deny file should look similar to this:

```
#
# hosts.deny    This file describes the names of the hosts which are
#               *not* allowed to use the local INET services, as decided
#               by the '/usr/sbin/tcpd' server.
#
# The portmap line is redundant, but it is left to remind you that
# the new secure portmap uses hosts.deny and hosts.allow.  In particular
# you should know that NFS uses portmap!
swat:ALL EXCEPT 127.0.0.1
```

If you made any modification to those two files you need to restart inetd. This can be done by executing the commands:

/etc/rc.d/init.d/init stop

/etc/rc.d/init.d/init start

If you did everything without errors you are ready to use SWAT. To start SWAT point your favorite Web browser to the Internet address of your Samba server on port 901, as you can see in Figure 136.

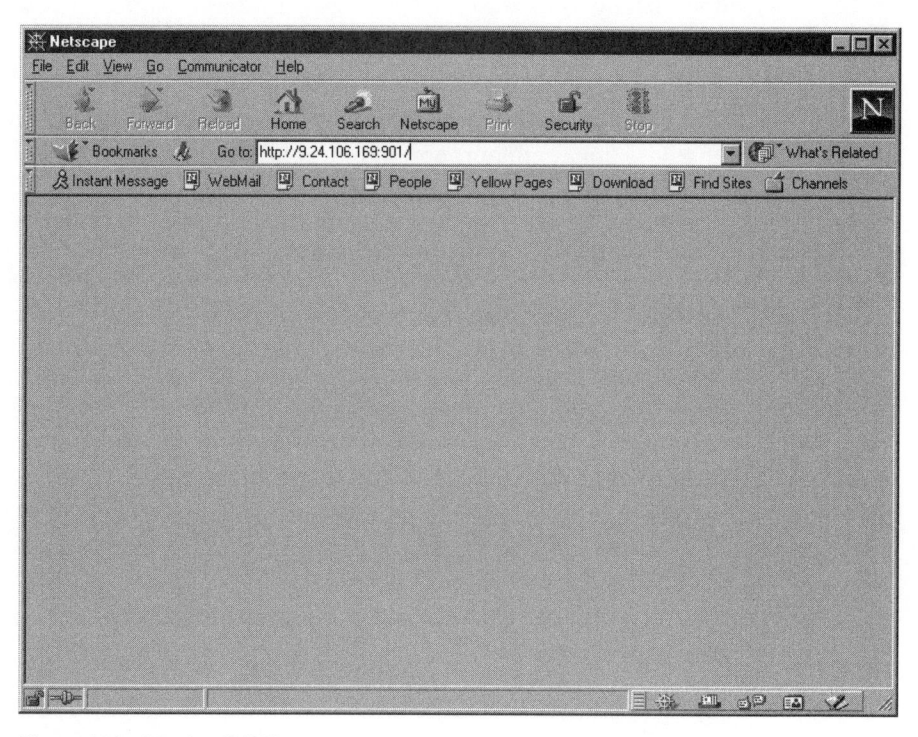

Figure 136. Starting SWAT

After you load the home page of SWAT, you will see a window similar to Figure 137.

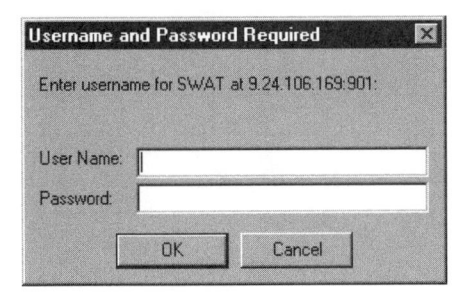

Figure 137. User authorization for SWAT

Type in the username and password of the Linux user defined on your Linux server. Click **OK** to continue. You will see a window similar to Figure 138.

— **Stop** —

Any Linux user can access SWAT, but only a root user can make changes.

Remember, when you are logging on to SWAT from a remote machine, you are sending passwords in plain text. This can be a security issue, so we recommend that you do SWAT administration locally only.

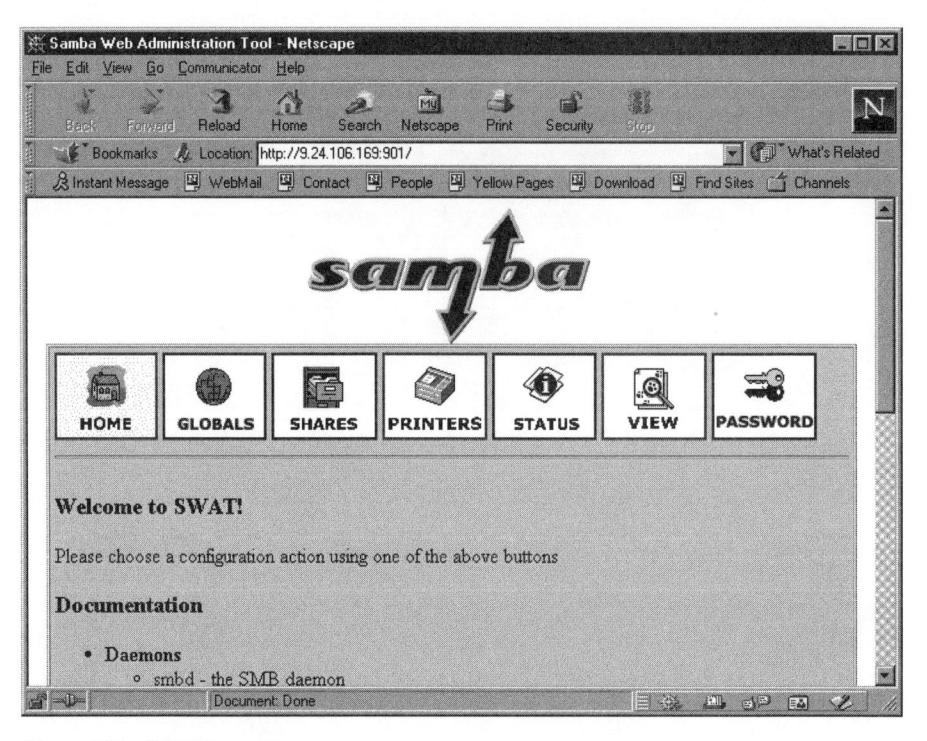

Figure 138. SWAT home page

As you can see in Figure 138, you have seven categories available:

1. Home - here you can find all the documentation you need about Samba.
2. Globals - here you can view and modify global parameters from the smb.conf configuration file.
3. Shares - here you can view, modify, and add shares.
4. Printers - here you can view, modify and add printers.
5. Status - here you can check the current status of your Samba server.
6. View - here you can view current configuration of the smb.conf configuration file.
7. Passwords - here you can manage passwords for the Samba server.

Now we will briefly describe the functions available in SWAT.

> **Note**
>
> You can reach any of the seven functions on all SWAT Web pages. There are always icons for the functions on the top of each page.
>
> After you make changes to smb.conf configuration file, the Samba server must be restarted.

4.2.4.1 Globals

When you click the **Globals** icon in the main SWAT window, and you will see a window similar to Figure 139.

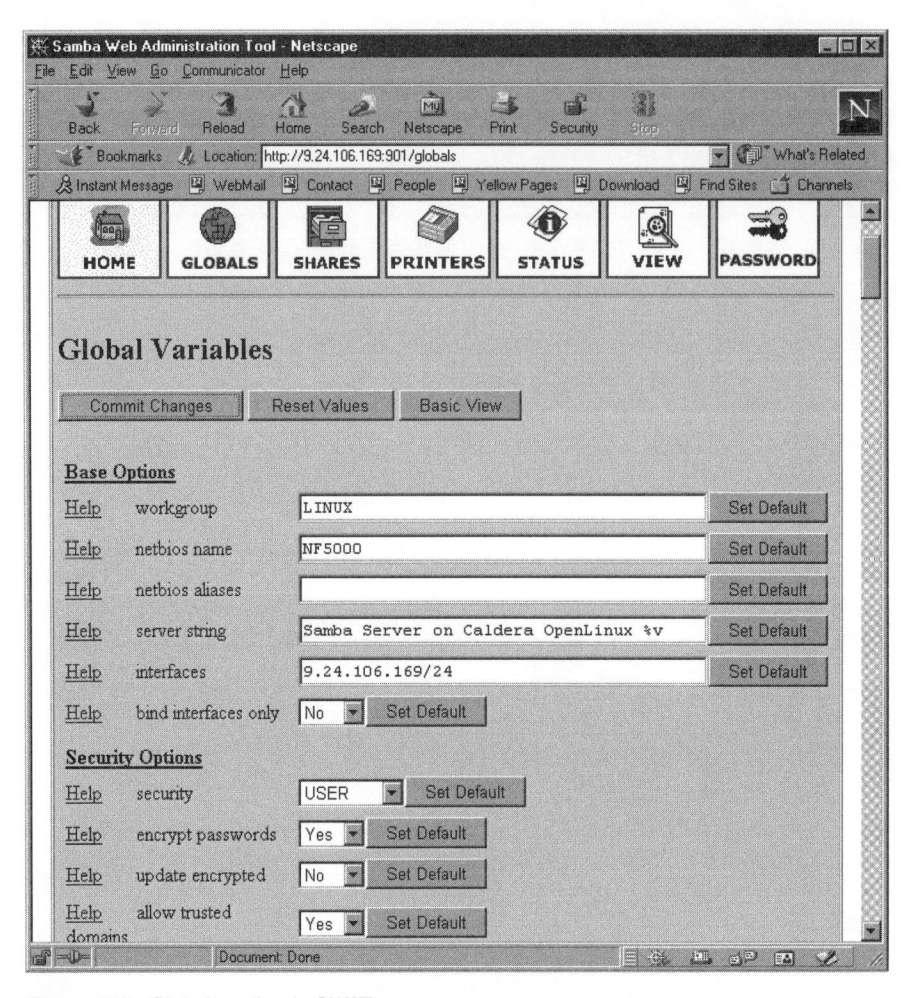

Figure 139. Global section in SWAT

In this window you can modify the global parameters for the Samba server. By default you will see the Basic View; if you want to see the Advanced View click **Advanced View**. In the Advanced View you have all options available, while in the Basic View you can change only the basic options. To return from the Advanced View to the Basic View ,click **Basic View.** After you have made your changes you can save them by clicking **Commit changes.** If you get a pop-up window similar to Figure 140, which warns you that you are sending non-secure information over the network, you can easily select **Continue** if you are working locally or if you know that your network is secure.

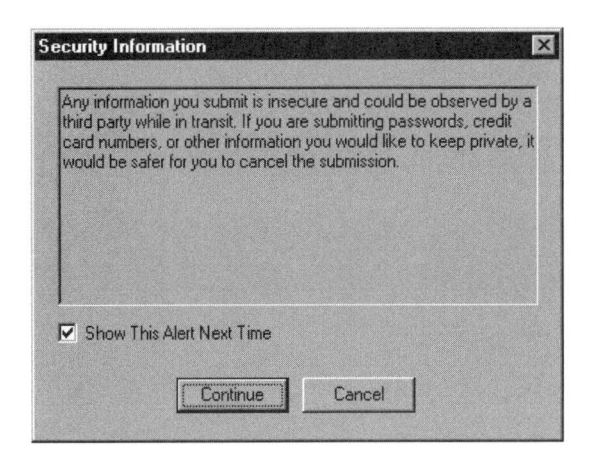

Figure 140. Security warning

4.2.4.2 Shares

When you click the **Shares** icon on any of the SWAT Web pages, you will see a window similar to Figure 141.

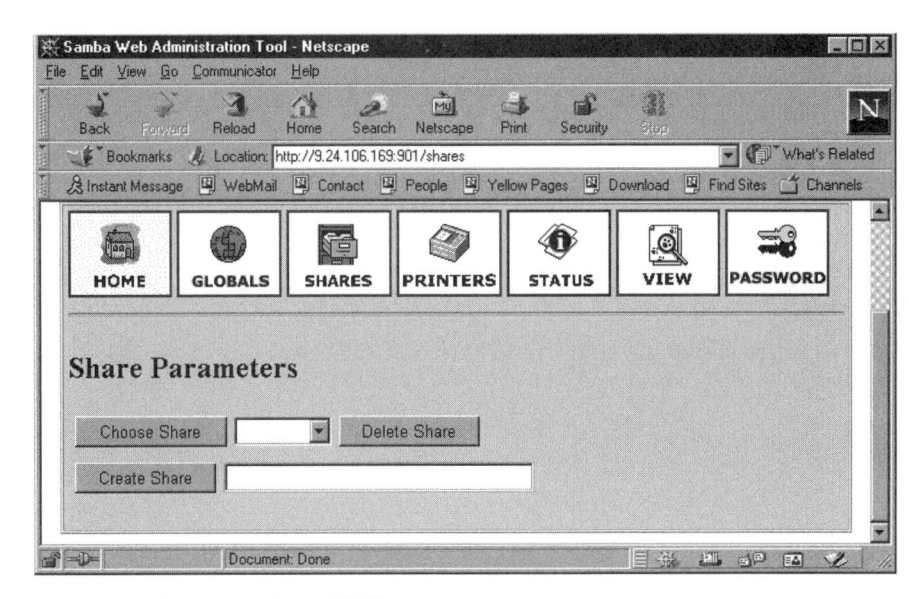

Figure 141. Shares section in SWAT

Here you can:

1. View the defined share
1. Delete share

1. Create a new share

4.2.4.3 Viewing or modifying an existing share

To view an already defined share, select the share from the field to the right of the **Choose Share** button, similar to Figure 142.

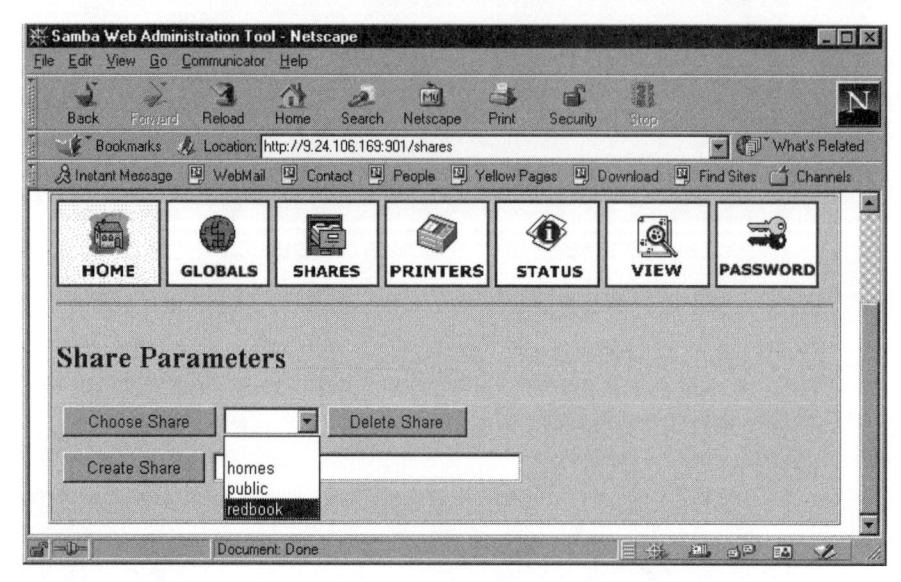

Figure 142. Choosing a share to view

After you have selected the share, click **Choose Share** to view the share properties. You will see a window similar to Figure 143.

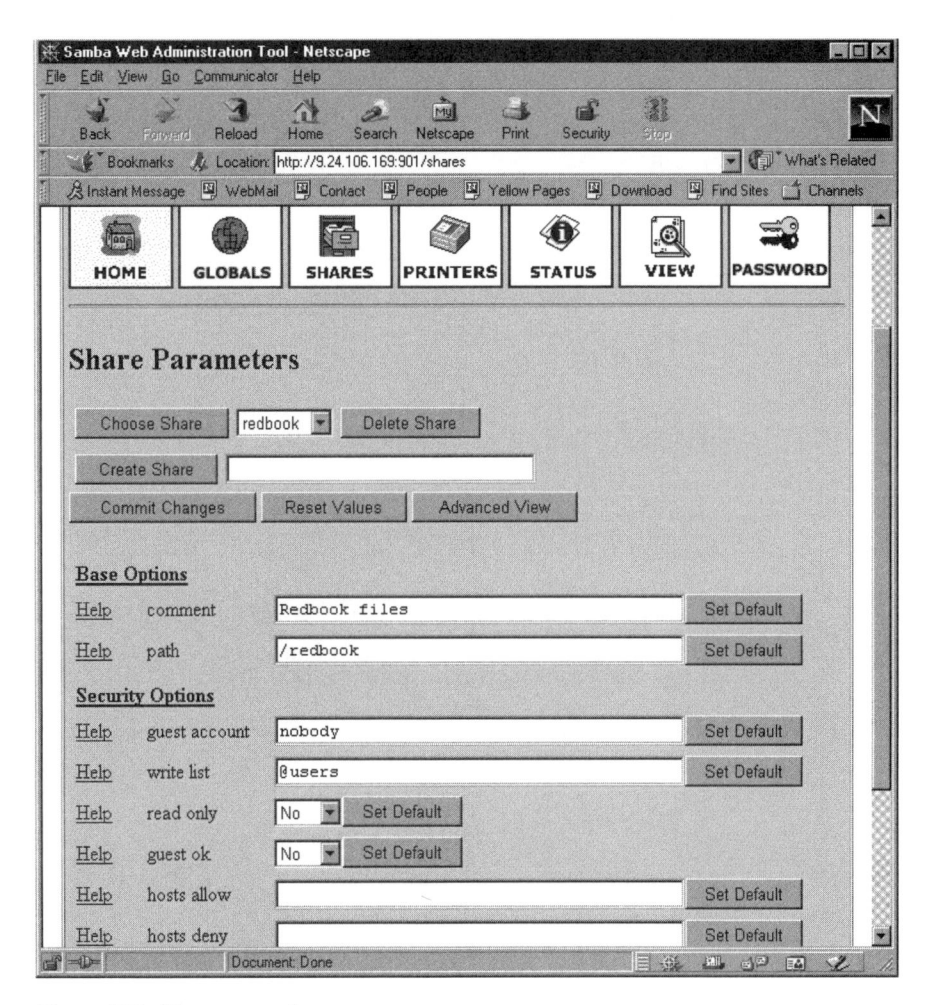

Figure 143. Share properties

If you want to view all available parameters, click **Advanced View.** In this view you can also make changes and save them by clicking **Commit Changes.**

4.2.4.4 Deleting an existing share

To delete an existing share you must first select an already defined share similar to Figure 142. Then click **Delete Share.**

— Stop —————————————————————————

The share is deleted immediately and without warning.

Chapter 4. Samba **143**

After you have deleted the share, the Samba server must be restarted.

4.2.4.5 Creating a new share

To create a simple share, follow these steps:

1. Create a directory that will be used for the share. You can do this by executing this command from the terminal:

   ```
   mkdir /home/public
   ```

   In our example we created a "public" directory in the "home" directory.

2. Make sure that the UNIX permissions are set correctly in that directory, so that only intended users have access rights to it.

3. In the shares view of the SWAT Web pages, type in the name of the share you are creating, similar to Figure 144.

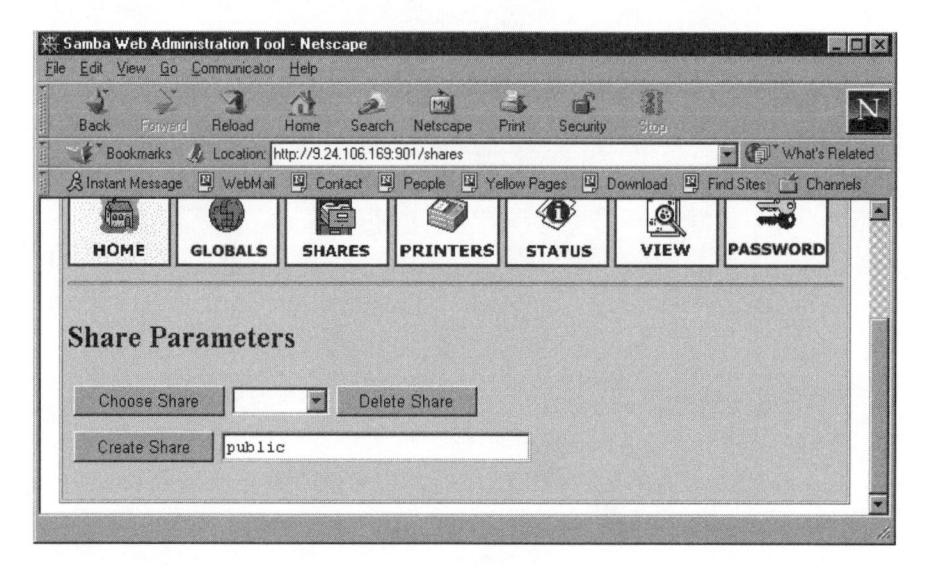

Figure 144. Entering the name for a new share

4. Click **Create Share** to continue, and you will see a window similar to Figure 145.

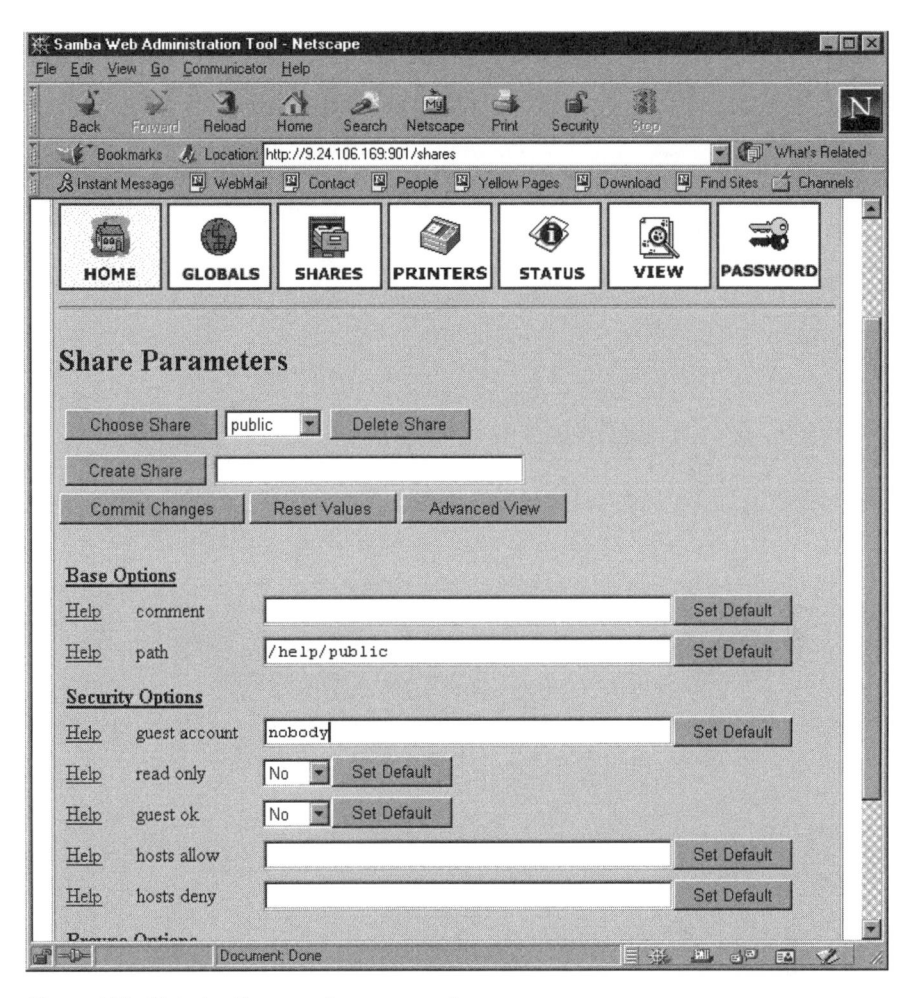

Figure 145. Entering the new share parameters

5. Fill in the needed parameters. If you need to set more advanced parameters, click **Advanced View** and you will see all available parameters. After you typed in all you want, click **Commit Changes** to save your new share.

6. You can see the changed smb.conf configuration file by selecting the **View** icon from the SWAT Web pages. You will see a window similar to Figure 146.

Chapter 4. Samba **145**

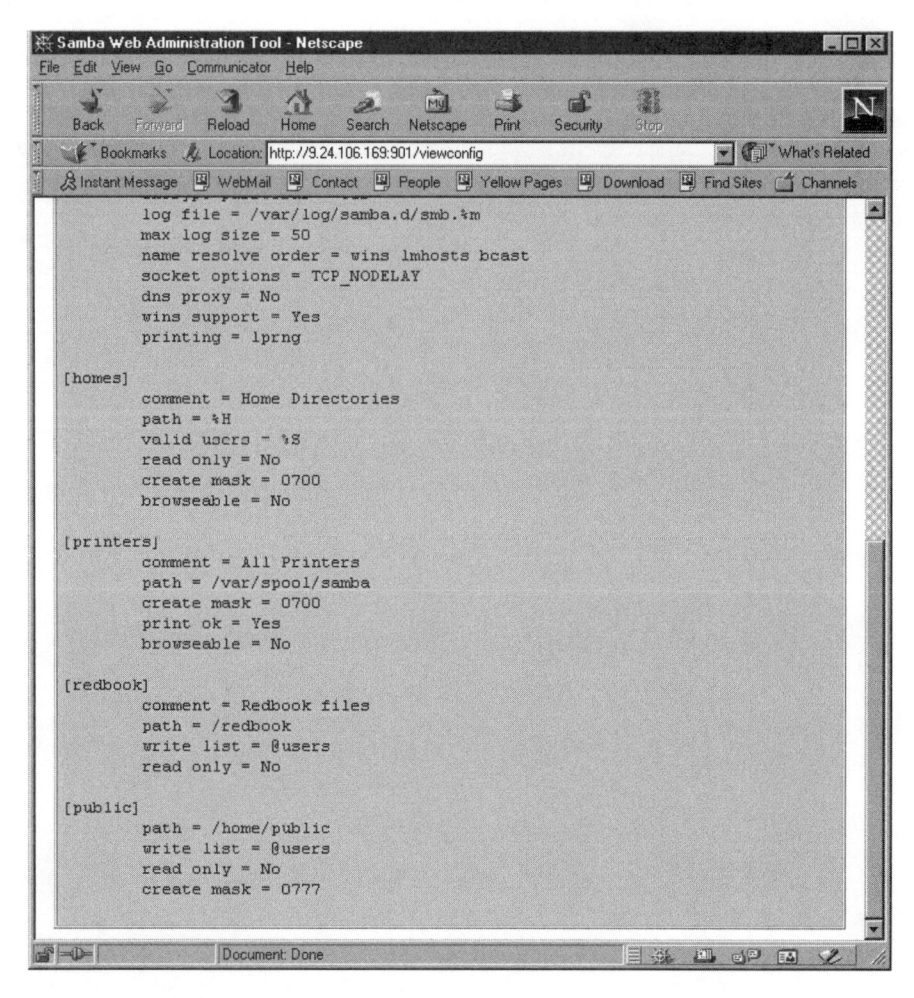

Figure 146. Viewing the smb.conf configuration file

7. Restart the Samba server.

Congratulations! You have just created your first usable share on the Samba server.

4.2.4.6 Restarting the Samba server

The Samba server can be restarted by clicking the **Start** icon on any SWAT Web pages. You will see a window similar to Figure 147.

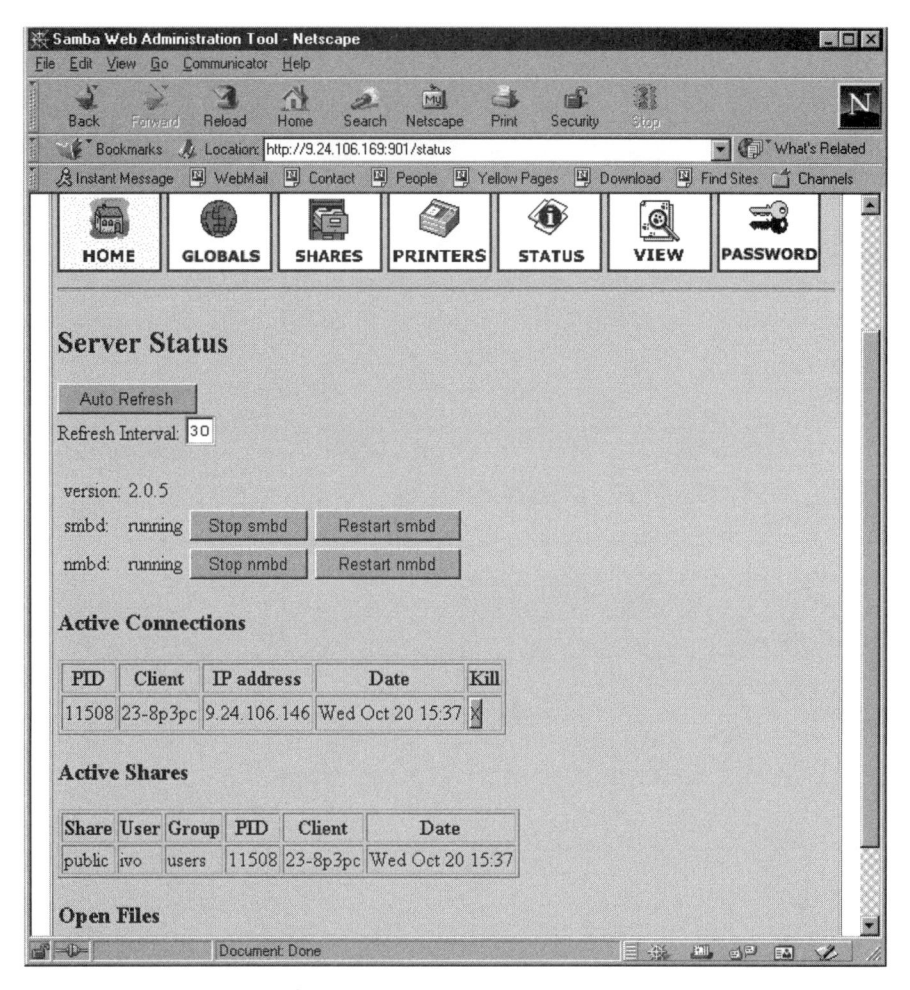

Figure 147. Restarting the Samba server

To restart the Samba server simply click **Restart smbd.** On this page you can also restart the WINS server by clicking **Restart nmbd.**

4.2.4.7 Printers

In the printer section you can view, modify, or add printers. The operations for handling printers are the same as for handling shares. You can access the printer settings by clicking the **Printers** icon on the SWAT Web page similar to Figure 148.

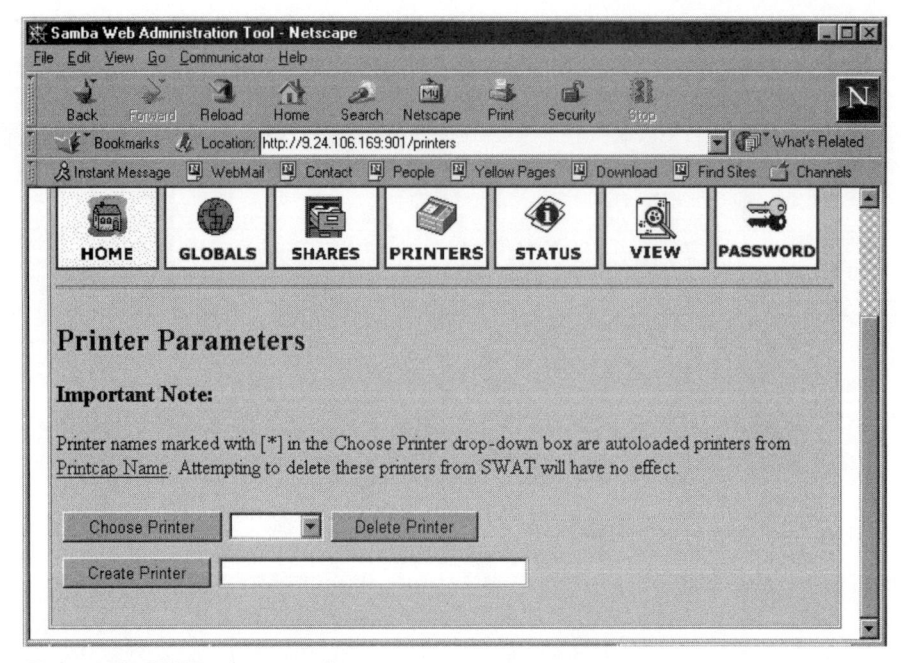

Figure 148. SWAT printers section

If you want to view the settings for a specific printer, select the printer from the list as you can see in Figure 149.

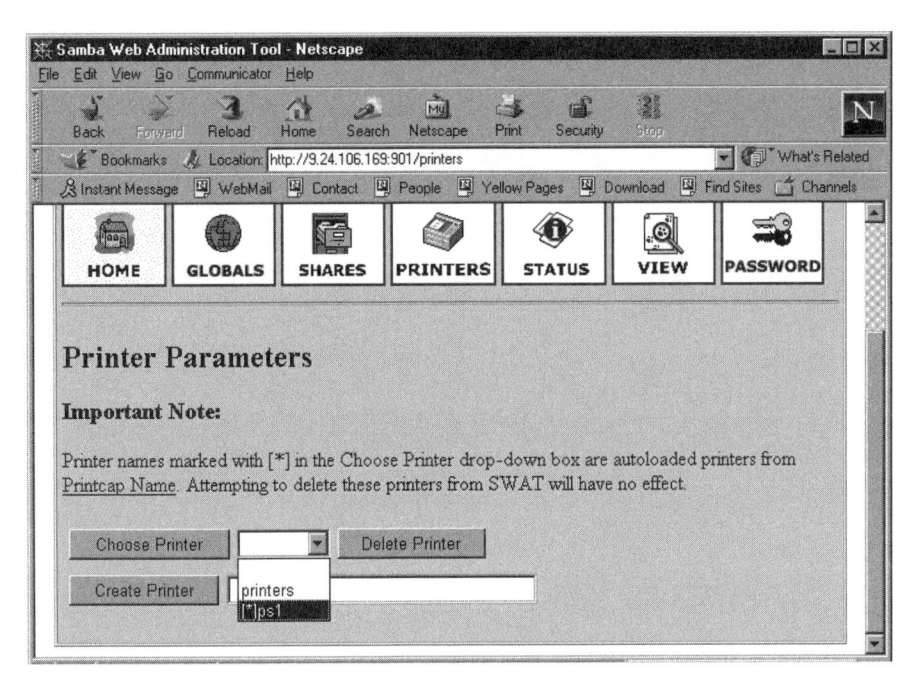

Figure 149. Selecting a printer

After you have selected the printer, click **Choose Printer** to view its properties. You will see a window similar to Figure 150.

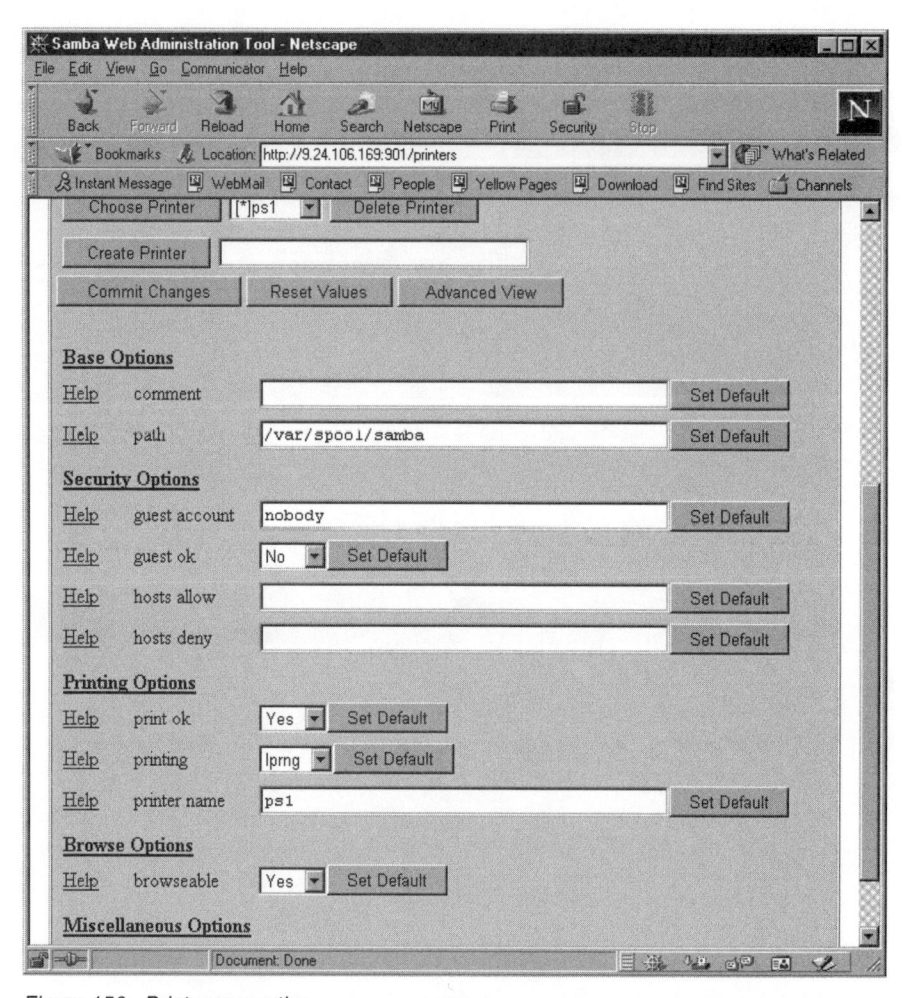

Figure 150. Printer properties

In this view you can also modify the printer properties. When you are done, save the settings by clicking **Commit Changes**.

4.2.4.8 Status

In this section you can check the status of the Samba server. Here you can view all the connections and open files. You can also start or restart the Samba server or just its components. You can access the printer settings by clicking the **Status** icon on the SWAT Web pages, as you can see in Figure 151.

150 Caldera OpenLinux and Netfinity Server Integration Guide

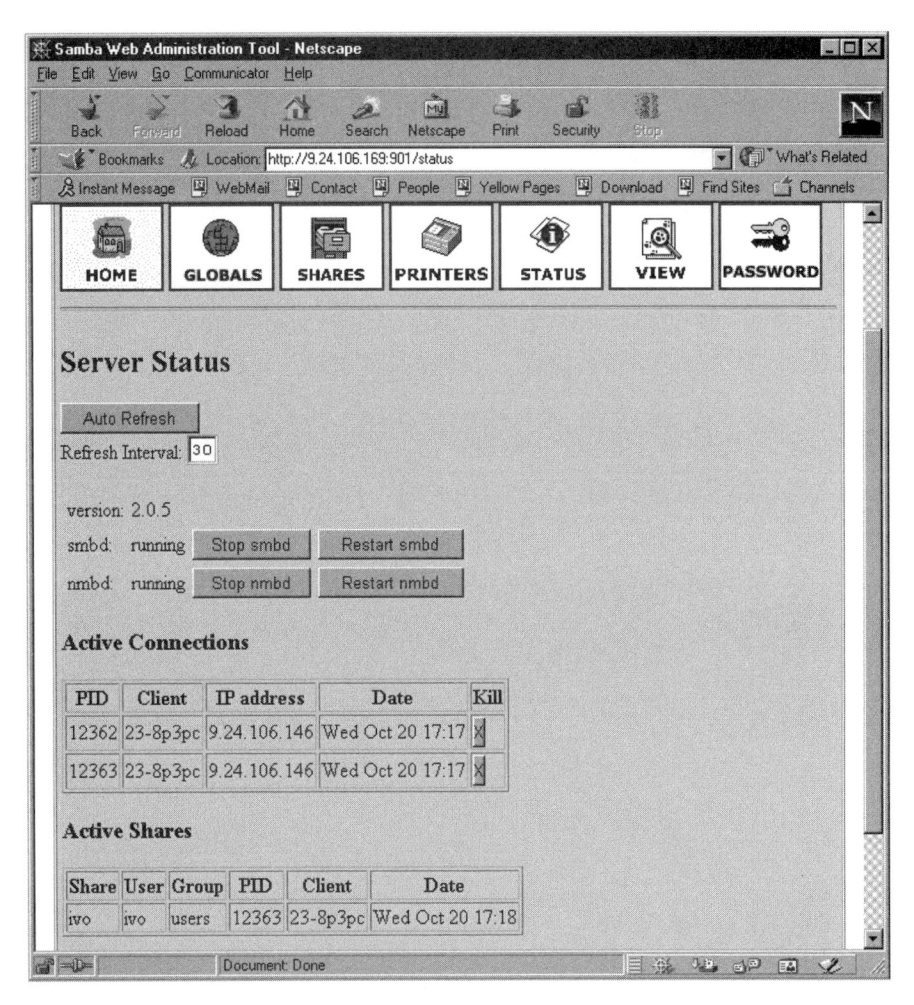

Figure 151. Status section

4.2.4.9 View

In this section you can view the current smb.conf configuration file. You can access printer settings by clicking the **View** icon on the SWAT Web pages similar to Figure 152.

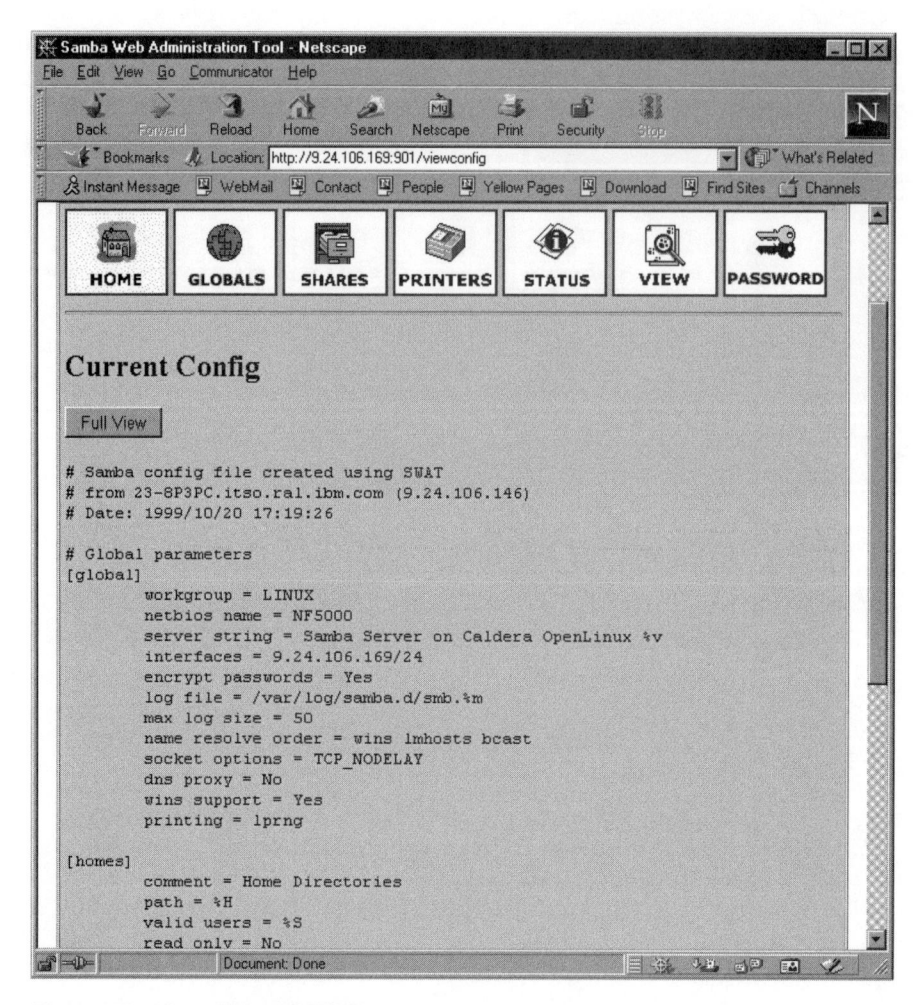

Figure 152. View section of SWAT

4.2.4.10 Password
In this section you can manage the passwords of all Samba users. You can access printer settings by clicking the **Password** icon on the SWAT Web pages similar to Figure 153.

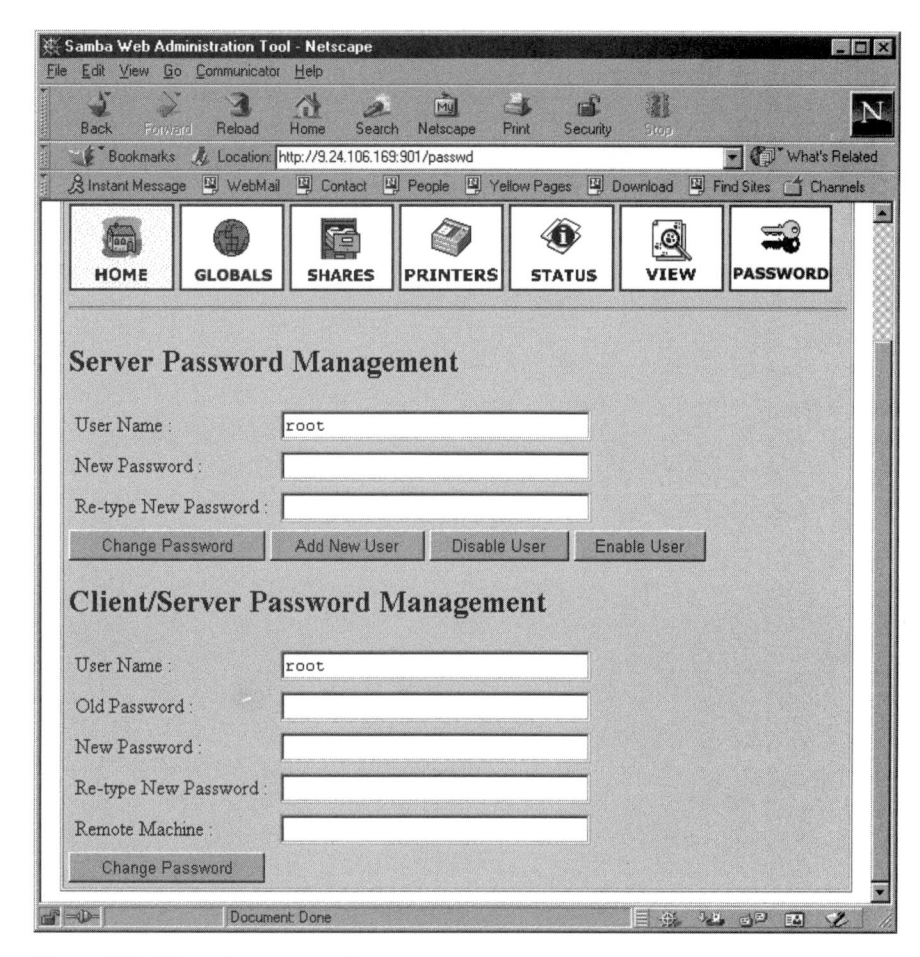

Figure 153. Managing passwords

4.3 Sources and additional information

You can find more information on the official Samba project Web site at:

`http://www.samba.org`

There are always good how-to documents on the Linux Documentation project home page:

`http://www.linuxdoc.org/`

Chapter 5. DNS - Domain Name Service

If you connect two or more computers to a network, they can share information and resources. However, these computers need to "talk in the same language" to be able to establish a connection. This "language" is called a network protocol. Today the most popular communication protocol is TCP/IP. This is the protocol that is being used on the Internet and in many local area networks as well.

Hosts in a TCP/IP network communicate with each other by using unique IP addresses. These addresses consist of four 8-bit numbers (octets) that are divided by dots. For example, host A has the address 192.168.99.1, while host B uses 122.68.29.5.

However, this addressing scheme is not very comprehensible to human beings and it is almost impossible to memorize a number of hosts by their IP addresses. Therefore a naming scheme has been invented.

Each host has a host name (for example fred) and belongs to a certain domain (for example snake-oil.com). Domains can be organized in a hierarchical fashion and can consist of different subdomains (for example marketing.snake-oil.com). The combination of a host name and its domain name is called a fully qualified domain name (FQDN) (for example fred.marketing.snake-oil.com). Since domains are hierarchical, it is possible to have more hosts with the same host name in different subdomains. Therefore, fred.marketing.snake-oil.com can be a different host from fred.management.snake-oil.com. If you want these hosts to be addressable from the Internet, you need to register your domain name with a central registry. There are several top-level domains, such as .com, .org or .net. In addition to these generic top-level domains, each country in the world has its own country code as the top-level domain. For example, Germany has .de, Denmark has .dk, and Finland uses .fi.

Since the hosts internally still use their IP addresses to communicate, there needs to be a mapping between host names and the corresponding IP address. There are two ways this can be implemented.

All host names of a network, including their IP addresses, are put into a static text file. This file has to be copied on each host that wants to communicate with the others by name. As soon as a host has been added or removed from the network, or an IP address or host name has changed, and the host files on all computers have to be adjusted accordingly. This can get very tedious, if the number of hosts reaches a certain amount.

This is where the Domain Name System (DNS) steps in. The following description of DNS is very simplified, but it should give you a rough picture of what DNS is all about.

Instead of maintaining a separate host file on each machine, there is a central server that carries a list of all hosts and IP addresses of its domain. All clients now send their host name resolution request to this central server instead of looking in a local table. The name server will look up the requested host name and return the respective IP address. The opposite is also possible: the client can also ask for a host name that belongs to a certain IP address. If a client asks for an IP address of another domain, the local domain name server will forward the request to the next name server above in its hierarchy, if it cannot answer the request by itself. Therefore changes to the table of host names have to be made at one central point only rather than on all participants of the network.

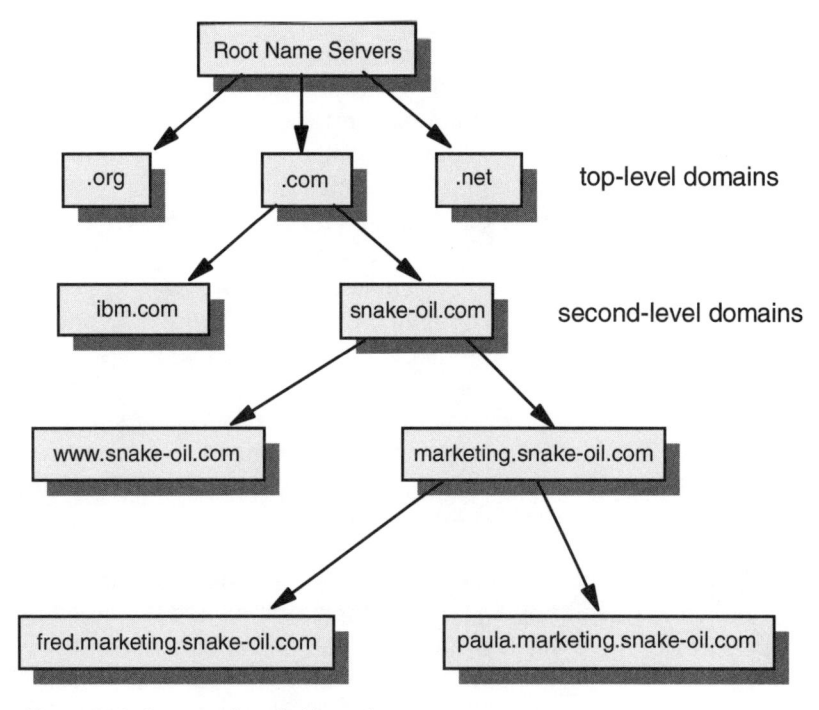

Figure 154. Internet domain hierarchy

This chapter will describe how to set up a name server for a local domain and how to maintain a host list for this domain.

5.1 Installation of software

The server that is supposed to be the DNS server needs to have a working TCP/IP network connection to the other hosts in its network first. The program that is responsible for this service is called named and belongs to the software package bind, which is coordinated by Paul Vixie for The Internet Software Consortium. There are two major versions of bind: bind4 and bind8. Caldera OpenLinux comes with the bind8 version. Before we continue, make sure that the following packages are installed:

- bind-8.1.2-1
- bind-utils-8.1.2-1

You can do this by starting kpackage from COAS tools as we explained in 2.5, "Adding and removing software packages using kpackage" on page 72. These packages are in the Network subsection under the Server section.

5.2 DNS sample configuration

Configuring DNS can be very complex, depending on the intended functionality. Covering this in depth is beyond the scope of this chapter. We will therefore focus on very a simplified example and recommend that you take a look at the very informative DNS how-to at:

```
http://www.linuxdoc.org/HOWTO/DNS-HOWTO.html
```

or at /usr/doc/howto/DNS-HOWTO.gz on your local filesystem for further information on DNS and bind.

We will construct a simple example. The company Snake Oil Ltd. wants to set up a local DNS server for their internal network (the internal IP address range is 192.168.99.xxx/24, a Class C network). They chose snake-oil.com as their local domain name. The network is also connected to the Internet. The name server will be configured to answer all requests about the local (internal) snake-oil.com domain and forward all other requests to the ISP's name server (ns.bigisp.com, fictional IP address 155.3.12.1) as a caching name server.

We begin with a simple example. At first the local DNS will be configured to act as a caching-only name server. This means that it forwards all requests to the Internet Service Provider's (ISP) name server(s) (forwarders) and caches all answers for further requests from its clients. This reduces the network traffic on the outside line.

Add the following lines in the /etc/resolv.conf file:

```
search snake-oil.com
nameserver 127.0.0.1
```

This will make sure that the server itself will use its local name server for host name resolution.

You can also do this using the Resolver tool from the COAS tools as we explained in 2.19, "Name resolution settings" on page 103 and the host name tool as we explained in 2.11, "Hostname" on page 90.

The name server's main configuration file is /etc/named.conf. Since most distributions ship with a very detailed sample configuration file, you might want to save this for further reference. We will create a new file from scratch. Start a text editor and create a new /etc/named.conf file according to the following example:

```
options {
        directory "/var/named";
        listen-on { any; };
        forward only;
        forwarders { 155.3.12.1; };
        sortlist {
                { localhost; localnets; };
                { localnets; };
        };
};
logging {
        category lame-servers { null; };
        category cname { null; };
};
zone "localhost" IN {
        type master;
        file "localhost.zone";
        check-names fail;
        allow-update { none; };
};
zone "0.0.127.in-addr.arpa" IN {
        type master;
        file "127.0.0.zone";
        check-names fail;
        allow-update { none; };
};
```

Replace the IP address in the `forwarders` field with your ISP's name server IP address.

You also need to create a /var/named/localhost.zone file as follows:

```
$ORIGIN localhost.
@                       1D IN SOA       @ root (
                                        42              ; serial (d. adams)
                                        3H              ; refresh
                                        15M             ; retry
                                        1W              ; expiry
                                        1D )            ; minimum

                        1D IN NS        @
                        1D IN A         127.0.0.1
```

Furthermore, create a /var/named/127.0.0.zone file with the following content:

```
$ORIGIN 0.0.127.in-addr.arpa.
@                       1D IN SOA       localhost. root.localhost. (
                                        42              ; serial (d. adams)
                                        3H              ; refresh
                                        15M             ; retry
                                        1W              ; expiry
                                        1D )            ; minimum

                        1D IN NS        localhost.
1                       1D IN PTR       localhost.
```

Your network clients should all be configured to query the local DNS server's IP address instead of your ISP's name server.

You can now start the server with the command:

```
/etc/rc.d/init/named start
```

Check the /var/log/messages file for the startup messages. The name server should now resolve DNS queries from its clients by forwarding them to the ISP's name server. You can verify this with the `host <somehostname>` and `nslookup` commands.

If you want DNS to start automatically when the Linux server is started, follow the instructions in 4.2.3, "Starting Samba as startup service" on page 134, but instead of selecting **SMB server process (samba)** you select **Internet domain nameserver (named)**. After you enabled DNS to run as a service it will start automatically when the Linux server boots up.

In the following step, this server should now also act as a primary name server for the local domain snake-oil.com. Stop the name server with this command:

```
/etc/rc.d/init/named stop
```

Edit the file /etc/named.conf so it looks like the following example:

```
options {
        directory "/var/named";
        listen-on { any; };
        forward only;
        forwarders {9.24.106.15;};
        sortlist {
                { localhost; localnets; };
                { localnets; };
        };
};
logging {
        category lame-servers { null; };
        category cname { null; };
};
zone "." {
        type hint;
        file "root.hint";
};
zone "localhost" IN {
        type master;
        file "localhost.zone";
        check-names fail;
        allow-update { none; };
};
zone "0.0.127.in-addr.arpa" IN {
        type master;
        file "127.0.0.zone";
        check-names fail;
        allow-update { none; };
};
zone "snake-oil.com" {
        type master;
        file "snake-oil.zone";
};
zone "99.168.192.IN-ADDR.APRA" {
        type master;
        file "snake-oil.rev";
};
```

We have now added the zone files (the databases) needed for our local domain "snake-oil.com". The file /var/named/snake-oil.zone is responsible for the mapping of host names to IP addresses.

```
;
; Zone file for snake-oil.com
;
@         IN       SOA     ns.snake-oil.com. hostmaster.snake-oil.com. (
                           199910011    ; serial, todays date + todays serial #
                           8H           ; refresh, seconds
                           2H           ; retry, seconds
                           1W           ; expire, seconds
                           1D )         ; minimum, seconds
;
                   NS      ns                ; Inet Address of nameserver
                   MX      10 mail           ; Primary Mail Exchanger
                   MX      20 mail.bigisp.com. ; Secondary Mail Exchanger
;
localhost          A       127.0.0.1
gw                 A       192.168.99.1
ns                 A       192.168.99.2
fred               A       192.168.99.3
mail               A       192.168.99.4
ftp                A       192.168.99.5
www                A       192.168.99.6
```

You should also create the zone file /var/named/snake-oil.rev. This is necessary for reverse name lookups, for example, if you need to resolve an IP address to its name.

```
@         IN       SOA     ns.snake-oil.com. hostmaster.snake-oli.com. (
                           199910011 ; Serial, todays date + todays serial
                           8H       ; Refresh
                           2H       ; Retry
                           1W       ; Expire
                           1D)      ; Minimum TTL
                   NS      ns.snake-oil.com.
1                  PTR     gw.snake-oil.com.
2                  PTR     ns.snake-oil.com.
3                  PTR     fred.snake-oil.com.
4                  PTR     mail.snake-oil.com.
5                  PTR     ftp.snake-oil.com.
6                  PTR     www.snake-oil.com.
```

Now let the name server reload its configuration again by running `rcnamed restart`. Take a look at the messages in the /var/log/messages file. If everything went well, you should see messages similar to the following:

```
Oct 26 18:03:20 ns named[14870]: starting
Oct 26 18:03:20 ns named[14870]: cache zone "" (IN) loaded (serial 0)
Oct 26 18:03:20 ns named[14870]: master zone "localhost" (IN) loaded (serial 42)
Oct 26 18:03:20 ns named[14870]: master zone "0.0.127.in-addr.arpa" (IN) loaded (serial
Oct 26 18:03:20 ns named[14870]: master zone "snake-oil.com" (IN) loaded (serial 199910
Oct 26 18:03:20 ns named[14870]: master zone "99.168.192.IN-ADDR.APRA" (IN) loaded (ser
199910011)
Oct 26 18:03:20 ns named[14870]: listening on [127.0.0.1].53 (lo)
Oct 26 18:03:20 ns named[14870]: listening on [9.24.105.210].53 (eth0)
Oct 26 18:03:20 ns named[14870]: Forwarding source address is [0.0.0.0].1041
Oct 26 18:03:20 ns named[14871]: Ready to answer queries.
```

Your name server should now correctly resolve host names for the snake-oil domain as well.

5.3 Configuration tips

Use the listen-on directive in the options section of the named.conf file. For each interface a name server listens on, a pair of filehandles are opened. On a busy name server, saving every filehandle is a big win.

Check the /var/log/messages file from time to time for errors. Named is pretty verbose in its error messages.

If you are constantly adding, removing or just making modifications to your zone records, you might want to have a look at the nsupdate tool, which also belongs to the bind8 package.

Chapter 6. DHCP - Dynamic Host Configuration Protocol

With the ever-decreasing number of IP addresses available, along with the headache of maintaining static IPs, DHCP has become a necessity in most TCP/IP computing environments.

6.1 What is DHCP?

DHCP stands for Dynamic Host Configuration Protocol. When using TCP/IP, a computer system needs a unique IP address to communicate with other computer systems. Without DHCP, the IP address must be entered manually at each computer system. DHCP lets network administrators distribute IP addresses from a central location without having to actively manage each individual address.

With DHCP, IP addresses are distributed though pools usually broken up by subnets. Leases are given out for a specific time period for each address. The process of managing leases is all done by the DHCP server. Once a lease has expired the DHCP server will try to contact the client or the client will contact the server to renew the lease. If the server cannot contact the client, the IP address is returned to the pool and available for the next client in need of an address.

6.2 Why should I use DHCP?

In the past, for every device on a network you had to have a static IP address. With the increasing number of computers accessing the Internet, the pool of available addresses is quickly diminishing. Network administrators can significantly reduce the number of IP addresses they need by using DHCP.

Even with smaller networks, keeping track of individual IP addresses can be maintenance intensive. With DHCP, the server does all of the maintenance, mapping IP addresses to MAC addresses and tracking lease times. Administrators can adjust lease times, expand or reduce pools, and change gateways or DNS addresses, all from a central location.

6.3 Implementation on Linux

In this section we will discuss how to implement a DHCP server on Linux.

First we will install the DHCP server binaries. The package is available on the Caldera OpenLinux CD and is usually installed by default. You can verify this by executing kpackage as we described in 4.2, "Setting up the Samba server" on page 123. The dhcpd package is under the Boot subsection in the Server section. After you start kpackage you will see a window similar to Figure 155.

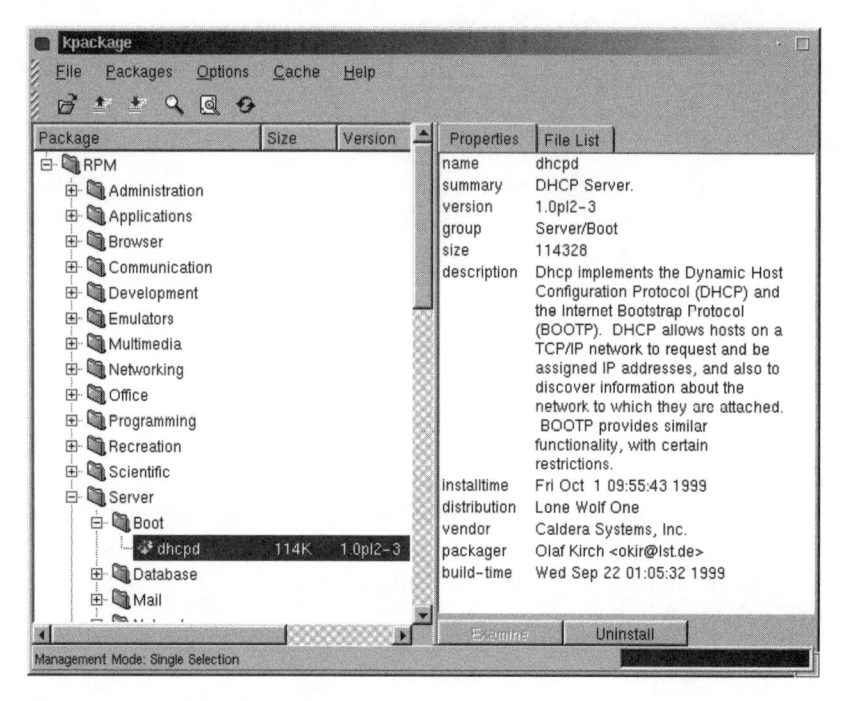

Figure 155. Verifying if the dhcpd package is installed

Using your editor of choice, change the /etc/dhcpd.conf file to meet your requirements.

The following sample of the dhcpd.conf file is rather simple. We designate a default lease time of 600 seconds (10 min.) but we will let clients request up to a 7200-second (2-hour) lease time. We include a recommended subnet mask of 255.255.255.0 and a broadcast address of 192.168.1.255. Other options we specify include a default gateway (router), two nameservers, and the domain.

For our subnet specifics we are using the private 192.168.1.0 class C subnet. For our DHCP pool we will be giving out addresses numbered from 15 to 100 for a total of 85 addresses. The rest can be used by static devices.

```
T#
# Configuration file for DHCP server.
# Please see /usr/doc/dhcpd-1.0p12 for examples,
# and view the manpage dhcpd.conf(5).
#
default-lease-time 600;
max-lease-time 7200;
option subnet-mask 255.255.255.0;
option broadcast-address 192.168.1.255;
option routers 192.168.1.254;
option domain-name-servers 192.168.1.1, 192.168.1.2;
option domain-name "ibm.com";

subnet 192.168.1.0 netmask 255.255.255.0 {
range 192.168.1.15 192.168.1.100;
}
```

You are not limited to a single subnet. You are allowed to have shared network-specific parameters, multiple subnet- specific parameters, group parameters, and host-specific parameters.

You can define multiple ranges, assign specific IP addresses based on the hardware address of the client, and specify a WINS server if needed.

More information is available from the dhcpd.conf man page.

The DHCP server needs a place to keep track of leases. This is done in the file /var/state/dhcpd.leases.

To start the DHCP server, type:

```
/etc/rc.d/init/dhcpd start
```

For debugging information, use the -d -f flags.

If you want the DHCP server to start automatically when the server is started follow the instructions in 4.2.3, "Starting Samba as startup service" on page 134, but instead of selecting **SMB server process (samba)** you select **DHCP and BOOTP boot server**.

Chapter 7. Apache and IBM HTTP Server

The Apache Web server is the most popular Web server software on today's Internet. According to the NetCraft Web server survey at http://www.netcraft.com/survey/, more than 55% of all surveyed Web servers (more than 7.3 million) were running a version of Apache (as of the time of this writing). Apache is a very successful collaborative Open Source project. The Web site for Apache is http://www.apache.org. Because of the free availability of the full source code, it is a very flexible and powerful Web server solution. There are also a lot of additional modules, which can be used in combination with the Apache main program. Some popular examples are PHP (PHP: Hypertext Preprocessor, an embedded HTML scripting language), mod_perl (an embedded perl interpreter) and mod_ssl for secure transactions. More Apache modules can be downloaded from the Apache Module Registry at:

http://modules.apache.org.

Some of key features of Apache are:

- Implements the latest protocols, including HTTP/1.1 (RFC2068).
- Is highly configurable and extensible with third-party modules.
- Can be customized by writing "modules" using the Apache module API.
- Provides full source code and comes with an unrestrictive license.
- Runs on most versions of UNIX (including Linux) without modification.
- DBM databases for authentication, which allow you to easily set up password-protected pages with enormous numbers of authorized user, without bogging down the server. A wide variety of SQL databases can be used for authentication too (using additional modules).
- Customized responses to errors and problems, which allow you to set up files, or even CGI scripts, which are returned by the server in response to errors and problems. For example, you can set up a script to intercept 500 server errors and perform on-the-fly diagnostics for both users and yourself.
- Multiple DirectoryIndex directives, which allow you to say DirectoryIndex index.html index.cgi, which instructs the server to either send back index.html or run index.cgi when a directory URL is requested, whichever it finds in the directory.
- Unlimited numbers of alias and redirect directives that may be declared in the config files.

- Content negotiation, the ability to automatically serve clients of varying sophistication and HTML level compliance, with documents which offer the best representation of information that the client is capable of accepting.
- Multi-homed servers, which allow the server to distinguish between requests made to different IP addresses (mapped to the same machine).

7.1 The IBM HTTP server

The IBM HTTP Server powered by Apache is based on the Apache HTTP Server. In addition to Linux, this HTTP Server also runs on AIX, Solaris and Windows NT. See the home page at:

```
http://www-4.ibm.com/software/webservers/httpservers/
```

IBM HTTP Server for Linux offers the following additional features:

- Remote Configuration: a browser-based configuration tool to allow manipulation of the server configuration via a GUI.
- SNMP Support: Simple Network Management Protocol (SNMP) is a well-established protocol for managing and gathering information about servers remotely. This new support allows IBM HTTP Server to be managed by the SNMP protocol.
- LDAP: The IBM HTTP Server Lightweight Directory Access Protocol (LDAP) plug-in allows authentication and authorization (which is required when accessing a protected resource) to be performed by an LDAP server, thereby greatly decreasing the administrative overhead for maintaining user and group information locally for each Web server.
- Machine Translation Support: This new function, when used with an available IBM Machine Translation Engine, enables the IBM HTTP Server to translate English Web pages into other languages without human intervention. This permits a Web site visitor to read the page in his native language, effectively broadening the reach of your Web site. IBM Machine Translation Engines are included in the WebSphere Application Server 3.0 and include German, Simplified Chinese and Traditional Chinese. Additional languages will be available in the future.
- Support for SSL secure connections: The IBM HTTP Server powered by Apache supports both the SSL Version 2 and SSL Version 3 protocols. This protocol, implemented using IBM security libraries, ensures that data transferred between a client and a server remains private. Once your server has a digital certificate, SSL-enabled browsers such as Netscape Navigator and Microsoft Internet Explorer can communicate securely with your server using the SSL protocol. The IBM HTTP Server powered by

Apache supports client authentication, configurable cipher specifications, and session ID caching for improving SSL performance on the UNIX platforms.

- Fast Response Cache Accelerator: The Cache Accelerator can dramatically improve the performance of the IBM HTTP Server powered by Apache when serving static pages, for example, text and image files. Because the Cache Accelerator cache is automatically loaded during server operation, you are not required to list the files to be cached in your server configuration file. In addition, the server will automatically recache changed pages and remove outdated pages from the cache. The Cache Accelerator provides support for caching on Web servers with single and multiple TCP/IP adapters.

7.2 Apache HTTP Server installation

Usually the Apache HTTP server is installed and started by default in the Caldera OpenLinux. You can verify that the Apache package is installed by running kpackage as we explained in 2.5, "Adding and removing software packages using kpackage" on page 72. The Apache server package is found by clicking **Server -> WWW**.

The Apache HTTP is usually automatically started on bootup. You can check this by examining the services that will start at server startup, as we described in 2.9, "Daemons (services)" on page 88. If you want Apache HTTP server to start at the server startup, enable the **Web server** service. To start, stop or reload Apache HTTP server (after a configuration change), run the script:

```
/usr/rc.d/init/httpd (start|stop).
```

In Caldera OpenLinux, Apache will serve HTML documents from the directory /home/httpd/html and CGI scripts from /home/httpd/cgi-bin. If you installed the PHP module (mod_php), it will also execute PHP code, if the file ends on .php3. The access log file is in /var/log/httpd/access_log, the error log file is /var/log/httpd/error_log. The Apache configuration files reside in the subdirectory /etc/httpd/conf.

If you now point your browser to the server's IP address, you should see the following start page (/home/httpd/html/index.html), when the Apache HTTP server is running:

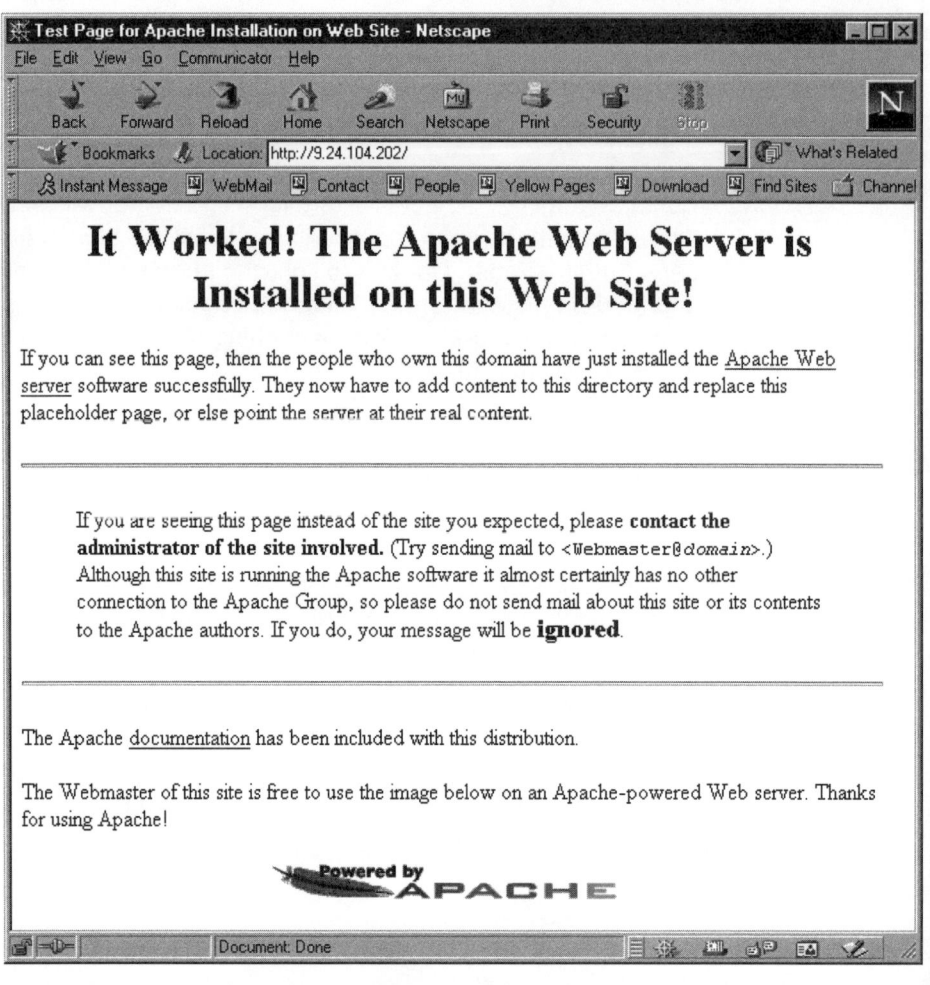

Figure 156. Apache startup page on Caldera OpenLinux

7.3 IBM HTTP Server installation

To install the IBM HTTP Server on Caldera OpenLinux, you need to perform the following steps.

For the IBM HTTP server and the remote administration capabilities, download the following tar files from the Web page:

```
http://www-4.ibm.com/software/webservers/httpservers/download.html
```

the HTTPServer.linux.glibc21.server.tar file contains the following packages:

- IBM_HTTP_Server-1.3.6-2.i386.rpm - the IHS Web server
- IBM_Apache_Source-1.3.6-2.i386.rpm - the Apache 1.3.6 sources
- Readme.httpserver - Installation notes

HTTPServer.linux.glibc21.admin.tar file contains the following packages:

- IBM_Admin_Server-1.3.6-1.i386.rpm - GUI administration server
- IBM_Admin_Server_Forms-1.3.6-1.i386.rpm - Web forms for the GUI

There are some additional packages like SNMP and SSL modules, that also can be installed. However, these will not be covered in this chapter. Please see the installation instructions at:

```
http://www-4.ibm.com/software/webservers/httpservers/doc/v136/readme_ht
tpserver.htm
```

After you have downloaded the "tarballs", move them to the directory /tmp and extract them with the command:

```
tar xvf HTTPServer.linux.glibc21.server.tar
tar xvf HTTPServer.linux.glibc21.admin.tar
```

This will extract the above-listed RPM files from the tar archive into the subdirectory /tmp/IHS. You now need to become the root user (if you not already are). To avoid resource conflicts, you first have to shut down the currently running Apache Web server (if installed), by executing the following command:

```
/etc/rc.d/init/httpd stop
```

Also make sure, that it will not be started again after the next reboot by disabling the Web server service in as we described in 2.9, "Daemons (services)" on page 88.

Now you need to install the packages with the following commands (assuming the packages reside in the current directory):

```
rpm -Uvh IBM_HTTP_Server-1.3.6-1.i386.rpm
rpm -Uhv IBM_Admin_Server-1.3.6-1.i386.rpm
rpm -Uhv IBM_Admin_Server_Forms-1.3.6-1.i386.rpm
```

The installation of the HTTP Server package will also attempt to start the server automatically. If it did not start, you might still have another HTTP server running. Stop this one first, and try to restart the IBM HTTP Server with the following command:

```
/etc/rc.d/init/ibmhttpd start
```

If no errors are present on the command line or in:

```
/opt/IBMHTTPServer/logs/error_log,
```

Try to open the new HTTP server's home page with your browser. You should see the following page:

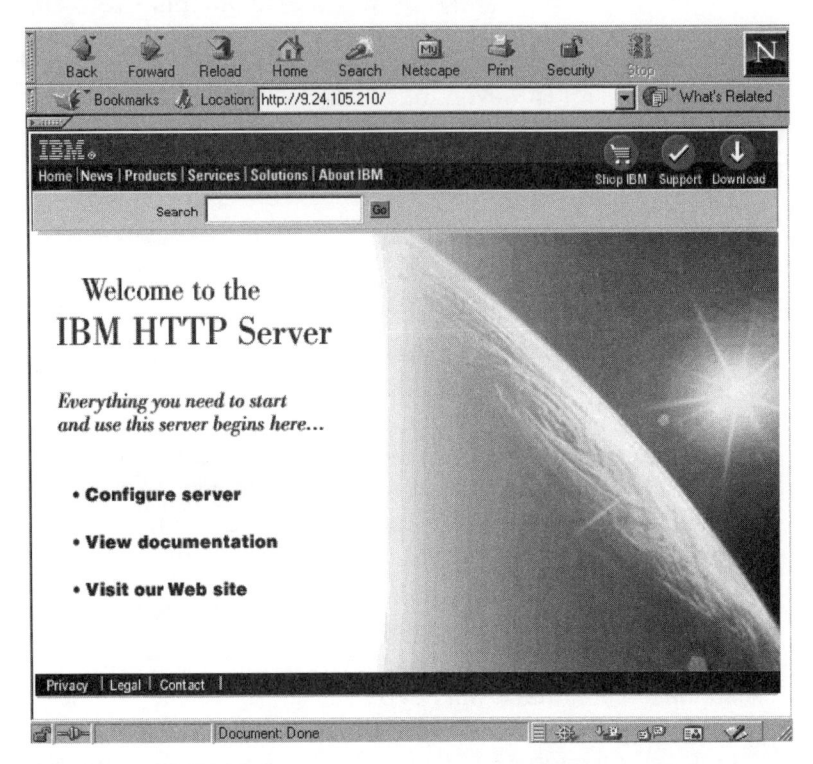

Figure 157. IBM HTTP Server startup page

If you still see the old Web server's startup page (see Figure 156), press Shift+Reload on the Netscape browser to force a reload of this page.

The basic installation of the IBM HTTP Server is now finished! In the default set up, it serves HTML pages from the directory /opt/IBMHTTPD/htdocs and CGI scripts from /opt/IBMHTTPD/cgi-bin. The log files reside in /opt/IBMHTTPD/logs.

7.3.1 Activating IBM HTTPD on system bootup

By default, the IBM HTTP Server has to be started manually after a system reboot. If you want to start it automatically, you have to add the startup script to the bootup procedure.

If you want this server to be started on bootup, you have to create the correct symbolic links in the directory /etc/rc.d/rc3.d (if you start the system in runlevel 3, the default runlevel), or /etc/rc.d/rc5.d (If you use the graphical login, runlevel 5). You can do this manually with the following commands:

```
cd /etc/rc.d/rc3.d

ln -s ../init.d/ibmhttpd ./S67ibmhttpd
ln -s ../init.d/ibmhttpd ./K01ibmhttpd


cd /etc/rc.d/rc5.d

ln -s ../init.d/ibmhttpd ./S67ibmhttpd
ln -s ../init.d/ibmhttpd ./K01ibmhttpd
```

This will start the IBM HTTP server in runlevel 2 and runlevel 3 and make sure, that it will be properly shut down when switching into another runlevel (for example, shutdown).

7.3.2 Setting up the Administration Server

You have to perform some preliminary steps before you can start using the Administration Server to be able to modify the configuration files of your IBM HTTP Server remotely.

The basic intent of the Administration Server tasks are to allow the Administration Server read/write/execute access to the necessary configuration files and one executable file. The Administration Server should obtain read/write access through a unique user ID and group, which must be created. The User and Group directives of the Administration Server's configuration file should be changed to the unique user ID and group. The Administration Server's configuration file's "group access permissions" should be changed to allow read/write "group access". In addition there is a utility program that should have "Group execute permissions" and "Set User ID Root permissions". This executable must run as root in order to request restarts for the IBM HTTP Server and the Administration Server.

To properly set up these prerequisites, these tasks can be performed by executing the script /opt/IBMHTTPserver/bin/setupadm. After the invocation, it will ask you a few questions and will give detailed information about each step it is performing. On Caldera OpenLinux the script fails to automatically create a new user and group for the Administration Server. The solution is to create a group and account with the COAS tools and then use those names during the setup of the Administration Server. After you do this enter the keywords marked in boldface in the following screens:

```
[root@nf5000 bin]# ./setupadm

***************************************************************
Please supply a User ID to run the Administration Server
We will create the USERID using System Administration tools
***************************************************************
[no default] -> account name you have created

***************************************************************
Please supply a GROUP NAME to run the Administration Server
We will create the Group using System Administration tools
***************************************************************
[no default] -> group name you have created

***************************************************************
Please supply the Directory containing the files for
which a change in the permissions is necessary.
***************************************************************
[default: /opt/IBMHTTPServer/conf] -> [Enter]

***************************************************************
We will flag 'SetUserID for Root' as well as
update the Group, Group access permissions and
Group execute permissions, for file:
        /opt/IBMHTTPServer/bin/admrestart

This interface is necessary for Administration Server requests
to restart manage webservers
YES(default)-      ENTER 1
NO         -       ENTER 2
***************************************************************
[default: YES  - 1] -> [Enter]
```

```
************************************************************
You may use WildCards (i.e *.conf)
Please supply a File Name for permission changes
Default will change file permissions for ALL files in directory
************************************************************
[default: ALL FILES] -> [Enter]


These are the file(s) and directory for which we will be changing
Group permissions:

-rw-r--r--   1 root     root         4137 Jul 29 15:02 admin.conf
-rw-r--r--   1 root     root         4137 Jul 29 15:02 admin.conf.default
-rw-r--r--   1 root     root         6246 Jul 29 15:02 admin.msg
-rw-r--r--   1 root     root            1 Jul 29 15:02 admin.passwd
-rw-r--r--   1 root     root        30990 Oct 22 08:43 httpd.conf
-rw-r--r--   1 root     root        30989 Jul 29 14:58 httpd.conf.default
-r--r-----   1 root     root        46360 Jul 29 14:58 httpd.conf.sample
-rw-r--r--   1 root     root        12441 Jul 29 14:58 magic
-rw-r--r--   1 root     root        12441 Jul 29 14:58 magic.default
-rw-r--r--   1 root     root         7350 Jul 29 14:58 mime.types
-rw-r--r--   1 root     root         7350 Jul 29 14:58 mime.types.default
drwxr-xr-x   2 root     root         1024 Oct 22 08:43 /opt/IBMHTTPServer/conf

This is the file for which we will be adding 'set user ID' permission for Root:

-rwsr-x---   1 root     root        46807 Jul 29 15:02 /opt/IBMHTTPServer/bin/ad
mrestart


**************************************************
CONTINUE - Perform Changes  ENTER 1
QUIT -     No Changes       ENTER 2
**************************************************
[default: QUIT - 2] -> 1
```

```
>>>Validating Group Name: 'nogroup'<<<
       Group Name: 'nogroup' already exists

>>>Validating UserID:wwwrun<<<
       UserID: 'wwwrun' already exists

>>>>>>>>>>>>>>>>>>>>>>>>>>>>>>>>>>>>>>>>>>>>>>>>>>>>>>>>
Changing Group:
CMD: 'chgrp   /opt/IBMHTTPServer/bin/admrestart'
<<<<<<<<<<<<<<<<<<<<<<<<<<<<<<<<<<<<<<<<<<<<<<<<<<<<<<<<


>>>>>>>>>>>>>>>>>>>>>>>>>>>>>>>>>>>>>>>>>>>>>>>>>>>>>>>>
Change Group permissions and Add SetUserID permission for Root:
CMD: 'chmod  4750 /opt/IBMHTTPServer/bin/admrestart'
>>>>>>>>>>>>>>>>>>>>>>>>>>>>>>>>>>>>>>>>>>>>>>>>>>>>>>>>


>>>>>>>>>>>>>>>>>>>>>>>>>>>>>>>>>>>>>>>>>>>>>>>>>>>>>>>>
Changing Group:
CMD: 'chgrp  nogroup /opt/IBMHTTPServer/conf /opt/IBMHTTPServer/conf/* '
<<<<<<<<<<<<<<<<<<<<<<<<<<<<<<<<<<<<<<<<<<<<<<<<<<<<<<<<


>>>>>>>>>>>>>>>>>>>>>>>>>>>>>>>>>>>>>>>>>>>>>>>>>>>>>>>>
Changing Group permissions:
CMD: 'chmod  g+rw /opt/IBMHTTPServer/conf /opt/IBMHTTPServer/conf/*'
<<<<<<<<<<<<<<<<<<<<<<<<<<<<<<<<<<<<<<<<<<<<<<<<<<<<<<<<
Here are the new file(s) and directory permissions:

drwxrwxr-x   2 root      nogroup        1024 Oct 22 08:43 /opt/IBMHTTPServer/conf
-rw-rw-r--   1 root      nogroup        4137 Jul 29 15:02 admin.conf
-rw-rw-r--   1 root      nogroup        4137 Jul 29 15:02 admin.conf.default
-rw-rw-r--   1 root      nogroup        6246 Jul 29 15:02 admin.msg
-rw-rw-r--   1 root      nogroup           1 Jul 29 15:02 admin.passwd
-rw-rw-r--   1 root      nogroup       30990 Oct 22 08:43 httpd.conf
-rw-rw-r--   1 root      nogroup       30989 Jul 29 14:58 httpd.conf.default
-r--rw----   1 root      nogroup       46360 Jul 29 14:58 httpd.conf.sample
-rw-rw-r--   1 root      nogroup       12441 Jul 29 14:58 magic
-rw-rw-r--   1 root      nogroup       12441 Jul 29 14:58 magic.default
-rw-rw-r--   1 root      nogroup        7350 Jul 29 14:58 mime.types
-rw-rw-r--   1 root      nogroup        7350 Jul 29 14:58 mime.types.default

Here is a file with 'set user ID' permission for Root:

-rwsr-x---   1 root      nogroup       46807 Jul 29 15:02 /opt/IBMHTTPServer/bin/ad
mrestart
Changes Completed
```

```
******************************************************************
Configuration file: '/opt/IBMHTTPServer/conf/admin.conf'
will be saved as '/opt/IBMHTTPServer/conf/admin.conf.13:48:05_295'
Do you wish to update the Administration Server Configuration file
CONTINUE    enter 1
EXIT        enter 2
******************************************************************
[default: QUIT - 2] -> 1
USER DONE
GRoup DONE
Successfully updated configuration file
Old configuration file saved as '/opt/IBMHTTPServer/conf/admin.conf.13:48:05_295
[root@nf5000 bin]#
```

To summarize the above steps: the Administration Server will be run with the user "wwwrun" and the group "nobody."

The Administration Server is basically just another Web server, running in parallel to the main IBM HTTP server(s). Therefore it has to be started separately and listens on another TCP port (8008 by default). By default, it has to be started manually. If you also want to start it on system bootup, you have to integrate the start script into the bootup procedure. Copy the file /opt/IBMHTTPServer/bin/adminctl to the directory /etc/rc.d/init.d and follow the steps described in 7.3.1, "Activating IBM HTTPD on system bootup" on page 173, using adminctl as the init script name instead of ibmhttpd.

The Administration Server is protected with a user name and password. You can create an entry in the password file /opt/IBMHTTPServer/bin/conf/admin.passwd by issuing the following command from inside the directory /opt/IBMHTTPServer/bin:

```
./htpasswd -m ../conf/admin.passwd <user name>
```

Enter the password for the required user name twice. It is possible to have more than one user name in this password file, if you need to differentiate between multiple administrators.

Now you can start the administration server by running the following command:

```
/opt/IBMHTTPServer/bin/adminctl start
```

After clicking the **Configure Server** link shown in Figure 157 on page 172, you need to enter the user name and password you defined for the Administration Server user. If entered correctly, you will see the welcome page of the Administration Server:

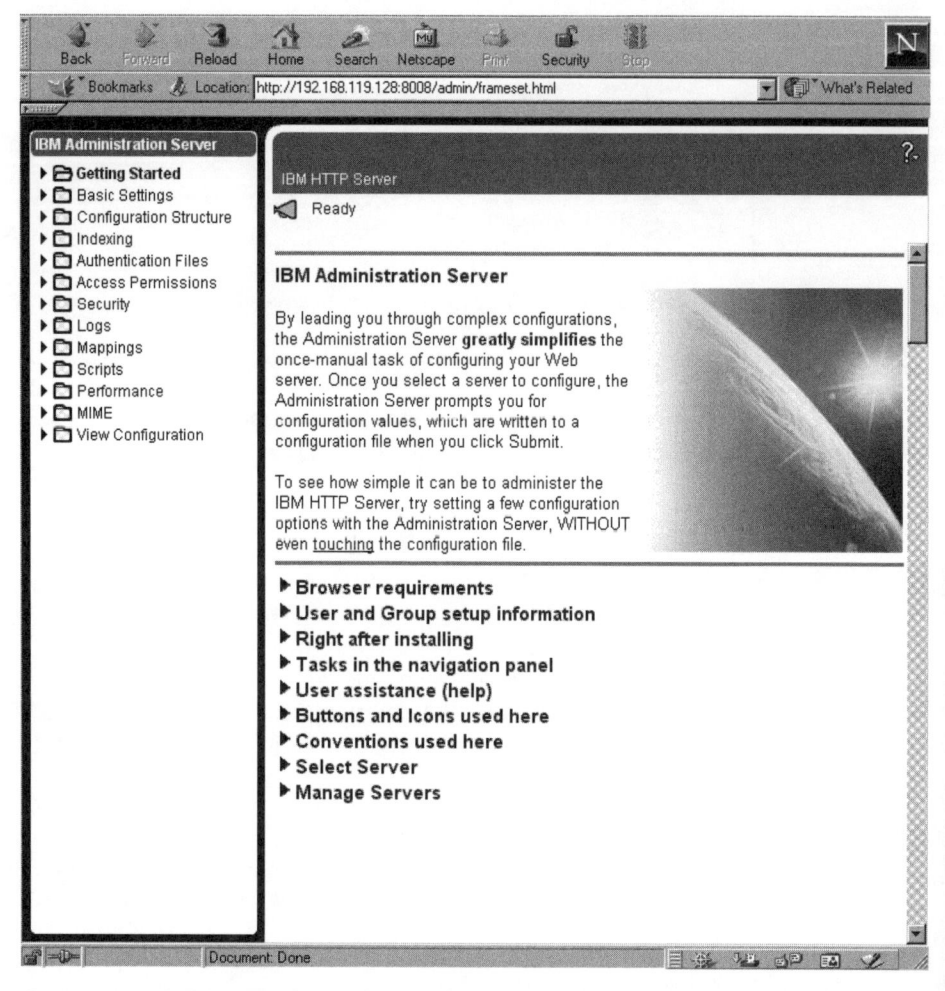

Figure 158. Administration Server startup window

You are now ready to start adjusting the configuration of your main Web server according to your needs. Please see the online documentation for help about the different configuration options.

7.4 General performance tips

Configuring Apache for maximum performance is dependent on many parameters. Apache is very flexible and gaining the best performance may require some research. A very informative document about Apache performance tuning can be found on the Apache Web site:

```
http://www.apache.org/docs/misc/perf-tuning.html
```

In short, experiment with the following options:

- Set FollowSymLinks option unless you really do not want it.
- Set AllowOverride to None unless you really need it.
- Explicitly list all DirectoryIndex file options from most to least commonly used.
- Tune KeepAliveTimeout starting with 3 ranging to 30 per content and connection types.
- Apache (and the IBM HTTP Server as well) uses multiple processes to handle individual requests. Tune StartServers starting with 64 increasing in steps of 32 until performance drops off. Tune MaxClients starting with the value of StartServers. **Note:** Scaling performance can fall off dramatically if Max Clients is too large!
- For SMP systems listening on a single socket, try recompiling after defining SINGLE_LISTEN_UNSERIALIZED_ACCEPT.

A helpful utility to benchmark your Apache server is ab. In its simplest form, you can call it like this:

```
ab http://www.your-server.com/index.html
```

The following are ab options:

```
[root@nf5000 user]# ab -h
Usage: ab [options] [http://]hostname[:port]/path
Options are:
    -n requests     Number of requests to perform
    -c concurrency  Number of multiple requests to make
    -t timelimit    Seconds to max. wait for responses
    -p postfile     File containg data to POST
    -T content-type Content-type header for POSTing
    -v verbosity    How much troubleshooting info to print
    -w              Print out results in HTML tables
    -x attributes   String to insert as table attributes
    -y attributes   String to insert as tr attributes
    -z attributes   String to insert as td or th attributes
    -V              Print version number and exit
    -k              Use HTTP KeepAlive feature
    -h              Display usage information (this message)
```

Chapter 8. Sendmail

Communicating with other people is one of the most desirable experiences in the human history. Sending electronic mail is a way to communicate with people all over the globe. Electronic mail can be more reliable, cheaper and faster than ordinary mail.

8.1 What is Sendmail?

As you can tell from the name, Sendmail is used to send mail. However, Sendmail is not sending old fashioned mail, but electronic mail, which becomes more important every day. But in spite of that, Sendmail is basically acting as a post office. It receives mail from a sender and passes the mail on to the recipient post office. At the recipient post office a local postman delivers the mail to the recipient mailbox. Sendmail is a powerful Mail Transport Agent (MTA) and is used to pass the mail to another MTA, which can be Sendmail or some other application capable of handling electronic mail.

8.2 What you can do with Sendmail

With Sendmail your Linux server can become a server for electronic mail. You can handle mail for users of a Linux server locally and users do not have to ask for mail accounts. The users on your Linux server will have their mailboxes locally and they will still be able to send mail to people anywhere. When you set up Sendmail, you can also offer mail service to the users which have accounts on the other network servers, which do not provide Internet mail service.

8.3 Before you begin

In the following sections we explain how to set up a mail server on your Linux server. In this explanation we will use our lab network setup, and all setup is related to this lab setup. You can easily adopt this to your existing installation. You can see our lab network in Figure 159. Before you proceed with the implementation you need to verify if these packages are installed:

- bind-8.1.2-1
- bind-utils-8.1.2-1
- sendmail-8.9.3-1
- sendmail-cf-8.9.3-1

You can do this by starting kpackage tool from COAS tools as we explained in 2.5, "Adding and removing software packages using kpackage" on page 72. These packages are in the **Network** and **Mail** subsections under the **Server** section. If the packages are not installed refer to the same package on how to install them.

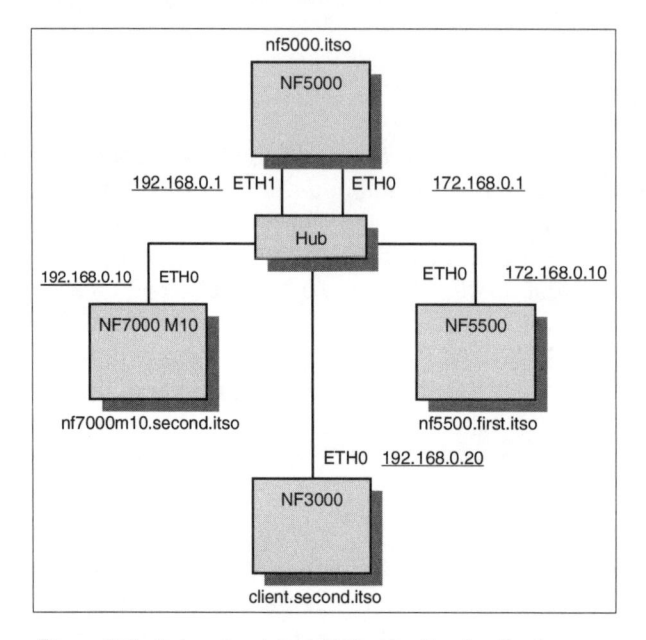

Figure 159. Lab network installation for Sendmail setup

> **Note**
>
> For successful operation of Sendmail you need the correct settings for the Domain Name System server (DNS). This means that you have to set up your own DNS correctly or have access to another DNS.

As you can see in Figure 159 our network consists of three domains:

1. Itso - this is the master (root) domain. All computers in this domain has a .itso extension. In this domain we have a server running the master (root) DNS.

2. First.itso - this is the first subdomain of the .itso domain. The main server in this domain is running the DNS for this domain and is also mail (Sendmail) server for the users of the domain.

3. Second.itso - this is the second subdomain of the .itso domain. The main server in this domain is running the DNS for this domain and is mail (Sendmail) server for the users of the domain.

All users of the mail server have user name/password definition on their domain server even if they are using other physical servers or workstations. They need this user name/password for accessing the mail. Each defined user has a mailbox on the mail server. He can reach his mailbox over the network with his client connecting to the mail server. When the connection is established, the user can download his messages to his workstation and delete them from the server. Or he can remotely connect to the server and read his mail on the server, but in this case the mail stays in the mailbox on the server.

When the users are using the server for mail only and they have their own workstations, the mail servers are setup with limited space for each mail box. That means that users have to download their mail regularly from the server to make room for the new messages. In the environment where users use the server for their operations the mailboxes are usually bigger. Users can still reach their mail remotely with the client, in that case they do not download the messages.

The most commonly used protocols for sending and delivering mail are SMTP/POP3. The Simple Mail Transfer Protocol (SMTP) is used for sending mail from the mail client and the Post Office Protocol (POP3) is for getting the mail from the mail server. Sendmail supports along with all other protocols also the SMTP and POP3 protocols. In our setup we used SMTP/POP3 protocols for the mail exchange.

Before we start describing how to set up a mail server, we will describe how to set up DNS for our lab network. That is because the correct DNS setup is important for successful operating of the mail server.

8.4 Network configuration

Each subdomain is on its own network. The "first.itso" domain is on the network 172.168.0.0 and "second.itso" domain is on the network 192.168.0.0. The server running the "itso" domain is acting as gateway for both subdomains.

We have the following network definitions:

1. The gateway server with two Network Interface Cards (NIC). The first NIC has an IP 172.168.0.1, the second IP has the IP 192.168.0.1. The server

has enabled IP Forwarding so it can acts as a gateway for subnetworks. This server is also DNS server for the "itso" domain.

2. The server for the "first.itso" domain has one NIC with IP address 172.168.0.10.
3. The server for the "second.itso" domain has one NIC with IP address 192.168.0.10.
4. The client in "second.itso" domain has one NIC with IP address 192.168.0.20
5. The client in "first.itso" domain has one NIC with IP address 172.168.0.20.

8.5 Setting up the DNS configuration

As mentioned before our lab network setup was created with a master (root) domain called ".itso" with two subdomains called ".first.itso" and ".second.itso". You can see this setup in Figure 160.

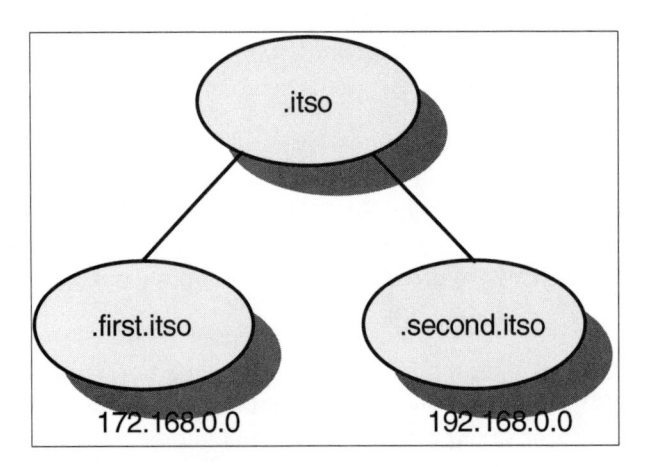

Figure 160. Domain setup

8.5.1 Setting up the root DNS

In this section we explain how we set up our root DNS server for the lab network setup. Before you start setting up the DNS server you need to check if the BIND package is installed. You can follow the instructions in 4.2, "Setting up the Samba server" on page 123, but instead of looking for the SAMBA package, you need to search for the BIND package. After you have verified that the BIND package is installed, you need to set up your system so DNS will start automatically when the Linux server is started. To do this follow the instructions in 4.2.3, "Starting Samba as startup service" on page 134, but instead of selecting **SMB server process (samba)**, select **Internet domain name server (named)**. After you have enabled DNS to run as a service it will start automatically when the Linux server boots up.

To set up the master (root) DNS for ".itso" domain follow these steps:

1. Create the /etc/named.conf file with the following entries:

```
// generated by named-bootconf.pl
options {
directory "/var/named";
/*
 * If there is a firewall between you and nameservers you want
 * to talk to, you might need to uncomment the query-source
 * directive below.  Previous versions of BIND always asked
 * questions using port 53, but BIND 8.1 uses an unprivileged
 * port by default.
 */
// query-source address * port 53;
};
//
// a caching only nameserver config
// we don't need root entry, because this DNS
// is root server for .itso domain
//
//zone "." {
//type hint;
//file "named.ca";
//};
zone "0.0.127.in-addr.arpa" {
type master;
file "named.local";
};
zone "itso" {
notify no;
type master;
file "itso";
};
zone "0.168.172.in-addr.arpa" {
notify no;
type master;
file "172.168.0";
};
zone "0.168.192.in-addr.arpa" {
notify no;
type master;
file "192.168.0";
};
```

As you can see we defined the zone file for the "itso" domain and the zone files for reverse address resolution for local, network 172.168.0.0 and network 192.168.0.0.

2. Create the directory /var/named.

Chapter 8. Sendmail   **185**

3. Create the zone file /var/named/itso with the following entries:

```
@       IN      SOA     nf5000.itso. root.itso. (
                        1997022700 ; Serial
                        28800      ; Refresh
                        14400      ; Retry
                        3600000    ; Expire
                        86400 )    ; Minimum
;
 NS nf5000 ; Name Server
 MX 10 mail ; Mail Server
;
localhost A 127.0.0.1
nf5000 A 172.168.0.1
mail CNAME nf5000
first A 172.168.0.10
second A 192.168.0.10
second.itso. 86400 IN NS nf7000m10.second.itso.
nf7000m10.second.itso. 86400 IN A  192.168.0.10
first.itso. 86400 IN NS nf5500.first.itso.
nf5500.first.itso. 86400 IN A 172.168.0.10
```

We specified in this file that all requests for "first.itso" and "second.itso" go to the corresponding DNS servers in these domains.

4. Create the zone file /var/named/172.168.0. with the following entries:

```
@       IN      SOA     nf5000.itso. root.itso. (
                        1997022700 ; Serial
                        28800      ; Refresh
                        14400      ; Retry
                        3600000    ; Expire
                        86400 )    ; Minimum
                NS      nf5000.itso.
1.0.0.10.in-addr.arpa.    IN CNAME 1.0-255.0.168.172.in-addr.arpa.
172.168.0.10.in-addr.arpa. IN CNAME 172.0-255.0.168.172.in-addr.arpa.
;
0-255.0.168.172.in-addr.arpa.  86400 IN NS  nf5500.first.itso.
```

As you can see all requests for the reverse address resolution of the 172.168.0.0 network are passed on to the DNS in the "first.itso" domain. So when the DNS server gets a request for IP address in the network 172.168.0.0-255 it will pass this request to the DNS server that is serving this network. In our example, this is the DNS server for "first.itso" domain.

5. Create the zone file /var/named/192.168.0. with the following entries:

```
@           IN      SOA     nf5000.itso. root.itso. (
                                  1997022700 ; Serial
                                  28800      ; Refresh
                                  14400      ; Retry
                                  3600000    ; Expire
                                  86400 )    ; Minimum
            NS      nf5000.itso.
1.0.0.11.in-addr.arpa.    IN CNAME 1.0-255.0.192.168.in-addr.arpa.
10.0.0.11.in-addr.arpa.   IN CNAME 10.0-255.0.192.168.in-addr.arpa.
20.0.0.11.in-addr.arpa.   IN CNAME 20.0-255.0.192.168.in-addr.arpa.
;
0-255.0.192.168.in-addr.arpa.  86400 IN NS  nf7000m10.second.itso.
```

As you can see, all requests for the reverse address resolution of the 192.168.0.0 network are passed on to the DNS in the "second.itso" domain. So when the DNS server gets a request for an IP address in the network 192.168.0.0-255, it will pass this request to the DNS server which is serving this network. In our example this is the DNS server for the "second.itso" domain.

6. Create the zone file /var/named/named.local with the following entries:

```
@           IN      SOA     nf5000.itso. root.itso. (
                                  1997022700 ; Serial
                                  28800      ; Refresh
                                  14400      ; Retry
                                  3600000    ; Expire
                                  86400 )    ; Minimum
            NS      nf5000.itso.
1 IN PTR    localhost.
```

7. Your server is ready to be powered on. To start the server without restarting the operating system, which is the case in another very popular operating system, execute the command:

   /etc/rc.d/init/named start

Congratulations! You have just set up a fully functional DNS server. Get ready for more excitement when you will set up the DNS servers for the subdomains.

8.5.2 Setting up the DNS for the first subdomain

Before you start configuring DNS, you need to check if the DNS server is installed. You can do this following the instructions in 8.5.1, "Setting up the root DNS" on page 184.

After you checked all prerequisites, follow these steps to set up DNS for the "first.itso" domain:

1. Create the /etc/named.conf file with the following entries:

```
// generated by named-bootconf.pl
options {
directory "/var/named";
/*
 * If there is a firewall between you and nameservers you want
 * to talk to, you might need to uncomment the query-source
 * directive below.  Previous versions of BIND always asked
 * questions using port 53, but BIND 8.1 uses an unprivileged
 * port by default.
 */
// query-source address * port 53;
};
//
// a caching only nameserver config
//
zone "." {
type hint;
file "named.ca";
};
zone "0.0.127.in-addr.arpa" {
type master;
file "named.local";
};
zone "first.itso" {
notify no;
type master;
file "first.itso";
};
zone "0.168.172.in-addr.arpa" {
notify no;
type master;
file "0.168.172.in-addr.arpa";
};
zone "0-255.0.168.172.in-addr.arpa" {
type master;
file "0.168.172.in-addr.arpa";
             };
```

As you can see we defined the zone for the root domain "." and the zone for "first.itso" domain. We also defined zones for reverse address resolution for local network 172.168.0.0 and for network 172.168.0.0-255, which serve the requests from the root server. You can see the zone files for network 172.168.0.0 and network 172.168.0.0-255 are the same. We need two definitions because the first one (0.168.172) is for local requests and the second (0-255.0.168.172) is for resolving requests from the root server in case someone else requests reverse resolution in this network (172.168.0.0) from the root server. The root server will ask the server serving this network (172.168.0.0) for the information (in our example, the server for the "first.itso" domain). Refer to 8.5.1, "Setting up the root DNS" on page 184 to see how the root server setup is done to pass requests to servers in subdomains.

2. Create the directory /var/named.

3. Create the zone file /var/named/named.ca with the following entries:

```
.  3600000 IN NS nf5000.itso
nf5000.itso  3600000     A 172.168.0.1
```

In this file we define master (root) DNS in our network.

4. Create the zone file /var/named/first.itso with the following entries:

```
@       IN      SOA     nf5500.first.itso. root.first.itso. (
                                1997022700 ; Serial
                                28800      ; Refresh
                                14400      ; Retry
                                3600000    ; Expire
                                86400 )    ; Minimum
;
 NS nf5500 ; Name Server
 MX 10 mail ; Mail Server
;
localhost A 127.0.0.1
nf5500 A 172.168.0.10
mail CNAME nf5500
```

In this file we create definitions for all the computers in network 172.168.0.0.

5. Create the zone file /var/named/0.168.172.in-addr.arpa with the following entries:

```
@       IN      SOA     nf5500.first.itso. root.first.itso. (
                                1997022700 ; Serial
                                28800      ; Refresh
                                14400      ; Retry
                                3600000    ; Expire
                                86400 )    ; Minimum
                NS      nf5500.first.itso.
1 PTR nf5000.itso.
10 PTR nf5500.fisrt.itso.
```

In this file we define reverse address resolution for network 172.168.0.0.

6. Create the zone file /var/named/named.local with the following entries:

```
@       IN      SOA     nf5500.first.itso. root.first.itso.  (
                                1997022700 ; Serial
                                28800      ; Refresh
                                14400      ; Retry
                                3600000    ; Expire
                                86400  )   ; Minimum
                NS      nf5500.first.itso.
1       IN      PTR     localhost.
```

7. Start the server with the command:

   `/etc/rc.d/init/named start`

8.5.3 Setting up the DNS for the second subdomain

Before you start configuring DNS, you need to check if the DNS server is installed. You can do this by following the instructions in 8.5.1, "Setting up the root DNS" on page 184.

After you have checked all prerequisites, follow these steps to set up the DNS for the "second.itso" domain:

1. Create the /etc/named.conf file with the following entries:

```
// generated by named-bootconf.pl
options {
directory "/var/named";
/*
 * If there is a firewall between you and nameservers you want
 * to talk to, you might need to uncomment the query-source
 * directive below.  Previous versions of BIND always asked
 * questions using port 53, but BIND 8.1 uses an unprivileged
 * port by default.
 */
// query-source address * port 53;
};
//
// a caching only nameserver config
//
zone "." {
type hint;
file "named.ca";
};
zone "0.0.127.in-addr.arpa" {
type master;
file "named.local";
};
zone "second.itso" {
notify no;
type master;
file "second.itso";
};
zone "0.168.192.in-addr.arpa" {
notify no;
type master;
file "0.168.192.in-addr.arpa";
};
zone "0-255.0.192.168.in-addr.arpa" {
type master;
file "0.168.192.in-addr.arpa";
};
```

As you can see we defined the zone for the root domain "." and the zone for "first.itso" domain. We also defined zones for reverse address resolution for local, network 192.168.0.0 and for network 192.168.0.0-255, which serves the requests from the root server. You can see the zone files for network 192.168.0.0 and network 192.168.0.0-255 are the same. We need two definitions because the first one (0.168.192) is for local requests and the second (0-255.0.192.168) is for resolving requests from the root server in case someone else requests reverse resolution in this network (192.168.0.0) from the root server. The root server will ask the server serving this network (192.168.0.0) for the information (in our example, the server for the "first.itso" domain). Refer to 8.5.1, "Setting up the root DNS" on page 184 to see how root server setup is done to pass requests to servers in subdomains.

2. Create the directory /var/named.

3. Create the zone file /var/named/named.ca with the following entries:

```
. 3600000 IN NS nf5000.itso
nf5000.itso   3600000      A 192.168.0.1
```

In this file we define the master (root) DNS in our network.

4. Create the zone file /var/named/second.itso with the following entries:

```
@          IN       SOA      nf7000m10.second.itso. root.second.itso. (
                             1997022700 ; Serial
                             28800      ; Refresh
                             14400      ; Retry
                             3600000    ; Expire
                             86400 )    ; Minimum
;
 NS nf7000m10 ; Name Server
 MX 10 mail ; Mail Server
;
localhost A 127.0.0.1
nf7000m10 A 192.168.0.10
mail CNAME nf7000m10
client A 192.168.0.20
```

In this file we create definitions for all computers in network 192.168.0.0.

5. Create the zone file /var/named/0.168.192.in-addr.arpa with the following entries:

```
@          IN       SOA      nf7000m10.second.itso. root.second.itso.
           (                 1997022700 ; Serial
                             28800      ; Refresh
                             14400      ; Retry
                             3600000    ; Expire
                             86400 )    ; Minimum
                    NS       nf7000m10.second.itso.
1 PTR nf5000.itso.
10 PTR nf7000m10.second.itso.
20 PTR client.second.itso.
```

In this file we define reverse address resolution for network 192.168.0.0.

6. Create the zone file /var/named/named.local with the following entries:

```
@        IN      SOA     nf7000m10.second.itso. root.second.itso. (
                                 1997022700 ; Serial
                                 28800      ; Refresh
                                 14400      ; Retry
                                 3600000    ; Expire
                                 86400 )    ; Minimum
                 NS      nf7000m10.second.itso.
1        IN      PTR     localhost.
```

7. Start the server with the command:

   /etc/rc.d/init/named start

You now have three DNS servers running. The network is ready for the setup of the mail server.

8.5.4 Setting up Sendmail

All documentation on Sendmail will tell you that the Sendmail configuration file /etc/sendmail.cf is a nightmare for a network administrator. This is not entirely true; when you do not need any special features offered by Sendmail, the setup is fairly easy. You just need to modify the generic macro files slightly and recreate the new sendmail.cf with the "m4" macro processor. In this section we explain how to set up Sendmail for handling mail in its own domain. Caldera OpenLinux comes with generic macro file for Sendmail. The file is located in the /usr/share/sendmail/cf/cf and is called generic-col2.2.mc. This file just needs a little modification to become a working file on your server. Follow these steps to set up your mail servers:

1. Make a copy of Caldera OpenLinux generic macro file with the command:

   cp /usr/share/sendmail/cf/cf/generic-col2.2.mc
   /usr/share/sendmail/cf/cf/mydomain.mc

2. Add the following lines to mydomain.mc file:

   a. For the server in "first.itso" domain:

```
dnl ##############################################################
dnl # Definitions for sample domain
dnl # we define PSEUDONYMS, DEFAULT_HOST
define(`PSEUDONYMS', `nf5500.first.itso' `first.itso')
define(`DEFAULT_HOST', 'nf5500.first.itso')
dnl ##############################################################
```

   b. For the server in "second.itso" domain:

```
dnl ################################################################
dnl # Definitions for sample domain
dnl # we define PSEUDONYMS, DEFAULT_HOST
define(`PSEUDONYMS', `nf7000m10.second.itso' `second.itso')
define(`DEFAULT_HOST', 'nf7000m10.second.itso')
dnl ################################################################
```

3. Create a new sendmail.cf file with your domain file by executing the command:

```
/usr/bin/m4 /usr/share/sendmail/cf/m4/cf.m4
/usr/share/sendmail/cf/cf/mydomain.cf
/usr/share/sendmail/cf/feature/relay_entire_domain.m4 >
/etc/sendmail.cf
```

This can be a lot easier if your current directory is /usr/share/sendmail/cf:

```
/usr/bin/m4 m4/cf.m4 cf/mydomain.cf feature/relay_entire_domain.m4 >
/etc/sendmail.cf
```

As you can see we used two more files in order to create the configuration file:

   a. cf.m4 must be used, otherwise files will not be parsed correctly.

   b. relay_entire_domain.m4 is used to enable clients, which are accessing the mail server with remote clients, to send mail through this server.

4. Modify the /etc/sendmail.cw file:

   a. For the server in "first.itso" domain add the line:

   ```
   first.itso
   ```

   a. For the server in "second.itso" domain add the line:

   ```
   second.itso
   ```

   The /etc/sendmail.cw includes all aliases for your mail server. You need to include the domain name; otherwise, mail will be undeliverable.

5. Start the server with the command:

   ```
   /etc/rc.d/init.d/mta start
   ```

If you want Sendmail to start automatically when the server is started follow the instructions in 4.2.3, "Starting Samba as startup service" on page 134, but instead of selecting **SMB server process (samba)** you select **Mail Transfer Agent**.

You need to execute all the previous instructions on the servers in both domains (first.itso and second.itso) if you want to send mail from one domain to another.

8.5.4.1 Configure Sendmail for mail routing

By default Sendmail can deliver mail to a defined user if it can reach the mail server for the user's domain. So, for example, if you are on an internal network and your Sendmail server does not have direct connection to the Internet you can configure Sendmail to route mail through another reachable mail server, which is connected to the Internet. To do this you need to enter the appropriate values into the /etc/sendmail/mailertable file. For example, if you want to route the mail for `otherdomain.com` through `reachableserver`, then your /etc/sendmail/mailertable file will look similar to this:

```
#
# /etc/mailertable
#
# This file can be used to fine-tune sendmail's email routing.
# After you change this file, you must rebuild the DB file using
# /usr/sbin/makemap hash /etc/sendmail/mailertable < /etc/sendmail/mailer
#
otherdomain. smtp:reachableserver
```

This means that all mail for `otherdomain` will be routed to the `reachableserver` mail server with the SMTP protocol. The domain name must always have a "." dot at the end. With this setup you can route mail from server to server until it reaches its destination.

Whenever you modify the /etc/sendmail/mailertable file, you need to rebuild the /etc/sendmail/mailertable.db file, which is really the file used by Sendmail to perform routing tasks. You can do this by executing the command:

```
/usr/sbin/makemap hash /etc/sendmail/mailertable <
/etc/sendmail/mailertable
```

If you want all your mail to be routed to another server, you may do this by appending the following line to the /etc/sendmail/mailertable file:

```
smtp:smartserver
```

Where `smartserver` is the mail server that will handle all mail from your Sendmail server.

8.5.5 Setting up the mail client

Each mail user needs a user name/password on the server that is running mail server (in our case Sendmail). After the user has a user name/password, he can reach his mailbox remotely. In this section we show how to set up the Netscape mail setting for sending and receiving mail.

> **Note**
>
> The POP3 server must be installed and running before you can set up the client.

Follow these steps to set up the Netscape mail properties:

1. Start Netscape.
2. Select **Edit > Preferences > Mail & Newsgroups > Identity** and you will see a window similar to Figure 161.

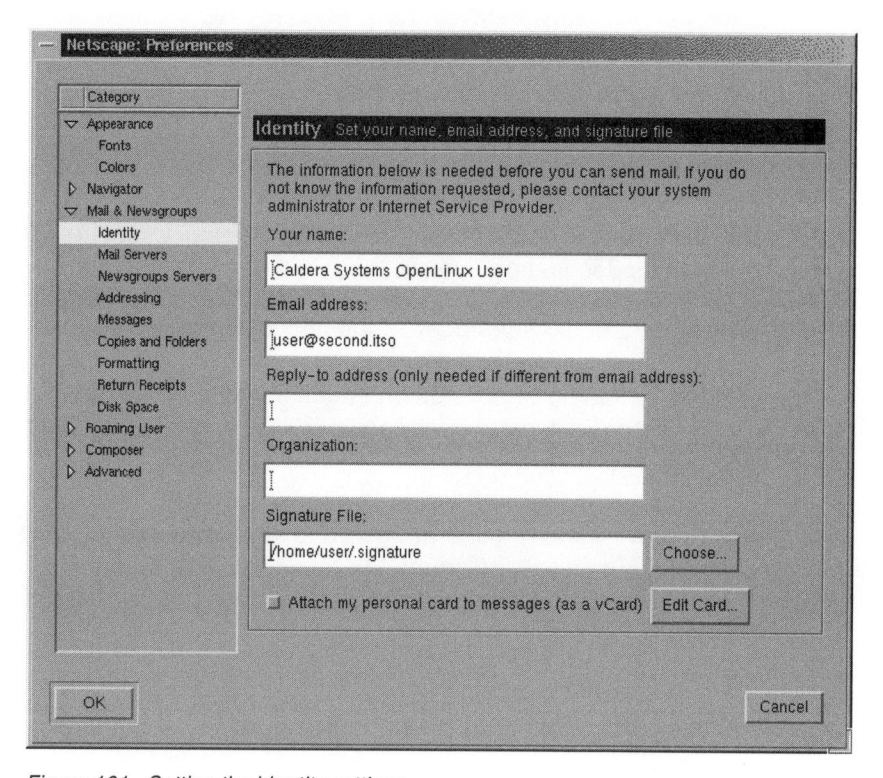

Figure 161. Setting the identity settings

3. Type in required values and select **Mail Servers.** You will see a window similar to Figure 162.

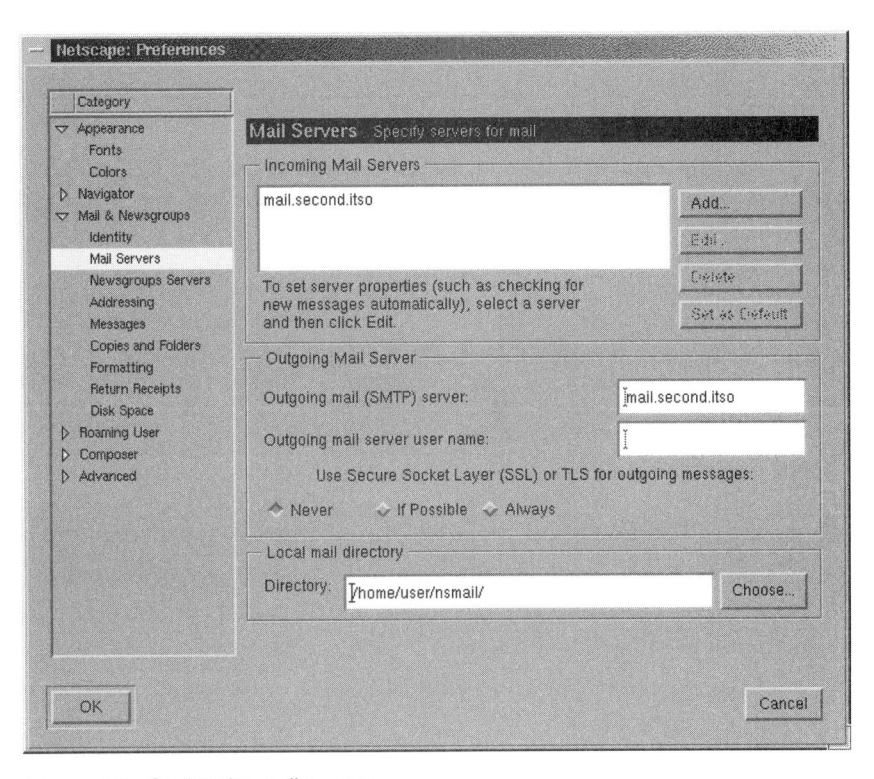

Figure 162. Setting the mail servers

4. In the Outgoing mail (SMTP) server field type your mail server address (in our example, "mail.second.itso").

5. In the Incoming Mail Server section, select the current server and click **Edit**, and you will see a window similar to Figure 163.

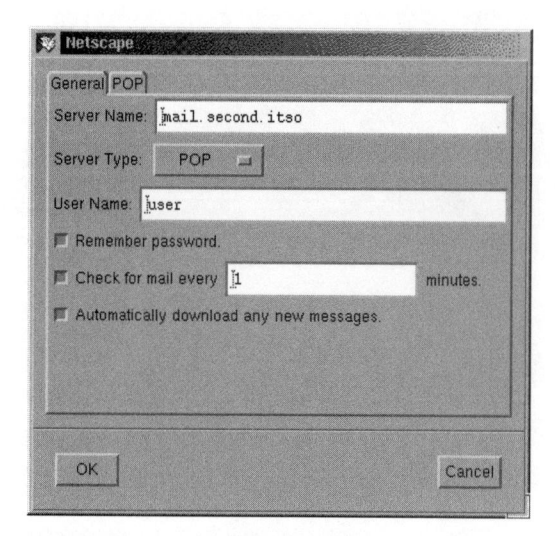

Figure 163. Setting POP3 server

6. In the Server Name field, type in the address of your mail server.

7. In the User Name field, type in your user name on the mail server. You can also configure some other options that will affect your mail reading. Click **OK** to continue.

8. When you are back in the Preferences window, click **OK** to store your new mail settings.

Now you are ready to send mail to all the users in the "first.itso" and "second.itso" domain.

8.6 Sources of additional information

You can find more information on the official Web site of the Sendmail project:

```
http://www.sendmail.org
```

And there are always good how-to documents at the Linux Documentation project Web site:

```
http://www.linuxdoc.org/
```

Chapter 9. LDAP - Lightweight Directory Access Protocol

LDAP has become a buzzword in the IT world. The exciting thing about LDAP and directory services is that they can be used for so many purposes. This chapter will give you a brief explanation of what LDAP is, what it can be used for, basic structures, and simple implementation on the Linux OS. This chapter merely scratches the surface of what is actually possible with LDAP.

9.1 What is LDAP?

LDAP stands for Lightweight Directory Access Protocol. LDAP has become an Internet standard for directory services that run over TCP/IP. LDAP is a client/server protocol for accessing a directory service. Originally designed as a front end for X.500 databases, LDAP is now commonly used in a stand-alone capacity. IBM, Netscape, Sun, Novell, Microsoft, and many other companies are incorporating LDAP into their directory structures.

9.1.1 Directory Services

A directory service is the collection of software, hardware, processes, policies, and administrative procedures involved in making the information in a directory available to the users of the directory.

A directory is similar to a database. However, directories and databases differ in the number of times they are searched and updated. Directories are tuned for being searched, while relational databases are geared toward maintaining data with a frequent number of updates.

Examples of directories would be the Yellow Pages, a card catalog, or an address book. Information is organized in a defined hierarchy and given attributes.

When we place a directory online, the data becomes dynamic in the sense that it can be easily updated and cross-referenced. Unlike printed material, any updates that occur are instantaneous for all users.

You can apply security to the directory so that only intended users can view, modify, or create data. This security can be based upon groups, individual users, or any other authentication scheme. The data can also be encrypted.

Directory services typically involve data distribution and replication. The advantages of distributing your directory services are performance, availability, and reliability. For a segmented network, distribution of servers containing the directory data improves performance by reducing network traffic and load on individual servers. By replicating your data on multiple servers you increase availability in case a single server should go down.

9.1.2 X.500

In the mid-1980s, the International Telecommunications Union (ITU, formerly the CCITT) and the International Organization for Standardization (ISO) merged their efforts on directory services standards and created X.500. The X.500 specifications consist of a series of recommendations on the concepts, models, authentication, distribution, attributes, objects, and replication that underlie an X.500 directory service.

Early X.500 implementations used a client access protocol known as DAP. DAP is thick, complicated, and difficult to implement for desktop computers. For all of these reasons other lighter-weight protocols were developed. As predecessors to LDAP, DIXIE and DAS were very successful. Out of this success a group from the Internet Engineering Task Force (IETF) began work on LDAP. The first Request for Change (RFC1487) describing LDAP was released in July 1993.

9.2 How can I use LDAP?

LDAP can allow system and network administrators to centrally manage users, groups, devices, and other data. IT decision makers can avoid tying themselves to a single vendor for applications and operating systems. Developers can use LDAP-based standards to ensure cross-platform integration.

Some practical applications of LDAP-based directory services include:

- Corporate address book
- User administration
- Domain Name System

9.3 LDAP basics

The LDAP information model is based on objects. Objects can be people, printers, servers, or just about anything you can think of. The most basic unit of the LDAP model is the entry. An entry is a collection of information about an object. Each entry belongs to an object class that determines required and optional attributes. Each attribute has a type and one or more values. The type describes the kind of information contained in the attribute and the value contains the actual data.

9.3.1 LDIF files

An LDIF file is the standard way of representing directory data in a textual format. This format can typically be used for importing and exporting directory data. The following is an LDIF file for loading the LDAP directory and adding a user in the Netscape roaming profiles directory:

```
dn: o=ibm.com
objectclass: top

dn: ou=People,o=ibm.com
objectclass: top
objectclass: organizationalUnit

dn: cn=username, ou=People, o=ibm.com
objectclass: top
objectclass: organizationalUnit
cn: username
userpassword: secret

dn: ou=Roaming,o=ibm.com
objectclass: top
objectclass: organizationalUnit

dn: nsLIProfileName=username,ou=Roaming,o=ibm.com
objectclass: top
objectclass: nsLIProfile
nsliprofilename: username
owner: cn=username,ou=People,o=ibm.com
```

Each LDAP entry must have a distinguished name (DN). The distinguished name is a unique key that refers to that entry specifically.

> **Note**
>
> When importing LDIF files, watch for additional white space, spelling, and case. OpenLDAP will treat all of these differently. Authentication errors can usually be linked back to errors with the LDIF file.

9.4 Implementation on Linux

Caldera OpenLinux comes with OpenLDAP package Version 1.2.3-1. This version will not work with the Netscape roaming profiles, which were used in our explanation of OpenLDAP.

Before you proceed with this chapter make sure that the original OpenLDAP package is not installed. You can do this by using the kpackage tool from the KDE menus. When you start kpackage, OpenLDAP can be found by clicking **Server -> Network**. You will see a window similar to Figure 164.

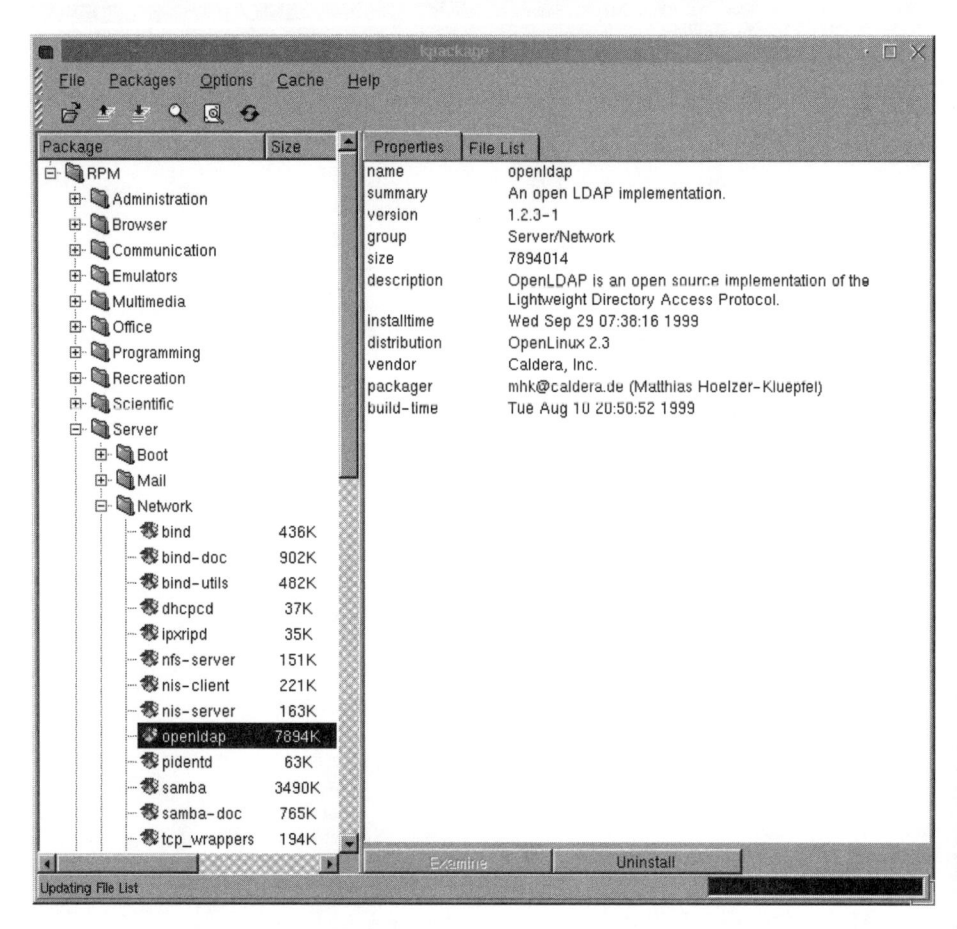

Figure 164. Checking if OpenLDAP is installed

Note

Do not forget to uninstall the originally installed OpenLDAP package if you want to use Netscape roaming profiles.

9.4.1 Downloading and installing OpenLDAP

Although Caldera OpenLinux includes a source package of OpenLDAP, a patch needs to be applied to the source before compilation. The recommended way is to download the latest stable version and the patch from the official OpenLDAP ftp site: `ftp://ftp.openldap.org`. The patch addresses inconsistencies between OpenLDAP and Netscape's LDAP implementations. The patch will not be incorporated into later releases of OpenLDAP. OpenLDAP's position is that their current implementation is more consistent with the LDAP precedent.

Download the latest stable version of OpenLDAP from:

```
ftp.openldap.org/pub/openldap
```

Download the Netscape patch (Albert-FitzPatrick-990519.gz) from:

```
ftp.openldap.org/pub/openldap/incoming/
```

Unpack OpenLDAP by typing:

```
tar -xvzf openldap-stable.tgz
```

Apply the patch before compilation and installation.

```
gunzip < Albert-FitzPatrick-990519.tar.gz > roaming.patch
cd ldap/servers/slapd
patch < ../../../roaming.patch
cd ../.. (ldap)
```

Begin the Installation procedures:

```
./configure
make depend
make
cd tests
```

The following step will test OpenLDAP. Pay attention to any errors.

```
make
cd ..
make install
```

OpenLDAP is now installed.

9.4.2 Roaming Profiles for Netscape

In order to set up roaming profiles we need the Netscape directory schema. You can download the roaming-073099.tar.gz file, which contains the slapd.oc.conf file, the slapd.at.conf file, and an excellent sample slapd.conf file, from:

```
http://www.openldap.org/incoming/roaming-073099.tar.gz
```

Or make the following additions to the slapd.oc.conf and slapd.ac.conf files. The following lines belong at the end of /usr/local/etc/openldap/slapd.oc.conf:

```
#from netscape to implement roaming access...
objectclass nsLIPtr
#       oid 2.16.840.1.113730.3.2.74
        requires
                objectclass
        allows
                nsLIPtrURL,
                owner


objectclass nsLIProfile
#       oid 2.16.840.1.113730.3.2.75
        requires
                objectclass,
                nsLIProfileName
        allows
                nsLIPrefs,
                uid,
                owner


objectclass nsLIProfileElement
#       oid 2.16.840.1.113730.3.2.76
        requires
                objectclass,
                nsLIElementType
        allows
                owner,
                nsLIData
                nsLIVersion


objectclass nsLIServer
#       oid 2.16.840.1.113730.3.2.77
        requires
                objectclass,
                serverhostname
        allows
                description,
```

```
                cn,
                nsServerPort,
                nsLIServerType,
                serverroot
```

> **Note**
>
> Make sure that you comment out the oid entries in the slapd.oc.conf.

Add the following lines at the end of /usr/local/etc/openldap/slapd.at.conf:

```
# ns-mcd-li-schema.conf
#
# Netscape Mission Control Desktop Roaming Access schema
#
attribute nsLIPtrURL        2.16.840.1.113730.3.1.399       ces
attribute nsLIPrefs         2.16.840.1.113730.3.1.400       ces
attribute nsLIProfileName   2.16.840.1.113730.3.1.401       cis
attribute nsLIData          2.16.840.1.113730.3.1.402       bin
attribute nsLIElementType   2.16.840.1.113730.3.1.403       cis
attribute nsLIServerType    2.16.840.1.113730.3.1.404       cis
attribute nsLIVersion       2.16.840.1.113730.3.1.405       bin
attribute nsServerPort      2.16.840.1.113730.3.1.280 cis
```

More information on the Netscape directory schema and roaming profiles can be found at:

```
http://help.netscape.com/products/client/communicator/manual_roaming2.h
tml
```

Create the directory to store OpenLDAP server database files:

```
mkdir /usr/ldap_db
```

Modify your slapd.conf file to support roaming profiles. Replace `ibm.com` with the name of your organization.

```
#
# See slapd.conf(5) for details on configuration options.
# This file should NOT be world readable.
#
include /usr/local/etc/openldap/slapd.at.conf
include /usr/local/etc/openldap/slapd.oc.conf
schemacheck off
lastmod on
#referral ldap://ldap.itd.umich.edu

pidfile /usr/local/var/slapd.pid
```

```
argsfile /usr/local/var/slapd.args

###########################################################
# ldbm database definitions
###########################################################

database: ldbm
suffix "o=ibm.com"
directory /usr/tmp
rootdn "cn=root, o=ibm.com"
rootpw secret
# cleartext passwords, especially for the rootdn, should
# be avoid.  See slapd.conf(5) for details.
access to * by * write
access to * by * compare
access to * by * read
```

> **Stop**
>
> The permissions specified in the last three lines are extremely insecure and should only be used for testing purposes. See the slapd.conf man page for more information about setting up appropriate permissions for your environment.

9.4.3 Starting OpenLDAP server

To start the OpenLDAP server, you need to run the slapd program. Type the following command:

```
/usr/libexec/slapd (-d 255 for debugging information).
```

With slapd successfully running, we now need to load the initial database. Create an LDIF file like the one on page 201. Replace `Username` with your user name and `ibm.com` with your organization name.

Once you have created, for example, the entries.ldif file, add the data from that file to the database by executing the command:

```
/usr/local/bin/ldapadd -D "cn=root, o=ibm.com" -w secret -f entries.ldif
```

9.4.4 Configuring Netscape

The final step is to configure your Netscape browser.

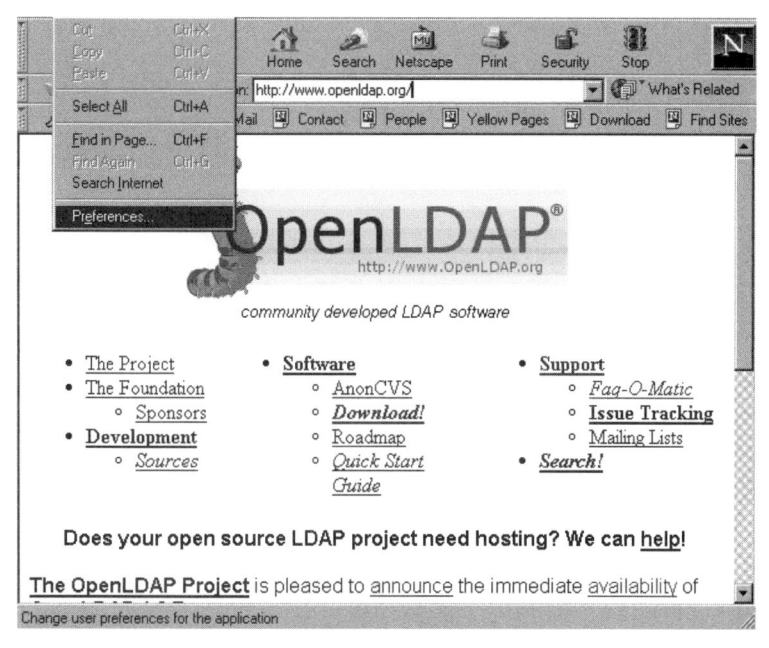

Figure 165. Configuring your browser

1. From the Edit drop-down menu, select **Preferences**.

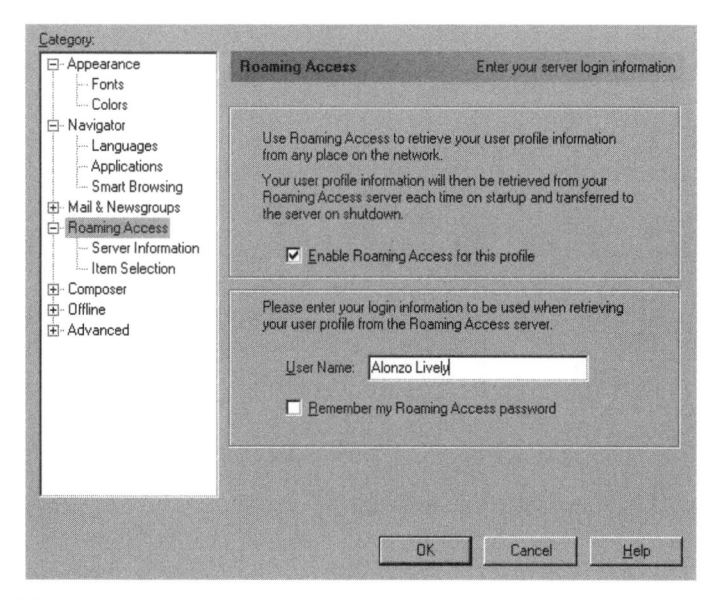

Figure 166. Configuring Netscape

Chapter 9. LDAP - Lightweight Directory Access Protocol

2. Click the **Roaming User** tab, and you will see a window similar to Figure 166.
3. Click the **Enable Roaming Access for this profile** check box.
4. Enter the user name.

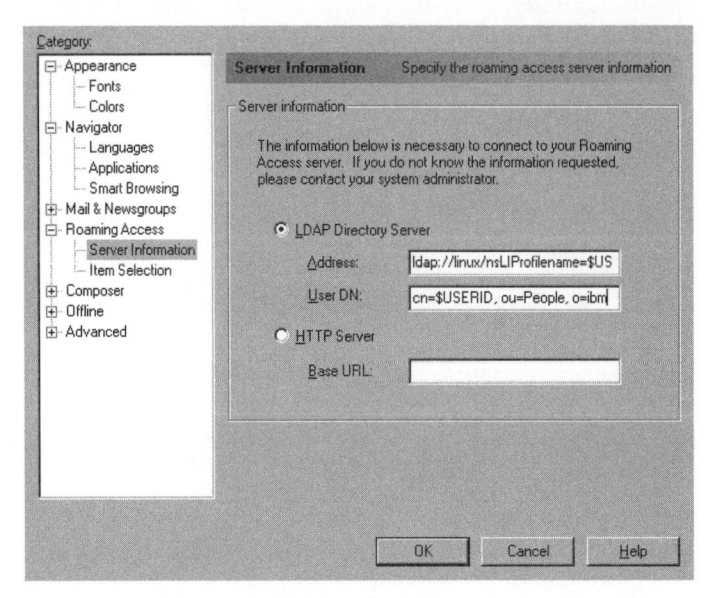

Figure 167. Configuring Netscape 2

5. Click **Server Information**, and you will see a window similar to Figure 167.
6. In the Address field under LDAP Directory Server, enter:

    ldap://linuxbox/nsLIProfilename=$USERID, ou=Roaming, o=ibm.com

    Replace `linuxbox` with the hostname of the OpenLDAP server and `ibm.com` with the name of your organization (specified in the slapd.conf).

7. In the User DN field under LDAP Directory Server, type in:

    cn=$USERID, ou=People, o=ibm.com

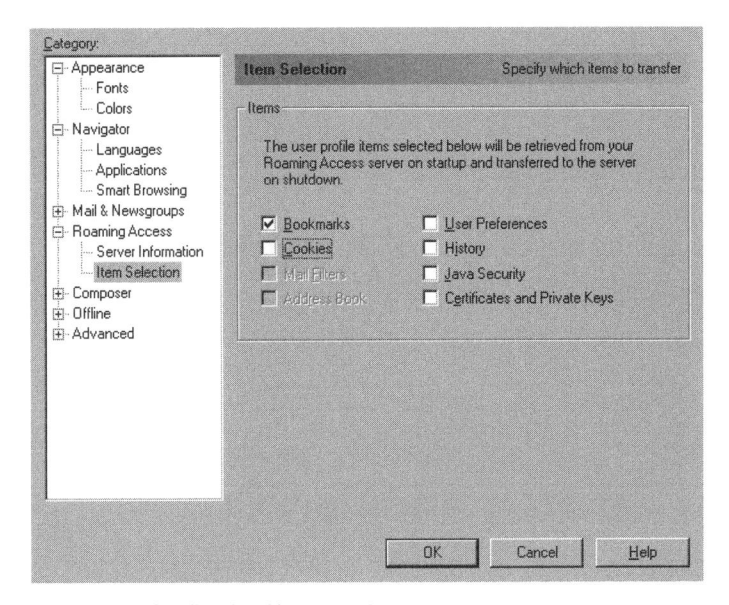

Figure 168. Configuring Netscape 3

8. Click **Item Selection**, and you will see a window similar to Figure 168.
9. Select the items you would like to synchronize with the OpenLDAP server.
10. Restart Netscape and you are are all set. Congratulations!

9.5 Sources of additional information

- LDAP how-tos are available from the Linux Documentation project Web site:

    http://www.linuxdoc.org

- OpenLDAP home page includes key information, including a post from Phil Allred regarding Netscape roaming profiles and OpenLDAP:

    http://www.OpenLDAP.org

- *Understanding and Deploying LDAP Directory Services,* by Timothy Howes, Mark Smith, and Gordon Good, Macmillan Publishing, 1999.

Chapter 10. NIS - Network Information System

In a distributed computing environment, maintenance of password files, groups, and host files can be a major task. Consistency is possibly the biggest difficulty. For example, when a user changes their password on one machine, ideally it would be propagated to any other machine they had accounts on. When a network is composed of hundreds or thousands of machines, this convenience becomes a necessity. NIS is one way of addressing some of these problems.

10.1 What is NIS?

Network Information System (NIS) is a service designed to provide a distributed database system for common configuration files. NIS servers manage copies of the database files. NIS clients request the information from the NIS server instead of using their own configuration files.

NIS is built on the client/server model. A NIS server contains data files called maps. These maps are owned by the NIS master and can only be updated by the master. There are NIS slave servers that replicate from the master. When there is a change to a master server's map, this change is then distributed to all the slave servers. Clients are hosts that request information from these maps but are not allowed to modify them.

10.2 How can I use NIS?

NIS is typically used to centrally manage commonly replicated configuration files. Examples of common configuration files are:

- /etc/hosts
- /etc/passwd
- /etc/group

10.3 Implementation on Linux

To introduce the concepts behind NIS, we will create a map of our password file kept on the NIS master server. This will allow users to log in to NIS clients without having to maintain an account on each box. Centralized administration is a key benefit of using NIS.

A note on security: Before deciding to put NIS in a production environment, please consider the security implications of passing sensitive data across the network. You may wish to take a look at NIS+, which has strong encryption as well as additional maintenance implications.

Packages that need to be installed for a NIS client and the NIS server:

- nis-client-2.0-8
- nis-server-2.0-8

The /etc/nsswitch.conf file determines the order of lookups performed.

Sample /etc/nsswitch.conf file:

```
# /etc/nsswitch.conf
#
# Name Service Switch configuration file.
#
passwd : compat
shadow : compat
group : compat
#
hosts : files dns nis
networks : nis files dns
#
ethers : nis files
protocols : nis files
rpc : nis files
services : nis files
```

> **Note**
>
> You should remove NIS reference from all the options where you do not use the NIS server for coordination.

10.3.1 NIS Server

The configuration files for the NIS server in Caldera OpenLinux are located in the directory /etc/nis. To set up a NIS server on your Caldera OpenLinux server, follow these steps:

1. Decide on a NIS domain name. This name does not need to be equal to the domain name of the server because it only has to be unique among adjacent domains, not worldwide.

2. Create a directory /etc/nis/nisdomainname. In our example we used domain name "nis.com". We created a directory by executing this command:

    `mkdir /etc/nis/nis.com`

3. You can define the NIS domain using COAS. Click on the **K** sign on the panel, select **COAS** -> **Network** -> **TCP/IP** -> **NIS**. See Figure 169.

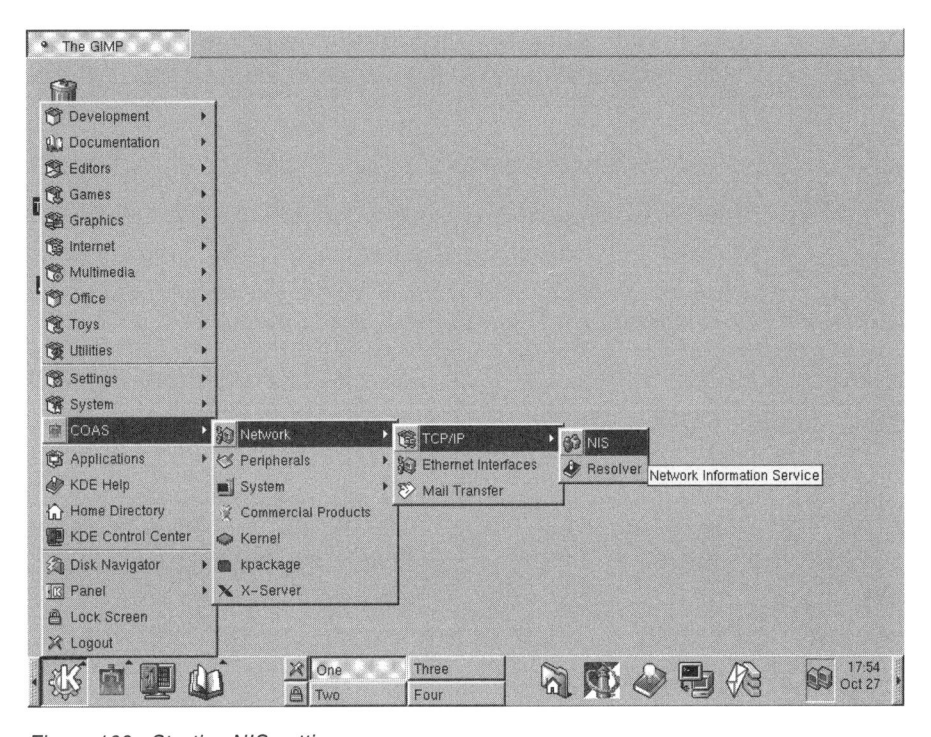

Figure 169. Starting NIS settings

After the NIS configuration is started you will see a window similar to Figure 170.

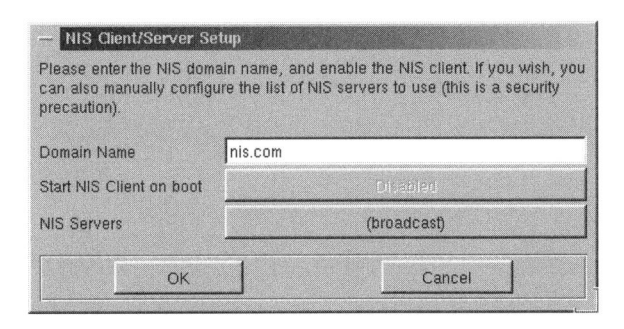

Figure 170. NIS properties

4. In the Domain Name field, type in your domain name. In our example type in `nis.com`.

Chapter 10. NIS - Network Information System **213**

5. Click **OK** to continue, **Save** on the next window and to finish select **Done** on the last window or wait until the window closes automatically.

6. Create symbolic links of all files you want to have shared in the local network into /etc/nis/nisdomainname. In our example we want to have password and group files distributed, so we created symbolic links for these files:

   ```
   ln -s /etc/passwd /etc/nis/nis.com/passwd
   ln -s /etc/shadow /etc/nis/nis.com/shadow
   ln -s /etc/group /etc/nis/nis.com/group
   ```

7. Copy /etc/nis/.nisupdate.conf.sample to the directory for your domain, in our example /etc/nis/nis.com, with the filename changed to .nisupdate.conf, by executing the command:

   ```
   cp /etc/nis/.nisupdate.conf.sample /etc/nis/nis.com/.nisupdate.conf
   ```

   This file is used to update or create maps used by the NIS server. Edit this file for the maps you want.

8. Run /etc/nis/nis_update. You will see a window similar to Figure 171. By executing this command all NIS domain directories are scanned and the files for the NIS server are created in the directory /var/nis.

```
[root@nf5000 nis]# ls -l
total 13
drwx------   2 root     root         1024 Oct 27 18:00 nis.com
-rwxr-xr-x   1 root     root         8453 Feb  4  1999 nis_update
-rw-r--r--   1 root     root          808 Oct 27 17:58 passwd
-rw-------   1 root     root          540 Oct 27 17:58 shadow
-rw-r--r--   1 root     root           64 Sep 10  1996 shells
[root@nf5000 nis]# ./nis_update
Processing domain nis.com
Updating nis.com/passwd
Updating nis.com/group
[root@nf5000 nis]#
```

Figure 171. After executing nis_update

Do this every time one of the files used by NIS server changes. If you examine this script you can find examples of which files to put into the NIS environment as well.

9. Start the NIS server by executing the command:

   ```
   /etc/rc.d/init/nis-server start
   ```

If you want the NIS server to start automatically when the server is started, follow the instructions in 4.2.3, "Starting Samba as startup service" on page 134, but instead of selecting **SMB server process (samba)** select **NIS--Network Information Service (server part)**.

Take a look at /var/yp/securenets. This file defines the access rights to your NIS server. By default it is set to give access to everyone. Change it accordingly (see man securenets).

To test our NIS server setup we will use the `rpcinfo` command:

```
rpcinfo -u localhost ypserv
```

You should see:

```
program 100004 version 1 ready and waiting
program 100004 version 2 ready and waiting
```

To test our NIS master server, we need to set up a client to run ypbind, which is a client for NIS servers.

10.3.2 NIS Client

The client can be set up with COAS. Follow these steps to set up the NIS client:

1. Start the NIS configuration as we described in 10.3.1, "NIS Server" on page 212. When you start the NIS configuration you will see a window similar to Figure 172.

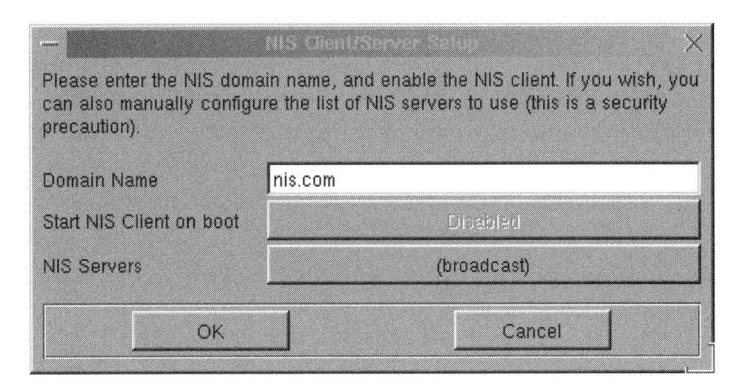

Figure 172. Configuring the NIS client

2. In the Domain Name field, type in the NIS domain name.
3. Click the **NIS Servers** button. You will see a window similar to Figure 173.

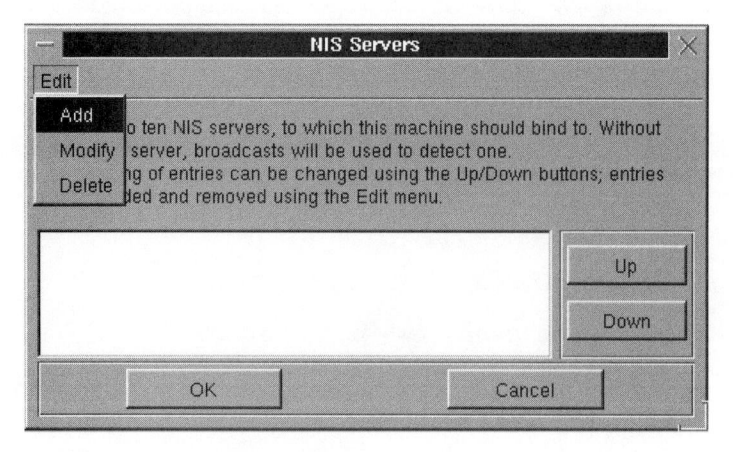

Figure 173. Adding NIS server

4. In **Edit** menu select **Add.** You will see a window similar to Figure 174.

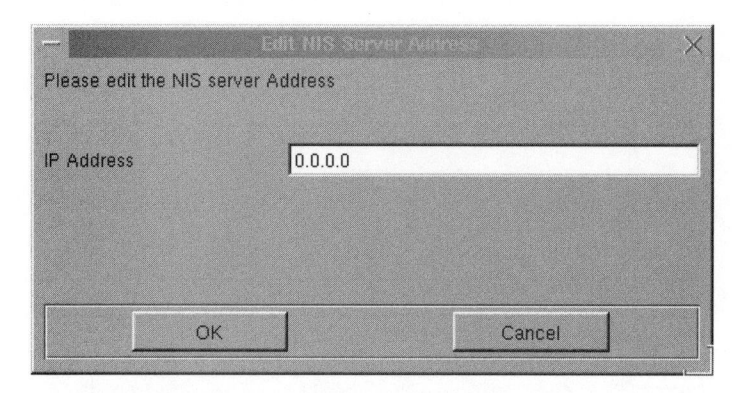

Figure 174. Specifying the address of NIS server

5. Type in the hostname or the IP address of your NIS server. Click **OK** to continue. You will see a window similar to Figure 175.

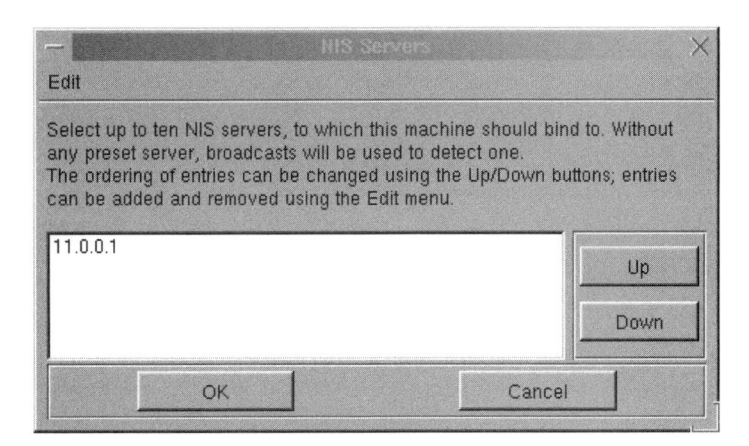

Figure 175. After defining the NIS server

6. Click **OK** to continue. Select **Save** at the next window, and you will see that your NIS client will be restarted. Click **Done** to finish the setup or wait until the window closes automatically.

7. Start the NIS client by executing the command:

   /etc/rc.d/init/nis-client start

If you want the NIS client to start automatically when the server is started follow the instructions in 4.2.3, "Starting Samba as startup service" on page 134, but instead of selecting **SMB server process (samba)** select **NIS--Network Information Service (client part)**.

To test our NIS configuration we will use the ypcat command:

   ypcat passwd

You should see output similar to Figure 176.

```
[root@test2 /root]# ypcat passwd
john:$1$Zx1Q62xM$XtP3v8/gPirZVQKK5/0hC1:501:501::/home/john:/bin/bash
ayne:$1$t/sEma1W$nLzLUZDsAUICeaXAg3f2z/:502:502::/home/ayne:/bin/bash
karri:$1$SZ5F27Vc$gI5Gc6.yDDjwLC42jSwCR1:507:510::/home/karri:/bin/bash
otto:$1$ctpEVbLK$W8Z9rX.SndoUTaqWyxCUu.:501:504::/home/otto:/bin/bash
bob:$1$NLcH9/fP$zbmyKDzEcH37ENu9hB22C.:502:505::/home/bob:/bin/bash
sammy:$1$HFgmti3X$H8d11enyorUkj10Ba8/pm/:508:511::/home/sammy:/bin/bash
tina:$1$xow9ZBpk$CGD5jBgBy5Xe11.pnI2BQ1:504:507::/home/tina:/bin/bash
ivo:$1$0MaQooFS$Hp1C3BW8msWPbL65AT1YE.:505:508::/home/ivo:/bin/bash
nancy:$1$2Z9axj.Y$WZcW/evEbx63eMzhzvuwt/:506:509::/home/nancy:/bin/bash
korry:$1$SZ5F27Vc$gI5Gc6.yDDjwLC42jSwCR1:507:510::/home/korry:/bin/bash
steve:$1$YFNxznca$fOF2yRGDu/b83elC8UF8j.:503:506::/home/steve:/bin/bash
[root@test2 /root]#
```

Figure 176. Executing ypcat passwd

Now to really test the machine, log in to a NIS client using an account that is on the NIS master server. When you log in, you should see the following:

```
Caldera OpenLinux(TM)
Version 2.3-Lone Wolf One
Copyright 1996-1999 Caldera Systems, Inc.

login: ivo
Password:
Last login: Wed Oct 27 19:22:03 1999 from 9.24.106.49 on ttyp1
No directory /home/ivo!
Logging in with home = "/".
bash$
```

Figure 177. No home directory

Since Ivo's home directory is not defined on the client box, but only on the NIS master server, we get an error when logging in. This can be fixed by creating a home directory for Ivo on the client box if necessary. Another option would be to use NFS in conjunction with NIS to automatically mount Ivo's home directory.

10.4 Sources of additional information

For further information or trouble-shooting, the NIS how-to by Thorsten Kukuk is a good place to start. Find it at
`http://www.metalab.unc.edu/pub/Linux/docs/HOWTO/NIS-HOWTO`

Managing NFS and NIS by Hal Stern is also a good resource.

Chapter 11. NFS - Network File System

Network File System (NFS) is a product developed by Sun Microsystems that allows you to share directories across the network. The directory mounts become transparent to you. You access the mounted directories just like you do any directory or filesystem on your computer. The mounting process is the same as for any filesystem or partition that you want to mount on your system. The basic foundation of this is the mount command.

In order to share directories across the network you will need two basic things:

- The system sharing the data must allow you to have access.
- The system that is using the data must originate the request and allow the mount to happen.

Both concepts will be discussed in this chapter.

11.1 The NFS process

First you need to verify that the NFS RPM package has been loaded. RPM is short for Red Hat Package Manager and is a common way of installing packages in Linux. You can do this with the command:

```
rpm -ql nfs-server
```

You will see the results as in Figure 178. This gives a listing of the contents of the RPMs that are installed when NFS is installed. NFS may have been installed by default when you first set up the system by choosing a package that included it. You can also verify if the package is installed with the kpackage utility from the COAS tools as we described in 2.5, "Adding and removing software packages using kpackage" on page 72. The nfs-server package is found by clicking **Server -> Network**.

You can install NFS manually by either using the kpackage utility or by using the following commands:

```
mount /mnt/cdrom
rpm -i /mnt/cdrom/Packages/RPMS/nfs-server-2.2beta44-3
```

The NFS package should now be installed. Now you can repeat the earlier rpm command to verify that the package is installed.

```
[root@nf5000 user]# rpm -ql nfs-server
/etc/rc.d/init.d/nfs
/etc/sysconfig/daemons/nfs
/usr/doc/nfs-server-2.2beta44
/usr/doc/nfs-server-2.2beta44/NEWS
/usr/doc/nfs-server-2.2beta44/README
/usr/man/man5/exports.5.gz
/usr/man/man8/mountd.8.gz
/usr/man/man8/nfsd.8.gz
/usr/man/man8/rpc.mountd.8.gz
/usr/man/man8/rpc.nfsd.8.gz
/usr/sbin/rpc.mountd
/usr/sbin/rpc.nfsd
[root@nf5000 user]#
```

Figure 178. Checking NFS rpms

NFS makes use of several daemons (services). Those daemons are:

- portmap - is the process that converts Remote Procedure Call (RPC) program numbers into Defense Advanced Research Projects Agency (DARPA) protocol port numbers. When a client wishes to make an RPC call to a given program number (for example, the NFS server), it will first contact portmap on the server machine to determine the port number where RPC packets should be sent.

- rpc.mountd - This handles the exporting of NFS filesystems. It looks in the /etc/exports file to figure out what to do with mount requests from various hosts.

- rpc.nfsd - this provides the user level part of the NFS process.

You can verify that the rpc.nfsd, rpc.mountd and portmap daemons are running as shown in Figure 179.

```
# ps ax | grep nfs
  323 ?          SW      0:00 [nfsd]
  324 ?          SW      0:00 [nfsd]
  325 ?          SW      0:00 [nfsd]
  326 ?          SW      0:00 [nfsd]
  327 ?          SW      0:00 [nfsd]
  328 ?          SW      0:00 [nfsd]
  329 ?          SW      0:00 [nfsd]
  330 ?          SW      0:00 [nfsd]
  662 ttyp1     S       0:00 grep nfs
#
# ps ax | grep mount
  313 ?          SW      0:00 [rpc.mountd]
  673 ttyp1     S       0:00 grep mount
#
# /etc/rc.d/init.d/portmap status
portmap (pid 192) is running...
```

Figure 179. Verifying the NFS daemons

If the portmap daemon is not running, you need to start it up first before you start up the NFS daemons. You can do this with the command:

```
/etc/rc.d/init.d/portmap start
```

Once the portmap daemon is running, you can start up the NFS daemons with the command:

```
/etc/rc.d/init.d/nfs start
```

When you start up the NFS daemon you will see the results in Figure 180.

```
[root@nf5000 user]# /etc/rc.d/init.d/nfs start
Starting NFS services:  mountd nfsd.
```

Figure 180. Starting up NFS

> **Note**
>
> If the /etc/exports file does not exist or is empty, the NFS daemons will not start. Information on setting up the /etc/exports file is in 11.2, "Allowing NFS access to data" on page 224.

To stop the NFS server you use the command:

```
/etc/rc.d/init.d/nfs stop
```

The results are shown in Figure 181. You will notice that same processes are shut down, but not necessarily in the same order.

```
[root@nf5000 user]# /etc/rc.d/init.d/nfs start
Starting NFS services:   mountd nfsd.
```

Figure 181. Stopping the NFS Server

You can restart the NFS process with the command:

    /etc/rc.d/init.d/nfs restart

This can also be used to restart the NFS process if you have made changes to the configuration files.

11.2 Allowing NFS access to data

You can give NFS access to a filesystem by setting it up in the /etc/exports file. The file is set up on the exporting server. You can create a sample file entry by opening the /etc/exports file. Then you can add an entry like:

    /usr/local/share myserver.mydomain.com(ro)

This says that the directory /usr/local/share is only accessible to the server myserver.mydomain.com.

> **Note**
>
> When exporting a filesystem you need to be sure that the exporting server can recognize and access the server that is in the /etc/exports file. You can verify this with the command:
>
> ping server_name
>
> where server_name is the name of the server you are trying to access. Otherwise, the NFS commands may hang.

There are a number of options you can set up in the /etc/exports file. Some of them are listed in Table 19.

You need to be sure that the exporting server can recognize the server name.

Table 19. Access options

Access options	
ro read only	Only permits reading
rw read write	Permits reading and writing. If both ro and rw are specified, rw takes priority.
root_squash client	Anonymous user (nobody) access from client.
no_root_squash client	Access request privileges per the privileges of the client root. Useful for diskless clients.
squash_uids and squash_gids	Specify a list of UIDs or GIDs that should be subject to anonymous mapping. A valid list of IDs looks like this: squash_uids=0-15,20,25-50
all_squash all access	Processes all requests for access as anonymous user.
anonuid=uid	root_squash or all_squash when options are set will assign a group ID to an anonymous user request.
anonuid=gid	root_squash or all_squash when options are set will assign a group ID to an anonymous user request.

A sample /etc/exports file is shown in the man pages for exports and in Figure 182.

```
# sample /etc/exports file
/                   master(rw) trusty(rw,no_root_squash)
/projects           proj*.local.domain(rw)
/usr                *.local.domain(ro) @trusted(rw)
/home/joe           pc001(rw,all_squash,anonuid=150,anongid=100)
/pub                (ro,insecure,all_squash)
/pub/private        (noaccess)
```

Figure 182. A sample /etc/exports file

The lines in the sample /etc/exports file are explained as follows:

- `# sample /etc/exports file`

    This is just a comment. Any line or character string can be converted to a comment and disabled by entering a # symbol. Everything from that point to the end of the line is considered to be a comment.

- `/              master(rw) trusty(rw,no_root_squash)`

    This says that the root directory (/) is exported to the servers:

    > `master` - whose rights are read-write.

    > `trusty` - whose rights are read-write and the access rights of the client root can be the same as the server's root.

- `/projects      proj*.local.domain(rw)`

    The directory /projects is accessible read-write to all servers whose names match the pattern proj*.local.domain. This includes proj.local.domain, proj1.local.domain, projprojproj.local.domain and so forth.

- `/usr           *.local.domain(ro) @trusted(rw)`

    Any systems whose hostname ends in .local.domain is allowed read-only access. The @trusted netgroup is allowed read-write access.

- `/home/joe      pc001(rw,all_squash,anonuid=150,anongid=100)`

    The directory /home/joe is accessible to pc001 for read-write access; all requests for access are processed as an anonymous user. The anonymous UID number is set to 150 and the anonymous group ID is set to 100. This is useful when using a client that is running PCNFS or an equivalent NFS process on the PC. Since the PC IDs do not necessarily map to the UNIX IDs, this allow the proper file attributes to be set.

- `/pub           (ro,insecure,all_squash)`

    The directory /pub is accessible as read-only. It says that option in this entry also allows clients with NFS implementations that do not use a reserved port for NFS and process all requests as an anonymous user.

- `/pub/private   (noaccess)`

    The directory /pub/private does not allow any NFS access.

11.3 Accessing data remotely with NFS

To mount a remote filesystem on your local system the mount point must exist. The mount process does not create the mount point automatically. The process of making the mount point is to use the Linux `mkdir` command. To make the /usr/local/share mount point, enter:

```
mkdir /usr/local/share
```

Typically you do not need to worry about file attributes and ownership when making an NFS mount point. The NFS access rights will usually supersede any rights established for the directory.

Once you have created the mount point, then you can use the mount command as follows:

```
mount -t nfs nfs_host:share_dir local_mount_dir
```

where:

- `-t nfs` — Says to do the mount as an NFS mount. This is now optional because if you explicitly specify the directory to be mounted as host:directory the `mount` command knows that it is an NFS mount.
- `nfs_host:share_dir` — The `nfs_host` is the host that is exporting the filesystem to be shared and `share_dir` is the actual directory that is to be shared.
- `local_mount_dir` — Is the directory on the local host where the remote directory is going to be mounted. As mentioned earlier, this mount point must exist.

11.4 Allowing NFS access to data with GUI

In Caldera OpenLinux you can also mount the NFS resources using a graphical user interface. We explained this in 2.10.1, "Mounting an NFS volume" on page 90.

Chapter 12. Packet filtering with IP Chains

Whenever you connect your computer to today's Internet world you are exposed to intruders from the outside. There are thousands of hackers just waiting to get into your computer to do damage or maybe to steal information. Therefore you need protection against them!

12.1 What is packet filtering?

As you can tell from the name, packet filtering is a kind of a filter, filtering the data coming to your computer. Packet filtering is one method commonly used in firewall implementations. With packet filtering you can implement a firewall that will protect your computer from the outside world.

Because everybody wants to communicate sooner or later you need to connect your private network to the Internet. At that point it is time to think about security. You can also use a firewall on a single computer which is for example connected to the Internet through a dial-up line. When you install a firewall to protect your internal network every computer that wants to talk to a computer on the internal network, must ask the firewall for permission. If the permission is not granted, access is denied.

12.2 What can you do with Linux packet filtering?

With Linux packet filtering you can do many things. Let us describe a few of them here:

- You can protect your internal network connected to the Internet from outside intruders.
- You can perform Network Address Translation (NAT), which allows internally connected computers without a registered Internet address to reach the Internet resources.
- You can filter the information going in or out of your internal network or just one computer.
- You can use your Linux server as a gateway between two different types of network, for example connecting token-ring and Ethernet worlds. This can be a cheap solution in comparison to buying an expensive router to this job.
- You can share your dial-up Internet connection with others.

12.3 What do you need to run packet filtering?

To set up a packet filter server with IP Chains, your Linux installation needs to meet requirements:

1. You need kernel Version 2.2.x or higher. It is recommended that you use the latest available stable version. The kernel has to be compiled with appropriate modules for IP Forwarding, IP Masquerading, and IP Firewalling. We recommend that you compile all your networking options and available modules. If you want to use your Linux server as a router, enable IP - optimize as router not host. This will also increase the routing performance.
2. Loadable kernel modules Version 2.1.121 or newer
3. IP Chains 1.3.8 or newer

The default installation of Caldera OpenLinux meets all these requirements except that the kernel is not optimized to be used as a router. So if you want to increase the performance of the routing process, you should recompile the kernel and choose the **IP - optimize as router not host** option.

12.4 Network configuration for a packet filtering implementation

In this section we will describe our lab network setup for implementing a packet filtering solution.

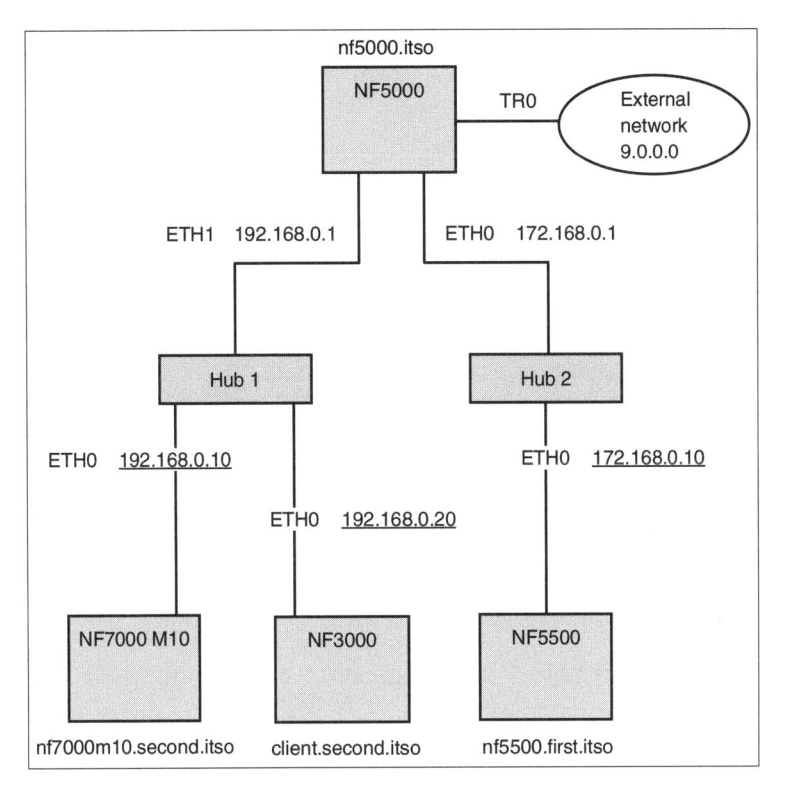

Figure 183. Lab network setup for firewall solution

Figure 183 shows our network setup:

- A Netfinity 5000 with three Network Interface Cards (NIC) is acting as a gateway. The NICs have the following settings:
    - Eth0 - 192.168.0.1
    - Eth1 - 172.168.0.1
    - Tr0 - 9.24.104.202
- A Netfinity 5500 with one NIC and the following settings:
    - Eth0 - 192.168.0.10, default gateway 192.168.0.1
- A Netfinity 7000M10 with one NIC and the following settings:
    - Eth0 - 172.168.0.10, default gateway 172.168.0.1
- A Netfinity 3000 with one NIC and the following settings:
    - Eth0 - 172.168.0.20, default gateway 172.168.0.1

You can see we have two separate networks, 192.168.0.0 and 172.168.0.0. These networks are connected to a Linux server that is acting as a gateway (router). You see that our gateway is connected to the Internet with a registered IP address. We enabled IP Forwarding on the server that was acting as a gateway.

12.5 How to permanently enable IP Forwarding

In Caldera OpenLinux the network process is started by executing this script during the server startup:

```
/etc/rc.d/init/network
```

The IP Forwarding is not enabled by default. To enable it, open the file /etc/rc.d/init/network and find the line:

```
: ${IPFORWARDING:=no}
```

and change it to:

```
: ${IPFORWARDING:=yes}
```

You need to restart network to activate the change. You can do this by executing the commands:

```
/etc/rc.d/init/network stop

/etc/rc.d/init/network start
```

Now your server is ready to act as a router. You can try this by pinging to the tr0 interface 9.24.104.202 from the machine on 172.168.0.0 network. If the ping is successful your router is working correctly. You will see a window similar to Figure 184.

```
[root@client /root]# ping 9.24.104.202
PING 9.24.104.202 (9.24.104.202): 56 data bytes
64 bytes from 9.24.104.202: icmp_seq=0 ttl=255 time=0.7 ms
64 bytes from 9.24.104.202: icmp_seq=1 ttl=255 time=0.3 ms
64 bytes from 9.24.104.202: icmp_seq=2 ttl=255 time=0.3 ms
64 bytes from 9.24.104.202: icmp_seq=3 ttl=255 time=0.3 ms
64 bytes from 9.24.104.202: icmp_seq=4 ttl=255 time=0.3 ms

--- 9.24.104.202 ping statistics ---
5 packets transmitted, 5 packets received, 0% packet loss
round-trip min/avg/max = 0.3/0.3/0.7 ms
[root@client /root]#
```

Figure 184. PING after enabling IP Forwarding

12.6 Your first IP Chains success

Now when your router is working, let us make use of it. It does not make sense to have a router without deploying it. We would like to access the external network 9.0.0.0 from the internal network 172.168.0.0. How can we do this? By using the IP Masquerading function of IP Chains. Follow these steps on the gateway server to set up the File Transport Protocol (FTP) access from internal network 172.168.0.0 to external network 9.0.0.0:

1. Create module dependency information for all modules by executing the command:

    ```
    /sbin/depmod -a
    ```

2. Load the module for proper FTP masquerading:

    ```
    /sbin/modprobe ip_masq_ftp
    ```

    If you want to use another protocol, such as Real Audio and Internet Relay Chat (IRC), you can load the modules for them also.

3. Set up the timeout for IP Masquerading:

    ```
    /sbin/ipchains -M -S 8000 20 200
    ```

    The parameters have the following meaning:

    a. `8000` - timeout value for TCP sessions in seconds

    b. `20` - timeout value for TCP sessions after a FIN packet in seconds

    c. `200` - timeout value for UDP packets in seconds

    You can adjust these settings to meet your needs.

4. Change built-in policy for forwarding by disabling it for all IP addresses:

    ```
    /sbin/ipchains -P forward DENY
    ```

5. Add the policy for enabling the forwarding with masquerading for your internal networks:

    ```
    /sbin/ipchains -A forward -s 192.168.0.0/24 -j MASQ
    /sbin/ipchains -A forward -s 172.168.0.0/24 -j MASQ
    ```

You are ready to try your setup. From the computer on the network 172.168.0.0, execute the command:

```
/usr/bin/ftp server
```

Where ftp `server` is the FTP server on the external network (in our example 9.0.0.0). You will see a window similar to Figure 185.

```
[root@client /root]# ftp 9.24.106.49
Connected to 9.24.106.49.
220 TPIV02 IBM TCP/IP for OS/2 - FTP Server ver 19:29:50 on Sep  2 1998 ready.
Name (9.24.106.49:root): ivo
331 Password required for ivo.
Password:
230 User ivo logged in.
Remote system type is OS/2.
ftp>
```

Figure 185. FTP after IP Masquerading setup

You have just enabled access from internal networks to an external network.

12.7 How packets travel through a gateway

In this section we will explain how IP Chains work. You can see the path of a packet coming into your server in Figure 186.

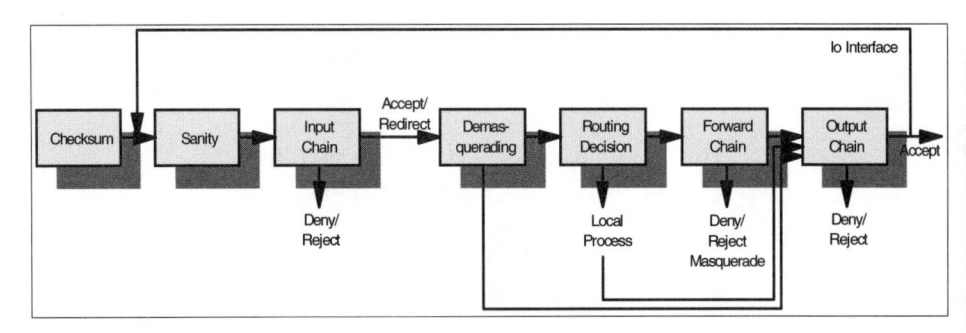

Figure 186. How the packet is traveling

Here are short descriptions of each stage:

- Checksum - this is to test if the packet is corrupted or not.
- Sanity - Malformed packets are denied here.
- Input chain - This is the first real packet checking point. Packets can be rejected, denied or accepted.
- Demasquerade - If the packet is a reply to a previously masqueraded packet, it is demasqueraded and goes directly from here to output chain.
- Routing decision - Routing code decides if this packet is for a local process or should be forwarded to a remote machine.
- Local process - a process running on the server can receive packets after a routing decision step, and can then send the packets, which go through a routing decision step and then to the output chain.

- lo interface - if packets from local process are destined for local process, they will go through the output chain with interface set to "lo", then they will return to the input chain with interface "lo". The "lo" interface is usually called the loopback interface.
- Local - if the packet is not created by the local process, then forward the chain is checked.
- Forward chain - this is the checkpoint for all packets passing through this server to another.
- Output chain - this a checkpoint for all packets just before they are sent out.

As you can see from Figure 186, you have three places where you can check the packets in your server:

a. Input chain
b. Forward chain
c. Output chain

With the /sbin/ipchains command you can set up your rules for packet checking.

> **Note**
>
> By default, all checking policies are set to Accept. This means that all packets can come in, go through or go out from your server without any restrictions.

You can see the current checking policies by executing:

/sbin/ipchains -L

You will see a window similar to Figure 187.

```
[root@client /root]# ipchains -L
Chain input (policy ACCEPT):
Chain forward (policy ACCEPT):
Chain output (policy ACCEPT):
[root@client /root]#
```

Figure 187. Listing the default IP Chains policies

12.8 Using IP Chains

With the /sbin/ipchains command, you can create, change or delete your own policies for checking packets or you can modify built-in policies. You cannot delete the built-in chains, but you can append your rules to the existing chains or even create your own chains.

To manage whole chains you can use the parameters described in Table 20.

Table 20. Parameters for managing whole chains

Parameter	Description
-N	Create a new chain
-X	Delete an empty chain
-P	Change policy for a built-in chain
-L	List the rules in a chain
-F	Flush the rules out of a chain
-Z	Zero the packets and byte counters on all rules in a chain

For manipulating rules inside the chain you can use the parameters explained in Table 21.

Table 21. Parameters for managing rules in the chain

Parameter	Description
-A	Append new rule to a chain
-I	Insert a new rule in a chain at some position
-R	Replace a rule at some position in a chain
-D	Delete a rule at some position in a chain

And there are more operations for managing masquerading. They are described in Table 22.

Table 22. Parameters for managing masquerading

Parameter	Description
-M -L	List the currently masqueraded connections
-M -S	Set masquerading timeout values

12.8.1 How to create a rule

The most common syntax for the creating a new rule is:

```
/sbin/ipchains -A input -s source -p protocol -j action
```

The parameters are described in Table 23.

Table 23. IPChains parameters

Parameter	Description
-A	Append a new rule to the chain
source	IP address or hostname of the source
protocol	Type of the protocol to which one a rule is applied
action	What will happen with the packet: 1) ACCEPT - packet will be accepted 2) REJECT - packet will be rejected 3) DENY - packet is dropped since it was not received 4) MASQ - packet will be masqueraded 5) REDIRECT - packet is redirected to local port 6) RETURN - fall off the chain immediately

> **Note**
>
> Redirecting packets to a local port using the REDIRECT action makes sense only in combination with masquerading for a transparant proxy server.

For example, if you want to create a rule for denying the ICMP protocol packets, which are used when you execute the ping command, for a specific IP address you will do this by executing the command:

```
/sbin/ipchains -A input -s IP_address -p icmp -j DENY
```

If you omit the protocol definition, all the packets will be denied. So for example if you want to block the access to your machine from the network 172.168.0.0 with subnet mask 255.255.255.0 you can do this by executing the command:

```
/sbin/ipchains -A inout -s 172.168.0.0/255.255.255.0 -j DENY
```

or with:

```
/sbin/ipchains -A input -s 172.168.0.0/24 -j DENY
```

As you can see, the subnet mask can be specified with the number of used bits for that mask.

The command for not allowing any traffic from your server to the network 172.168.0.0 with subnet mask 255.255.255.0 will look like this:

```
/sbin/ipchains -A output -d 172.168.0.0/24 -j DENY
```

Chapter 12. Packet filtering with IP Chains **237**

Here we used the "-d" parameter for specifying the destination address.

12.8.1.1 Using the inversion flag

With some of the parameters, you can use the inversion option "!". This means that the rule will be applied to everything else except to the parameters specified after "!". For example, if you want to deny packets that come from all IP addresses except from network 192.168.0.0 with subnet mask 255.255.255.0 you can to this by executing the command:

```
/sbin/ipchains -A input -s ! 192.168.0.0/24 -j DENY
```

> **Note**
>
> The rules you made are not permanent, so next time you restart the server they are gone.

12.8.2 Making the rules permanent

For making the rules permanent you have two scripts available that can make your life easier. To save all the rules you created, you can execute the command:

```
/sbin/ipchains-save > filename
```

If you execute this command withouta file name, the rules will be sent to the standard output.

You can then restore the saved rules by executing the command:

```
cat filename | /sbin/ipchains-restore
```

So if you want your saved rules to be enabled whenever you start your system, add the following line to the /etc/rc.d/rc.local file:

```
cat filename | /sbin/ipchains-restore
```

12.9 Sources of additional information

You can find more information on the official Linux IP Firewall Chains page at:

```
http://www.rustcorp.com/linux/ipchains
```

And there are always good how-to documents on the Linux Documentation Project home page:

```
http://www.linuxdoc.org/
```

Chapter 13. Backup and Recovery

Even though the hardware and software components used in today's IT industry are becoming more and more reliable, we still need to protect our data. To protect your data you need a backup solution. The most popular media for the backup are tapes, but in these days you can also create backup on other media, such as CDRW or CD-ROM.

It may seem obvious that backing up and restoring data quickly is critical, but many administrators leave this task at the end of the "to do" list until it is too late. With the ease of use of the commercially available backup utilities available from Microlite and BRU utility, there is no need to wait.

13.1 Microlite BackupEDGE

BackupEDGE is a complete backup solution for the Linux platform. It is easy to use and still very robust. With BackupEDGE you can safely archive every file, directory, device node and special file on your file systems. Unlike standard UNIX tar files which ignore many important files, BackupEDGE also verifies every byte of the data written to the tape to ensure the tape is an accurate reflection of your data. Below are the features provided by Microlite BackupEDGE software:

- Data Compression - automatic data compression is supported.
- Menu Interface - almost all functions can be accessed through an intuitive menu system.
- Remote Tape Drive Support - you can back up computers across the network.
- High Performance - advanced double buffering and variable block factors.
- Virtual File Support - you can back up virtual (sparse) files.
- Multi-Volume / Multi-Device Archives - automatic spanning across multiple volumes or devices.
- Wildcard Support - when selecting files you can use a wildcard.
- Raw Device Backups - you can archive an entire raw device/partition to tape.
- Master / Incremental Backups
- Unattended Operation - you can perform a master backup or back up only the changed files.

BackupEDGE is designed to operate on Linux kernels 2.x and there are available versions for several types of libraries.

In the following sections we will describe how to install, configure and use the Microlite BackupEDGE backup software.

> **Note**
>
> We recommend that you do not connect tape devices to the IBM ServeRAID controller. Use a separate SCSI controller for the tape devices.

13.1.1 Installing Microlite BackupEDGE

Before you install BackupEDGE you must identify the device entry for your backup device. Usually tape devices under Linux are assigned in device nodes `/dev/st0, /dev/st1...` a no rewind device is created for each tape device, which is `/dev/nst0, /dev/nst1...` In our example we used `/dev/st0` as the tape device and `/dev/nst1` as the no-rewind device.

In our example we used a diskette as the installation medium. To install the product follow these steps:

1. Log in as root.
2. Change the directory to root "/".
3. Insert the diskette with the product in the floppy drive and execute the command:

   `tar xvf /dev/fd0`

   Where `/dev/fd0` is your floppy device.

4. Execute the following command to finish the installation:

   `/tmp/init.edge`

   You will see a window similar to Figure 188.

```
BackupEDGE Enhanced Data Archiving System
..................................................
Portions [c] Copyright 1987 - 1999 by Microlite Corporation
Portions [c] Copyright 1987 - 1999 by UniTrends Software Corporation
            All Rights Reserved

System:  Linux 2.x (Uses glibc [libc.so.6] and stdc++.so.2.9)
BackupEDGE Version:     01.01.07 - 1999-11-02

BackupEDGE has been activated for 90 days.
Temporary activation will expire on January 31, 2000.
Please run /usr/lib/edge/bin/edge.activate
to register your product.

Please copy /usr/lib/edge/bin/S88edge into your startup
rc directory or onto the end of your /etc/rc file.
This program removes the edge.progress file during system startup.

Fast File Restore Option Has Been Installed.  Please Run
/usr/lib/edge/bin/edge.resmgr To Test For Fast File Restore Capability!

BackupEDGE Installation Complete!
Press [Enter] To Continue
```

Figure 188. Completing the installation

Now you are ready to use the product.

13.1.2 Configuring the tape devices

Before you can start to make backups you need to define your backup device. To accomplish this follow these steps:

1. Start the edge.resmgr resource manager by executing the command:

   /usr/lib/edge/bin/edge.resmgr

   You will see a window similar to Figure 189.

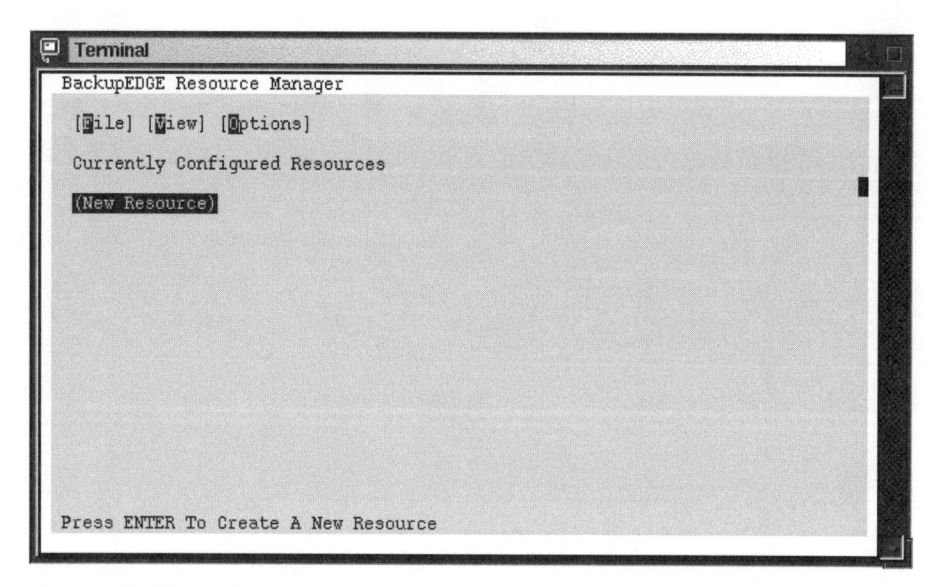

Figure 189. Starting the resource manager

2. Select **New resource** and press Enter. You will see a window similar to Figure 190.

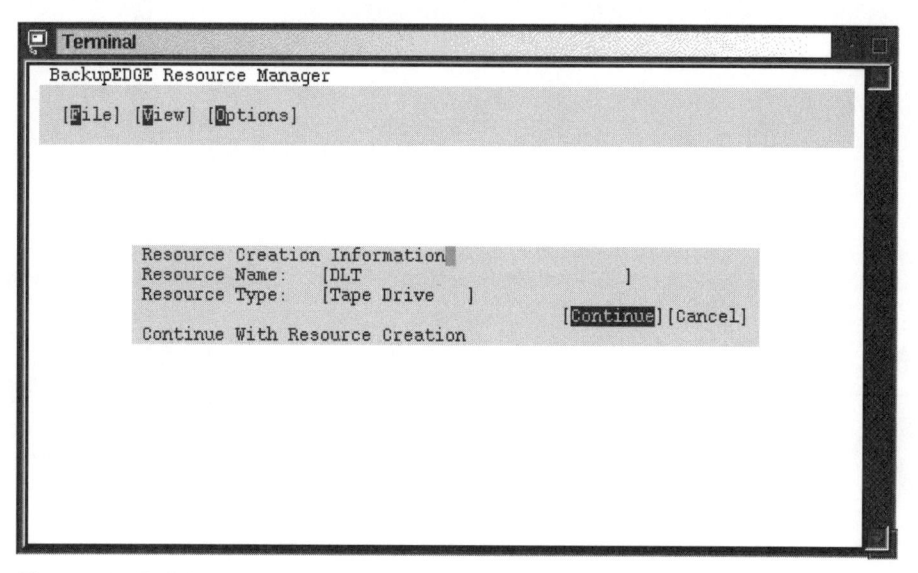

Figure 190. Defining the resource name

3. Type in the resource name and select a resource type. Then select **Continue** to go on. You will see a window similar to Figure 191.

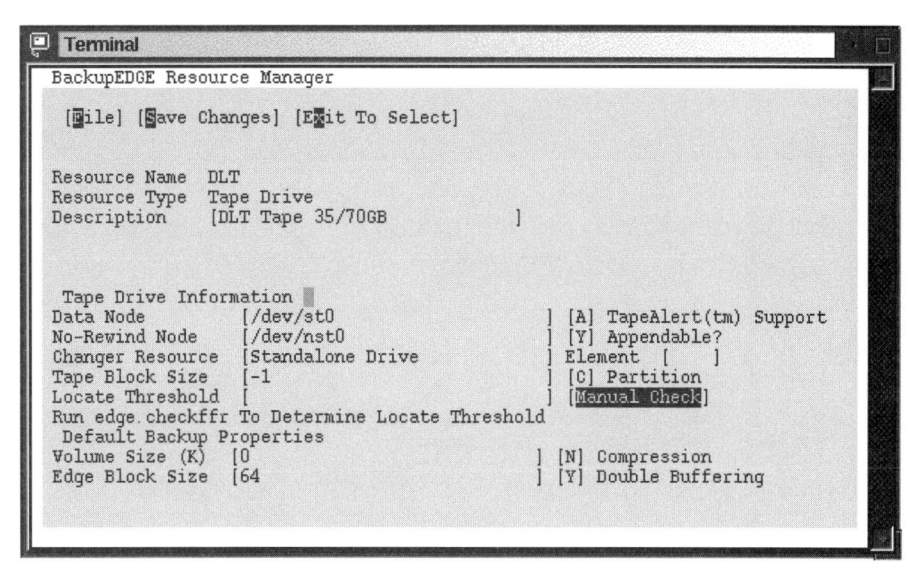

```
Terminal
BackupEDGE Resource Manager
 [File] [Save Changes] [Exit To Select]

 Resource Name   DLT
 Resource Type   Tape Drive
 Description     [DLT Tape 35/70GB          ]


  Tape Drive Information
 Data Node           [/dev/st0              ] [A] TapeAlert(tm) Support
 No-Rewind Node      [/dev/nst0             ] [Y] Appendable?
 Changer Resource    [Standalone Drive      ] Element  [    ]
 Tape Block Size     [-1                    ] [C] Partition
 Locate Threshold    [                      ] [Manual Check]
 Run edge.checkffr To Determine Locate Threshold
  Default Backup Properties
 Volume Size (K)     [0                     ] [N] Compression
 Edge Block Size     [64                    ] [Y] Double Buffering
```

Figure 191. Parameters for the tape

4. Type in the description, data node and no-rewind node. In our example, the data node is /dev/st0 and no-rewind node is /dev/nst0. You can leave all other fields as default.

5. Select **Manual Check** to define other parameters automatically. You will see a window similar to Figure 192.

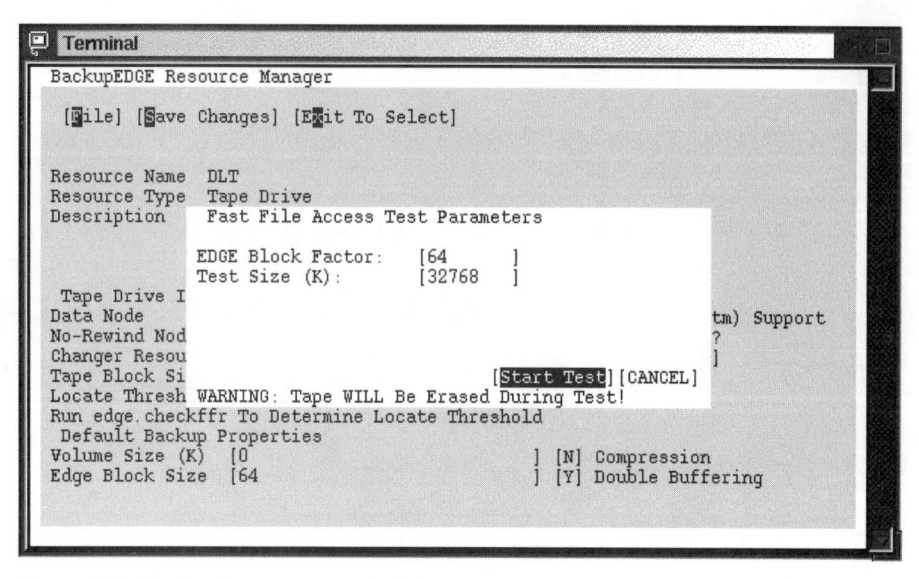

```
Terminal
BackupEDGE Resource Manager

 [File] [Save Changes] [Exit To Select]

 Resource Name   DLT
 Resource Type   Tape Drive
 Description     Fast File Access Test Parameters

                 EDGE Block Factor:    [64    ]
                 Test Size (K):        [32768 ]
 Tape Drive I
 Data Node                                                  tm) Support
 No-Rewind Nod                                              ?
 Changer Resou                                              ]
 Tape Block Si                              [Start Test][CANCEL]
 Locate Thresh  WARNING: Tape WILL Be Erased During Test!
 Run edge.checkffr To Determine Locate Threshold
 Default Backup Properties
 Volume Size (K)  [0                         ] [N] Compression
 Edge Block Size  [64                        ] [Y] Double Buffering
```

Figure 192. Setting the parameters for tests

6. Here you can select the block factor and the test size. Select **Start Test** to continue. You will see a window similar to Figure 193.

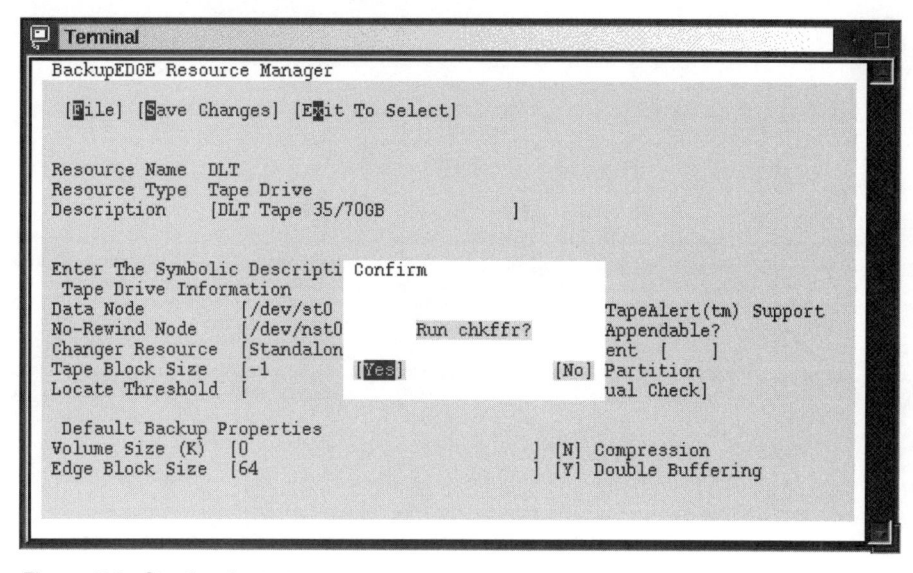

```
Terminal
BackupEDGE Resource Manager

 [File] [Save Changes] [Exit To Select]

 Resource Name   DLT
 Resource Type   Tape Drive
 Description     [DLT Tape 35/70GB            ]

 Enter The Symbolic Descripti  Confirm
 Tape Drive Information
 Data Node        [/dev/st0                    TapeAlert(tm) Support
 No-Rewind Node   [/dev/nst0       Run chkffr? Appendable?
 Changer Resource [Standalon                   ent [   ]
 Tape Block Size  [-1         [Yes]      [No]  Partition
 Locate Threshold [                            ual Check]

 Default Backup Properties
 Volume Size (K)  [0                         ] [N] Compression
 Edge Block Size  [64                        ] [Y] Double Buffering
```

Figure 193. Starting the tests

244 Caldera OpenLinux and Netfinity Server Integration Guide

> **Stop**
>
> Performing this test will destroy all data on the tape.

7. Select **Yes** to continue. You will see a window similar to Figure 194.

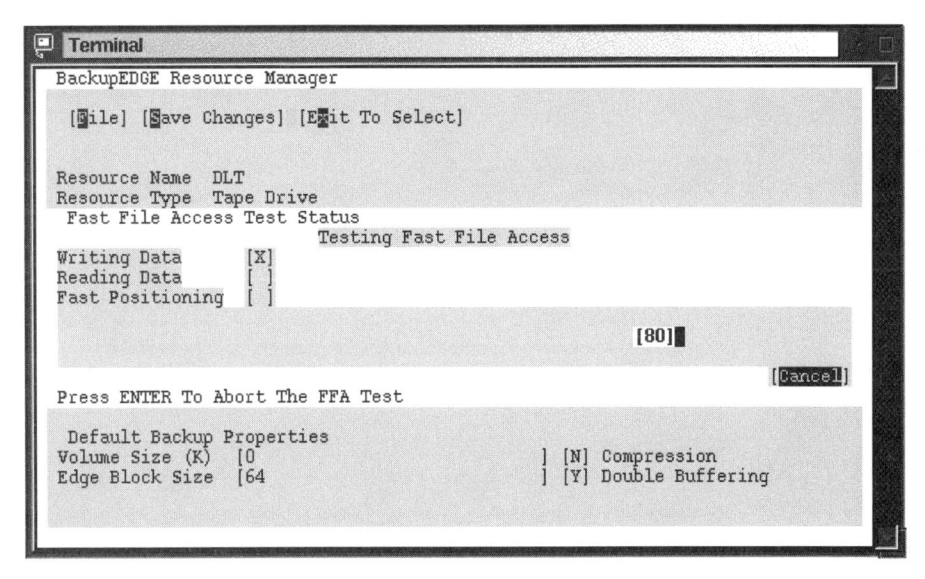

```
Terminal
BackupEDGE Resource Manager

 [File] [Save Changes] [Exit To Select]


 Resource Name   DLT
 Resource Type   Tape Drive
  Fast File Access Test Status
                         Testing Fast File Access
 Writing Data     [X]
 Reading Data     [ ]
 Fast Positioning [ ]

                                                [80]
                                                             [Cancel]
 Press ENTER To Abort The FFA Test

 Default Backup Properties
 Volume Size (K)  [0                ]  [N] Compression
 Edge Block Size  [64               ]  [Y] Double Buffering
```

Figure 194. Performance test

After the test is done you will see a window similar to Figure 195.

Chapter 13. Backup and Recovery **245**

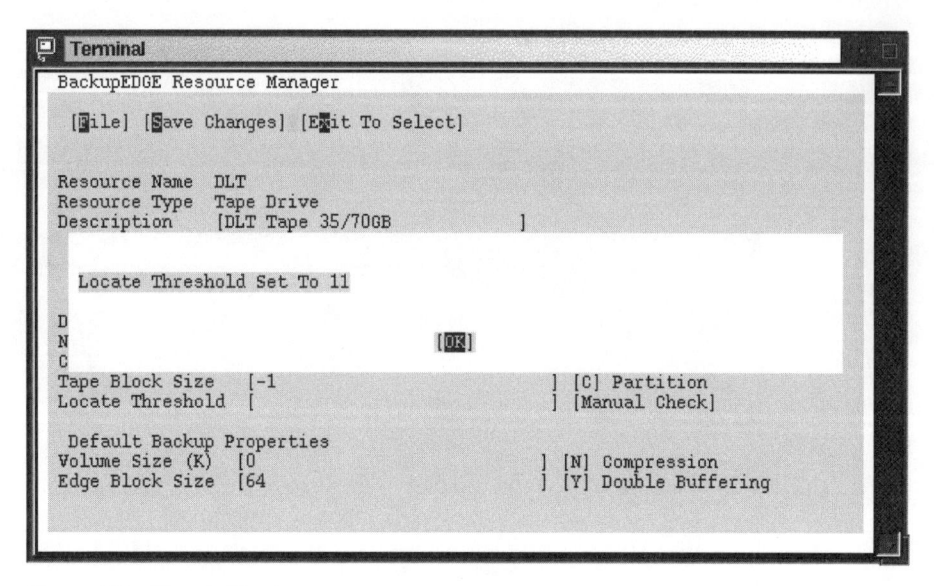

```
Terminal
BackupEDGE Resource Manager
  [File] [Save Changes] [Exit To Select]

  Resource Name   DLT
  Resource Type   Tape Drive
  Description     [DLT Tape 35/70GB         ]

  ┌─────────────────────────────────────────────┐
  │  Locate Threshold Set To 11                 │
  D                                             │
  N                              [OK]           │
  C                                             │
  Tape Block Size  [-1            ]  [C] Partition
  Locate Threshold [              ]  [Manual Check]

   Default Backup Properties
  Volume Size (K) [0              ]  [N] Compression
  Edge Block Size [64             ]  [Y] Double Buffering
```

Figure 195. Threshold value

8. After the test is done you will see the proposed value for the threshold. Click **OK** to continue. You will be back in the parameters definition window similar to Figure 192 on page 244. Here you need to define four more parameters:

   - Volume Size

   - EDGE Block Size - the default size is 64 for a 32 KB buffer.

   - Compression

   - Double Buffering - with multiple buffers you can increase the backup speed.

9. Save the changes by selecting **Save Changes.** You will see a window similar to Figure 196.

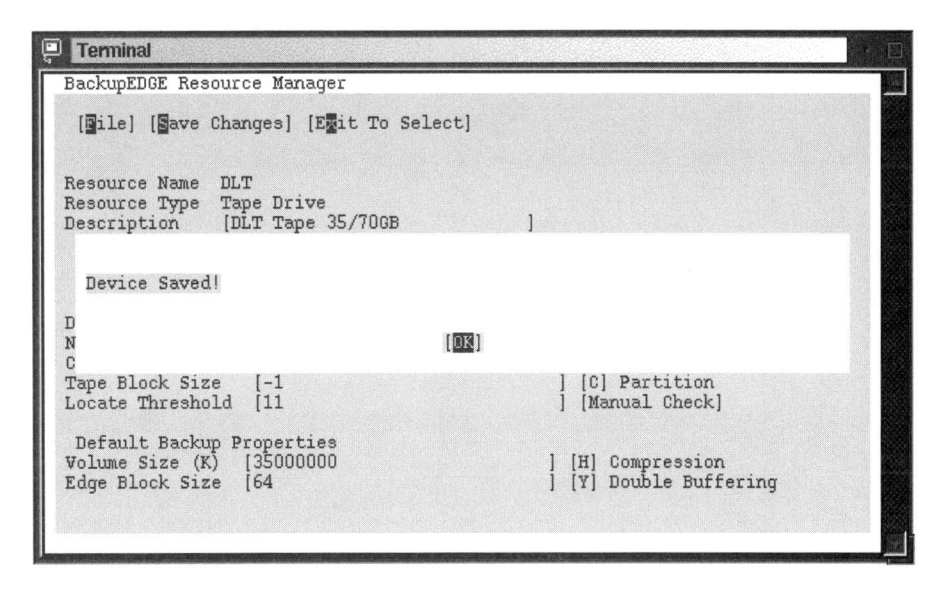

Figure 196. Saving the device definitions

13.1.3 Defining the devices for making backups

Now that the hardware device is configured, you need to tell the backup software which device to use for each user performing backups. If you are logged in as root, you will define devices for the root user. Usually this is the only user doing backups on the system. Follow these steps to enable the device you defined in the resource manager for backup:

1. Start the edge.config configuration menu by executing the command:

   /usr/bin/edge.config

   You will see a window similar to Figure 197.

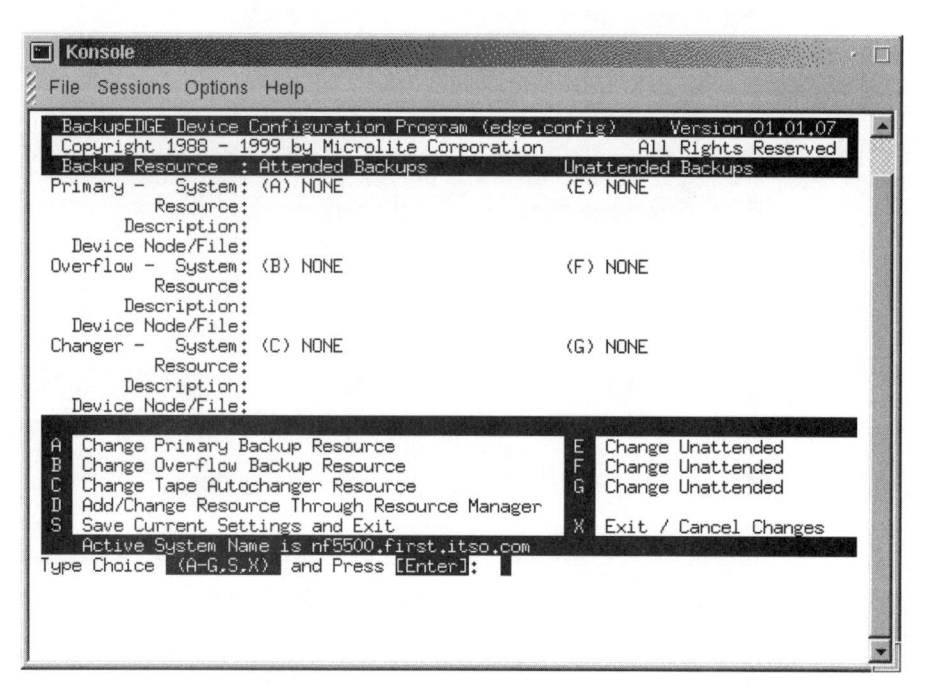

```
┌─ Konsole ─────────────────────────────────────────────────┐
│ File  Sessions  Options                              Help │
│ ┌───────────────────────────────────────────────────────┐ │
│ │ BackupEDGE Device Configuration Program (edge.config)    Version 01.01.07 │ │
│ │ Copyright 1988 - 1999 by Microlite Corporation          All Rights Reserved │ │
│ │ Backup Resource  : Attended Backups              Unattended Backups │ │
│ │ Primary -    System: (A) NONE                    (E) NONE │ │
│ │            Resource:                                      │ │
│ │         Description:                                      │ │
│ │     Device Node/File:                                     │ │
│ │ Overflow -   System: (B) NONE                    (F) NONE │ │
│ │            Resource:                                      │ │
│ │         Description:                                      │ │
│ │     Device Node/File:                                     │ │
│ │ Changer -    System: (C) NONE                    (G) NONE │ │
│ │            Resource:                                      │ │
│ │         Description:                                      │ │
│ │     Device Node/File:                                     │ │
│ │┌─────────────────────────────────────────────────────────┐│ │
│ ││ A  Change Primary Backup Resource      E  Change Unattended ││ │
│ ││ B  Change Overflow Backup Resource     F  Change Unattended ││ │
│ ││ C  Change Tape Autochanger Resource    G  Change Unattended ││ │
│ ││ D  Add/Change Resource Through Resource Manager             ││ │
│ ││ S  Save Current Settings and Exit      X  Exit / Cancel Changes ││ │
│ ││    Active System Name is nf5500.first.itso.com              ││ │
│ │└─────────────────────────────────────────────────────────┘│ │
│ │ Type Choice  (A-G,S,X)  and Press  [Enter]: ▮            │ │
│ └───────────────────────────────────────────────────────┘ │
└───────────────────────────────────────────────────────────┘
```

Figure 197. Device Configuration

2. Here you need to define the devices for attended and unattended backups.

3. Type in A and press Enter to define the device for attended backups. You will see a window similar to Figure 198.

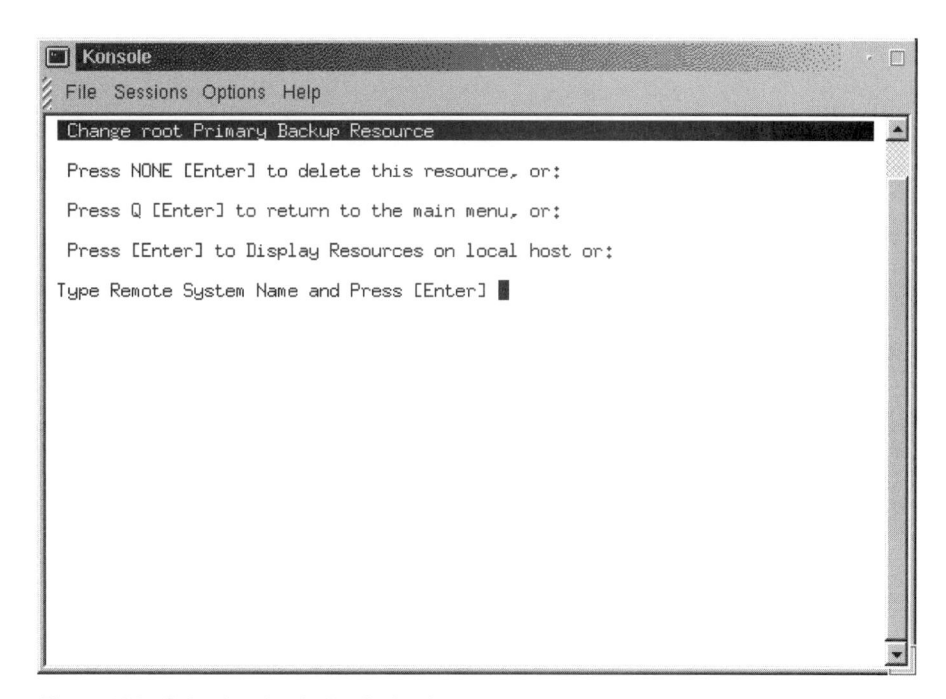

```
Konsole
File  Sessions  Options  Help
Change root Primary Backup Resource
Press NONE [Enter] to delete this resource, or:
Press Q [Enter] to return to the main menu, or:
Press [Enter] to Display Resources on local host or:
Type Remote System Name and Press [Enter]
```

Figure 198. Selecting the device for backup

4. Press Enter to continue. At the next window you will see all defined backup devices. Type in the device you want and press Enter to continue. You will see a window similar to Figure 199.

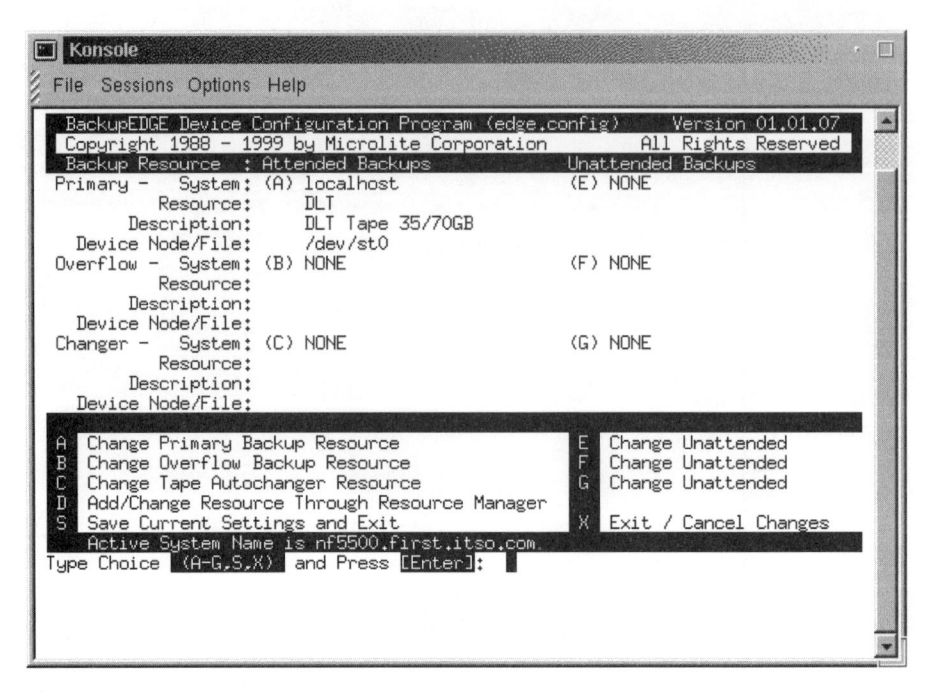

Figure 199. After definition of attended backup device

5. Follow steps from 1- 4 for the unattended device.

You are now ready to make backups of your important files.

13.1.4 Initializing the tape

Before you start making backups you should initialize the tape. To do this follow these steps:

1. Start the edgemenu program by executing command:

   /usr/bin/edgemenu

   You will see a window similar to Figure 200.

```
Terminal

[File] [Backup] [Restore] [Verify] [Admin] [Schedule]
                                   [Define Resources]
                                   [Set Default Backup Resources]
                                   [Initialize Tapes]
                                   [Changer Control]
                                   [Activate BackupEDGE]
                                   [Edit Registration]
                                   [Make RecoverEDGE Media]
                                   Do BackupEDGE Initialization

Primary Resource   : nf5500:drive!DLT (/dev/st0) (DLT Tape 35/70GB)
Overflow Resource: NONE
Changer Resource  : NONE
Primary : Compress: Hard, Tape Block:   -1, Edge Block:   64, Partition: -1
Overflow: N/A
Last Master Backup: Tue Nov  2 14:20:15 1999
Local Machine: nf5500.first.itso.com  Administering: nf5500.first.itso.com
```

Figure 200. EDGEMENU main menu

2. In the Admin menu select **Initialize Tapes.** You will see a window similar to Figure 201.

```
Terminal

[File] [Backup] [Restore] [Verify] [Admin] [Schedule]

              Initialize Tape in Primary Resource



                        [Initialize Tape]

Primary Resource   : nf5500:drive!DLT (/dev/st0) (DLT Tape 35/70GB)
Overflow Resource: NONE
Changer Resource  : NONE
Primary : Compress: Hard, Tape Block:   -1, Edge Block:   64, Partition: -1
Overflow: N/A
Last Master Backup: Tue Nov  2 14:20:15 1999
Local Machine: nf5500.first.itso.com  Administering: nf5500.first.itso.com
```

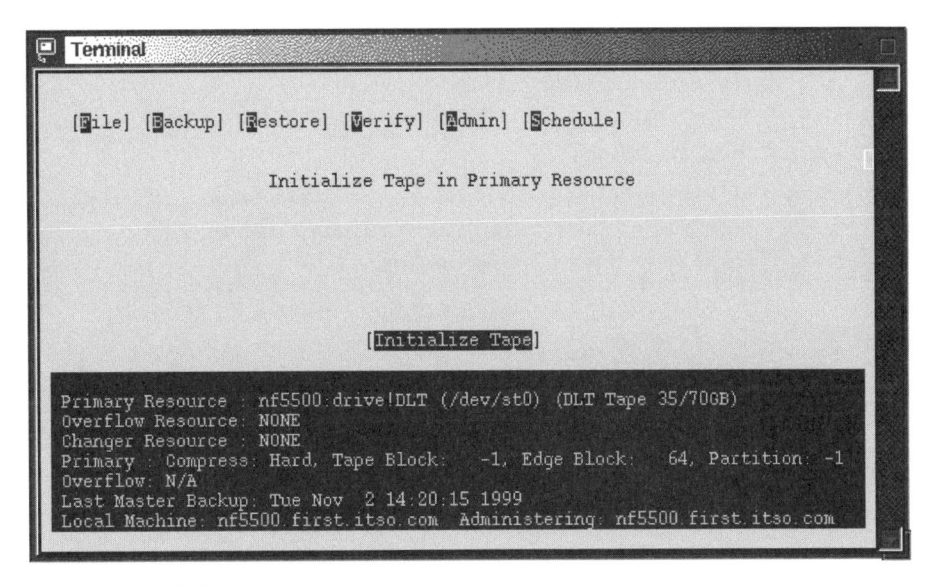

Figure 201. Initializing the tape

3. Select **Initialize Tape** and press Enter. The tape will be initialized. You will get a message that tape is successfully initialized. Press Enter to continue.

You can check the tape properties by selecting **Show Tape Label** in the Verify menu. You will see a window similar to Figure 202.

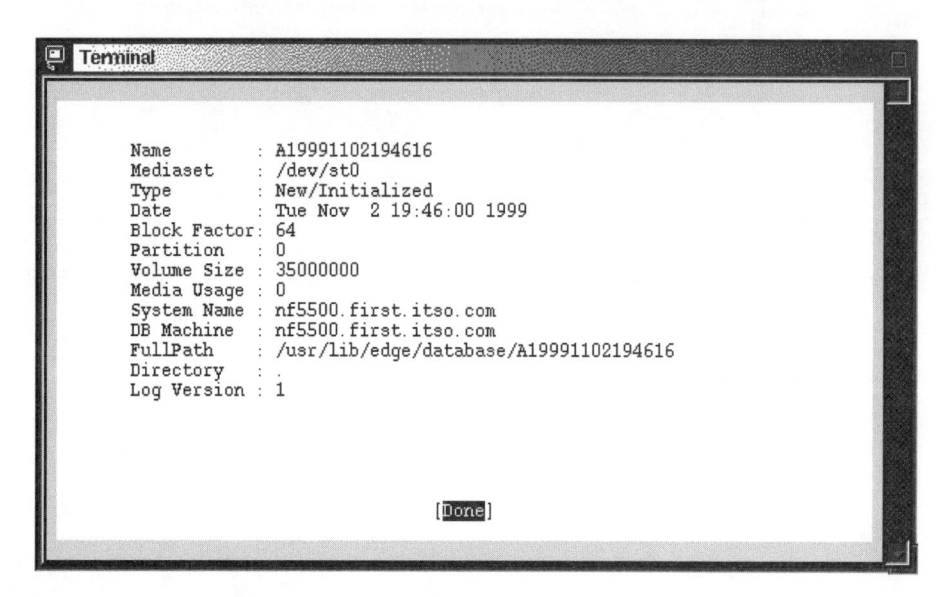

```
Name         : A19991102194616
Mediaset     : /dev/st0
Type         : New/Initialized
Date         : Tue Nov  2 19:46:00 1999
Block Factor : 64
Partition    : 0
Volume Size  : 35000000
Media Usage  : 0
System Name  : nf5500.first.itso.com
DB Machine   : nf5500.first.itso.com
FullPath     : /usr/lib/edge/database/A19991102194616
Directory    : .
Log Version  : 1
```

Figure 202. Tape information

13.1.5 Your first backup

In this section we will show how to make backups of desired files or directories. You can perform backups in the edgemenu utility. Follow these steps to make a sample backup:

1. Start the edgemenu program by executing command:

    /usr/bin/edgemenu

    You will see a window similar to Figure 203.

[Figure 203 screenshot]

Figure 203. Starting the backup

2. In the Backup menu, select **Backup Files / Dirs,** and you will see a window similar to Figure 204.

[Figure 204 screenshot]

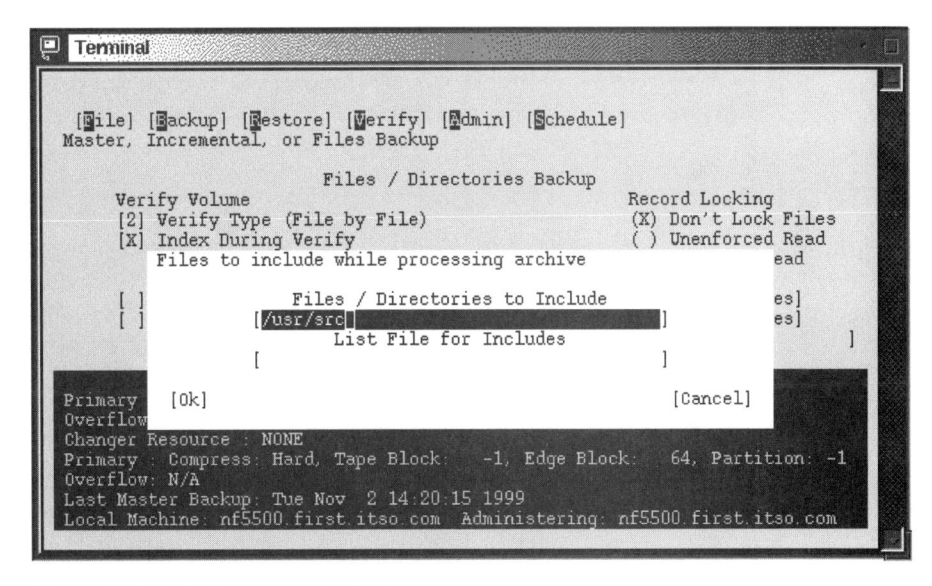

Figure 204. Selecting source for backup

3. In the Files / Directories to Include field, type in the files or directories you want to back up. In our example we want to make backups of the directory

/usr/src. Select **OK** to continue. You will see a window similar to Figure 205.

Figure 205. Backup in progress

After the backup is finished you will see a window similar to Figure 206.

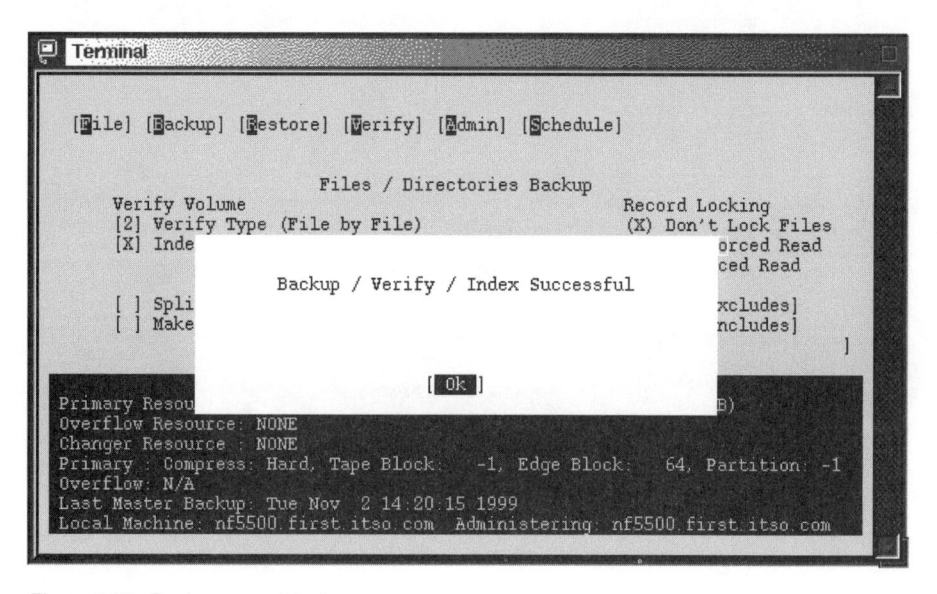

Figure 206. Backup completed

You will also see a backup report similar to Figure 207.

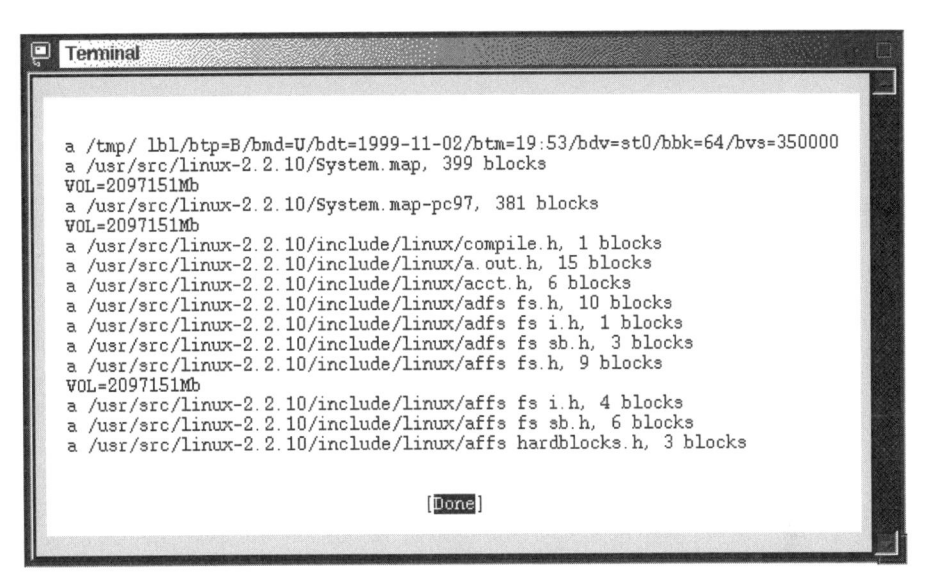

```
a /tmp/ lbl/btp=B/bmd=U/bdt=1999-11-02/btm=19:53/bdv=st0/bbk=64/bvs=350000
a /usr/src/linux-2.2.10/System.map, 399 blocks
VOL=2097151Mb
a /usr/src/linux-2.2.10/System.map-pc97, 381 blocks
VOL=2097151Mb
a /usr/src/linux-2.2.10/include/linux/compile.h, 1 blocks
a /usr/src/linux-2.2.10/include/linux/a.out.h, 15 blocks
a /usr/src/linux-2.2.10/include/linux/acct.h, 6 blocks
a /usr/src/linux-2.2.10/include/linux/adfs fs.h, 10 blocks
a /usr/src/linux-2.2.10/include/linux/adfs fs i.h, 1 blocks
a /usr/src/linux-2.2.10/include/linux/adfs fs sb.h, 3 blocks
a /usr/src/linux-2.2.10/include/linux/affs fs.h, 9 blocks
VOL=2097151Mb
a /usr/src/linux-2.2.10/include/linux/affs fs i.h, 4 blocks
a /usr/src/linux-2.2.10/include/linux/affs fs sb.h, 6 blocks
a /usr/src/linux-2.2.10/include/linux/affs hardblocks.h, 3 blocks
```

Figure 207. Backup report

You have just made your first backup and your files are safe now!

13.1.6 Restoring single files or directories

In this section we show how to recover files from the backup. We are assuming that you are recovering files on the same server as you made the backup from, and with the same user ID. You can perform recovery from the same utility as backups. Follow these steps to recover files:

1. Start the edgemenu program by executing command:

    /usr/bin/edgemenu

    You will see a window similar to Figure 203.

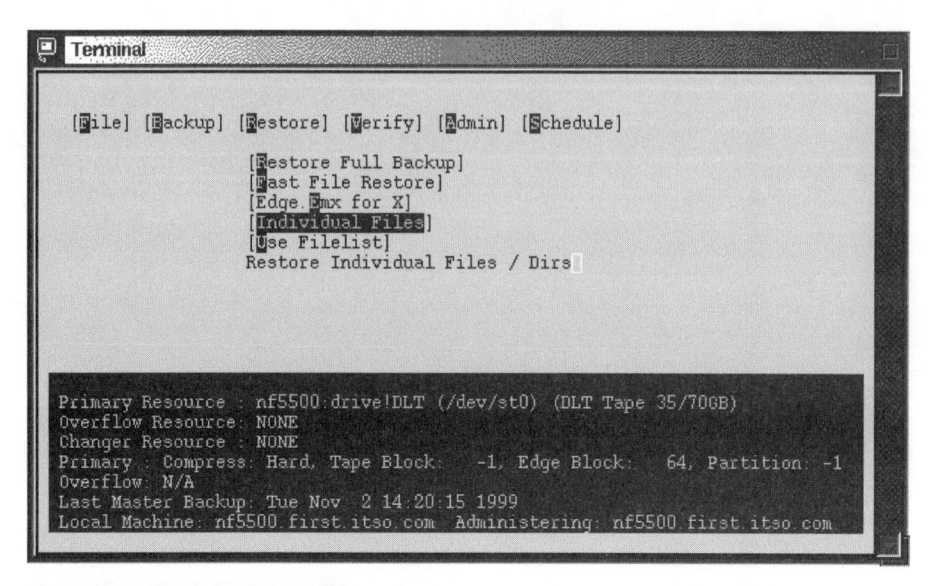

Figure 208. Starting the recovery

2. Select **Restore ->Individual Files**, and you will see a window similar to Figure 204 on page 253.

3. Select the files or directories to restore. Select **OK** to continue, and you will see a window similar to Figure 209.

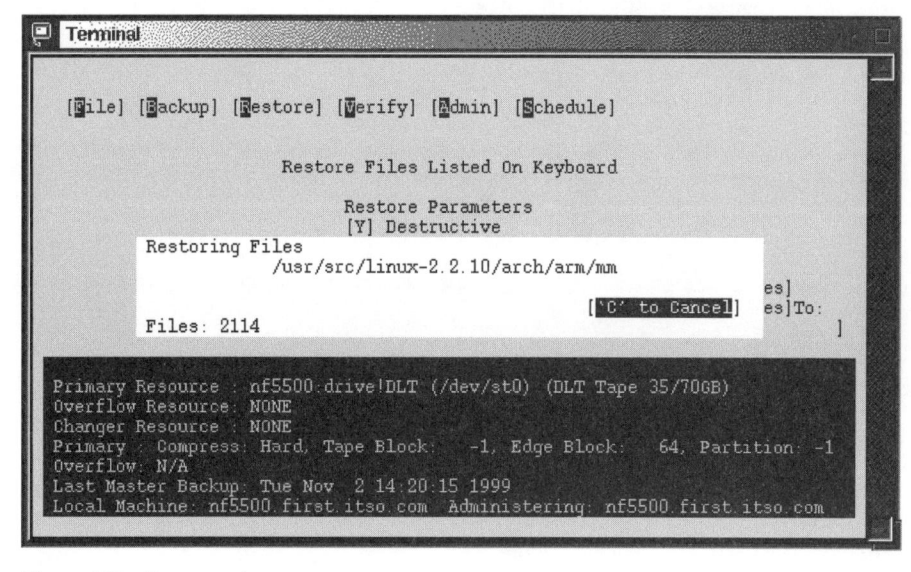

Figure 209. Recovery in progress

When the recovery is completed you will see a window similar to Figure 210.

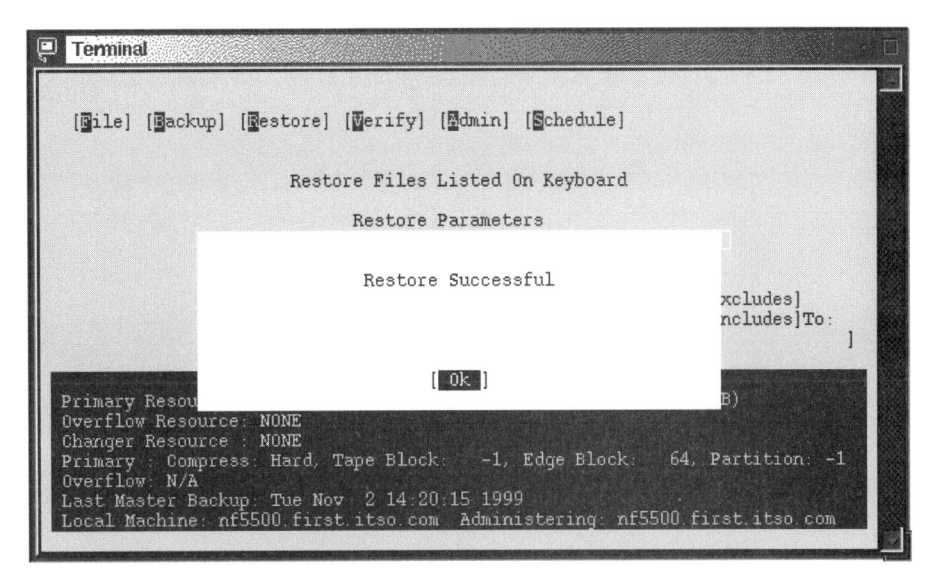

Figure 210. Recovery completed

Select **OK** to continue and you will see a recovery report similar to Figure 211.

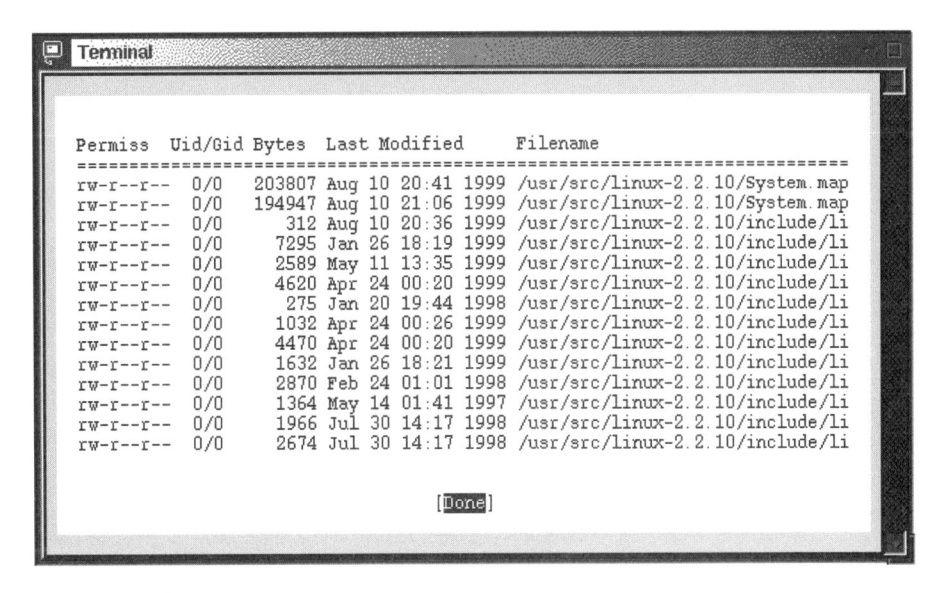

Figure 211. Recovery report

Chapter 13. Backup and Recovery   257

Your files were recovered successfully!

13.1.7 Master and incremental backups

Usually system administrators perform so-called master and incremental backups. The master backup is a backup of all files on the system. Incremental backup is a backup of only those files that have changed from the last master backup. When you need to restore your data, restore the master backup and the last incremental backup. BackupEDGE can perform different types of incremental backups. Refer to the BackupEDGE manual for more information. Master and incremental backups can be performed from the edgemenu utility.

To perform a master backup follow these steps:

1. Start the edgemenu program by executing command:

   /usr/bin/edgemenu

   You will see a window similar to Figure 203 on page 253.

2. Select **Backup -> Master Backup,** and you will see a window similar to Figure 212.

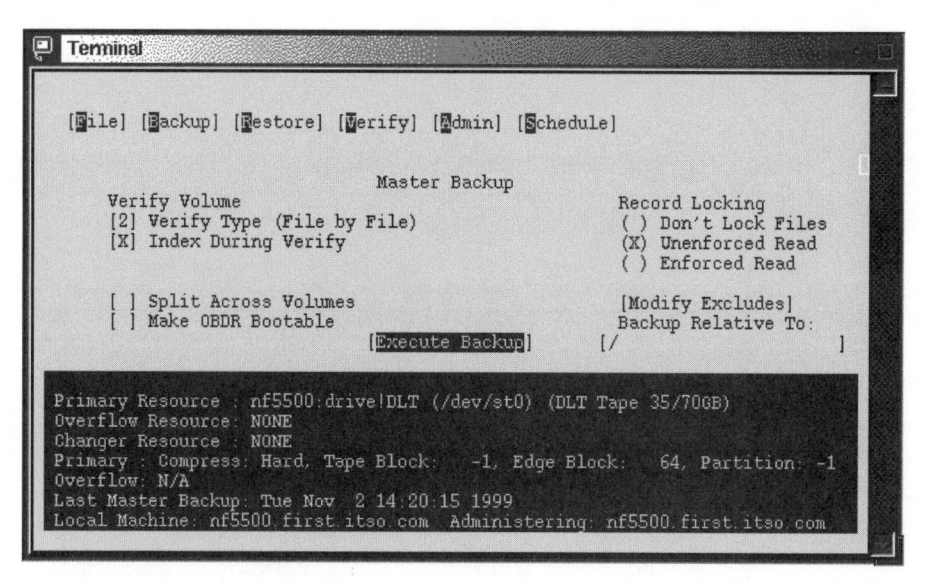

Figure 212. Staring Master Backup

3. Choose options you want and select **Execute Backup** to start the backup. You will see a window similar to Figure 213.

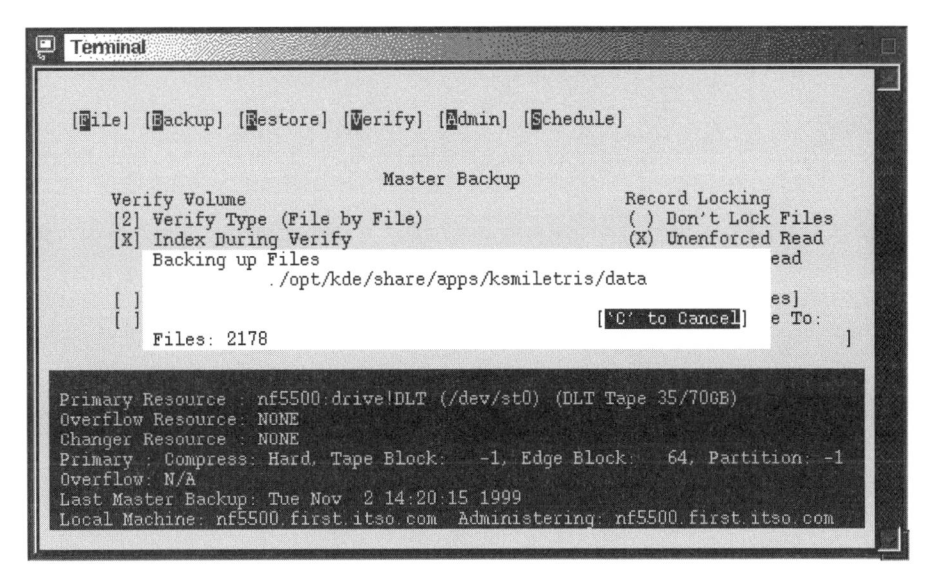

Figure 213. Master backup in progress

When the backup is finished you will see a window similar to Figure 214.

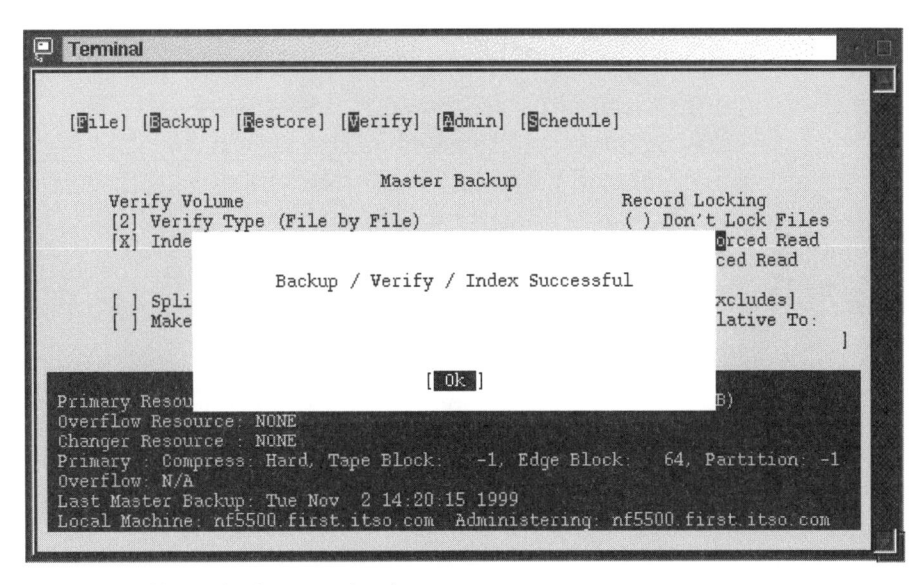

Figure 214. Master backup completed

Select **OK** to finish the operation, and you will see a backup report similar to Figure 215.

Chapter 13. Backup and Recovery 259

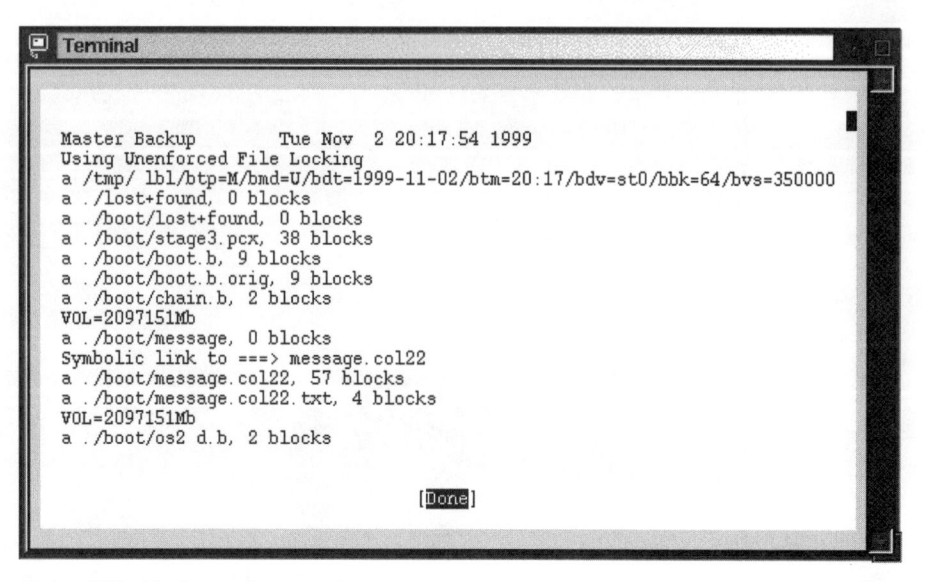

```
Master Backup           Tue Nov  2 20:17:54 1999
Using Unenforced File Locking
a /tmp/ lbl/btp=M/bmd=U/bdt=1999-11-02/btm=20:17/bdv=st0/bbk=64/bvs=350000
a ./lost+found, 0 blocks
a ./boot/lost+found, 0 blocks
a ./boot/stage3.pcx, 38 blocks
a ./boot/boot.b, 9 blocks
a ./boot/boot.b.orig, 9 blocks
a ./boot/chain.b, 2 blocks
VOL=2097151Mb
a ./boot/message, 0 blocks
Symbolic link to ===> message.col22
a ./boot/message.col22, 57 blocks
a ./boot/message.col22.txt, 4 blocks
VOL=2097151Mb
a ./boot/os2 d.b, 2 blocks

                    [Done]
```

Figure 215. Master backup report

To perform incremental backups select **Backup -> Incremental Backup** . Then follow the instructions in the window; they are similar to the ones for master backup.

13.1.8 Restoring master and incremental backups

To restore master and incremental backups you can use the edgemenu utility. When you start the utility you will see a window similar to Figure 216.

Figure 216. Starting Restore Full Backup

Select **Restore -> Restore Full Backup**, and you will see a window similar to Figure 217.

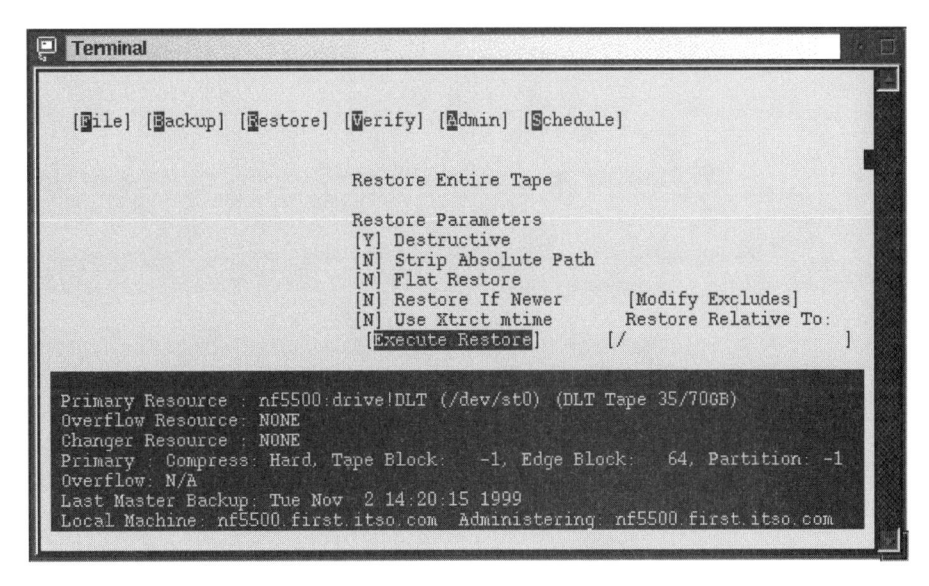

Figure 217. Full Backup restore options

Choose your options and select **Execute Restore** to start restoring files.

Chapter 13. Backup and Recovery   **261**

13.1.9 Performing scheduled backups

To perform scheduled backups you can use the utility included with BackupEDGE. This utility is called edge.nightly. To start this utility execute the command:

```
/usr/lib/edge/bin/edge.nightly
```

But before you can use scheduled backups you need to define them. To do this follow these steps:

1. Start the edgemenu.
2. Select **Schedule -> Nightly Scheduling.** You will see a window similar to Figure 218.

```
BackupEDGE Nightly Archive Setup Menu (edge.cronset)        Version 01.01.07
Copyright 1988 - 1999 by Microlite Corporation              All Rights Reserved
Choice:     Setting                              Current        Last
   A        BackupEDGE Backup Type               OFF            OFF
   B        Backup Time (24 hour format)
   C        Mail Notification To                 OFF            OFF
   D   (t)  Backup On Sundays
   E   (t)  Backup On Mondays
   F   (t)  Backup On Tuesdays
   G   (t)  Backup On Wednesdays
   H   (t)  Backup On Thursdays
   I   (t)  Backup On Fridays
   J   (t)  Backup On Saturdays
   K        Verify After Backup
   L        Index After Backup                   YES            YES
   M        Send Diagnostic Output To
   N        Print Backup Results To              DISABLED

   S        Save Settings - Create New Cron Entry
   X        Exit - Abandon Changes - Use Last Entries
      (t)   Toggles Entry (YES or NO)                      1999-11-04 13:41:00
Please Type Letter of Your Selection and Press [ENTER]
```

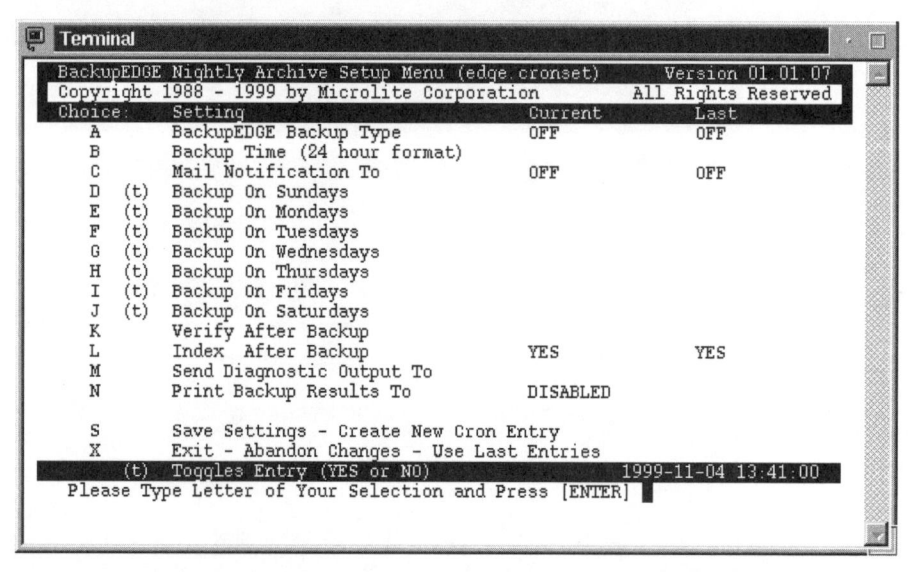

Figure 218. Schedule setup

3. Here you can define the schedule for your backups. You need to define the type and time of the backup. To define the type of the backup select **A** and press Enter, and you will see a window similar to Figure 219.

```
Terminal
Backup Type: Master, Incremental, or None (I/M/N) ?
Press [ENTER] for None :
```

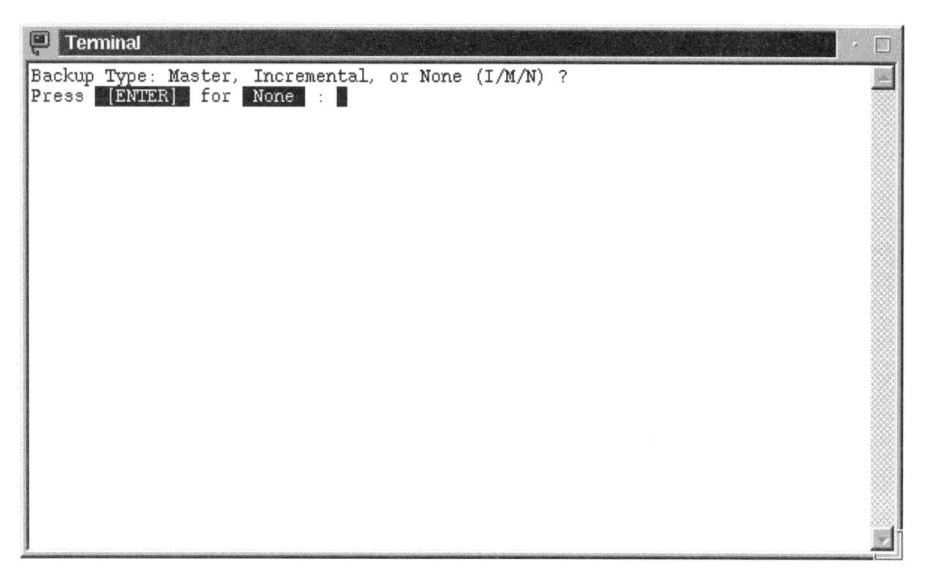

Figure 219. Defining the type of the backup

4. Specify the type of the backup you want to perform. In our example we selected **M** for master backup. You will be returned to the main window.

> **Note**
>
> You cannot mix master and incremental backups. If your master backup fits on one tape cartridge we recommend that you do a master backup daily. If your master backup will not fit on one tape cartridge, do a manual master backup once a week and do incremental backups daily.

5. Next you need to specify the time of everyday backup by selecting **B** and pressing Enter. You will see a window similar to Figure 220.

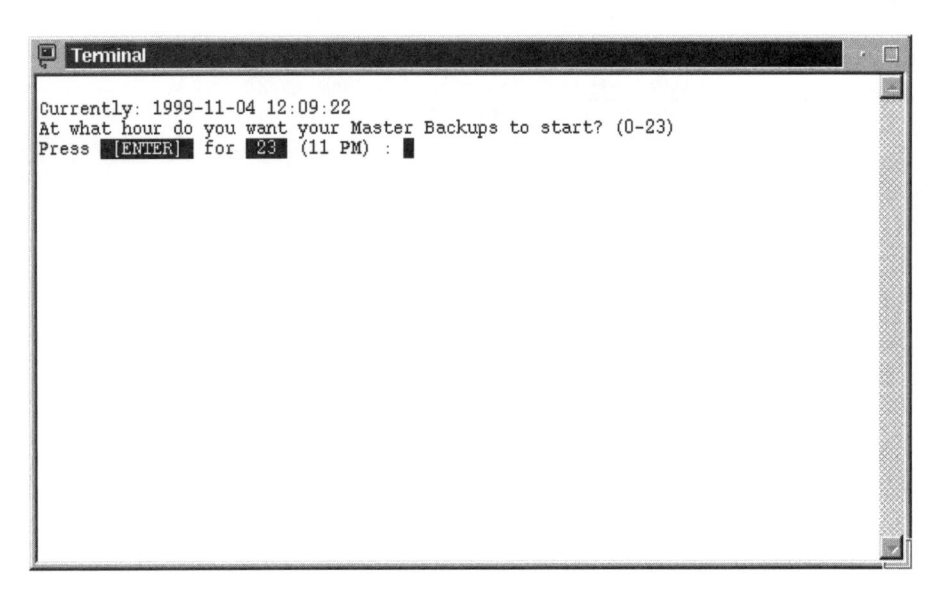

```
Currently: 1999-11-04 12:09:22
At what hour do you want your Master Backups to start? (0-23)
Press [ENTER] for 23 (11 PM) :
```

Figure 220. Setting the time

6. Define the time for your backups. You will see a window similar to Figure 221.

```
BackupEDGE Nightly Archive Setup Menu (edge.cronset)    Version 01.01.07
Copyright 1988 - 1999 by Microlite Corporation          All Rights Reserved
Choice:   Setting                               Current         Last
   A       BackupEDGE Backup Type               Master          Master
   B       Backup Time (24 hour format)         12:30           12:30
   C       Mail Notification To                 root            root
   D  (t)  Backup On Sundays                    YES             YES
   E  (t)  Backup On Mondays                    YES             YES
   F  (t)  Backup On Tuesdays                   YES             YES
   G  (t)  Backup On Wednesdays                 YES             YES
   H  (t)  Backup On Thursdays                  YES             YES
   I  (t)  Backup On Fridays                    YES             YES
   J  (t)  Backup On Saturdays                  YES             YES
   K       Verify After Backup                  BIT             BIT
   L       Index  After Backup                  YES             YES
   M       Send Diagnostic Output To            /dev/null
   N       Print Backup Results To              DISABLED

   S       Save Settings - Create New Cron Entry
   X       Exit - Abandon Changes - Use Last Entries
        (t) Toggles Entry (YES or NO)                   1999-11-04 12:27:39
Please Type Letter of Your Selection and Press [ENTER]
```

Figure 221. After schedule definition

7. Select **S** and press Enter to save the settings. The configuration program will create an entry in the cron database for executing the edge.nightly

utility. From now on, cron will execute the backup utility as you defined in the previous steps.

> **Note**
>
> Before you start using scheduled backups you need to copy the file /usr/lib/edge/bin/S88egde to the /etc/rc.d/rc2.d directory. This script will clear all zombie PIDs from the edge.nightly on the system restart.

You can also start edge.nightly from your own scripts. When you start it from a command line or a script, you have to be logged in as root. After the edge.nightly is started it will perform an immediate backup.

13.2 Microlite RecoverEDGE

By using RecoverEDGE tools you can create emergency recovery diskettes to rebuild your system in the case of disaster. RecoverEDGE handles the details of reconstructing your FDisk, divvy, and/or slice tables, rebuilding your filesystems and restoring your data, even if your hard drive size and/or geometry have changed. RecoverEDGE uses your live system backups, so there is no need to shut down your system in order to protect it. You can even restore your system over the network.

With RecoverEDGE restoring the system is very easy. To recover the system you should follow these tasks:

1. Identify and correct the cause of the failure.
2. Boot from the RecoverEDGE disks.
3. Reconfigure your filesystems.
4. Restore your backups.
5. Shut down and reboot.
6. System is ready to use.

> **Note**
>
> RestoreEDGE uses your master and incremental backups for recovery, so the accuracy of the data depends on these backups.

13.2.1 Creating the RecoverEDGE boot disks

Before you can use RecoverEDGE for disaster recovery you should build a set of boot disks. To create the boot disks follow these steps:

1. Start the utility for creating RecoverEDGE boot diskettes:

   /usr/bin/re2

   You will see a window similar to Figure 222.

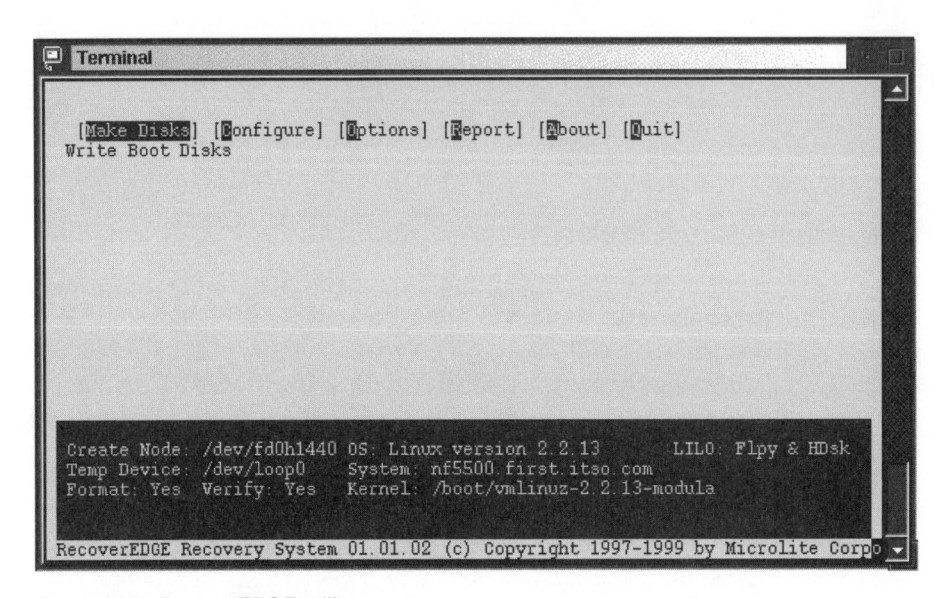

Figure 222. RecoverEDGE utility

2. Select the **Configure** option and press Enter, and you will see a window similar to Figure 223.

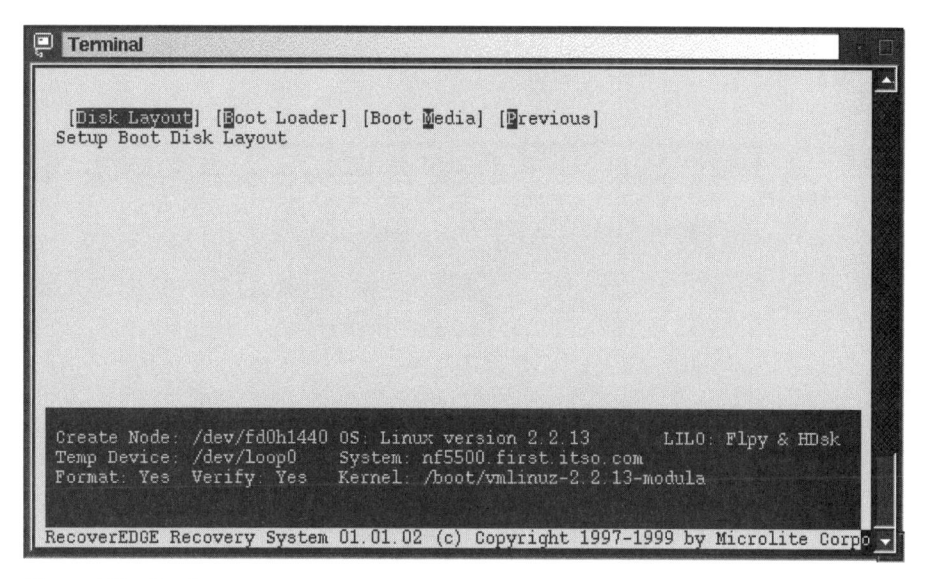

Figure 223. Configure menu

3. Select the **Disk Layout** option and press Enter, and you will see a window similar to Figure 224.

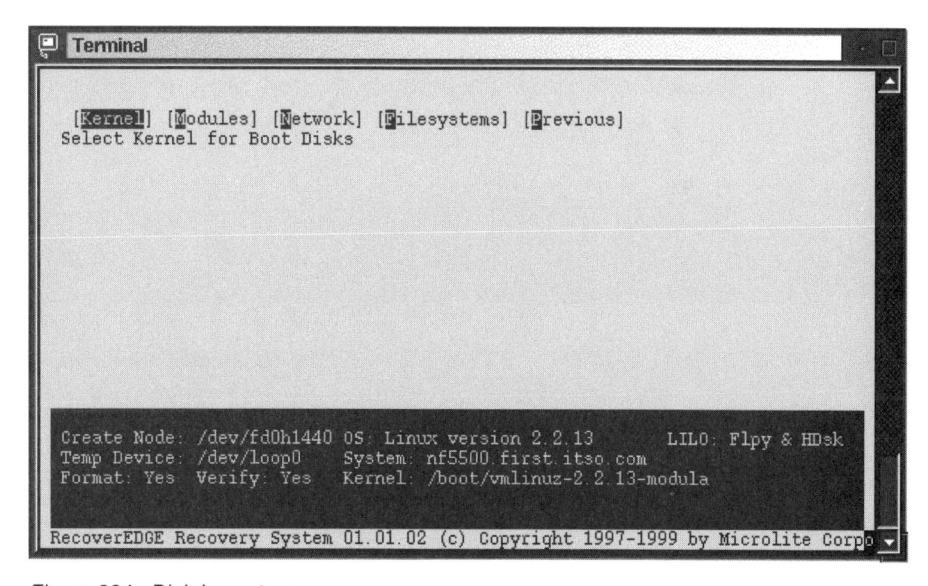

Figure 224. Disk Layout menu

4. Here you can configure the kernel, modules, network and the filesystems for your RecoverEDGE boot disks. Select **Kernel** option and you will see a window similar to Figure 225.

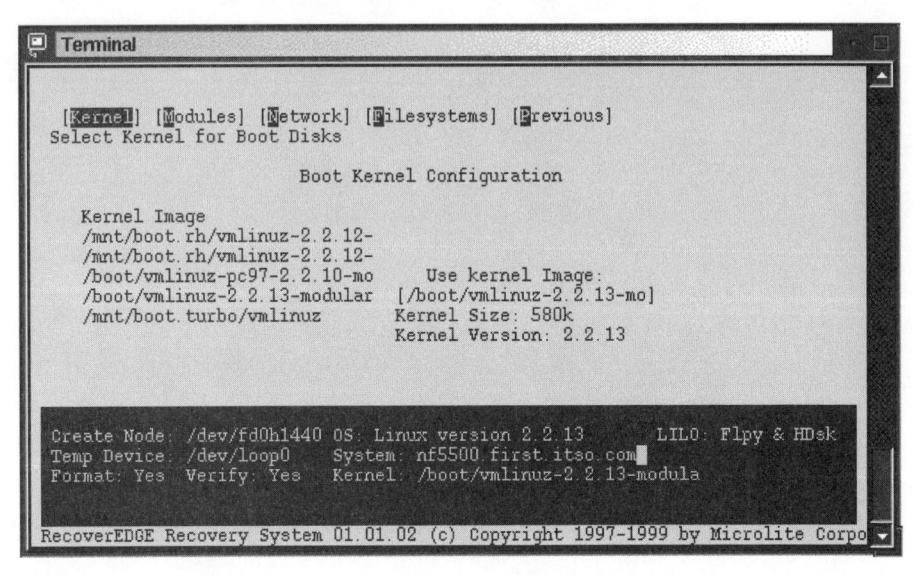

```
Terminal

[Kernel] [Modules] [Network] [Filesystems] [Previous]
Select Kernel for Boot Disks

                    Boot Kernel Configuration

   Kernel Image
   /mnt/boot.rh/vmlinuz-2.2.12-
   /mnt/boot.rh/vmlinuz-2.2.12-
   /boot/vmlinuz-pc97-2.2.10-mo     Use kernel Image:
   /boot/vmlinuz-2.2.13-modular     [/boot/vmlinuz-2.2.13-mo]
   /mnt/boot.turbo/vmlinuz          Kernel Size: 580k
                                    Kernel Version: 2.2.13


   Create Node: /dev/fd0h1440  OS: Linux version 2.2.13      LILO: Flpy & HDsk
   Temp Device: /dev/loop0     System: nf5500.first.itso.com
   Format: Yes  Verify: Yes    Kernel: /boot/vmlinuz-2.2.13-modula

RecoverEDGE Recovery System 01.01.02 (c) Copyright 1997-1999 by Microlite Corpo
```

Figure 225. Kernel options

Here you define which kernel will be used for creating the diskette.

5. Return to the previous stage and select **Modules** and press Enter, and you will see a window similar to Figure 226.

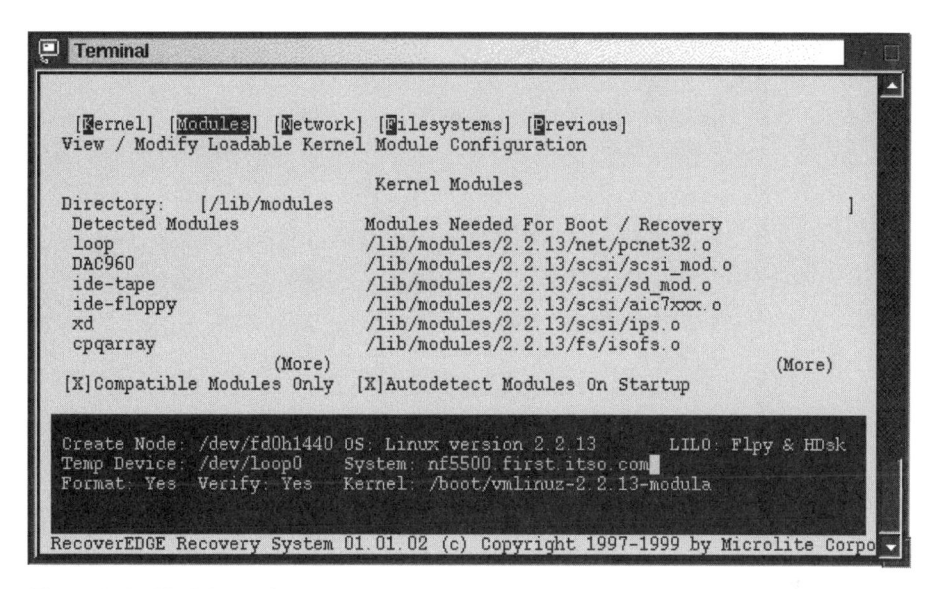

```
[Kernel] [Modules] [Network] [Filesystems] [Previous]
View / Modify Loadable Kernel Module Configuration
                              Kernel Modules
Directory:    [/lib/modules                                              ]
 Detected Modules          Modules Needed For Boot / Recovery
  loop                      /lib/modules/2.2.13/net/pcnet32.o
  DAC960                    /lib/modules/2.2.13/scsi/scsi_mod.o
  ide-tape                  /lib/modules/2.2.13/scsi/sd_mod.o
  ide-floppy                /lib/modules/2.2.13/scsi/aic7xxx.o
  xd                        /lib/modules/2.2.13/scsi/ips.o
  cpqarray                  /lib/modules/2.2.13/fs/isofs.o
             (More)                                        (More)
 [X]Compatible Modules Only  [X]Autodetect Modules On Startup

 Create Node: /dev/fd0h1440 OS: Linux version 2.2.13     LILO: Flpy & HDsk
 Temp Device: /dev/loop0    System: nf5500.first.itso.com
 Format: Yes  Verify: Yes   Kernel: /boot/vmlinuz-2.2.13-modula

RecoverEDGE Recovery System 01.01.02 (c) Copyright 1997-1999 by Microlite Corpo
```

Figure 226. Modules options

Here you define which modules will be used for building the initial ramdisk for the recovery system. In the Directory field you can specify the path to the modules which corresponds to the kernel you defined for booting. If you choose the option **Autoprobe Modules at Startup**, RecoverEDGE will load currently loaded modules.

> **Note**
>
> Do not forget to include the module for tape drives.

6. Return to the previous stage and select **Network** and press Enter, and you will see a window similar to Figure 227.

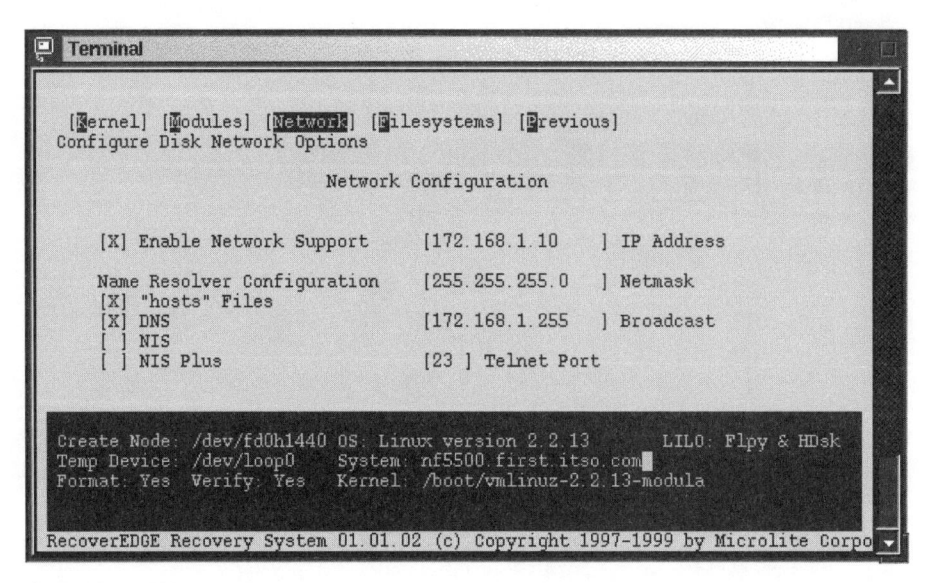

```
   [Kernel] [Modules] [Network] [Filesystems] [Previous]
   Configure Disk Network Options

                        Network Configuration

     [X] Enable Network Support    [172.168.1.10   ] IP Address

     Name Resolver Configuration   [255.255.255.0  ] Netmask
     [X] "hosts" Files
     [X] DNS                       [172.168.1.255  ] Broadcast
     [ ] NIS
     [ ] NIS Plus                  [23 ] Telnet Port


   Create Node:  /dev/fd0h1440  OS: Linux version 2.2.13         LILO: Flpy & HDsk
   Temp Device:  /dev/loop0      System: nf5500.first.itso.com
   Format: Yes   Verify: Yes     Kernel: /boot/vmlinuz-2.2.13-modula

   RecoverEDGE Recovery System 01.01.02 (c) Copyright 1997-1999 by Microlite Corpo
```

Figure 227. Network options

Here you define you network setup in case you will restore the system from a tape device on the network. You do not need this if you have a locally attached tape.

7. Return to the previous stage and select **Filesystems** and press Enter, and you will see a window similar to Figure 228.

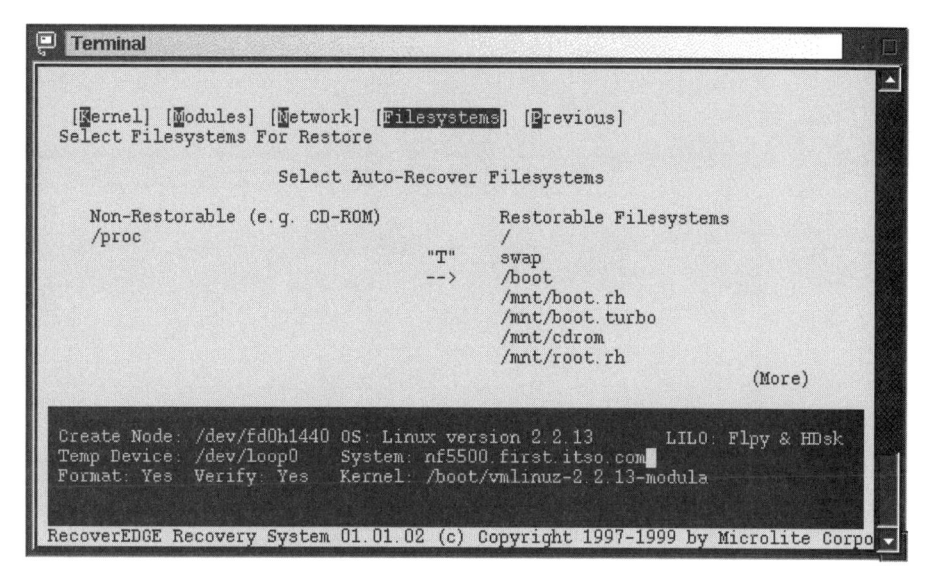

```
[Kernel] [Modules] [Network] [Filesystems] [Previous]
Select Filesystems For Restore

               Select Auto-Recover Filesystems

 Non-Restorable (e.g. CD-ROM)       Restorable Filesystems
 /proc                              /
                            "T"     swap
                            -->     /boot
                                    /mnt/boot.rh
                                    /mnt/boot.turbo
                                    /mnt/cdrom
                                    /mnt/root.rh
                                                        (More)

Create Node: /dev/fd0h1440 OS: Linux version 2.2.13     LILO: Flpy & HDsk
Temp Device: /dev/loop0    System: nf5500.first.itso.com
Format: Yes  Verify: Yes   Kernel: /boot/vmlinuz-2.2.13-modula

RecoverEDGE Recovery System 01.01.02 (c) Copyright 1997-1999 by Microlite Corpo
```

Figure 228. Filesystems options

Here you define which mounted filesystems will be recovered.

8. Return to the configuration panel and select the **Boot Loader** option and press Enter. You will see a window similar to Figure 229.

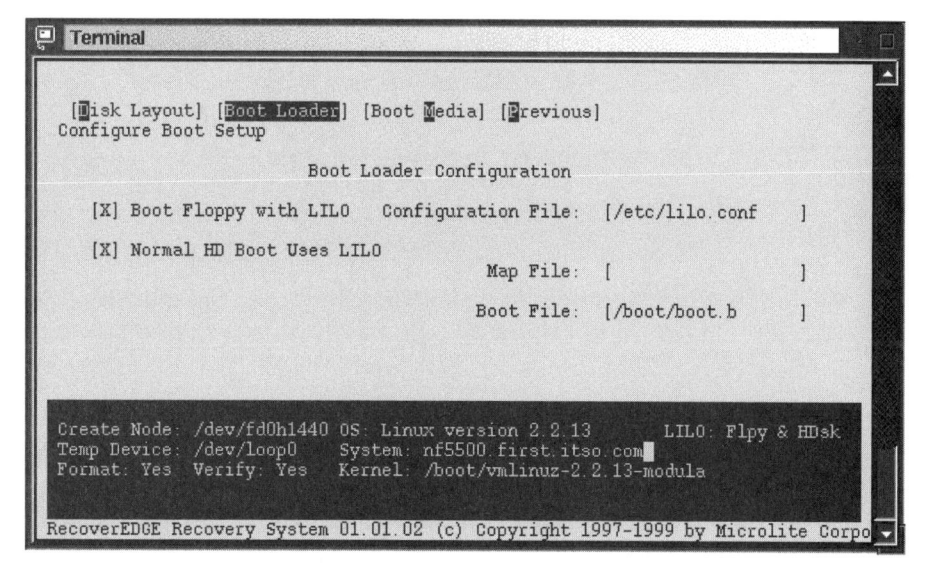

```
[Disk Layout] [Boot Loader] [Boot Media] [Previous]
Configure Boot Setup

                  Boot Loader Configuration

 [X] Boot Floppy with LILO    Configuration File: [/etc/lilo.conf  ]

 [X] Normal HD Boot Uses LILO
                                        Map File:  [               ]

                                        Boot File: [/boot/boot.b   ]

Create Node: /dev/fd0h1440 OS: Linux version 2.2.13     LILO: Flpy & HDsk
Temp Device: /dev/loop0    System: nf5500.first.itso.com
Format: Yes  Verify: Yes   Kernel: /boot/vmlinuz-2.2.13-modula

RecoverEDGE Recovery System 01.01.02 (c) Copyright 1997-1999 by Microlite Corpo
```

Figure 229. Boot Loader options

Here you define options for the Boot Loader.

9. Return to the configuration panel and select the **Boot Media** option and press Enter. You will see a window similar to Figure 230.

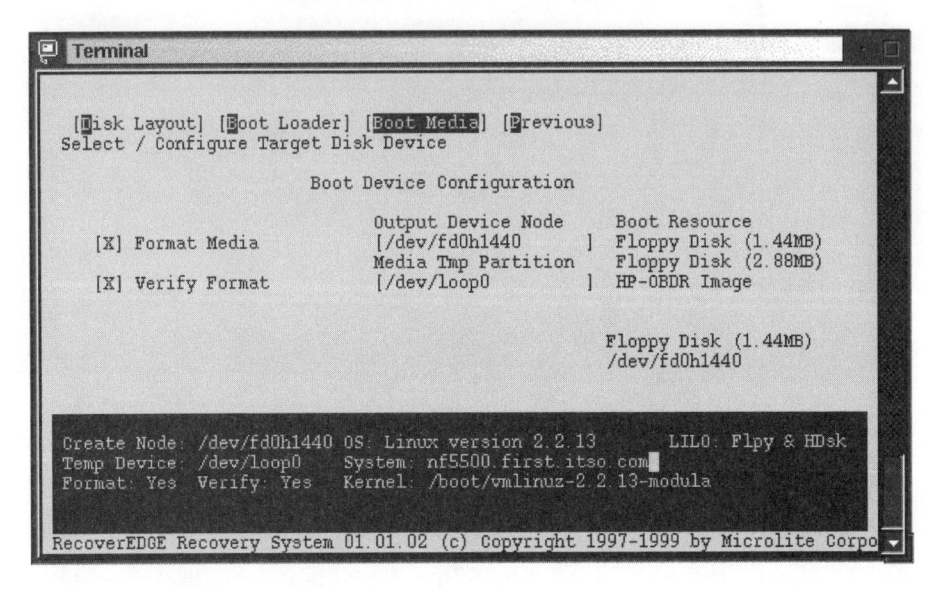

```
Terminal

[Disk Layout] [Boot Loader] [Boot Media] [Previous]
Select / Configure Target Disk Device

              Boot Device Configuration
                       Output Device Node     Boot Resource
  [X] Format Media     [/dev/fd0h1440    ]    Floppy Disk (1.44MB)
                       Media Tmp Partition    Floppy Disk (2.88MB)
  [X] Verify Format    [/dev/loop0       ]    HP-OBDR Image

                                              Floppy Disk (1.44MB)
                                              /dev/fd0h1440

Create Node: /dev/fd0h1440 OS: Linux version 2.2.13      LILO: Flpy & HDsk
Temp Device: /dev/loop0   System: nf5500.first.itso.com
Format: Yes  Verify: Yes   Kernel: /boot/vmlinuz-2.2.13-modula

RecoverEDGE Recovery System 01.01.02 (c) Copyright 1997-1999 by Microlite Corpo
```

Figure 230. Boot Media options

Here you define how the boot diskettes will be created.

Before you can make the diskettes you need to modify the configuration file of RecoverEDGE utility. To do this open the /usr/lib/edge/recover2/OSFILES file.

Make the following changes in that file:

a. Delete the line /bin/ash.

b. Change the line /lib/ld.so to /lib/ld-linux.so.1.9.9

10. After you configured all settings return to the main window and select **Make Disks.** You will be prompted to insert three diskettes.

> **Notes**
>
> If you get an error that diskettes cannot be created, the probable cause is that images are too big. Try to reduce the number of loaded modules or even make a special kernel just for this purpose, throwing out all unnecessary things.

After the diskettes are created you are ready to deal with a disaster on your system. But before it really happens, try to boot from these diskettes and verify if your tape device is recognized.

13.2.1.1 Verifying the RecoverEDGE boot diskettes

To verify the diskettes, boot from the first diskette and follow instructions on the window. When the system is started you will get a RecoverEDGE main menu. Select **Utilities -> Tape Drive**.

In the Tape Device Node field, you see the defined tape device. Go to the Test Tape Drive field and test your tape device. If the test is successful your recovery set is ready to use.

13.2.2 Recovering from total crash

To recover from a disaster crash follow these steps:

1. Resolve all hardware problems.

> **Note**
>
> Before restoring the system, initialize the Master Boot Records of all disks drives.

2. Boot the server from the first RecoverEDGE boot diskette.

3. When you are prompted to insert the root diskette, insert the second RecoverEDGE boot diskette. After the diskette is loaded, RecoverEDGE will start.

4. Select **Restore -> One Touch**. Follow the instructions on the window to complete recovery.

> **Note**
>
> For recovery you will use your master and incremental backups.

5. When all files are backed up, press a key to get back to the main window. All the filesystems will be then synchronized and the LILO will be set up and executed.

6. Before you reboot, switch to console 2 by pressing Alt+F2 and execute the following commands to check the fstab file for correct entries for your system:

```
mount /dev/sdb6 /mount
cat /mount/etc/fstab
```

In our example sdb6 is our root partition; you should use your root partition here.

That is all there is to it. Your restored system is ready to use.

13.3 More information on Microlite

For information on advanced features, consult the *Microlite User's Guide* or the Microlite Web site at:

```
http://www.microlite.com/
```

13.4 BRU

BRU is a Backup and Restore Utility with significant enhancements over other common utilities such as tar, cpio, volcopy and dump. BRU is designed to work with most backup devices, including cartridge, 4mm DAT, 8mm (Exabyte) and 9-track tape drives.

BRU includes incremental backups, full backups, multivolume archives, distribution and updates, error detection and recovery, random access capabilities, file comparisons, file overwrite protection, and increased speed over previous versions.

13.4.1 Installing BRU

Before we begin we need to know the following:

1. The device name of our tape drive. Typically under Caldera OpenLinux this will be /dev/st0.

2. The size of our backup medium in megabytes.

To install BRU from the floppy drive with the `tar` command do the following:

```
cd /tmp
tar xvf /dev/fd0
./install
```

Follow the prompts regarding readme files and licenses until you come to the following window:

```
###############################################################
Creating New /etc/brutab file.  This file will contain
information about devices on your system.
###############################################################


Please select backup devices from the following list
or enter Q when you are done.

a) 1/4 Inch Catridge Tape Drive
b) 4mm DAT Tape Drive
c) 8mm (Exabyte) Tape Drive
d) DLT (Digital Linear Tape)
e) Other
q) Quit


What is the type of this device: _
```

Figure 231. Selecting your backup devices

1. Select all of your backup devices and then enter Q when you are done.
2. You will now be asked to enter your BRU serial number.
3. When input correctly, you will be asked if you would like to install the X11 interface. Select **Y**.

The installation program needs to create an xbru directory. You can select a path or accept the default /usr/local/.

The installation program will install executables in a user-specified directory. The default is /usr/local/bin.

> **Note**
>
> The key configuration file is /etc/brutab. Consult the *BRU User's Guide* for advanced information. Do not edit unless you know what you are doing.

BRU is now installed.

13.4.2 Basic commands

The basic command structure for BRU is:

```
# bru modes [control options] [selection options] [files]
```

where BRU is the command or program followed by the mode specifying backup, restore, or various queries. Control options specify devices and buffer size. Selection options control which files or directories to work with. Files is the specified target of the bru command.

13.4.2.1 Basic backup
To back up a single file /home/ayne/.profile:

```
# bru -c -vvvv -G /home/ayne/.profile
```

To back up the complete directory /home/ayne:

```
# bru -c -vvvv -G /home/ayne
```

To back up the entire system:

```
# bru -c -vvvv -G /
```

13.4.2.2 Basic restore
To restore a single file /home/ayne/.profile:

```
# bru -x -vvvv -ua -w /home/ayne/.profile
```

To restore the complete directory /home/ayne:

```
# bru -x -vvvv -ua -w /home/ayne
```

To restore the entire system:

```
# bru -x -vvvv -ua -w /
```

13.4.2.3 Basic verification and listing commands
The -i mode can be used in conjunction with a backup command or by itself. The -i mode reads each block of data and verifies the check sum of the block. If used with the verbosity options (-vvvv), BRU will give a complete listing of the contents of an archive.

The -G mode displays the archive header block which contains detailed information on the archive including the command used to create the archive. See the *BRU User's Guide* for more information.

The -GG mode displays the contents of the on-tape directory. This mode can only be used if the archive was created with the -G option.

13.4.3 X interface
To use BRU's X interface, you will need to be in an X-Windows environment. Type xbru.

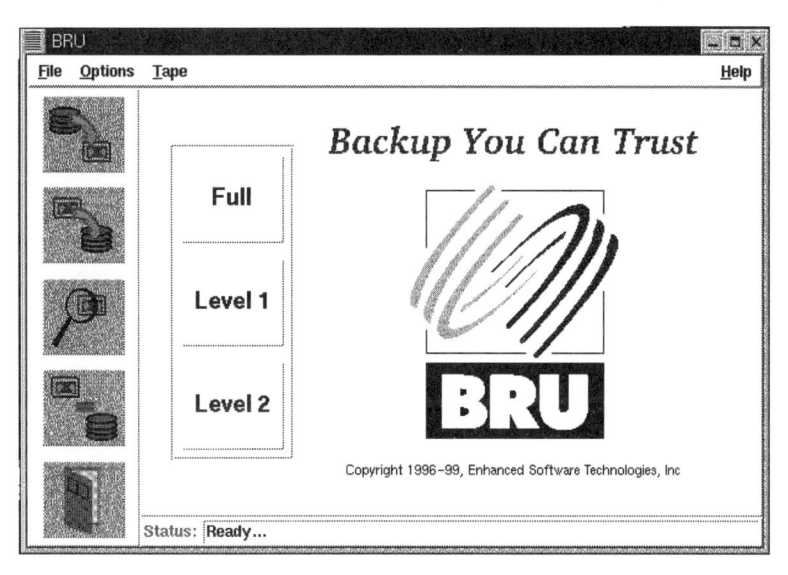

Figure 232. XBRU

You will see a figure similar to Figure 232.

From this interface you can:

- Create and restore backups.
- Create save, and load backup definitions.
- Schedule backups.
- List and verify the contents of archives.
- View the BRU log.

13.4.4 The big buttons

The three main buttons (Full, Level 1 and, Level 2) are shortcuts to various levels of backing up your system, directories, or individual files.

- Select **Full** to backup all the files in the user's home directory, or if the user is root, the entire system.
- Select **Level 1** to execute a backup for the same files as listed above on the condition that files have been modified since the previous full backup. If no previous full backup has been done, this will be considered a full backup.
- Select **Level 2** to execute a backup for the same files as listed above on the condition that files have been modified since the previous level 1

backup. If no previous level 1 backup has been done, this will be considered a level 1 backup.

13.4.4.1 Creating archives

Creating archives with BRU's X interface is simple. Click the **Backup** button to bring up the Backup File Selection interface (Figure 233).

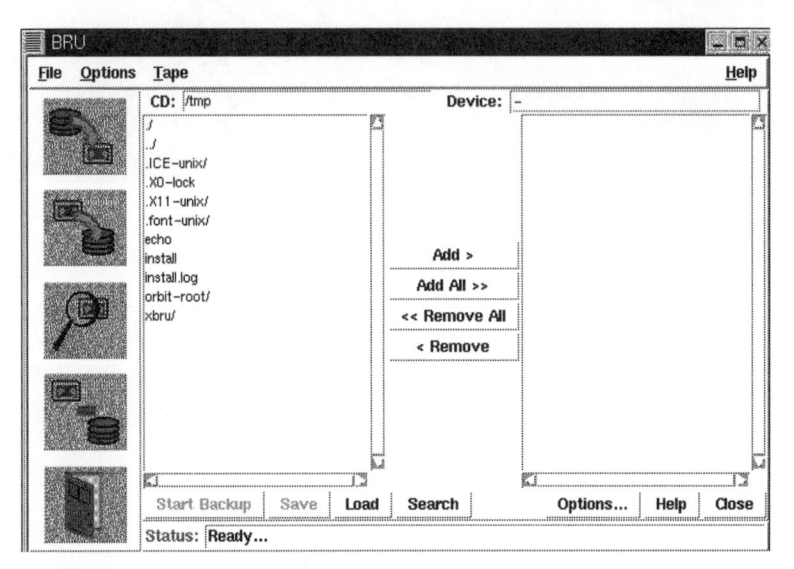

Figure 233. Creating an archive

The box on the left displays the contents of the current directory. You can change the current directory by clicking in the upper right hand corner of the window and editing the CD entry.

You can add or remove files and directories from the backup list by selecting them and clicking the appropriate button.

BRU also provides a search function. Click the **Search** button to bring up a dialog box prompting you for a search string. This string can contain typical wildcards.

Backup Definitions are a way to define a set of commonly used backup options or preferences for use at a future time. You can create definitions for use with the backup scheduler or simply use the default selections.

After you have selected the files and directories that you wish to back up, click the **Continue** button.You will be led through a series of dialog boxes regarding your overwriting, appending, and labeling preferences for the archive. The backup will proceed by presenting you with an estimated time to completion and a progress window.

13.4.4.2 Scheduling

To access the scheduling feature, select **File -> Scheduler**.

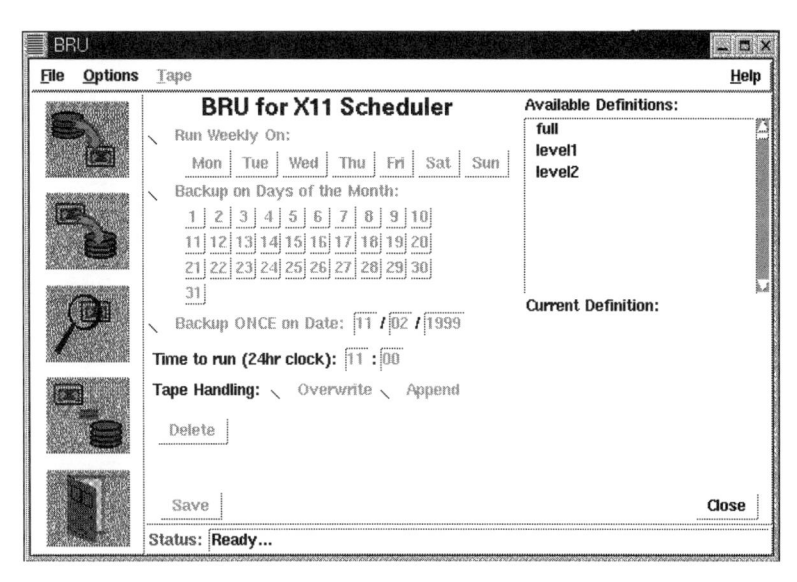

Figure 234. Scheduler

BRU provides a scheduling utility to automate the backup process for the busy administrator. There are three predefined definitions: Full, Level 1, and Level 2. These are the same definitions used in 13.4.4, "The big buttons" on page 277. You can create your own definitions in the Creating Archives interface.

From the BRU for X11 Scheduler interface, you can set scheduled backups based on weekly, monthly, or single dates. The scheduler is very flexible. In order to take advantage of the scheduling options, you must save your desired schedule configuration and verify that the scheduler is being run from cron. To verify or add the cron entry, log in as root and type:

```
crontab -e
```

Insert the following line:

```
0/5 * * * * /usr/local/bin/bruschedule
```

If you chose a different path for the binaries during installation, change the entry accordingly.

Save the crontab entry. You can now schedule backups.

13.4.4.3 Restoring files

Restoring files with BRU's X interface is simple. BRU will retrieve the contents of the archive when you click the **Restore** button. After scanning the archive, the Restore File Selection interface (similar to Figure 233) will appear.

> **Note**
>
> If the on-tape directory is not in the archive, then BRU must scan the entire archive to get a listing. This can be very time consuming. When creating an archive, use the -G option to create the on-tape directory.

The box on the left displays the contents of the current directory that is stored on the tape. You can change the current directory by clicking in the upper right hand corner of the window and editing the CD entry.

You can add or remove files and directories from the backup list by selecting them and selecting the appropriate button.

When you have selected all of the files and directories that you wish to restore, click the **Restore** button. A progress window will show each file as it is restored.

13.4.4.4 Listing and verifying archives

For listing the contents of an archive, BRU gives you three options:

1. Header - This option shows the archive header record which lists the label, creation date, version, and serial number. For more information on the Header, consult the *BRU User's Guide.*

2. Filenames only - This option displays the on-tape directory. If the archive was created without using the -G option, BRU will scan the entire archive to create a list of files. You will be prompted before this occurs as this can be a lengthy process.

3. Full details - This option scans the entire archive for details such as file names, permissions, owners, size, modification times, etc. This process can be time consuming.

For verifying archives, BRU gives you two options:

1. Checksum Verification - When archives are written, a checksum is calculated for each block of data. The checksum is stored in the header of each block. Checksum verification will read each block, recalculate the

checksum, and compare the checksum to the value in the header. Each file will be listed as it is verified, along with any errors found. If no errors are found, you know you have an accurate backup.

2. Differences Verification - BRU compares the files in the archive to the files on the hard drive. Any differences, such as modification times, size, or files in the archive that are nonexistent on the hard drive are noted. An end of differences notice will be listed when the verification is complete.

13.4.5 Summary

For information on advanced features consult your *BRU User's Guide* or the BRU Web site at:

```
http://www.estinc.com/
```

Appendix A. RAID levels

This appendix has been included for the convenience of our readers who are unfamiliar with the disk subsystem technology known as RAID. We anticipate that this will be a small percentage of our readership, because RAID is an important technology that most people implementing business-critical IT systems probably know about. RAID is mentioned in many places throughout this book and a basic appreciation of its features and benefits will help you to understand why.

Even those who know about RAID already will be interested to hear about the new RAID-5E level supported by IBM's latest ServeRAID adapter.

A.1 What is RAID?

Although very commonly implemented using SCSI disks, RAID is independent of the specific disk technology being used. IBM Netfinity servers have RAID controllers that support SCSI, Fibre Channel, and SSA disk subsystems. In addition, Windows NT supports its own software-based RAID, although this is not often used, as much of the performance gained from having a dedicated hardware RAID controller is lost.

A typical RAID disk subsystem will have between two and six physical disks that are accessed by the processor by way of a specialized RAID controller adapter. The controller makes the array appear as a single large virtual disk to the processor. Because this disk has six completely independent head mechanisms for accessing data (in the case of a six-drive array), the potential for improved performance is immediately apparent. In the optimal situation, all six heads could be providing data to the system without the need for the time-consuming head-seeks to different areas of the disk that would be necessary were a single physical disk being used.

However, the primary intent of a RAID implementation is to prevent the system served by the array from being affected by critical hard disk failures. Several different implementations of RAID have been defined and are referred to as levels. Each level has different characteristics and these levels allow a choice to be made to best meet the cost, security, and performance desired. The three most common implementations are levels 0, 1, and 5. These are the levels available with all of IBM's disk subsystems supported by Netfinity servers, namely SCSI, SSA, and Fibre Channel. The Netfinity ServeRAID-3HB Ultra2 SCSI adapter introduces a new enhanced RAID-5 described in A.1.5, "RAID-5 enhanced" on page 291.

A.1.1 RAID-0

RAID-0, sometimes referred to as disk striping, is not really a RAID solution since there is no redundancy in the array at all. The disk controller merely stripes the data across the array so that a performance gain is achieved. This is illustrated in Figure 235:

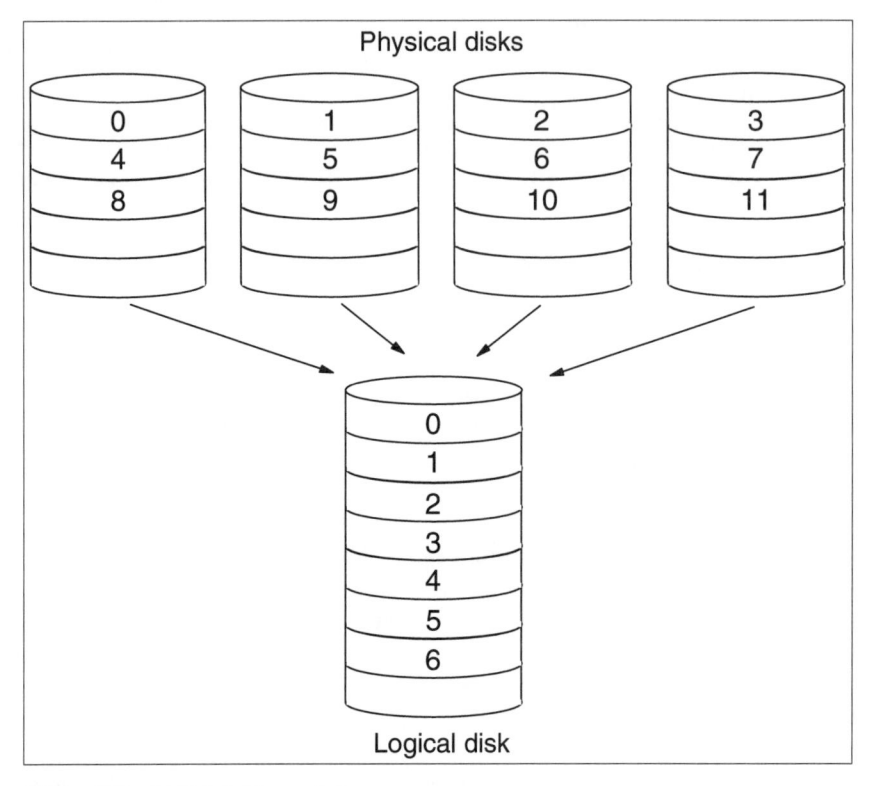

Figure 235. RAID-0 implementation

It is common for a striped disk array to map data in blocks with a stripe size that is an integer multiple of real drive track capacity. For example, IBM's ServeRAID adapters allow stripe sizes of 8 KB, 16 KB, 32 KB or 64 KB, selectable during initialization of the array. Applications get better performance if their data I/O size matches the stripe size of the array so it is recommended that you take this into consideration when defining your RAID sets.

Advantages:

- Performance improvement in many cases.
- All disk space available for data.

Disadvantages:

- No redundancy.

A.1.2 RAID-1 and RAID-1E

RAID-1, or disk mirroring, offers true redundancy. Each stripe is duplicated, or mirrored, on another disk in the array. In its simplest form, there are two disks where the second is a simple copy of the first. If the first disk fails then the second can be used without any loss of data. Some performance enhancement is achieved by reading data from both drives. Certain operating systems, including Windows NT, provide direct support for disk mirroring. There is a performance overhead, however, as the processor has to issue duplicate write commands. Hardware solutions where the controller handles the duplicate writes are preferred.

When more than two disks are available, the duplication scheme can be a little more complex to allow striping with disk mirroring, also known as Enhanced RAID-1. An example is shown in Figure 236:

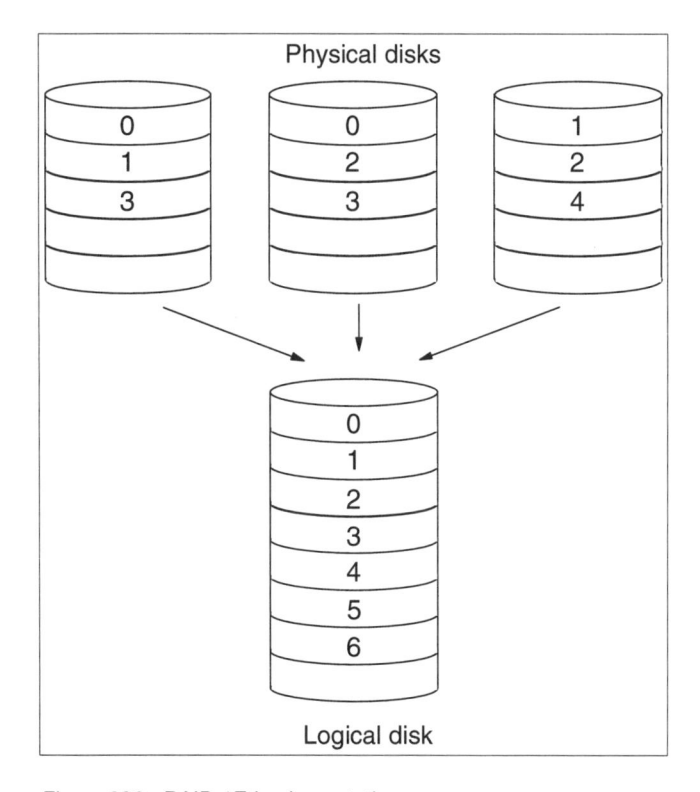

Figure 236. RAID-1E implementation

As you can see, any one disk can be removed from the array without loss of information because each data stripe exists on two physical disks. The controller detects a failed disk and redirects requests for data from the failed drive to the drive containing the copy of the data. When a drive has failed, the replacement drive can be rebuilt using the data from the remaining drives in the array.

When a disk fails, there is only one copy of the data that was on the failed disk available to the system. The system has lost its redundancy, and if another disk fails, data loss is the result. To avoid this, failed disks should be replaced as soon as possible. The controller then rebuilds the data that was on the failed disk from the remaining drives and writes it to the new disk, restoring the redundancy.

To avoid having to manually replace a failed disk, IBM's Netfinity ServeRAID controllers implement *hot spare* disks. A hot spare disk is held idle until a failure occurs, at which point the controller immediately starts to rebuild the lost data onto the hot spare, minimizing the time when redundancy is lost. The controller continues to provide data to the system while the rebuild takes place.

When you replace the failed drive, its replacement becomes the array's new hot spare.

Advantages:

- Performance improvement in many cases.
- Redundancy. A drive can fail without loss of data.

Disadvantages:

- Cost. The logical disk has only half the capacity of the physical disks.

A.1.3 RAID-10

As we have seen, RAID-1 offers the potential for performance improvement as well as redundancy. RAID-10 is a variant of RAID-1 that effectively creates a mirror copy of a RAID-0 array.

In large disk subsystems that require, for example, two external storage enclosures, it would be beneficial to ensure that mirrored data exists in both units. This would allow an entire unit, including its power supply or connecting cables, to fail without interrupting operation. RAID-10 does just this by allowing one RAID-0 array to be contained in one of the enclosures and its mirror copy in the other. A diagram of a RAID-10 configuration is shown below:

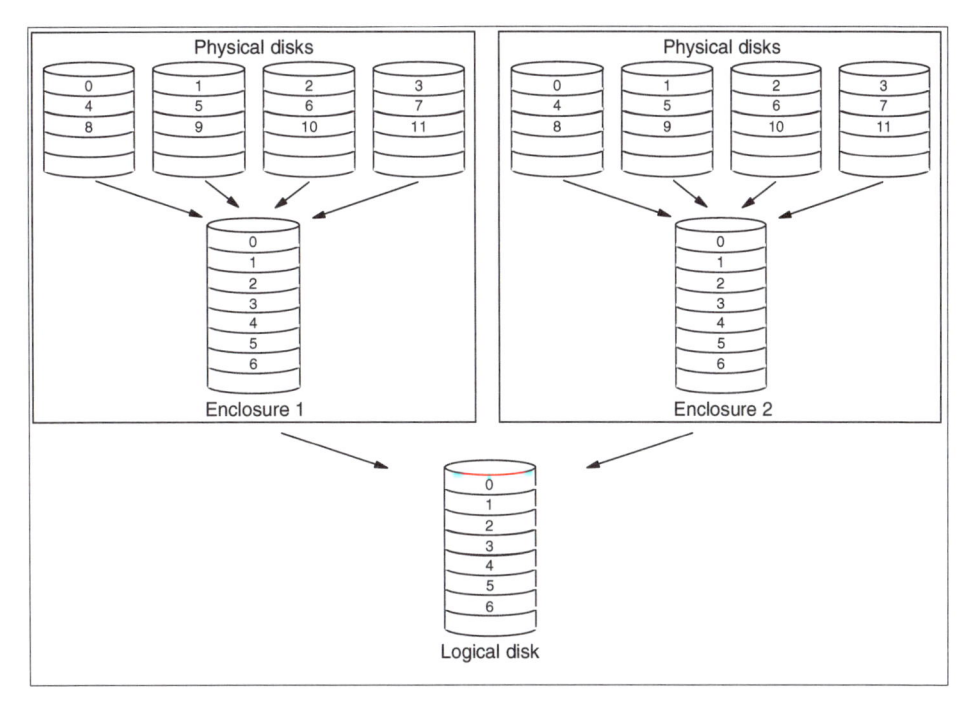

Figure 237. RAID-10 configuration

RAID-10 configurations are supported by the IBM Netfinity Fibre Channel RAID Controller Unit.

Advantages:

- Performance improvement in many cases.
- Redundancy. A drive can fail without loss of data.
- Provides fault tolerance for disk enclosures.

Disadvantages:

- Cost. The logical disk has only half the capacity of the physical disks.
- Slightly less flexible than RAID-1E (requires an even number of disks).

A.1.4 RAID-5

RAID-5 is one of the most capable and efficient ways of building redundancy into the disk subsystem. The way redundancy is implemented, capacity loss is equal to one of the drives in the array and data striping provides the read performance gains from RAID-0 and RAID-1. The principles behind RAID-5 are very simple and are closely related to the parity methods sometimes used for computer memory subsystems. In memory, the parity bit is formed by evaluating the number of 1 bits in a single byte. For RAID-5, if we take the example of a four-drive array, three stripes of data are written to three of the drives and the bit-by-bit parity of the three stripes is written to the fourth drive.

As an example, we can look at the first byte of each stripe and see what this means for the parity stripe. Let us assume that the first byte of stripes 1, 2, and 3 are the letters A, B, and G respectively. The binary code for these characters is 01000001, 01000010 and 01000111 respectively.

We can now calculate the first byte of the parity block. Using the convention that an odd number of 1s in the data generates a 1 in the parity, the first parity byte is 01000100 (see Table 24). This is called Even Parity because there is always an even number of 1s if we look at the data and the parity together. Odd parity could have been chosen; the choice is of no importance as long as it is consistent.

Table 24. Generation of parity data for RAID-5

Disk 1 "A"	Disk 2 "B"	Disk 3 "G"	Disk 4 Parity
0	0	0	0
1	1	1	1
0	0	0	0
0	0	0	0
0	0	0	0
0	0	1	1
0	1	1	0
1	0	1	0

Calculating the parity for the second byte is performed using the same method, and so on. In this way, the entire parity stripe for the first three data stripes can be calculated and stored on the fourth disk.

The presence of parity information allows any disk to fail without loss of data.

In the above example, if drive 2 fails (with B as its first byte) there is enough information in the parity byte and the data on the remaining drives to reconstruct the missing data. The controller has to look at the data on the remaining drives and calculate what drive 2's data must have been to maintain even parity. Because of this, a RAID-5 array with a failed drive can continue to provide the system with all the data from the failed drive.

Performance will suffer, of course, because the controller has to look at the data from all drives when a request is made to the failed one. However, that is better than losing the system completely. A RAID-5 array with a failed drive is said to be critica, since the loss of another drive will cause lost data. For this reason, the use of hot spare drives in a RAID-5 array is as important as in RAID-1.

The simplest implementation would always store the parity on disk 4 (in fact, this is the case in RAID-4, which is hardly ever implemented for the reason about to be explained). Disk reads are then serviced in much the same way as a level 0 array with three disks. However, writing to a RAID-5 array would then suffer from a performance bottleneck. Each write requires that both real data and parity data are updated. Therefore, the single parity disk would have to be written to every time any of the other disks were modified. To avoid this, the parity data is also striped, as shown in Figure 238, spreading the load across the entire array.

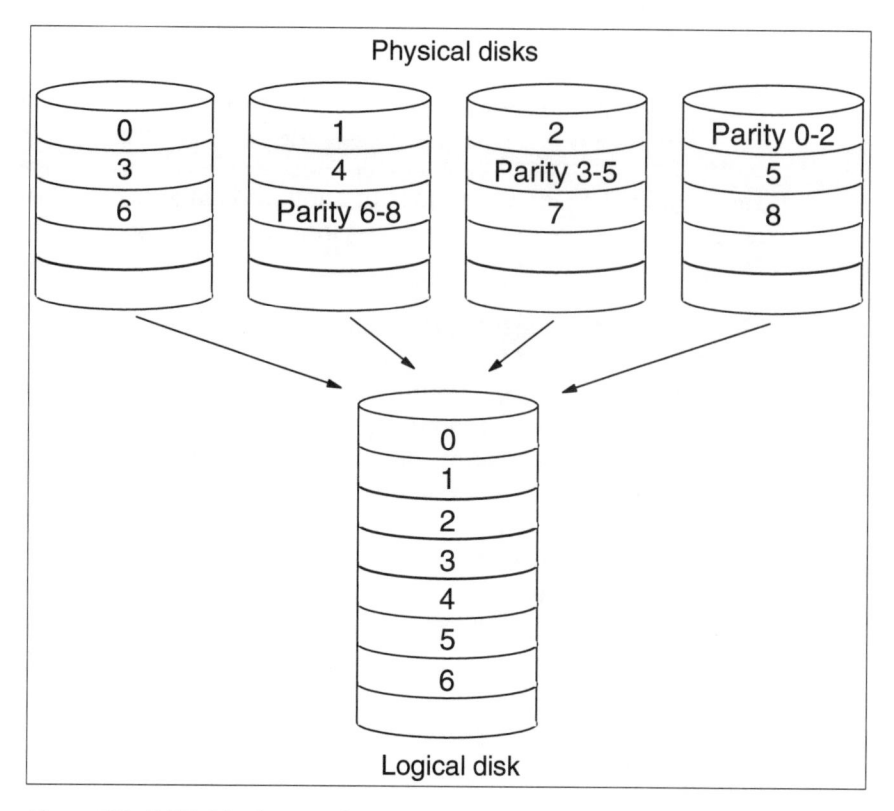

Figure 238. RAID-5 implementation

The consequence of having to update the parity information means that for every stripe written to the virtual disk, the controller has to read the old data from the stripe being updated and the associated parity stripe. Then the necessary changes to the parity stripe have to be calculated based on the old and the new data. All of this complexity is hidden from the processor, but the effect on the system is that writes are much slower than reads. This can be offset to a greater or lesser extent by the use of a cache on the RAID controller. IBM's ServeRAID controllers have cache as standard, which is used to hold the new data while the calculations are being performed. Meanwhile, the processor can continue as though the write has taken place. Battery backup options for the cache, available for some controllers, mean that data loss is kept to a minimum even if the controller fails with data still in the cache.

Advantages:

- Performance improvement in many cases.
- Redundancy. A drive can fail without loss of data.

- Storage overhead is equal to the size of only one drive.

Disadvantages:
- Overhead associated with writes can be detrimental to performance in applications where the write/read ratio is high. A controller cache can alleviate this.

A.1.5 RAID-5 enhanced

RAID-5 Enhanced (RAID-5E) puts hot spare drives to work to improve reliability and performance. A hot spare is normally inactive during array operation and is not used until a drive fails. By utilizing unallocated space on the drives in the array, a virtual distributed hot spare (DHS) can be created to improve reliability and performance. Figure 239 shows normal operation of a RAID-5E array. The data areas of the individual disks shown contain the application data and stripe parity data as for a normal RAID-5 array:

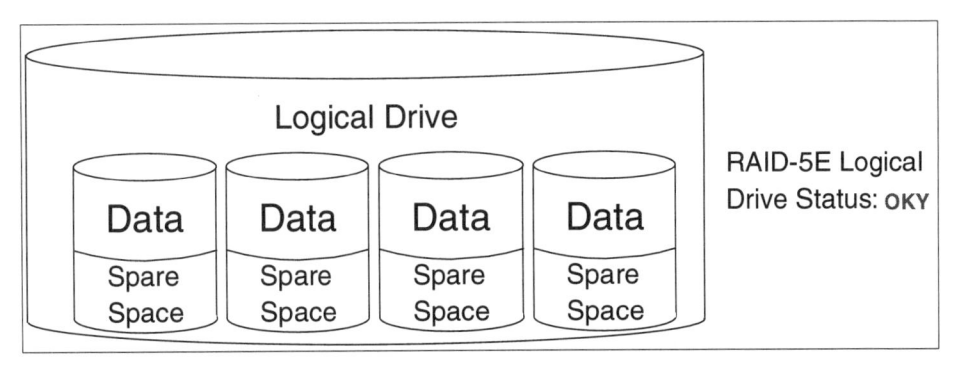

Figure 239. RAID-5E array: normal operation

In the event of a physical drive failing, its status will change to Defunct Disk Drive (DDD) and the ServeRAID adapter will start rearranging the data the disk contained into the spare space on the other drives in the array, provided there is enough space, of course.

Appendix A. RAID levels   **291**

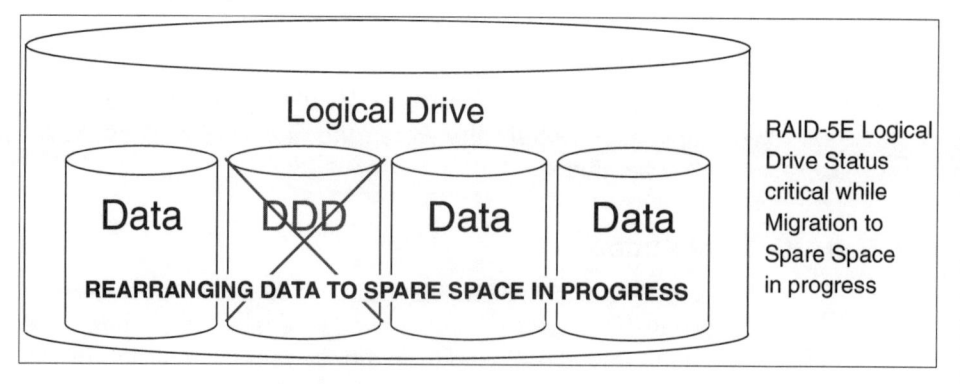

[Figure: Logical Drive with Data, DDD (failed), Data, Data disks. REARRANGING DATA TO SPARE SPACE IN PROGRESS. RAID-5E Logical Drive Status critical while Migration to Spare Space in progress]

Figure 240. RAID-5E array: single physical disk failure

During the migration of data, the logical drive will be in a critical, nonredundant state. As soon as all the data is rearranged, the logical drive will be marked OKY (Okay) and have full redundancy again. This is illustrated in Figure 241.

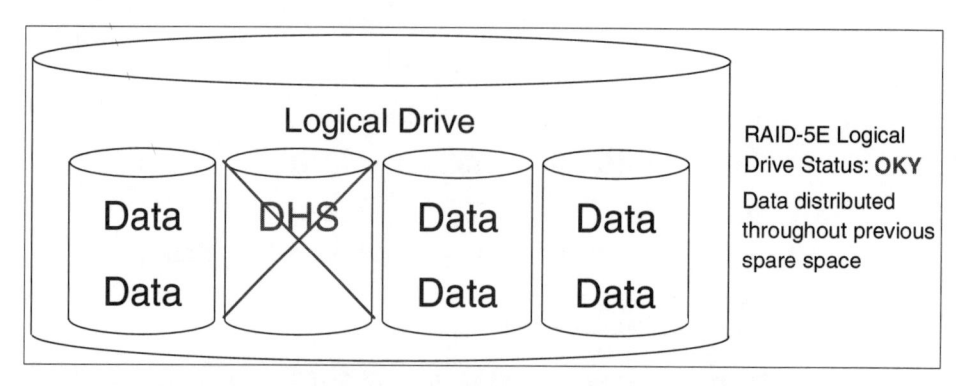

[Figure: Logical Drive with Data/Data, DHS (removed), Data/Data, Data/Data. RAID-5E Logical Drive Status: OKY. Data distributed throughout previous spare space]

Figure 241. RAID-5E array: data distributed throughout previous spare space

In the event of a second physical disk failure before the previously failed disk has been replaced, illustrated in Figure 242, normal RAID-5 procedures will be taken to provide service to the system through the checksum calculations described in A.1.4, "RAID-5" on page 287.

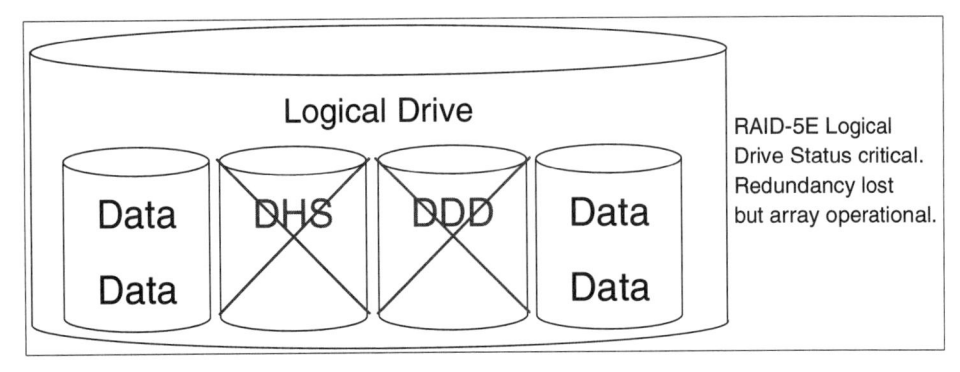

Figure 242. RAID-5E array: second physical disk failure

Advantages (compared to RAID-5):

- 15 - 20% performance improvement for smaller arrays with typical data transfer size.
- Protects data, even in the event of a two-drive failure.

Disadvantages:

- Migration time.

Design characteristics:

- One RAID-5E logical drive per array.
- Minimum of four physical drives in array configured for RAID-5E logical drive.

A.1.6 Orthogonal RAID-5

Orthogonal RAID-5 is an enhancement of RAID-5 in the sense that it is powered by more than one disk controller and hence improves both reliability and performance.

The performance of a disk subsystem depends on more than just the underlying performance of the disks. Multiple requests to one disk or across one adapter will typically take longer to satisfy than the same number of requests to multiple disks across multiple adapters.

In addition, the overall reliability of a standard RAID-5 system is dependent on the reliability of the one disk adapter to which all of the disks are connected. Orthogonal RAID-5 solves both of these concerns by grouping the disk arrays orthogonally to the disk adapters, SCSI buses, and power cables.

This would normally be implemented as a four-drive orthogonal RAID-5 array, where each disk would be connected to a different adapter and SCSI bus.

The result of this is that any one component of the disk subsystems, not just a disk drive, can fail with no loss of data and no interruption to system operation.

A.1.7 Performance

With different parameters affecting your RAID solution it is virtually impossible to find the perfect combination without measuring live throughput. Increasing redundancy also increases price and possibly lowers performance due to added overhead, which could be solved with more or faster controllers, again increasing the price.

As you can see in Figure 243 on page 295, speed is a significant issue when deciding on RAID level. The numbers shown in this figure and in Figure 244 on page 296 are based on benchmark testing performed by IBM's Netfinity server development team. Specific systems may not show precisely the same performance ratios but the figures are representative of typical performance data.

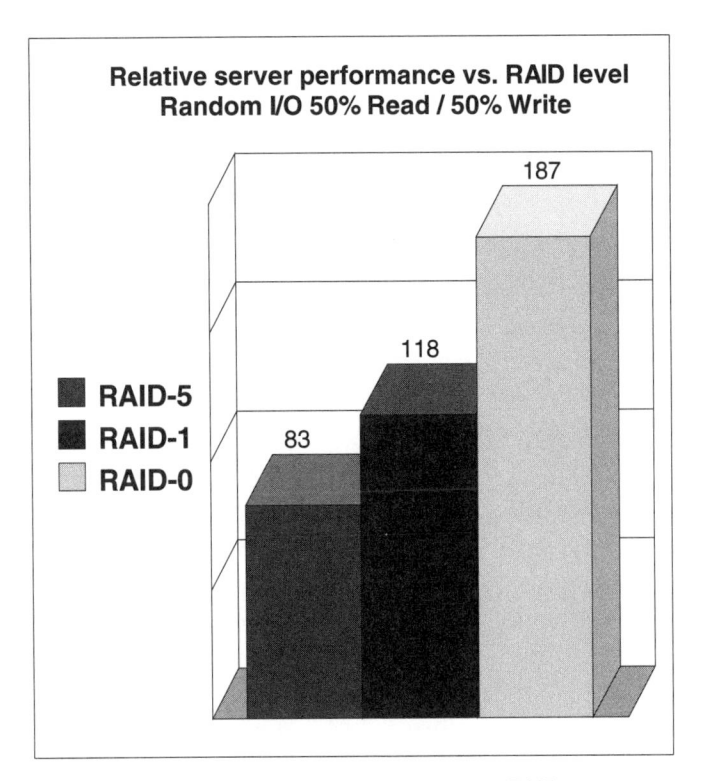

Figure 243. Relative server performance versus RAID strategy

It is important to point out that the speed difference in Figure 243 is mainly due to the same number of drives being used for all tests. Generally, the more drives you use in your array, the faster it gets, but it also requires your RAID controller to be able to attach more drives when using RAID-1 or RAID-5 to get optimal performance.

Using the same number of drives:

- RAID-0 gives up to 50% more throughput than RAID-1.
- RAID-1 gives up to 50% more throughput than RAID-5.

The above test was done using a worst-case scenario with 50% reads and 50% writes. A high write/read ratio adversely affects the performance of RAID-1 and RAID-5 arrays, so throughput improves with a higher percentage of reads, which is generally more common in a real-world environment.

- While increasing the number of drives boosts performance, it also increases the price. Figure 244 on page 296 shows what happens with I/O throughput when we add drives to a RAID-0 array.

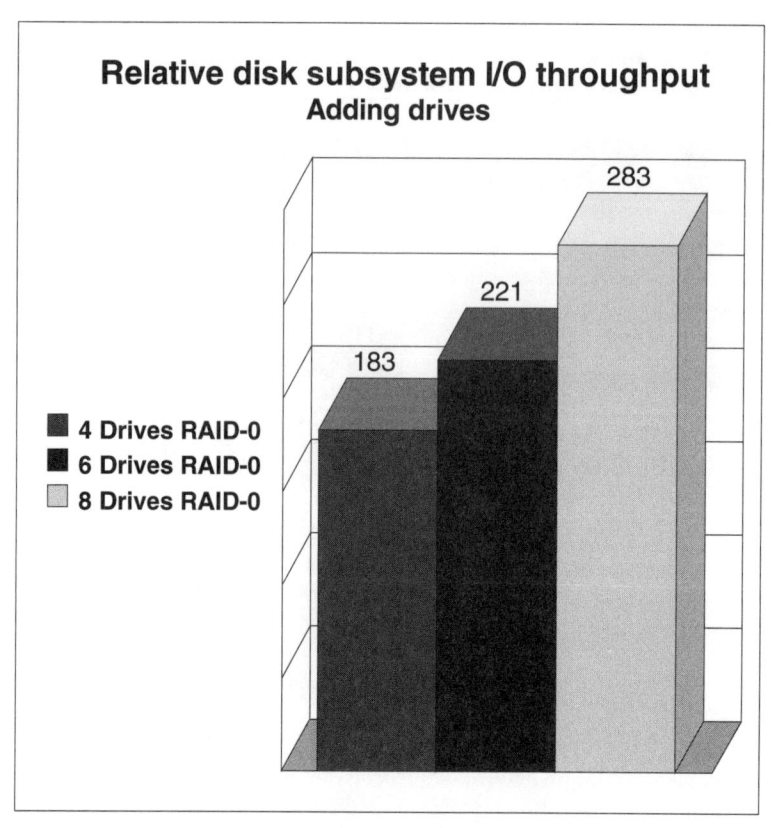

Relative disk subsystem I/O throughput
Adding drives

- 4 Drives RAID-0: 183
- 6 Drives RAID-0: 221
- 8 Drives RAID-0: 283

Figure 244. Adding drives to an array

Server throughput improves up to 50% when the number of drives is doubled for a RAID-0 and similar gains are shown for RAID-1 and RAID-5.

A.1.8 Recommendations

Before configuring your array you have to decide on a stripe size for the array. When configuring for maximum performance, Table 25 shows some rules of thumb:

Table 25. Recommended stripe configurations for ServeRAID adapters

Environment	Stripe size	Read-ahead
Groupware (Lotus Notes, Exchange)	16 KB	ON
Database Server (Oracle, SQL Server, DB/2)	16 KB	OFF
File Server (Windows NT 4.0, NetWare 4.1x)	16 KB	ON

Environment	Stripe size	Read-ahead
Web Server	8 KB	OFF
Other	8 KB	ON

A.1.9 Summary

RAID is an excellent and proven technology for protecting your data against the possibility of hard disk failure. IBM has a range of RAID controllers that bring the benefits of the technology to our Netfinity servers. As Intel-based servers become more and more critical to our customers' businesses, they are demanding the reliability provided by RAID.

Here is a quick summary of the different RAID levels we have covered in this appendix:

RAID-0: Block interleave data striping without parity

- Best performance of all RAID levels
- Drive seek times and latencies effectively reduced by parallel operation
- Significantly outperforms single large disk

RAID-1: Disk mirroring

- Fast and reliable but requires 100% disk space overhead
- Two copies of data maintained
- No performance degradation with a single disk failure
- Writes are slower than a single disk, reads are quicker

RAID-1E: Data stripe mirroring

- All the benefits of RAID-1
- Provides mirroring with an odd number of drives

RAID-10: Mirrored RAID-0 arrays

- All the benefits of RAID-1
- Can provide fault tolerance for entire storage enclosures

RAID-5: Block interleave data striping with distributed parity

- Best for random transactions
- Poor for large sequential reads if request is larger than block size
- Block size is the key to performance; must be larger than typical request size

- Performance degrades in recovery mode, that is, when a single drive has failed

RAID-5E: RAID-5 with distributed hot spare

- All the benefits of RAID-5
- 15 - 20% performance improvement for smaller arrays
- Protects data, even in the event of a two-drive failure

Orthogonal RAID-5: RAID-5 with multiple orthogonal disk adapters

- All the benefits of RAID-5
- Improved performance (due to load being spread across disk adapters)
- Improved reliability due to redundancy of disk adapters and disks

Table 26 gives you a summary of RAID performance characteristics:

Table 26. Summary of RAID performance characteristics

RAID level	Capacity	Large transfers	I/O rate	Data availability
RAID-0	Excellent	Very Good	Very Good	Poor[1]
RAID-1/1E	Moderate	Good	Good	Good
RAID-10	Moderate	Good	Good	Very Good
RAID-5	Very Good	Very Good	Good	Good
RAID-5E	Very Good	Very Good	Good to Very Good	Very Good
Orthogonal RAID-5	Very Good	Very Good	Good	Very Good

[1] Availability = MTBF of one disk divided by the number of disks in the array

If you want to learn more about RAID, the RAID Advisory Board, of which IBM is an active member, exists to standardize terminology and provide information about RAID technology. Its Web site can be found at the following URL:

    http://www.raid-advisory.com/

Appendix B. Working video modes for IBM Netfinity servers

In this appendix you can find some working modes for the Xfree86 servers for IBM Netfinity servers. All working graphics cards in IBM Netfinity servers use the XFree86 SVGA server. So before you do a video card probe, select the SVGA server. These are the modes tested in our working environment. If you want, you can try to find another working mode by yourself. This can be a time-consuming job. Good luck!

- Netfinity 3000

    Modeline "1152x864/70Hz" 92 at 24bpp

- Netfinity 3500M10

    Modeline "1024x768/70Hz" 75 at 16bpp

- Netfinity 5000

    Modeline "800x600/72Hz" 50 at 16bpp

- Netfinity 5600

    Modeline "800x600/85Hz" 60.75 at 24bpp

- Netfinity 5500 M10

    Modeline "1024x768/70Hz" 75 at 8bpp

- Netfinity 5500 M20

    Use XFree86 VGA server

- Netfinity 7000 M10

    Use XFree86 VGA server

- Netfinity 8500R

    Modeline "1152x864/70Hz" 92 at 24bpp

Appendix C. Recommendations for disk partitions

In Table 27 you can see recommended values for the partition sizes.

Table 27. Suggested partition and file system scheme

File system	Minimum (in MB)	Recommended (in MB)
/boot	10	25
swap	=RAM	=RAM*2
/	50	100
/usr	1000	1500
/var	25	128
/tmp	1	128
/opt	1	512
/home	5	2048

Appendix D. Hardware issues for IBM Netfinity servers

In this appendix we explain what you need to consider when you install Caldera OpenLinux on IBM Netfinity servers. This is because Caldera OpenLinux 2.3 and eServer have some limitations when installing on IBM Netfinity servers. Below you can find some hints for installing Caldera OpenLinux on IBM Netfinity servers:

1. Netfinity 3000

    - Although S3 Trio3D graphics chip is supported in XFree86 3.3.4 included in Caldera OpenLinux 2.3 and XFree 3.3.5 included in eServer, only some modes are working.

2. Netfinity 3500M10

    - S3 Savage4 graphics chip is not supported in XFree86 3.3.4 included in Caldera OpenLinux 2.3, so you can only use VGA server.
    - S3 Savage4 graphics chip is supported in XFree86 3.3.5 included in Caldera OpenLinux eServer, but only some modes are working.

3. Netfinity 5000

    - Caldera OpenLinux 2.3 install does not recognize the CD-ROM, so it is impossible to install from CD-ROM.
    - S3 Trio64V2 GX graphics chip is supported in XFree86 included in Caldera OpenLinux eServer, but only some modes are working.

4. Netfinity 5600

    - S3 Trio64 3D graphics chip is supported in XFree86 3.3.4 included in Caldera OpenLinux 2.3 and in XFree86 3.3.5 included in Caldera OpenLinux eServer, but only some modes are working.
    - AMD Am79C973 onboard Ethernet adapter is not supported in kernels up to 2.2.12.

5. Netfinity 5500 M10

    - S3 Trio64V2 GX graphics chip is supported XFree 3.3.4 included in Caldera OpenLinux 2.3 and in XFree 3.3.5 included in Caldera OpenLinux eServer, but only some modes are working.

6. Netfinity 5500 M20

    - S3 Trio64V2 GX graphics chip is supported XFree 3.3.4 included in Caldera OpenLinux 2.3 and in XFree 3.3.5 included in Caldera OpenLinux eServer, but because of the implementation on planar board only VGA server is working

7. Netfinity 7000 M10

    - S3 Trio64V2 GX graphics chip is supported XFree 3.3.4 included in Caldera OpenLinux 2.3 and in XFree 3.3.5 included in Caldera OpenLinux eServer, but only some modes are working, but because of the implementation on planar board only VGA server is working.

8. Netfinity 8500R

    - S3 Trio3D graphics chip is supported in XFree 3.3.4 included in Caldera OpenLinux 2.3 and in XFree 3.3.5 included in Caldera OpenLinux eServer, but only some modes are working.

Appendix E. Sample smb.conf SAMBA configuration file

```
# This is the main Samba configuration file. You should read the
# smb.conf(5) manual page in order to understand the options listed
# here. Samba has a huge number of configurable options (perhaps too
# many!) most of which are not shown in this example
#
# Any line which starts with a ; (semi-colon) or a # (hash)
# is a comment and is ignored. In this example we will use a #
# for commentry and a ; for parts of the config file that you
# may wish to enable
#
# NOTE: Whenever you modify this file you should run the command "testparm"
# to check that you have not many any basic syntactic errors.
#
#==================== Global Settings ==========================
[global]

# workgroup = NT-Domain-Name or Workgroup-Name
   workgroup = LINUX
   netbios name = NF5000


# server string is the equivalent of the NT Description field
   server string = Samba Server on Caldera OpenLinux %v


# This option is important for security. It allows you to restrict
# connections to machines which are on your local network. The
# following example restricts access to two C class networks and
# the "loopback" interface. For more examples of the syntax see
# the smb.conf man page
;   hosts allow = 192.168.1. 192.168.2. 127.

# If you want to automatically load your printer list rather
# than setting them up individually then you'll need this
   load printers = yes

# you may wish to override the location of the printcap file
;   printcap name = /etc/printcap

# It should not be necessary to specify the print system type unless
# it is non-standard. Currently supported print systems include:
# bsd, sysv, plp, lprng, aix, hpux, qnx
   printing = lprng


# Uncomment this if you want a guest account, you must add this to
/etc/passwd
```

305

```
# otherwise the user "nobody" is used
;   guest account = pcguest

# this tells Samba to use a separate log file for each machine
# that connects
  log file = /var/log/samba.d/smb.%m

# Put a capping on the size of the log files (in Kb).
  max log size = 50

# Security mode. Most people will want user level security. See
# security_level.txt for details.
   security = user
# Use password server option only with security = server
;    password server = <NT-Server-Name>

# Password Level allows matching of _n_ characters of the password for
# all combinations of upper and lower case.
;   password level = 8
;   username level = 8

# You may wish to use password encryption. Please read
# ENCRYPTION.txt, Win95.txt and WinNT.txt in the Samba documentation.
# Do not enable this option unless you have read those documents
  encrypt passwords = yes
  smb passwd file = /etc/samba.d/smbpasswd

# The following are needed to allow password changing from Windows to
# update the Linux sytsem password also.
# NOTE: Use these with 'encrypt passwords' and 'smb passwd file' above.
# NOTE2: You do NOT need these to allow workstations to change only
#        the encrypted SMB passwords. They allow the Unix password
#        to be kept in sync with the SMB password.
;   unix password sync = Yes
;   passwd program = /usr/bin/passwd %u
;   passwd chat = *New*UNIX*password* %n\n *ReType*new*UNIX*password* %n\n


*passwd:*all*authentication*tokens*updated*successfully*

# Unix users can map to different SMB User names
;   username map = /etc/samba.d/smbusers

# Using the following line enables you to customise your configuration
# on a per machine basis. The %m gets replaced with the netbios name
# of the machine that is connecting
;    include = /etc/samba.d/smb.conf.%m
```

```
# Most people will find that this option gives better performance.
# See speed.txt and the manual pages for details
   socket options = TCP_NODELAY

# Configure Samba to use multiple interfaces
# If you have multiple network interfaces then you must list them
# here. See the man page for details.
;   interfaces = 192.168.12.2/24 192.168.13.2/24
   interfaces = 9.24.106.169/24

# Configure remote browse list synchronisation here
#  request announcement to, or browse list sync from:
#a specific host or from / to a whole subnet (see below)
;   remote browse sync = 192.168.3.25 192.168.5.255
# Cause this host to announce itself to local subnets here
;   remote announce = 192.168.1.255 192.168.2.44

# Browser Control Options:
# set local master to no if you don't want Samba to become a master
# browser on your network. Otherwise the normal election rules apply
;   local master = no

# OS Level determines the precedence of this server in master browser
# elections. The default value should be reasonable
;   os level = 33

# Domain Master specifies Samba to be the Domain Master Browser. This
# allows Samba to collate browse lists between subnets. Don't use this
# if you already have a Windows NT domain controller doing this job
;   domain master = yes

# Preferred Master causes Samba to force a local browser election on
startup
# and gives it a slightly higher chance of winning the election
;   preferred master = yes

# Use only if you have an NT server on your network that has been
# configured at install time to be a primary domain controller.
;   domain controller = <NT-Domain-Controller-SMBName>

# Enable this if you want Samba to be a domain logon server for
# Windows95 workstations.
;   domain logons = yes

# if you enable domain logons then you may want a per-machine or
# per user logon script
```

```
# run a specific logon batch file per workstation (machine)
;    logon script = %m.bat
# run a specific logon batch file per username
;    logon script = %U.bat

# Where to store roving profiles (only for Win95 and WinNT)
#         %L substitutes for this servers netbios name, %U is username
#         You must uncomment the [Profiles] share below
;    logon path = \\%L\Profiles\%U

# All NetBIOS names must be resolved to IP Addresses
# 'Name Resolve Order' allows the named resolution mechanism to be
specified
# the default order is "host lmhosts wins bcast". "host" means use the unix
# system gethostbyname() function call that will use either /etc/hosts OR
# DNS or NIS depending on the settings of /etc/host.config,
/etc/nsswitch.conf
# and the /etc/resolv.conf file. "host" therefore is system configuration
# dependant. This parameter is most often of use to prevent DNS lookups
# in order to resolve NetBIOS names to IP Addresses. Use with care!
# The example below excludes use of name resolution for machines that are
NOT
# on the local network segment
# - OR - are not deliberately to be known via lmhosts or via WINS.
 name resolve order = wins lmhosts bcast

# Windows Internet Name Serving Support Section:
# WINS Support - Tells the NMBD component of Samba to enable it's WINS
Server
    wins support = yes

# WINS Server - Tells the NMBD components of Samba to be a WINS Client
#Note: Samba can be either a WINS Server, or a WINS Client, but NOT both
;    wins server = w.x.y.z

# WINS Proxy - Tells Samba to answer name resolution queries on
# behalf of a non WINS capable client, for this to work there must be
# at least one WINS Server on the network. The default is NO.
;    wins proxy = yes

# DNS Proxy - tells Samba whether or not to try to resolve NetBIOS names
# via DNS nslookups. The built-in default for versions 1.9.17 is yes,
# this has been changed in version 1.9.18 to no.
    dns proxy = no

# Case Preservation can be handy - system default is _no_
# NOTE: These can be set on a per share basis
```

```
;   preserve case = no
;   short preserve case = no
# Default case is normally upper case for all DOS files
;   default case = lower
# Be very careful with case sensitivity - it can break things!
;   case sensitive = no

#=========================== Share Definitions
==============================
[homes]
   comment = Home Directories
; this gives access to a 'Public' sub-directory in each user's home...
; (it is named 'public' as it is intended to be used by other sharing
; technologies (like NetWare, appletalk) too and may get disclosed due
; to weak protocols! -- hmm, are there less secure protocols than NFS? :)
   path = %H
   valid users = %S
   browseable = no
;   user = %S
;   only user = yes
   writable = yes
   create mask = 0700

# Un-comment the following and create the netlogon directory for Domain
Logons
; [netlogon]
;   comment = Samba Network Logon Service
;   path = /home/samba/netlogon
;   guest ok = yes
;   writable = no
;   share modes = no


# Un-comment the following to provide a specific roving profile share
# the default is to use the user's home directory
;[Profiles]
;    path = /home/samba/profiles
;    browseable = no
;    guest ok = yes


# NOTE: If you have a BSD-style print system there is no need to
# specifically define each individual printer
[printers]
   comment = All Printers
   path = /var/spool/samba
   browseable = no
```

Appendix E. Sample smb.conf SAMBA configuration file **309**

```
# Set public = yes to allow user 'guest account' to print
   guest ok = no
   writable = no
   printable = yes
   create mask = 0700

# A publicly accessible directory, but read only, except for people in
# the "users" group
[public]
   comment = Public Stuff
   path = /home/public
   browseable = yes
   public = yes
   writable = yes
   printable = no
# access may be controlled by these options
;  read list = user1, user2, @group
;  valid users = user1, user3
   write list = @users,@root

# Other examples.
#
# This one is useful for people to share files, BUT
# access to '/tmp' or '/var/tmp' should *not* be given lightly,
# as this can (still) pose a security threat!
# Better use a dedicate sub-directory to /(var/)tmp or something
# like a [public] share!
;[tmp]
;   comment = Temporary file space
;   path = /tmp
;   read only = no
;   public = yes

[redbook]
   comment = Redbook files
   path = /redbook
   browseable = yes
   printable = no
   writable = yes
   write list = @users

# A private printer, usable only by fred. Spool data will be placed in fred's
# home directory. Note that fred must have write access to the spool directory,
# wherever it is.
;[fredsprn]
```

```
;       comment = Fred's Printer
;       valid users = fred
;       path = /homes/fred
;       printer = freds_printer
;       public = no
;       writable = no
;       printable = yes

# A private directory, usable only by fred. Note that fred requires write
# access to the directory.
;[fredsdir]
;       comment = Fred's Service
;       path = /usr/somewhere/private
;       valid users = fred
;       public = no
;       writable = yes
;       printable = no

# a service which has a different directory for each machine that connects
# this allows you to tailor configurations to incoming machines. You could
# also use the %u option to tailor it by user name.
# The %m gets replaced with the machine name that is connecting.
;[pchome]
;       comment = PC Directories
;       path = /usr/pc/%m
;       public = no
;       writable = yes

# A publicly accessible directory, read/write to all users. Note that all
files
# created in the directory by users will be owned by the default user, so
# any user with access can delete any other user's files. Obviously this
# directory must be writable by the default user. Another user could of
course
# be specified, in which case all files would be owned by that user instead.
;[public]
;       path = /usr/somewhere/else/public
;       public = yes
;       only guest = yes
;       writable = yes
;       printable = no

# The following two entries demonstrate how to share a directory so that
two
# users can place files there that will be owned by the specific users. In
this
# setup, the directory should be writable by both users and should have the
```

```
# sticky bit set on it to prevent abuse. Obviously this could be extended to
# as many users as required.
;[myshare]
;    comment = Mary's and Fred's stuff
;    path = /usr/somewhere/shared
;    valid users = mary fred
;    public = no
;    writable = yes
;    printable = no
;    create mask = 0765
```

Appendix F. Special notices

This publication is intended to help customers, business partners and IBM employees implement Caldera OpenLinux on Netfinity servers. The information in this publication is not intended as the specification of any programming interfaces that are provided by OpenLinux or Netfinity. See the PUBLICATIONS section of the IBM Programming Announcement for Netfinity for more information about what publications are considered to be product documentation.

References in this publication to IBM products, programs or services do not imply that IBM intends to make these available in all countries in which IBM operates. Any reference to an IBM product, program, or service is not intended to state or imply that only IBM's product, program, or service may be used. Any functionally equivalent program that does not infringe any of IBM's intellectual property rights may be used instead of the IBM product, program or service.

Information in this book was developed in conjunction with use of the equipment specified, and is limited in application to those specific hardware and software products and levels.

IBM may have patents or pending patent applications covering subject matter in this document. The furnishing of this document does not give you any license to these patents. You can send license inquiries, in writing, to the IBM Director of Licensing, IBM Corporation, North Castle Drive, Armonk, NY 10504-1785.

Licensees of this program who wish to have information about it for the purpose of enabling: (i) the exchange of information between independently created programs and other programs (including this one) and (ii) the mutual use of the information which has been exchanged, should contact IBM Corporation, Dept. 600A, Mail Drop 1329, Somers, NY 10589 USA.

Such information may be available, subject to appropriate terms and conditions, including in some cases, payment of a fee.

The information contained in this document has not been submitted to any formal IBM test and is distributed AS IS. The use of this information or the implementation of any of these techniques is a customer responsibility and depends on the customer's ability to evaluate and integrate them into the customer's operational environment. While each item may have been reviewed by IBM for accuracy in a specific situation, there is no guarantee that the same or similar results will be obtained elsewhere. Customers attempting to adapt these techniques to their own environments do so at their own risk.

Any pointers in this publication to external Web sites are provided for convenience only and do not in any manner serve as an endorsement of these Web sites.

The following terms are trademarks of the International Business Machines Corporation in the United States and/or other countries:

AIX	AS/400
DB2	Home Director
IBM	Netfinity
OS/2	RS/6000
ServeRAID	SP
System/390	TechConnect
WebSphere	XT

The following terms are trademarks of other companies:

Caldera, the C-logo, OpenLinux, and DR-DOS are either registered trademarks or trademarks of Caldera, Inc.

LINUX is a registered trademark of Linus Torvalds.

C-bus is a trademark of Corollary, Inc. in the United States and/or other countries.

Java and all Java-based trademarks and logos are trademarks or registered trademarks of Sun Microsystems, Inc. in the United States and/or other countries.

Microsoft, Windows, Windows NT, and the Windows logo are trademarks of Microsoft Corporation in the United States and/or other countries.

PC Direct is a trademark of Ziff Communications Company in the United States and/or other countries and is used by IBM Corporation under license.

ActionMedia, LANDesk, MMX, Pentium and ProShare are trademarks of Intel Corporation in the United States and/or other countries.

UNIX is a registered trademark in the United States and other countries licensed exclusively through The Open Group.

SET and the SET logo are trademarks owned by SET Secure Electronic

Transaction LLC.

Other company, product, and service names may be trademarks or service marks of others.

Appendix G. Related publications

The publications listed in this section are considered particularly suitable for a more detailed discussion of the topics covered in this redbook.

G.1 International Technical Support Organization publications

For information on ordering these ITSO publications see "How to get IBM Redbooks" on page 321.

- *Linux for WebSphere and DB2 Servers*, SG24-5850
- *Netfinity and Red Hat Linux Integration Guide*, SG24-5853
- *Netfinity and SuSE Linux Integration Guide*, SG24-5863
- *Netfinity and TurboLinux Integration Guide*, SG24-5862

G.2 Redbooks on CD-ROMs

Redbooks are also available on the following CD-ROMs. Click the CD-ROMs button at `http://www.redbooks.ibm.com/` for information about all the CD-ROMs offered, updates and formats.

CD-ROM Title	Collection Kit Number
System/390 Redbooks Collection	SK2T-2177
Networking and Systems Management Redbooks Collection	SK2T-6022
Transaction Processing and Data Management Redbooks Collection	SK2T-8038
Lotus Redbooks Collection	SK2T-8039
Tivoli Redbooks Collection	SK2T-8044
AS/400 Redbooks Collection	SK2T-2849
Netfinity Hardware and Software Redbooks Collection	SK2T-8046
RS/6000 Redbooks Collection (BkMgr)	SK2T-8040
RS/6000 Redbooks Collection (PDF Format)	SK2T-8043
Application Development Redbooks Collection	SK2T-8037
IBM Enterprise Storage and Systems Management Solutions	SK3T-3694

G.3 Other publications

These publications are also relevant as further information sources:

- *Understanding and Deploying LDAP Directory Services,* by Timothy Howes, Mark Smith, and Gordon Good, ISBN: 1578700701

- *The Linux NIS(YP)/NYS/NIS+ HOWTO* by Thorsten Kakuk, found at: http://metalab.unc.edu/pub/Linux/docs/HOWTO/NIS-HOWTO.
- *Managing NFS and NIS,* by Hal Stern, ISBN 0937175757

G.4 Referenced Web sites

- http://www.suse.com/Support/Doku/FAQ
- http://www.redbooks.ibm.com
- http://www.pc.ibm.com/us/netfinity/tech_library.html
- http://www.pc.ibm.com/support
- http://www.networking.ibm.com
- http://www.developer.ibm.com/welcome/netfinity/serveraid.html
- http://www.isc.org
- http://www.kde.org
- http://www.rpm.org
- http://linux.powertweak.com
- http://tune.linux.com
- http://www.tunelinux.com
- http://www.linux-mandrake.com/lothar
- http://www.textuality.com/bonnie
- http://www.netperf.org/netperf/NetperfPage.html
- http://www.samba.org
- http://www.linuxdoc.org
- http://www.linuxdoc.org/HOWTO/DNS-HOWTO.html
- http://www.netcraft.com/survey
- http://www.apache.org
- http://www-4.ibm.com/software/webservers/httpservers/download.html
- http://www-4.ibm.com/software/webservers/httpservers/doc/v136/
- http://www.apache.org/docs/misc/perf-tuning.html
- http://modules.apache.org
- http://www.sendmail.org
- http://www.openldap.org/incoming/roaming-073099.tar.gz

- http://help.netscape.com/products/client/communicator/manual_roaming2.html
- http://www.openldap.org
- http://metalab.unc.edu/pub/Linux/docs/HOWTO/NIS-HOWTO
- http://www.rustcorp.com/linux/ipchains
- http://www.estinc.com
- http://www.microlite.com
- http://www.raid-advisory.com
- http://www.elink.ibmlink.ibm.com/pbl/pbl
- http://w3.itso.ibm.com
- http://w3.ibm.com

How to get IBM Redbooks

This section explains how both customers and IBM employees can find out about ITSO redbooks, redpieces, and CD-ROMs. A form for ordering books and CD-ROMs by fax or e-mail is also provided.

- **Redbooks Web Site** `http://www.redbooks.ibm.com/`

    Search for, view, download, or order hardcopy/CD-ROM redbooks from the redbooks Web site. Also read redpieces and download additional materials (code samples or diskette/CD-ROM images) from this redbooks site.

    Redpieces are redbooks in progress; not all redbooks become redpieces and sometimes just a few chapters will be published this way. The intent is to get the information out much quicker than the formal publishing process allows.

- **E-mail Orders**

    Send orders by e-mail including information from the redbooks fax order form to:

	e-mail address
In United States	usib6fpl@ibmmail.com
Outside North America	Contact information is in the "How to Order" section at this site: `http://www.elink.ibmlink.ibm.com/pbl/pbl`

- **Telephone Orders**

United States (toll free)	1-800-879-2755
Canada (toll free)	1-800-IBM-4YOU
Outside North America	Country coordinator phone number is in the "How to Order" section at this site: `http://www.elink.ibmlink.ibm.com/pbl/pbl`

- **Fax Orders**

United States (toll free)	1-800-445-9269
Canada	1-403-267-4455
Outside North America	Fax phone number is in the "How to Order" section at this site: `http://www.elink.ibmlink.ibm.com/pbl/pbl`

This information was current at the time of publication, but is continually subject to change. The latest information may be found at the redbooks Web site.

IBM Intranet for Employees

IBM employees may register for information on workshops, residencies, and redbooks by accessing the IBM Intranet Web site at `http://w3.itso.ibm.com/` and clicking the ITSO Mailing List button. Look in the Materials repository for workshops, presentations, papers, and Web pages developed and written by the ITSO technical professionals; click the Additional Materials button. Employees may access `MyNews` at `http://w3.ibm.com/` for redbook, residency, and workshop announcements.

IBM Redbooks fax order form

Please send me the following:

Title	Order Number	Quantity

First name _____ Last name _____

Company _____

Address _____

City _____ Postal code _____ Country _____

Telephone number _____ Telefax number _____ VAT number _____

☐ Invoice to customer number _____

☐ Credit card number _____

Credit card expiration date _____ Card issued to _____ Signature _____

We accept American Express, Diners, Eurocard, Master Card, and Visa. Payment by credit card not available in all countries. Signature mandatory for credit card payment.

List of abbreviations

AIX	advanced interactive executive	IBM	International Business Machines Corporation
BIOS	Basic Input/Output System	IDE	integrated drive electronics
BOOTP	boot protocol	IETF	Internet Engineering Task Force
bpp	bits per pixel	I/O	input/output
BRU	Backup and Restore Utility	IP	Internet Protocol
CGI	Common Gateway Interface	IPX/SPX	Internet Packet exchange/Sequenced Packet exchange
CIFS	Common Internet File System	IRC	Internet Relay Chat
COAS	Caldera Open Administration System	ISA	Industry Standard Architecture
CPU	central processing unit	ISDN	integrated-services digital network
DARPA	Defense Advanced Research Projects Agency	ISO	International Organization for Standardization
DAT	digital audio tape	ITSO	International Technical Support Organization
DHCP	Dynamic Host Configuration Protocol	ITU	International Telecommunications Union
DMA	direct memory access		
DNS	Domain Name Service	KB	kilobyte
FQDN	fully qualified domain name	KDE	K Desktop Environment
		LAN	local area network
FTP	file transport protocol	LDAP	Lightweight Directory Access Protocol
GB	gigabyte		
GPM	Gereral Purpose Mouse	LILO	Linux Loader
GUI	graphical user interface	MB	megabyte
HTML	Hypertext Markup Language	Mhz	megahertz
		mm	milimeter
HTTP	Hypertext Transfer Protocol	MTA	Mail Transfer Agent
Hz	Hertz	NAT	Network Address Translation

323

NFS	Network File System	TCP/IP	Transmission Control Protocol/Internet Protocol
NIC	Network Interface Card		
NIS	Network Information System	URL	Universal Resource Locator
PCI	Peripheral Component Interconnect	VGA	video graphics array
PCMCIA	Personal Computer Memory Card International Association	WINS	Windows Internet Name Service
		WWW	World Wide Web
PNP	Plug and Play		
POP	Post Office Protocol		
RAID	redundant array of imdependent disks		
RAM	random access memory		
RFC	Request for Comments		
RPC	Remote Procedure Call		
RPM	Red Hat Package Manager		
SCSI	small computer system interface		
SMB	Server Message Block		
SMBFS	Samba File System		
SMP	symmetric multiprocessing		
SMTP	Simple Mail Transfer Protocol		
SNMP	simple network management protocol		
SSA	serial storage architecture		
SSL	Secure Sockets Layer		
SVGA	super video graphics array		
SWAT	Samba Web Administration Tool		

Index

A
accounts 79
 managing accounts 81, 85
Adaptec SCSI Controller 2
Apache 167
 installation 169
 performance tips 178

B
backup and recovery 239
basic system administration 65
 console 66
 KDE 68
 kpackage 72
 login 66
 package
  install 75
  uninstall 74
 RPM 77
 terminal 69
BIOS 2
BRU 274
 additional information 281
 basic backup 276
 basic commands 275
 basic restore 276
 creating archives 278
 installing 274
 restore 280
 schedule backup 279
 X interface 276

C
COAS 65, 69, 70, 72, 78
 accounts 79
  managing accounts 81
  managing groups 85
 daemons 88
 filesystem 89
 hostname 90
 kernel modules 106
 network 99
 peripherials 93
  mouse 94
  printer 95
 resources 91
 services 88
 time 92
custom setup 13

D
DARPA 222
DAS 200
DHCP 27, 163
 installation 163
 lease time 164
 token-ring 63
disk striping 284
disk subsystem
 See also RAID
 RAID performance 294
DIXIE 200
DNS 104, 155, 182
 configuration 157, 162
 installation 157

E
Ethernet 100

F
file/print 123
firmware 2
format partitions 20

H
hardware requirements 1
hostname 90

I
IBM HTTP Server 167, 168
 Administration Server 173
 installation 170
 performance tips 179
IETF 200
installation type 23
installing Linux 1, 3
 custom setup 13
 DHCP 27
 hardware issues 303
 installation type 20, 23

keyboard setup   7
language   5
LILO   28
logon   33
monitor setup   10
mouse setup   6
network setup   27
partitions   13, 14
root password   24
ServeRAID   33
Tetris   30
time zone   29
token-ring   61
video setup   8

K

KDE   68
kernel modules   106
keyboard   7
kpackage   72, 124
    check dependencies   76
    install   75
    replace file   76
    replace package   76
    test   76
    uninstall   74
    upgrade   76

L

language   5
LDAP   199
    additional information   209
    directory service   199
    installation   201
    Netscape   204
    Netscape configuration   206
    permissions   206
    starting   206
    X.500   200
LILO   28
logical drive   17
login   66
    console   66

M

Microlite BackupEDGE   239
    backup   252

features   239
incremental backup   258
incremental restore   260
initialize tape   250
installing   240
master backup   258
master restore   260
restore   255
schedule backup   262
tape device   241
Microlite RecoverEDGE   265
    boot diskette   266
    total crash recovering   273
monitor setup   10
mouse   94
mouse setup   6

N

network   99
network setup   27
NFS   221
    installation   221
    remote access   226
NIS   211
    additional information   219
    client   215
    installation   211, 212
    server   212

P

packet filtering with IP chains   229
    additional information   238
    dail-up Internet connection   229
    FTP masquerading   233
    gateway   229, 234
        checksum   234
        demasquerade   234
        forward chain   235
        input chain   234
        lo interface   235
        local process   234
        output chain   235
        routing decision   234
        sanity   234
    IP chains   235
    IP forwarding   232
    NAT   229
    network configuration   230

requirements 230
partition
   /boot 14
   home 14
Partitions
   swap 14
partitions 14
   /boot 15
   DOS/Windows 14
   extended 14, 16
      logical drive 17
   format 20
   Linux 14
   mounting points 15
   opt 14
   reset 18
   root 14
   sizes 301
   swap 14
   usr 14
   var 14
performance
   of RAID subsystems 294
performance tools 109
   Ktop 114
   Lothar 115
   Powertweak 110
   top 112
peripherals 93
Personal Systems Reference 1
POP3 183, 196
printer 95

R
RAID
   described 283
   level 0 (RAID-0) 284
   level 1 (RAID-1, RAID-1E) 285
   level 10 (RAID-10) 286
   level 5 (RAID-5) 287
   level 5 enhanced (RAID-5E) 291
   orthogonal RAID-5 293
   performance 294
   RAID Advisory Board 298
   recommendations 296
   software-based 283
   summary of RAID levels 297
   support for two disk failures 291

supported disk technologies 283
RFC 200
root password 24
RPC 222
RPM 77

S
Samba 123
   configuration 125
   global settings 126
   installation 123
   NetBIOS 126
   printer shares 133
   shares 130
   start 133
   stop 134
   SWAT 135
      logon 137
   WINS 123
Sendmail 181
   additional information 198
   configuration 193
   DNS configuration 184
   mail client 196
   mail routing 195
   MTA 181
   network configuration 183
   packages 181
   POP3 183, 196
   SMTP 183
ServeRAID 2, 33
   administration and monitoring program 56
   configuration 34
   driver 34
   firmware 2
   hot swap rebuild 43
   ipsadm 56
   ipsmon 55
   ipssend 36
      commands 36
      devinfo 42
      getconfig 36
      getstatus 41
      hsrebuild 43
      rebuild 47
      setstate 44
      synch 46
      unattended 46

  rebuild drive   47
  replace drive   48
  RPM   34
  synchronize logical drives   46
  unattended mode   46
  utility   34
SMTP   183
SWAT   135
  global settings   137, 139
  logon   137
  printers   147
  restart Samba   146
  Samba passwords   152
  Samba status   150
  shares   141

T

Tetris   30
time   92
time zone   29
token-ring   2, 61
  DHCP   63
  ibmtr   62
  ISA   62
  lanaid   63
  olympic   62
  PCI   62

V

video mode   299
  Netfinity 3000   299
  Netfinity 3500M10   299
  Netfinity 5000   299
  Netfinity 5500 M10   299
  Netfinity 5500 M20   299
  Netfinity 5600   299
  Netfinity 7000 M10   299
  Netfinity 8500R   299
video setup   8

W

Web site
  RAID Advisory Board   298

X

X.500   200
X-Windows   108

IBM Redbooks evaluation

Netfinity and Caldera OpenLinux Integration Guide
SG24-5861-00

Your feedback is very important to help us maintain the quality of ITSO redbooks. **Please complete this questionnaire and return it using one of the following methods:**

- Use the online evaluation form found at `http://www.redbooks.ibm.com/`
- Fax this form to: USA International Access Code + 1 914 432 8264
- Send your comments in an Internet note to `redbook@us.ibm.com`

Which of the following best describes you?
_ **Customer**   _ **Business Partner**   _ **Solution Developer**   _ **IBM employee**
_ **None of the above**

Please rate your overall satisfaction with this book using the scale:
(1 = very good, 2 = good, 3 = average, 4 = poor, 5 = very poor)

Overall Satisfaction			_____

Please answer the following questions:

Was this redbook published in time for your needs?		Yes___ No___

If no, please explain:

_____
_____
_____
_____

What other redbooks would you like to see published?

_____
_____
_____

Comments/Suggestions: **(THANK YOU FOR YOUR FEEDBACK!)**

_____
_____
_____
_____

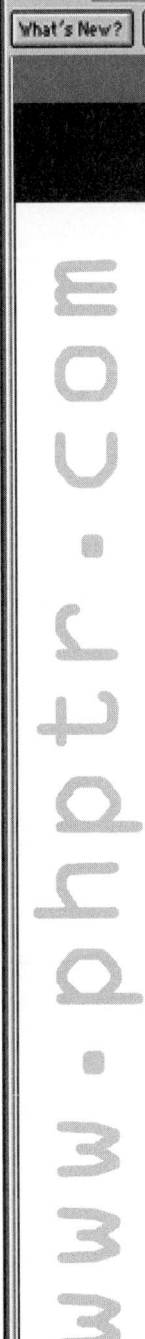

PRENTICE HALL
Professional Technical Reference
Tomorrow's Solutions for Today's Professionals.

Keep Up-to-Date with
PH PTR Online!

We strive to stay on the cutting-edge of what's happening in professional computer science and engineering. Here's a bit of what you'll find when you stop by **www.phptr.com**:

- **Special interest areas** offering our latest books, book series, software, features of the month, related links and other useful information to help you get the job done.

- **Deals, deals, deals!** Come to our promotions section for the latest bargains offered to you exclusively from our retailers.

- **Need to find a bookstore?** Chances are, there's a bookseller near you that carries a broad selection of PTR titles. Locate a Magnet bookstore near you at www.phptr.com.

- **What's New at PH PTR?** We don't just publish books for the professional community, we're a part of it. Check out our convention schedule, join an author chat, get the latest reviews and press releases on topics of interest to you.

- **Subscribe Today!** **Join PH PTR's monthly email newsletter!**

  Want to be kept up-to-date on your area of interest? Choose a targeted category on our website, and we'll keep you informed of the latest PH PTR products, author events, reviews and conferences in your interest area.

  Visit our mailroom to subscribe today! **http://www.phptr.com/mail_lists**